O9-ABI-376

EARLY CHILDHOOD EDUCATION SERIES

Leslie R. Williams, Editor
Millie Almy, Senior Advisor

ADVISORY BOARD: **Barbara T. Bowman, Harriet K. Cuffaro, Stephanie Feeney, Doris Pronin Fromberg, Celia Genishi, Dominic F. Gullo, Alice Sterling Honig, Elizabeth Jones, Gwen Morgan, David Weikart**

(Continued)

Reconceptualizing the Early Childhood Curriculum

BEGINNING THE DIALOGUE

Edited by

SHIRLEY A. KESSLER
BETH BLUE SWADENER

TEACHERS COLLEGE, COLUMBIA UNIVERSITY
New York and London

This book is dedicated to Mimi, our friend and mentor

Published by Teachers College Press, 1234 Amsterdam Avenue
New York, NY 10027

Copyright © 1992 by Teachers College, Columbia University
Chapter 7, copyright © 1992 by The University of Chicago. All rights reserved.

Library of Congress Cataloging-in-Publication Data

Reconceptualizing the early childhood curriculum : beginning the
    dialogue / edited by Shirley A. Kessler, Beth Blue Swadener.
        p.   cm.
    Includes bibliographical references and index.
    ISBN 0-8077-3199-4 (alk. paper). — ISBN 0-8077-3198-6 (alk. paper
: pbk.)
    1. Early childhood education—United States—Curricula. 2. Early
childhood education—United States—Philosophy.   I. Kessler,
Shirley A. II. Swadener, Beth Blue.
LB1139.4.R43   1992
372.21'0973—dc 20   92-18481

ISBN 0-8077-3199-4
ISBN 0-8077-3198-6 (pbk.)

Printed on acid-free paper
Manufactured in the United States of America

99 98 97 96 95 94 93 92   8 7 6 5 4 3 2 1

Contents

Foreword

A student in my Introduction to Teaching and Learning course completed the course evaluation as follows: "The problem with this course is that it raised more questions than it answered. At this point in my life I need answers, not questions." I put the evaluation on my wall because, although it was constructed as a criticism, it delighted me. Although I am twice as old as the students I typically teach and still yearn for answers, I have discovered so far *no* point at which answers are more important than questions. In fact, I have learned that there are no good answers without hard questions. Easy answers are invariably wrong, or at least partial.

This book asks hard questions, good questions. Like my course, it probably raises more questions than it answers, but they are wonderful, important questions to raise, the kind that challenge you to stop and think, reexamine, go back, reread and rethink. What are some of those questions and why do they matter?

One of the basic questions this book asks is why early childhood education is constructed and conceptualized the way it is. Whose interests are served and how? Could it be different? Would we want it to be? Central to this question is whose voices are typically presented in the process of thinking about school. Whose voices are omitted? And whose voices should be heard?

When my daughter Dalia was 6, her going-to-sleep ritual included snuggling and lots of talking. One night, delighting in the intensity and honesty of the stories she had been telling me, I remarked, "I love listening to you. What you have to say is so important." She looked up at me and responded, "Then how come at school when the children are talking the teacher asks: 'Is what you're talking about more important than what I'm talking about?' And you know, Mama, sometimes it is!"

My guess is that often it is. Sometimes, it seems, we forget what and whom education is supposed to be for, forget to ask children what school feels like, what they are learning, how it is for them. And we often neglect the voices of teachers as well. How do they experience teaching, what is hard for them, what is joyful, what needs to be changed? What can their voices tell us about the experience of schooling, about the ways our schools are failing to meet the needs of children, about school reform agendas?

One way to reconceptualize the early childhood curriculum, the goal of this book, is to ask a different set of questions than have typically been addressed. And perhaps the best way to *identify* those questions is to ask more people what those questions are, to represent multiple voices, particularly the voices of those most affected and often disregarded. If we heard different voices, we might hear a different story. We might hear, for example, about the plight of homeless children, about families in crisis who turn to teachers for support, about increasing demands and diminishing resources and how these are experienced by children and teachers.

We would hear different stories, and our research agendas and reform strategies might go far beyond the questions raised by discussions of the appropriateness of early phonics instruction in kindergarten or the utility of delaying school entry for young boys. But it is no accident that some voices are more clearly heard, some perspectives more likely than others to find representation. For a variety of reasons, the voices of women and children have been silenced; in a society that devalues both women and children, it is no wonder that early childhood education has been dismissed as "glorified babysitting," has had to struggle for legitimacy and respect, for validation and dignity. But recent efforts to "professionalize" the field may steer us equally wrong, may guarantee that certain voices still remain underrepresented.

If by professionalization we mean making early childhood education into a "business," a scientific enterprise, work "worthy of men," objective, serious, and quantifiable, then we may continue to shut out the voices of women and children, lose the potential to reformulate our research agendas and our institutional policies according to a different set of criteria. Our goal cannot be to validate early childhood education by making it resemble other "legitimate" enterprises; rather, we must reconceptualize what it means to be professional, what it means to be engaged in work worthy of respect and appreciation, what it means to devote one's life to young children. We must have a different vision of the importance of early childhood educators in creating communities of love and care, the earth-shattering importance of maintaining the possibilities of justice and equity through the ways in which we respond to young children.

This book is entitled *Reconceptualizing the Early Childhood Curriculum*, but, in some ways, that is too modest a title for this collection of essays. This book addresses what should be taught and who should decide, but it also addresses the social, political, and economic contexts in which such decisions are made, such change negotiated. This book addresses issues of curriculum in the broadest sense: what kind of a world do we want, and what is the role of early childhood educators in shaping that vision?

Several of the authors talk about and critique the notion of "developmentally appropriate practices," responding that such benchmarks may be narrow, inappropriate, and even misleading. But curriculum questions are embedded as much in issues of power and control; curriculum decisions are replete with assumptions about who the learners are and what they should learn, about who should decide, about empowerment and disempowerment.

One of my daughters attended a university-based, summer preschool, and her teacher met with me to share what they had identified as her curriculum goals for the session. They included the following:

Leora will learn to sort silverware and utensils and to name these appropriately.
Leora will learn to walk downstairs with alternating feet.
Leora will draw pictures with at least ten identifiable body parts.
Leora will learn to catch a ball with two hands without flinching.
Leora will learn to identify her waist and her heel when asked.

At first, I was puzzled, because none of these objectives seemed to have anything to do with the life or interests of the active, social 4-year-old I knew. The only specific thing *I* knew she was eager to learn was how to tie her shoes, and be rid of Velcro like the "big kids." But the source of these objectives became clearer when I was able to discern that these were the items she had "failed" on her developmental checklist assessment. We took care of "waist" and "heel" within two minutes; "Leora," I said, "this part here is called your 'waist' and this part of your foot is your 'heel.'" She was not particularly impressed, but repeated the words back to me. Frankly, I could not remember the last time anyone had asked *me* to point to my waist or my heel, but I let that pass. We took care of the "alternate feet on stairs" objective by pointing out to the teacher that Leora had been tested on the back stairs of an adult-sized university building, with stairs so wide that many adults struggled to do the alternating feet routine. I was more concerned about the other objectives, however. First of all, I loved the pictures that Leora drew: colorful and imaginative, they represented her world and her life. Why should she put ten identifiable body parts in everything she drew? Why did it matter? What would it do to her interest in art and drawing if counted body parts became the focus of every encounter with crayons and paper? Other objectives were equally troubling; yes, learning to catch a ball was important, but so was having fun with one. Maybe she would learn to catch when she was 5, maybe 6, maybe not until she was 8. But what would happen if she started to avoid ball play because she "wasn't good at it"? How would she approach playtime when it included focused lessons on ball catching, conducted one on one with a teacher, while other children were free to play with one another?

Why was the curriculum set by what she did not know? What would her school experience be like if it centered on those things she was not good at? How would others view her? How would she come to see herself? How would she view others who were more or less advanced, who worked on different objectives, all drawn from deficits and failures?

Beyond the critique of objective, deficit-driven educational objectives, education that is meaningless or marginalizing, there are even weightier issues. One of the critical questions addressed in this book centers on the school experiences of children who are identified as "lacking" or "deficient," and on the discrepancies between the kinds of educational programming and opportunities different children receive. Within early childhood settings, children get some of their earliest messages about who is of value and how we respond to differences, about who matters and who does not. That is where children's socialization to norms of justice and fairness begins, as well as their sense of how resources are and should be allocated, their notions of who is deserving.

Some children are provided with experiences and resources that will insure their future success; others receive little positive experience and poor preparation for transcending poverty or inequity. In preschools for children identified as "gifted," the curriculum is rich with possibility; children are encouraged to be creative and imaginative. The teachers assume that children have their own learning styles and agendas and respect children's individuality. In early childhood settings that serve children who are seen as "deficient," the curriculum is often much more skills-based and teacher-controlled. Children learn letters of the alphabet according to a prepackaged program, one a week: "A is for apple," "B is for ball." In one progressive, child-centered preschool setting, a child who chose to watch a game the first few times it was played was described as a "child who learns best through observation." In a program for "disadvantaged children," a child displaying similar behavior was labeled as "noncompliant" and became the subject of a behavior modification program: "Jason will join the game within two minutes four out of five times." In one setting, children's individuality was respected, in the other, differences were characterized as deviations from the norm, needing to be remediated.

Children do not come to school with equal resources or privilege, and once they are there, they do not receive equal or equally appropriate educations. This book asks us to think about the role of early childhood education in responding to these differences, challenges us to think about the effects, not the intentions, of various program models or curricular decisions. Many of the chapters in this book transcend early childhood issues to address questions of race relations, prejudice reduction, peace education, feminist pedagogy, and democratic schooling. We are asked to think seriously about the world we have created for children and the world these children will then create for us. We are urged to think about early childhood education as though it really mattered, as though our pedagogy could make a difference in addressing inequities and injustice.

When my daughter Dalia was 2, I struggled one evening getting her into her pajamas. I put one arm into her blanket sleeper, she withdrew the other; I put her foot in, she pulled her arm out. We became locked in battle, until she looked up at me and said, "You don't understand, I don't want to be cooperative, I want to have a struggle." Already, at 2, she was responding to my impositional behavior (*I* controlled bedtime, *I* chose the pajamas) with whatever resistance she could muster. As annoyed as I was, I knew that her strength and spirit would serve her well, would be necessary in a world that often does not respect or honor the choices of people considered of little value.

In many ways, as educators, we have become complicit in perpetuating various forms of societal oppression; we have implemented educational policies against our better judgment; we have graded and tracked children even though we knew at some level that it was wrong; we have used materials that did not represent the children we taught. We have found it difficult to think transformatively about education, about alternative possibilities for envisioning just and equitable schools. We have suffered from limited imaginations, a paucity of allies, and a shortfall of courage. We have been overburdened and underresourced, devalued and unsupported. My challenge to readers of this book is to continue to struggle; if our cooperation means going along with and not challenging poverty, racism, sexism, and disempowering teaching models, then we must struggle. At this point our best potential for doing better, for resisting external, ill-conceived reform efforts, is to think critically about early childhood education, to struggle against reform agendas that disempower those they purport to help. To do this we will need courage and power, and we will need allies. We will need to learn to talk about early childhood education in ways that connect it with real issues and real people, with real struggles. This book represents an important beginning to that process.

Mara Sapon-Shevin

Introduction
Reconceptualizing Curriculum

This is a book about curriculum. Since the early 1980s many of us who have examined early childhood education from the perspective of curriculum theory have begun to ask questions regarding the early childhood curriculum. Taking a historical perspective, we asked ourselves how the early childhood curriculum had come to be what it is. We wondered why there is the current debate about what are considered "developmentally appropriate" versus "developmentally inappropriate" practices in early childhood classrooms or settings. We asked whether all early childhood curriculum decisions should be made primarily from the perspective of developmental theory or if other theoretical frameworks might benefit our thinking about curriculum. We wondered about the relationship between psychological/developmental theory and the major curriculum question: What knowledge is of most worth? Perhaps the exclusive focus of research in early childhood education on developmental theory limited the possibilities for the early childhood curriculum (e.g., Jipson, 1991; O'Laughlin, 1991). We also asked ourselves whose voices were represented in prescriptions for early childhood pedagogy and whose interests were being served by the curriculum. We wondered, too, what vision of the future was embedded in the curriculum we advocated and implemented.

These questions came to us partly as the result of the location of our scholarly work within the broad field of curriculum studies. As curriculum generalists, we became aware of alternative theoretical perspectives or paradigms (Cherryholmes, 1988; Kuhn, 1970; Lather, 1991; Popkewitz, 1986; Witherell & Noddings, 1991) from which to conduct educational research and examinations of the early childhood curriculum. We became especially interested in examining the early childhood curriculum from an interpretive, critical, and feminist point of view, and wondered what the implications of alternative theoretical perspectives were for current research and practice in early childhood education. Thus we organized several forums to examine these questions and issues, which included sessions at the Annual Bergamo Conference on Curriculum Theory and Classroom Practice in 1989, the annual meeting of the American Educational Research Association in 1990, a special topic issue of *Early Education and Development* (April, 1991), companion articles in *Early Childhood Research Quarterly* (Bredekamp, 1991; Kessler, 1991), and two national conferences on Reconceptualizing Research and Practice in Early Childhood Education held in Madison, Wisconsin, in October 1991 and Chicago, Illinois, in September 1992.

In examining the above questions we drew upon much of the curriculum scholarship completed over the past 20 years in the United States (e.g., Apple, 1979, 1982; Grumet, 1988; Pinar, 1975, 1988), which represented attempts to "reconceptualize" ways of examining and understanding the school curriculum. This scholarship rejected the "traditional" approach to curriculum planning and deliberation associated with the work of Ralph Tyler (1949). Educators who identified with this group of "reconceptualists" (Pinar, 1975) sought an alternative to Tyler's "technical/rational" (Eisner, 1985) approach to curriculum planning, which emphasized behavioral objectives, direct instruction, and achievement testing and argued for a "reconceptualization" of curriculum discourse by illuminating the philosophical, historical, and political dimensions of what was taught and learned in school.

In addition, of vital interest to this scholarship was the issue of social inequality and the role that schools played in re-creating the unequal class, race, and gender relationships that existed in the wider society (Apple, 1979, 1982; Beyer & Apple, 1988; Weis, 1987; Whitty, 1977; Willis, 1978; Young, 1971). This research offered an alternative to the "input/ output" research design for examining the "educability" of low-income children of color, for example, by focusing on the "process" of schooling, in particular the school curriculum and teacher–pupil interaction (Karabel & Halsey, 1979), to study the ways in which social inequalities were produced and reproduced in schools (Apple, 1979). Thus the object of study within this genre of research was the school curriculum, including the formal body of knowledge that was "transmitted" in schools, as well as the tacit learnings acquired by students as a result of their interaction with teachers and the structures and norms that constituted everyday life in classrooms (e.g., Jackson, 1968). Early research in this genre focused on the school knowledge presented to children from working- versus middle-class backgrounds (Anyon, 1981; Keddie, 1971; McNeil, 1986). Over the years, however, more attention was paid to gender and the role of schools in producing sex differences in school achievement and the unequal gender relationships that existed in the larger society (Belenky, Clinchy, Goldberger, & Tarule, 1986; Grumet, 1988; Kelly & Nihlen, 1982). Currently, issues of racism, ableism, heterosexism, and other "parallel oppressions" have been addressed in the sociology of education and feminist literature (e.g., Ellsworth, 1989; Lather, 1986, 1991; Sears, 1990; Sleeter, 1991).

Thus we situated our queries about the early childhood curriculum within what has been referred to as the "sociology of the curriculum," a discipline emanating from the sociology of knowledge, which had its roots in England in the work of Karl Mannheim (Karabel & Halsey, 1979). This perspective assumes that knowledge is a social construction, created by individuals to help them make sense of their world and to answer questions that interest them. Therefore knowledge is not objective or neutral, but belongs to individuals and is, therefore, tied to their interests. More recently, themes within the sociology of the curriculum have included political analysis, aesthetic criticism, phenomenological and feminist studies (Pinar, 1988), as well as discussions of the role of technology and curriculum (Beyer & Apple, 1988).

In the following sections we provide an overview of issues within curriculum theory and related literature in order to provide a context for the chapters that follow. We begin with a discussion of the "Tyler rationale" (Kliebard, 1975) to lay the groundwork for a philosophical and political critique of an early childhood curriculum rationalized on the basis of developmental theory. Next, we offer alternative perspectives on the term *curriculum* itself and suggest varying orientations or theories of curriculum.[1] This discussion is followed by a brief orientation to historical perspectives on the curriculum, a brief overview of a "critically" oriented sociology of the curriculum, a discussion of feminist and interpretive perspectives, and a description of the role students and teachers play in the intended and especially the operational curriculum (Eisner, 1985). Finally, as we describe the overall organization of the book, we raise several broad issues and themes to serve as advance organizers for the chapters in this volume.

THE TYLER RATIONALE

The dominant approach to curriculum planning follows the outline described by Ralph Tyler (1949) in a series of lectures he delivered at the University of Chicago. According to this model, the curriculum maker addresses four primary questions:

1. What educational purposes should the school seek to attain?
2. What educational experiences can be provided that are likely to attain these purposes?
3. How can these educational experiences be organized?

4. How can we determine whether these purposes are being attained?

Furthermore, according to Tyler, the goals of the curriculum should be determined by examining the needs and interests of the student, studies of contemporary life, and recommendations from subject-matter experts. These goals are then to be filtered through a psychological and philosophical screen to ensure that they are appropriate to the developmental level of the student and what the community thinks is worthwhile. Early childhood educators traditionally have advocated that the curriculum be determined from the examination of the needs and interests of the learner, and this seems to be the position endorsed in the National Association of Early Childhood Education (NAEYC) position paper on "developmentally appropriate practices" (Bredekamp, 1987, 1991).

In using the learner as a source of curriculum objectives, Tyler recommends examining his or her "needs" and "interests." These findings are then to be compared to a standard of what was "normal" or "good" before being adopted as objectives for the curriculum. Tyler (1949) states:

> Studies of the learner suggest educational objectives only when the information about the learner is compared with some desirable standard, some conception of acceptable norms, so that the difference between the present condition of the learner and the acceptable norm can be identified. This difference or gap is what is generally referred to as a need. . . . Need in this sense is the gap between what is and what should be. (pp. 6, 8)

Obviously, what is needed in the call for developmentally appropriate practices is the articulation of those very standards. We need to ask ourselves: What are the acceptable norms that guide our work with young children? What are the desirable standards for children's development to which educators aspire? What should children become? (Biber, 1984).

To determine the interests of students, Tyler (1949) recommends observing students, interviewing them and their parents, administering questionnaires, and so forth. Once again these findings are to be compared to some standard or criteria of what is desirable before being adopted as goals and objectives for the curriculum. In other words, the interests of students are not legitimate until they are compared with what is desirable. Thus, in the final analysis, information about students' needs and interests that have validity for the curriculum are based on concepts of normality and desirability, not "objective" data.

Furthermore, Kliebard (1975) argues, the other two sources of curriculum (recommendations from subject-matter experts and from studies of contemporary life) are similarly value-laden. For example, the knowledge that is selected for the curriculum can serve the purposes of the average student or the would-be scholar. Aspects of contemporary life (e.g., driver's education, computer literacy, AIDS education) that are included in the curriculum depend on what the community believes is important. Each of the sources of the curriculum Tyler identified involves a process of valuing at the onset. Therefore philosophy is not simply the screen through which objectives should be filtered, but the primary basis for determining those very objectives: what needs and interests of the students have validity for the curriculum, what knowledge should be selected from subject-matter specialists, and what needs of society have priority. Tyler's "rationale" (Kliebard, 1975) has been further criticized because it focuses attention on the "how" in planning the curriculum, ignoring the important questions dealing with values and priorities, that is, the question of what should be taught and why (Eisner, 1985).

If one accepts the argument that curriculum decisions are based on beliefs about what it is important to know and what the child and the community need, we must alter the discourse about developmentally appropriate practices from an examination of what exists, in the empirical sense (in this case a child's developmental level), to a consideration of what should be, in terms of what is considered normal, desirable, and good. Axiology (a branch of philosophy that addresses the question of what is valuable) and ethics (which is concerned with examining what is good and evil) are, therefore, central to all choices about curriculum (Schubert, 1986).

WHAT IS CURRICULUM?

In addition to highlighting the axiological and ethical dimensions of curriculum, many scholars are beginning to question the very notion of what the curriculum is, how it became what it is, and how it is enacted. The popular view is that curriculum is what appears in the textbooks for a particular grade level or in the teachers' planbook, and/or what is taught. Others think of curriculum as what students experience and how students' experiences relate to their personal biographies, their relationship with the teacher, and/or social structures in the larger society, such as the economy, one's class position, race, gender, or first language.

Schubert (1986) prefers the terms *images* or *characterizations* of curriculum, rather than *definitions*, because "they denote a broader conceptualization than the label for a thing" (p. 26). Drawing upon the immense and diverse literature on curriculum, Schubert summarizes and categorizes several images of curriculum: curriculum as "content or subject matter," "a program of planned activities," "intended learning outcomes," "experience," "discrete tasks and concepts," "an agenda for social reconstruction," and "currere" (personal biography) (pp. 26–33). Cornbleth (1990) defines curriculum as "contextualized social process," highlighting the illusive, complex, and varied nature of what children experience in school. Kliebard (1980) argues that the various definitions or images of curriculum actually represent different, and usually conflicting, value orientations and priorities for accomplishing particular political agendas. For example, "curriculum as intended learning outcomes" is a phrase that conjurs up images of behavioral objectives, scope and sequence charts, and teacher-centered classrooms. On the other hand, "curriculum as experience" calls to mind a Deweyian, personalized, child-centered approach to early childhood education. Each image of curriculum offers a description of what curriculum *is* as well as what the curriculum *should be*. Thus implicit in the very way one conceives curriculum are prescriptions for educational practice.

Instead of images of curriculum, Eisner (1985), for example, sets forth five basic "orientations" toward curriculum, three of which are instructive for purposes here. Eisner's categories of "personal relevance" and "development of cognitive processes" suggest a curriculum that corresponds to the assumptions and values of the developmentally appropriate practices position. The "development of cognitive processes" orientation aims to help children strengthen their intellectual powers and to learn how to learn. In the "personal relevance" category the goal of the school is to provide a rich environment so that the child is able to find what he or she needs in order to grow. One metaphor to describe this orientation toward curriculum is the metaphor of "growth" (Kliebard, 1975).

Eisner's "curriculum as technology" orientation corresponds to the inappropriate practices described in the NAEYC guidelines. Tyler's rationale is the blueprint for developing curriculum from this perspective. As previously discussed, this model deemphasizes the role of philosophy in curriculum planning. Curriculum deliberation focuses on the means for achieving educational goals, not on the examination of the ends themselves. Offshoots of this orientation toward curriculum are such practices as educational accountability, behavior analysis, grouping and tracking, state-mandated testing, the alignment of curricula to match tested content, the call for national goals, and state and international comparison of educational achievement. Kliebard (1975) applies the metaphor of "production" to this orientation toward curriculum. From this perspective the student is seen as raw material that is transformed into some kind of product by the skilled technician (the teacher). Plans for the end product are carefully predetermined, and the subject is carefully shaped to meet design specifications.

While none of Eisner's (1958) orientations exist in pure form, each suggests parameters within which one thinks about the aims and content of the curriculum, the role of the teacher, and the criteria used to assess the quality of schooling. These orientations highlight the enormous differences between those advocating what NAEYC calls "appropriate" versus "inappropriate" practices: differences in beliefs as to the purposes of schooling, what knowledge is of most worth, the design of educational programs, the teacher–pupil relationship, and so forth. If we recognize the philsophical differences that underlie prescriptions for educational practice, we would prepare a different set of arguments for a discussion with those who favor practices incompatible with traditional child-centered methods.

Curriculum Theory

Curriculum theory has been defined as "prescriptive" and/or "descriptive" (Eisner, 1985; Schubert, 1986), the former based on normative data, the latter on so-called objective data. Prescriptive curriculum theory articulates and promotes what ought to be. It asks, "What is worthwhile to know, how do we know it is worthwhile, and how can its worth be justified?" (Schubert, 1986, p. 41). Examples of prescriptive curriculum theory in early childhood education abound, such as DISTAR, the Montessori method, High Scope, and open education. Descriptive theory, on the other hand, describes what exists empirically. Research that examines how children develop and/or learn is an example of descriptive curriculum theory. Many argue that statements advocating *what ought to be* taught cannot be determined from empirical data, or an examination of *what is*. Prescriptive theory involves the illumination and articulation of what is valuable or good—issues that cannot be addressed by relying solely on what is known about the natural or physical world. For example, child development research does not tell us to include in the social studies curriculum such topics as Martin Luther King, Jr., and the civil rights movement, women's history, peace and conflict management, or the nonstereotypic treatment of Native Americans and other people of color, rather than the more traditional topics that focus on the child's expanding environment: the home, neighborhood, community, and so forth. In both cases, what is taught in the social studies curriculum depends on what the teacher or curriculum planner thinks is important. As Spodek (1989) put it, "What children need to know or ought to know is not determined by what children are capable of knowing."

Since the inception of curriculum as a field of study in the early 1920s, most of the research and writing has focused on the technical aspects, or the "how to" in planning educational programs. As we stated earlier, this concern with the technical aspect of curriculum planning, the "how to" rather than the "what to teach" and "why," has obscured the philosophical underpinnings of curriculum discourse and analysis. However, we want to argue that since all curriculum decisions involve assumptions about the nature of knowledge, about what is valued and considered important, as well as answers to the question of how to live "the good life," philosophical analysis is central to all discussions about the curriculum. As Schubert (1986) puts it, "The difficult task of judging the defensibility of claims about knowledge and values becomes philosophy" (p. 119). As Bloch points out in Chapter 1, early childhood research and discourse have focused almost exclusively on developmental theory, preventing us from asking fundamental curriculum questions and from seeing our work from alternative perspectives (Kessler, 1991).

Historical and Political Perspectives

Other branches of "reconceptualist" thinking focus on the historical (e.g., Kliebard, 1986) and political (e.g., Beyer & Apple, 1988) nature of curriculum discourse and analysis. It has been argued that the field of education is ahistorical, and this is especially true with regard to the history of curriculum. However, in the last two decades, several scholars have focused on this issue, and there now exists a growing body of literature that is examining the relationship between the curriculum of today and that which preceded it. Barry Franklin, Herbert Kliebard, and Steven Selden (Pinar, 1988), Nanch Benham-Barbour (1986), Marianne Bloch (1987), and Bernard Spodek (in press) are just a few of the individuals who have undertaken a close examination of the past in order to contextualize current approaches to the study of curricula. For example, Kleibard (1975) claims that the three sources of the curriculum Tyler identified in 1949 actually represent different "doctrines" of education and political commitments. Thus adherents to various beliefs can be viewed as a kind of political interest group, or a lobby for a particular set of values. Kliebard (1986) identified four such interest groups that existed by the 1890s: The "humanists," who valued the traditional subject areas; the "social efficiency educators," who advocated basing the curriculum on the needs of society; and the "social meliorists," who sought to improve society through education. The final group described by Kliebard was the "developmentalists," whose chief spokesperson was G. Stanley Hall, the father of the child study movement, who advocated the examination of the learner for answers about what should be taught. Kliebard (1986) concludes:

> The twentieth century became the arena where these four versions of what knowledge is of most worth and of the central functions of schooling were presented and argued. No single interest group ever gained absolute supremacy, although general social and economic trends, periodic and fragile alliances between groups, the national mood, and local conditions and personalities affected the ability of these groups to influence school practice as the twentieth century progressed. In the end, what became the American curriculum was not the result of any decisive victory by any of the contending parties, but a loose, largely unarticulated, and not very tidy compromise. (p. 29)

Seen from a historical perspective, the current debate between those advocating what the NAEYC calls "appropriate" versus "inappropriate" practices, for example, can be viewed as a debate between two or more different interests groups lobbying for a particular set of values, taking different political positions, and representing different philosophical schools of thought. What appears to be a debate between those who are well informed by current research in child development and those who are not is, in reality, a debate between individuals who hold different values about the purposes of schooling, what counts as legitimate knowledge, and presumably the nature of the good life and the just society. Therefore, to argue for appropriate practices, one must not claim superior knowledge of child development research but recognize the fundamentally philosophical and political differences that exist between those who hold a personal relevance versus technological conception of curriculum, or favor developmentally appropriate versus inappropriate practices.

A Critical Sociology of the Curriculum

A critical sociology of the curriculum emphasizes the political context of the school curriculum. In doing so it combines a sociological perspective on knowledge production with the Neo-Marxist notion of "interests." An important component of this theory is the relationship between knowledge and power (Apple, 1982; Weis, 1987; Wexler, 1990). Its major tenets are as follows (Young, 1971):

1. Certain forms of knowledge have more status than other forms.
2. Knowledge is distributed unequally, such that students from higher-status families achieve more or receive more of the high-status knowledge.
3. School knowledge is viewed as belonging to a particular group, and control of knowledge is seen as a means by which that group maintains its dominant position in society.

Research within this "paradigm" (Kuhn, 1970) examines the ways in which a different curriculum is presented to students of different social classes, and several studies conclude that a different "type" of knowledge is indeed presented to students from the working class compared to those from the professional class, and to children in classrooms where white, middle-class students predominate compared to those largely made up of children of color (e.g., Anyon, 1981; Goodlad, 1984; Keddie, 1971; Oakes, 1985; Page & Valli, 1990).

Feminist and Interpretive Perspectives

Other rapidly growing theoretical strands within curriculum studies (as reflected in several of the chapters in this volume) are found in the diverse paradigms and interpretive forms in feminist literature. Advocating for the inclusion and validity of "multiple voices," feminist perspectives, and illumination of women's "ways of knowing," researchers such as Belenky and her colleagues (1986), Casey (1990), Gilligan (1982), Greene (1988), Jipson (1991), Miller (1990), Noddings (1984, 1989), and Witherell and Noddings (1991) have utilized a rich variety of reconceptualist or critical research and philosophical paradigms. Such approaches have included life history and autobiographical accounts, as well as phenomenological/interpretive studies based on teachers' (and mothers') own descriptions and understanding of their work with children. Other perspectives have included philosophical and ethical analyses, such as the ethic of care (Noddings, 1984); "maternal" metaphors in teaching, such as that which is described in Madeline Grumet's book *Bitter Milk* (1988); and liberatory or transformational "possibilities," as facilitated through collaboration between teachers and researchers (e.g., Ayers, 1989; Holly, 1989; Miller, 1990).

Other feminist scholars working within the curriculum theory field (e.g., Ellsworth, 1989; hooks, 1989; Jipson & Munro, 1991; Lather, 1986, 1991; Polakow, 1992) have increasingly used post-structuralist or post-modern perspectives emphasizing multivocality and extending earlier phenomenological and interpretive work. Such analyses also raise issues of women of color, lesbians and gays, silencing, and challenges of working across affinity groups (e.g., Ellsworth, 1989; Lather, 1991). Such analyses have not been limited to an emphasis on the roles of gender in the power relations of education and society but have sought to be inclusive of issues of race, sexual orientation, class, language and dialect, culture, physical characteristics, religion, and age, as well as other potential sources of marginalization, silencing, or oppression.

Students' Effect on the Teacher and the Curriculum

One of the criticisms of the sociology of the curriculum is that it oversimplified the analysis of the educational and/or socialization process and the reproduction of the social relations characteristic of the larger society (e.g., Wexler, 1990). Early research within this tradition depicted students as overly determined by the educational system. However, we all know that students are not passive in the educational process. A considerable body of literature describes the ways that students have been active in influencing the teacher and the curriculum (Cornbleth, 1990; Kessler, 1986; Swadener, 1991).

Early behavior-coding studies have described the ways in which students affect teachers' self-evaluations (Jenkins & Deno, 1969); the quantity and quality of verbal interactions (Sherman & Cormier, 1974); and the frequency with which teachers directed questions to them (Noble & Nolan, 1976). Evidence also supports the view that students influence the curriculum by affecting teachers' decisions about what to teach (Taylor, 1975). Shavelson and Stern (1981) found that students' achievement level and "participation" were significant influences on teachers' planning and the decisions they made while in the act of teaching. Furthermore, we know that children negotiate their participation in the classroom (Cornbleth, 1990) and often are purposely included in the development of curriculum meanings (Swadener, 1991). McCutcheon (1980) reported that students sometimes behaved in such a way as to create events or experiences that were outside what the teacher had planned. Furthermore, John Eggleston (1977) claimed that it was in the area of the hidden curriculum (Apple & King, 1977; Jackson, 1968; Willis, 1978) that pupils had the most influence or effect. By rejecting the normative values within the social system of the classroom, students can contribute to the teachers' formation of a negative view of them and perhaps lead teachers to expect less of them in terms of achievement.

In addition, several studies reported on the importance of an informal subculture within schools that exerted a significant influence on what was taught and what was learned. For example, Gracey (1972) described the beginnings of an informal subculture in a kindergarten where students resisted the strong imposition of routines and constructed a kind of knowing that excluded the teacher, knowledge which comprised an element of their culture, embodying their values and interests. Currently, the sociology of the curriculum perspective recognizes these kinds of reactions to the curriculum and rejection of attempts to socialize the young, and the process of schooling is now recognized as a complex, context-bound, interactive process which defies easy description and analysis.

ORGANIZATION OF THE BOOK

We have organized the chapters that follow around several broad themes that we consider critical to the reconceptualization of the early childhood curriculum. The book is divided into four parts that reflect these issues and themes. Chapters are summarized at the beginning of each part.

Part I, *Alternative Perspectives on Prevailing Theory and Practice*, extends the historical and theoretical background begun in the Introduction, including more detailed discussions of curriculum theory, a critical history of dominant paradigms in early childhood research, and the importance of context in understanding early childhood curricula. Part II, *Critical and Feminist Perspectives on Early Childhood Education*, focuses on topics and themes drawn from critical and feminist theory and further clarifies the relationship between critical and feminist theory and curriculum. Among the issues made problematic in this part are questions concerning whose interests are being served by the curriculum and whose voices have been silenced. Part III, *Issues of Cultural and Linguistic Pluralism*, places issues of power, silencing, and the reproductive aspects of early education in multiple cultural contexts. Although issues of race, class, gender, and linguistic diversity are addressed in other parts of the book, the chapters in Part III place these issues in the *foreground*. Part IV, *Voices from the Field: Teacher Narratives and Collaborative Work*, reflects some of both the earliest and the most recent work in curriculum theory and early childhood education, as it brings into the dialogue the voices, concerns, and contributions of teachers and those collaborating directly with teachers for curriculum change. Their stories, struggles, and successes document the type of work that will be required in order to truly reconceptualize the early childhood curriculum where it is enacted in an ongoing gestalt of very real events.

As you read the chapters to follow, we invite you to consider a number of major issues in the reconceptualization of the early childhood curriculum. These include questions such as "What knowledge should be included in the curriculum, and what form should pedagogy take?" and "Whose voices are represented by what is taught and experienced in school, and whose interests are being served?" Finally, we hope to bring to the center of our discussions an analysis of the visions for the future and of the "good life" for children and families that are embedded within our work to foster alternative perspectives on the early childhood curriculum. We will return to these fundamental curriculum questions in the Epilogue.

NOTE

1. Much of the discussion which follows was published in the June 1991 issue of *Early Childhood Research Quarterly*. Reprinted with the permission of Ablex Publishing Corporation.

REFERENCES

Anyon, J. (1981). Social class and school knowledge. *Curriculum Inquiry, 2*, 3–42.

Apple, M. W. (1979). *Ideology and curriculum*. Boston: Routledge and Kegan Paul.

Apple, M. W. (1982). *Education and power*. Boston: Routledge and Kegan Paul.

Apple, M. W., & King, N. A. (1977). What do schools teach? *Curriculum Inquiry, 6*, 341–357.

Ayers, W. (1989). *The good preschool teacher*. New York: Teachers College Press.

Belenky, M. F., Clinchy, B. Mc., Goldberger, N. R., & Tarule, J. M. (1986). *Women's ways of knowing: The development of self, voice, and mind*. New York: Basic Books.

Benham-Barbour, N. (1986, April). *Families as educators: Historical perspectives on parent involvement*. Paper presented at the annual meeting of the American Educational Research Association, San Francisco.

Beyer, L. W., & Apple, M. W. (1988). *The curriculum: Problems, politics, and possibilities*. Albany: State University of New York Press.

Biber, B. (1984). *Early education and psychological development*. New Haven, CT: Yale University Press.

Bloch, M. N. (1987). Becoming scientific and professional: An historical perspective on the aims and effects of early education. In T. S. Popkewitz (Ed.), *The formation of school subjects* (pp. 25–62). Basingstoke, England: Falmer.

Bredekamp, S. (1987). *Developmentally appropriate practice in early childhood programs serving children from birth through age 8.* Washington, DC: National Association for the Education of Young Children.

Bredekamp, S. (1991). Redeveloping early childhood education: A response to Kessler. *Early Childhood Research Quarterly, 6,* 199–209.

Casey, K. (1990). Teacher as mother: Curriculum theorizing in the life histories of contemporary women teachers. *Cambridge Journal of Education, 20,* 301–320.

Cherryholmes, C. (1988). *Power and criticism: Poststructural investigations in education.* New York: Teachers College Press.

Cornbleth, C. (1990). *Curriculum in context.* New York: Falmer.

Eggleston, J. (1977). *The sociology of the school curriculum.* Boston: Routledge and Kegan Paul.

Eisner, E. W. (1985). *The educational imagination.* New York: Macmillan.

Ellsworth, E. (1989). Why doesn't this feel empowering? *Harvard Educational Review, 59,* 297–324.

Gilligan, C. (1982). *In a different voice: Psychological theory and women's development.* Cambridge, MA: Harvard University Press.

Goodlad, J. I. (1984). *A place called school: Prospects for the future.* New York: McGraw-Hill.

Gracey, H. L. (1972). *Curriculum or craftsmanship.* Chicago: University of Chicago Press.

Greene, M. (1988). *The dialectic of freedom.* New York: Teachers College Press.

Grumet, M. (1988). *Bitter milk.* Amherst: University of Massachusetts Press.

Holly, M. L. (1989). *Writing to grow.* Portsmouth, NH: Heinemann.

hooks, b. (1989). *Talking back: Thinking feminist, thinking black.* Boston: South End Press.

Jackson, P. (1968). *Life in classrooms.* New York: Holt, Rinehart and Winston.

Jenkins, J. R., & Deno, S. L. (1969). Influence of student behavior on teacher's self-evaluations. *Journal of Educational Psychology, 60,* 439–442.

Jipson, J. (1991). Developmentally appropriate practice: Culture, curriculum, connections. *Early Education and Development, 2,* 120–136.

Jipson, J., & Munro, P. (1991). Fictions of the maternal/what's real: The deconstruction of life history as curricular text. In J. I. Erdman & J. G. Henderson (Eds.), *Critical discourse on current curriculum issues* (pp. 141–165). Chicago: Mid-West Center for Curriculum Studies.

Karabel, J., & Halsey, A. H. (1979). Educational research: A review and an interpretation. In J. Karabel & A. H. Halsey (Eds.), *Power and ideology in education* (pp. 1–85). New York: Oxford University Press.

Keddie, N. (1971). Classroom knowledge. In M. F. Young (Ed.), *Knowledge and control: New directions for the sociology of education* (pp. 133–160). London: Collier-Macmillan.

Kelly, G. P., & Nihlen, A. S. (1982). Schooling and the reproduction of patriarchy: Unequal workloads, unequal rewards. In M. W. Apple (Ed.), *Cultural and economic reproduction in education* (pp. 162–180). Boston: Routledge and Kegan Paul.

Kessler, S. A. (1986). *The child's effect on the kindergarten curriculum.* Unpublished doctoral dissertation, University of Wisconsin-Madison.

Kessler, S. A. (1991). Alternative perspectives on early childhood education. *Early Childhood Research Quarterly, 6,* 183–197.

Kliebard, H. (1975). Reappraisal: The Tyler rationale. In W. Pinar (Ed.), *Curriculum theorizing: The reconceptualists* (pp. 70–83). Berkeley: McCutchan.

Kliebard, H. (1980). Personal communication.

Kliebard, H. (1986). *The struggle for the American curriculum.* London: Routledge and Kegan Paul.

Kuhn, T. S. (1970). *The structure of scientific revolutions.* Chicago: University of Chicago Press.

Lather, P. (1986). Research as praxis. *Harvard Educational Review, 56,* 257–277.

Lather, P. (1991). *Getting smart: Feminist research and pedagogy with/in the postmodern.* New York: Routledge and Kegan Paul.

Lubeck, S. (1985). *Sandbox society: Early schooling in black and white America.* New York: Falmer.

McCutcheon, G. (1980). How do elementary school teachers plan their courses? *Elementary School Journal, 81,* 4–23.

McNeil, L. (1986). *Contradictions of control: School structure and school knowledge.* New York: Routledge and Kegan Paul.

Miller, J. L. (1990). *Creating spaces and finding voices: Teachers collaborating for empowerment.* Albany: State University of New York Press.

Noble, C. G., & Nolan, J. D. (1976). Effect of student verbal behavior on classroom teacher behavior. *Journal of Educational Psychology, 68,* 342–346.

Noddings, N. (1984). *Caring: A feminine approach to ethics and moral education.* Berkeley: University of California Press.

Noddings, N. (1989). Educating moral people. In M. M. Brabeck (Ed.), *Who cares?: Theory, research, and educational implications of the ethic of care* (pp. 216–232). New York: Praeger.

Oakes, J. (1985). *Keeping track: How schools structure inequality.* New Haven, CT: Yale University Press.

O'Laughlin, M. (1991, October). *Rethinking early childhood education: A sociocultural perspective.* Paper presented at the Reconceptualizing Research in Early Childhood Education Conference, Madison, WI.

Page, R., & Valli, L. (1990). *Curriculum differentiation: Interpretive studies in U.S. secondary schools.* Albany: State University of New York Press.

Pinar, W. F. (Ed.). (1975). *Curriculum theorizing: The reconceptualists.* Berkeley: McCutchan.

Pinar, W. F. (Ed.). (1988). *Contemporary curriculum discourses.* Scottsdale, AZ: Gorsuch Scarisbrick.

Polakow, V. (1992). *Lives on the edge: Single mothers and their children in the other America*. Chicago: University of Chicago Press.

Popkewitz, T. S. (1986). *Paradigm and ideology in educational research*. Basingstoke, England: Falmer.

Schubert, W. H. (1986). *Curriculum: Perspective, paradigm, and possibility*. New York: Macmillan.

Sears, J. (1990, April). *Political, ethical, and methodological issues in conducting research on homosexuality*. Paper presented at the annual meeting of the American Educational Research Association, Boston.

Shavelson, R. J., & Stern, P. (1981). Research on teacher's pedagogical thoughts, judgments, decisions, and behavior. *Review of Educational Research, 51*, 455–498.

Sherman, T. M., & Cormier, W. H. (1974). An investigation of the influence of student behavior on teacher behavior. *Journal of Applied Behavior Analysis, 7*, 11–21.

Sleeter, C. E. (Ed.). (1991). *Empowerment through multicultural education*. Albany: State University of New York Press.

Spodek, B. (1989). What should we teach kindergarten children? (Cassette Recording 612-89121). Alexandria, VA: Association for Supervision and Curriculum Development.

Spodek, B. (in press). Early childhood curriculum and the social definition of knowledge. In M. N. Bloch & G. G. Price (Eds.), *Essays on the history of early childhood education*. Norwood, NJ: Ablex.

Swadener, B. B. (1991, November). *Beyond democracy: Young children as consensus decision makers in a Friends school*. Paper presented at the annual meeting of the American Anthropological Association, Chicago.

Taylor, P. H. (1975). A study of curricular influences in a mid-western elementary school. In P. H. Taylor (Ed.), *Aims, influences and change in the primary school curriculum*. Windsor, Ontario: N.F.E.R.

Tyler, R. W. (1949). *Basic principles of curriculum and instruction*. Chicago: University of Chicago Press.

Weis, L. (Ed.). (1987). *Class, race, and gender in American education*. Albany: State University of New York Press.

Wexler, P. (1990). *Social analysis of education: After the new sociology*. New York: Routledge and Kegan Paul.

Whitty, G. (1977). Sociology and the problem of radical educational change: Notes towards a reconceptualization of the 'new' sociology of education. In M. F. D. Young & G. Whitty (Eds.), *Society, state and schooling* (pp. 112–137). Sussex, England: Falmer.

Willis, P. E. (1978). *Learning to labour*. Westmead, England: Saxon House.

Witherell, C., & Noddings, N. (Eds.). (1991). *Stories lives tell: Narrative and dialogue in education*. New York: Teachers College Press.

Young, M. F. D. (1971). An approach to the study of curricula as socially organized knowledge. In M. F. D. Young (Ed.), *Knowledge and control* (pp. 19–46). London: Collier-Macmillan.

PART I

ALTERNATIVE PERSPECTIVES ON PREVAILING THEORY AND PRACTICE

The chapters in this section place early childhood research and practice in historical, social, theoretical, and cultural contexts. Marianne Bloch's chapter was placed first in this volume because it provides perhaps the broadest perspective on the use of developmental theory to plan, implement, and evaluate early childhood programs. Bloch takes issue with the current emphasis in early childhood research on positivist traditions or theories of developmental psychology that marginalize research from other perspectives, such as critical social science, feminist, and postmodern theory. Her chapter explores the disciplinary and institutional history of early childhood education in an effort to explain the continuing lack of acceptance of critical science perspectives. She also discusses the costs of this past reliance on developmental theory for the future.

In Chapter 2 Shirley Kessler addresses the structural and sociocultural contexts of the early childhood curriculum by drawing upon Kathleen Wilcox's (1982) depiction of the layers of influence on the school curriculum, as well as Catherine Cornbleth's (1990) treatment of the specific components of contexts at each level. Kessler acknowledges the socialization function of schooling and draws upon the early work of Dreeban (1968) and Jackson (1968) to illustrate how schools teach a certain content as well as pass on the values, beliefs, and attitudes held by members of the dominant culture. She uses data from an early ethnographic study of how the child affects the curriculum (Kessler, 1986) to exemplify the layers of influence in two kindergarten classrooms. Finally, Kessler addresses the larger social context, in particular the role of the state in mandating the goals and outcomes of public schooling.

In Chapter 3 Nancy King continues with the emphasis on context in this volume by situating the play of children historically and culturally. King begins her chapter by describing factors—different from those outlined by Cornbleth—that comprise the classroom context of children's play: the physical, personal, curricular, and social contexts. Next, King lays out a fascinating description of views of play depicted in children's readers from 1900 to the 1950s. The final context illuminated by King's research deals with the cultural influences on children's play, particularly the Holocaust and the war play of young children today.

In Chapter 4 Elizabeth Graue illustrates the application of the sociology of knowledge to "readiness," arguing that readiness is not a characteristic of children but a social construction created by communities of educators to interpret the relationship between their perceptions of children's particular "academic" behaviors and the educational goals for kindergartners set by a particular community and its local school. Graue goes so far as to question whether there is such a thing as "readiness." Case studies of two communities are presented and the local policies relative to readiness depicted.

REFERENCES

Cornbleth, C. (1990). *Curriculum in context*. New York: Falmer.

Dreeben, R. (1968). *On what is learned in school*. Reading, MA: Addison-Wesley.

Jackson, P. (1968). *Life in classrooms*. New York: Holt, Rinehart and Winston.

Kessler, S. A. (1986). *The child's effect on the kindergarten curriculum*. Unpublished doctoral dissertation, University of Wisconsin–Madison.

Wilcox, K. (1982). Differential socialization in the classroom: Implications for equal opportunity. In G. Spindler (Ed.), *Doing the ethnography of schooling: Educational anthropology in action* (pp. 166–187). Chicago: Holt, Rinehart & Winston.

CHAPTER 1

Critical Perspectives on the Historical Relationship Between Child Development and Early Childhood Education Research

Marianne N. Bloch

The terms "critical theory," "interpretivist or symbolic research," or "post-modern" are rarely heard in seminar rooms, publications, or conferences focusing on early childhood education. Indeed, in recent years, the few scholars who identify with both these perspectives *and* early childhood education have called for and created their own forums for discussion of these issues.[1] Based on acceptance and visibility in typical early childhood education conferences and publications, many perceive their work to be unacceptable, unwelcome, or, at least, unrecognized. Indeed, with rare exceptions,[2] early childhood educators who fail to frame their research or research methods in the largely positivist traditions and theories of child development or developmental psychology find themselves marginalized in their own field because of their choice of alternative theories and methods that *are* considered legitimate outside early childhood education.

One[3] reason for the lack of recognition or acceptance of alternative theoretical and methodological perspectives in early childhood education is the century-long domination of psychological and child development perspectives in the field of early childhood education. A second reason relates to the important separate institutional histories of early childhood education and that of elementary education in the United States (Bloch, 1987). It is argued that these institutional separations were related to the

An earlier version of this chapter was published under the title "Critical Science and the History of Child Development's Influence on Early Education Research" in *Early Education and Development*, (1991), 2(2), 95–108. Reprinted by permission of Psychology Press.

growth of research using symbolic or interpretivist, critical, and, most recently, post-modern paradigms in schools of education, while early education, as a separate institution, typically in different university disciplines, remained tied to psychology, child development, and largely positivist and empirical-analytic paradigms in theory and method. This chapter explores the disciplinary and institutional histories of early childhood education in an effort to explain the continuing lack of acceptance of other theories and methods in early childhood education, while these approaches have attained recognition and substantial interest elsewhere.

The chapter is organized in several sections. In the first, I briefly describe what is meant by symbolic or interpretivist theory, critical theory, and post-modern paradigms in relation to empirical-analytic paradigms. In the second section, I try to trace the history of the development of child development and developmental psychology in relation to the growth of the field of early child education. In the final section of the chapter, I try to illuminate the costs to the field of continuing to exclude or marginalize alternative perspectives, such as those presented by critical theoretical frameworks and research.

ALTERNATIVE CONCEPTIONS OF THEORY AND SCIENCE

Popkewitz (1984) in *Paradigm and Ideology in Educational Research* describes the history of the social sciences and the development of three paradigms for research—"empirical-analytic" scientific frameworks (lawlike theories of social behavior), "symbolic" sciences (social life as rule making and rule governing), and "critical" sciences (social relations as historical expression)—that have emerged within the social sciences, and, especially, within educational research in the United States during the late twentieth century. Significantly, Popkewitz also situates the development of these paradigms within their historical and cultural periods of growth and legitimization in the United States and elsewhere. He attempts to show that these paradigms of research are distinguished by their assumptions concerning the definitions as well as the contestability of "knowledge," "science," "research," power, politics, and action. In addition, he suggests they have different underlying assumptions about the relationships between research and practice, research and action, researchers and their functions, and assumptions of objectivity and subjectivity of research. More recently, others (e.g., Ellsworth, 1989; Fraser, 1989; Lather, 1991; Popkewitz, 1991) have focused attention on feminist, post-structuralist, or post-modernist theories, and some have suggested that these theories represent a fourth paradigmatic approach to research and assumptions underlying research (e.g., Lather, 1991).

In this section I briefly describe some important distinctions in these different "ways of knowing" or establishing truth as science. I also illustrate theoretical differences of some importance within different paradigms (especially critical and post-modern) in order to illustrate significant differences within these fields (e.g., Apple, 1982; Cherryholmes, 1988; Ellsworth, 1989; Giroux, 1986; Giroux & McLaren, 1989; Lather, 1991; McCarthy & Apple, 1988). While the list and the descriptions are not exhaustive, and the category system, following Popkewitz (1984), seems to deny the interrelatedness of the issues and the categories, the section is meant to provide a beginning glance at some of the important areas of difference. Finally, it should be emphasized that the primary purpose of the section is to illustrate ways in which the dominance of positivist or empirical–analytic research traditions in early childhood education research has limited the way we conceive of and do research as well as practice in the field (also see Note 2 here). Those interested in more than an overview, however, should turn to primary sources cited within the text of the chapter.

Empirical–analytic sciences are characterized by Popkewitz (1984) as holding seven interrelated assumptions:

1. A theory that is universal and not bound to a specific context
2. A commitment to a disinterested science where the goals and values of people are independent of what may be expressed as scientific research by those people
3. A belief that the social world exists as a system of variables that are separable—that one can examine the parts of a system and make sense of one behavior by isolating and controlling variables, for example, without regard for the rest of the system (e.g., teacher praise as a single variable)
4. Formalized knowledge that must be operationalized and reliably judged before examination in research
5. A distinction between theory and practice, where theory and research should inform practice but not be directly linked to it
6. The frequent use of mathematics to test or examine the theory or hypotheses generated
7. An empirical–analytic paradigm typically aligned with positivist theory, stemming from Compte. In brief, it recognizes positive facts and stresses observable phenomena, as well as objective relations between these and the laws that determine them; positivism also is associated

with a reduction of emphasis on the causes or ultimate origins of phenomena that cannot be observed or examined within the context of research.

Symbolic science, or interpretivist science, focuses on intersubjectivities that are created through interactions among people, their discourse, and interpretations of meaning within specific contexts. The notion of theory shifts, in this paradigm, from a "search for lawlike regularities about the nature of social behavior to the identification of the social rules that underlie and govern the use of social 'facts'" (Popkewitz, 1984, p. 41).

Much of the original research stemmed from sociology, anthropology, or linguistics. Fieldwork associated with these and other disciplines (e.g., education) is frequently characterized as sociolinguistic, interpretative, qualitative, ethnographic, or microethnographic. Unlike the empirical–analytic sciences approach, subjective rather than objective conceptions and interpretations of reality are paramount. What is "real" and "valid" is determined through careful analysis of what is consensually agreed upon. Reliability is important insofar as there is agreement among individuals in meaning within a context, but the importance of a priori agreement related to the development of categories or codes to define behavior, a very important part of the empirical–analytic modes of research, is not as critical as shared meaning or interpretations within a context. Like empirical–analytic sciences, there is more of an emphasis on description than on practice or on politics; the relationships between research and practice and research and politics are debated more in critically-oriented research. Theory is built from the description and is nested in reinterpretations of meaning, but not in a broad structural or historical context.

The third approach cited by Popkewitz (1984), *critical theory or sciences*, has its roots in the Frankfurt School of sociological and philosophical inquiry. Research is to unravel the dynamics of contemporary society by illuminating assumptions and historical roots of current problems. Some Marxist and Neo-Marxist critical theories (e.g., Bowles & Gintis, 1976) examine the way in which philosophies and practices have determined what is taught in school and have served the "state" to reproduce class lines and economic relationships. Others (e.g., Apple, 1982; Apple & Weiss, 1983; McCarthy, 1988; McCarthy & Apple, 1988) have outlined a theory that is less deterministic and attempts to examine interrelationships among cultural, ideological, and economic relationships and race, class, and gender-related oppression. Critical theorists are purposefully political in their research, requiring themselves to admit that all research is politically biased, that no research or research methods are truly "objective." In doing so, they attempt to explicate the political theory that guides the research, focusing on the relationships between the state and classroom or pedagogy as legitimate and a critical part of the research question.

Other important differences exist, but they vary depending upon the researcher and the researched. Some emphasize the relationship between theory and praxis (e.g., Apple & Weiss, 1983; Lather, 1986) and have been leaders in examining personal and group "agency" and active resistance to outside forces. The concept of personal or group agency or resistance requires examination and contestation of overly deterministic models such as traditional Marxist economic analyses dictate (see Willis, 1977, as one example). Research methods have included critical ethnographies (see the recent review by Anderson, 1989) of classroom practice that has been interpreted as reproductive or productive of the same or new social relationships in society. Some research has used historical analysis to illuminate hidden assumptions in the development of educational policy or practice that have served to constrain educational practice and reproduce the place of the dominant class, race, and gender groups in society (e.g., Bloch, 1987; Kessler, 1991; Popkewitz, 1987; Swadener, 1991). Recent research has used teacher biography and oral history to illuminate similar themes and, most recently, to describe radical pedagogical practice aimed at transforming and restructuring relationships (e.g., Ayers, 1989; Goodson & Walker, 1991).

Finally, recent movements are summarized here under the title *postmodern*. This strand of social and educational theory focuses on the relation of language as well as media and other cultural images and the construction of practice. It includes a focus on the constructive role of language posed in a broad conceptualization of rules and standards by which speech is expressed (discourse). Language is not only an expression of human social affairs but also, as expressed, an expression of power and identity (Popkewitz, 1991). Cherryholmes (1988), for example, gives attention to the ways in which seemingly objective criteria of school practices are socially constructed and embody power relations through discourse. Feminist literature in education (e.g., Ellsworth, 1989; Fraser, 1989; Lather, 1986, 1991) considers discourse and the problem of literary and other forms of cultural representation in the formation of gender roles and power. This movement integrates multiple disciplines, including psychology, and turns attention away from Marxist theories that treat race, class, and gender as universal categories. It looks for plurality of interpretation. It is part of a broader rethinking of social, historical, and psychological theory and challenges structural theories that search for ultimate causes of oppression through, for example, universalized notions of race, class, and gender.

CHILD DEVELOPMENT AND ITS RELATIONSHIP TO EARLY CHILDHOOD EDUCATION: A HISTORICAL PERSPECTIVE

In the first part of this chapter, I suggest that the field of early childhood education has been linked to the psychological sciences, in particular, child development, for the majority of the twentieth century. I also suggest that few early childhood educators have begun to do scholarship outside the empirical–analytic science tradition that dominates as a paradigm within the psychological sciences; while more symbolic or qualitative studies of early education have emerged during the last decade (e.g., Heath, 1983; Lubeck, 1985), still relatively few (e.g., King, 1982) have worked from symbolic or, especially, critical science traditions. Indeed, today the empirical–analytic orientation to research still seems to have such dominance that special issues of journals (e.g., Swadener & Kessler, 1991) and special conferences (e.g., Ayers et al., 1991) are needed to bring early childhood education writers together on this topic.

At the elementary and secondary levels of education, critical theories, called *social melioration* theories by Kliebard (1986), became an important force in education in the late 1920s and 1930s (Kliebard, 1986; Popkewitz, 1984). While these perspectives lost ground for several decades after that period, critically-oriented theorists regained ground in the 1960s and had become a force in elementary and secondary education by the 1980s (Popkewitz, 1984). It is the influence of some of the research, writing, and teaching during this period (among the major influences have been Apple, 1982; Bowles & Gintis, 1976; Noddings, 1984) that has resulted in the emergence of a number of researchers who use critical (and now some post-modern) perspectives at the early childhood level.

Why did elementary and secondary education levels gradually incorporate more critical sciences into their research and traditions in the decades from 1960 to 1980 while early childhood education, until recently, did not? Although greater flexibility in methods were used in early education as some became interested in Jean Piaget's work and methodologies, as suggested earlier (see Note 2, this chapter), I believe that these shifts did not represent major changes in the examination of underlying assumptions as represented by symbolic, critical, or post-modern perspectives.

In the next section of this chapter, I describe the historical development of the strong relationship between psychology, child development, and early education. I also attempt to explain why early childhood and elementary and secondary education varied in their reliance on psychology and child development for definitions of theory, knowledge, research, and practice.

Becoming Scientific and Professional

During the late nineteenth and early twentieth centuries, the field of psychology was growing and attempting to utilize methods approaching the physical sciences (O'Donnell, 1985; Popkewitz, 1991). The field of child development, and the related field of early education, as these disciplines grew within universities during the first quarter of the twentieth century, attempted, in large part, to emulate psychology (for some exceptions during the 1920s and 1930s, see Antler, 1987; Bloch & Choi, 1990). To varying degrees, depending upon the place and person, there were attempts to use the "hard" physical sciences, and psychology's definition of science (typically personified in experimental psychology), as the model for truth, definitions of valuable knowledge, a way to get factual information about "normal" child development, and guidance for pedagogy. Those involved with using science to establish a base for greater knowledge about what to do with young children also aspired to be known as professionals in their respective fields of psychology, child development, or early education. Being "scientific" in theory, method of research, and pedagogical applications was part of becoming or appearing more professional, especially as many associated with child development or early education were associated with home economics and what was thought to be a female field.

In an earlier paper (Bloch, 1987), I described, in greater detail, the shift from a more introspective mode of inquiry and way of knowing about children, represented by Froebelian kindergartens in the late nineteenth century, to twentieth century "scientific" programs dictated by the philosophies of G. Stanley Hall, John Dewey, Edward Thorndike, and Patty Smith Hill. I claimed that in an effort to be "more scientific" and achieve status as a profession and as professionals, psychological researchers such as Hall turned toward what was perceived to be an "objective" psychology and attempts to study animal and child nature through their behavior.

Hall, as the leading American psychologist of the late nineteenth century (other than William James, his mentor), turned to child study as a scientific method and claimed that objective methods for examining children's natural development should be used to obtain information that could then guide pedagogy (O'Donnell, 1985). Hall trained numerous doctoral students in his methods and in the philosophies he also aligned with his objective notions of science. His students, according to O'Donnell, included one-half of the Ph.D.'s in psychology for the first twenty years of the history of the field in the United States. Terman, Dewey, Gesell, Baldwin, Burke, and Thorndike were among his students; Patty Smith Hill, Anna Bryant, and Colonel Francis Parker, whose Quincy, Massachusetts, curriculum he much admired, were among the psychologists and educators who attended Hall's seminars on child study and the new pedagogy. Students of Hall's were all influenced by the notions of a "scientific" study of children; science was radical and progressive; science was new; in certain circles, science was high in status and an earmark of a more professional approach to the study of the child and his education.

As a study of professionalization, it is important to see that Hall's notions, more or less intact, were used to begin the child development movement that related psychology to science, psychology to child development, and psychology to the study of pedagogy and curriculum.

While Hall's students all took somewhat different pathways (see O'Donnell, 1985), they retained the following beliefs:

1. In scientific (objective, rational, empirical) methods
2. That psychological studies of individuals and individual development and behavior were important
3. That observed "natural" development of children, their needs, interests, and impulses could be used to inform pedagogy
4. That philosophy should be, to some extent, separated from the science of psychology, child development research and knowledge, and educational pedagogy[4]

These beliefs resulted in a strong tie between psychology and pedagogy, especially at the early childhood level (Antler, 1987; Kliebard, 1986; Sears, 1975; Spodek, in press; Takanishi, 1982), and the continuing *dominant* belief in the possibility and worth of objective, nonintrospective, and nonphilosophical studies of children. The development of the child study movement and the growth of the field of child development in university settings were also strongly interrelated (Sears, 1975; Takanishi, 1982).

They also resulted, for Hall and some of his influential followers (Terman, Gesell, Baldwin, Burke, and, to a lesser extent, Hill), in a strong belief in biological determination and inherited abilities and nature. Ironically, Hall's attempt to claim an objective scientific approach to child study has been critiqued by many, since his strong reliance on recapitulation theory and Social Darwinistic survival of the fittest frameworks had strong biases and subjective as well as philosophical elements. Thus the belief in an objective science—while boldly acclaimed and adhered to in the history of child development and early childhood education—was not really true during Hall's time, and, indeed, is not true today (Kliebard, in press; Popkewitz, 1984).

Child development researchers, along with those in psychology and education in general, eventually rejected Hall's child study methods; however, the reasons for Hall's rejection varied by discipline. Those aspiring to develop the field of child development as a respected subdivision of psychology saw Hall's techniques as too "unscientific" because data had been gathered by imprecise means and by untrained parents and teachers. In order to appear more scientific within the fold of psychology, the majority of child development researchers turned even further toward experimental psychology as a model for research; the more objective, reliable, and controlled experiments and research could be, the better it was considered to be. In contrast, those in the fields of elementary and secondary education rejected Hall for very different reasons; these are described in the next section.

The Separate Institutional Histories of Early Education and Elementary Education

The ongoing development and variations in Hall's, Dewey's, Thorndike's, Watson's, Hill's, and others' theories as they relate to early educatioin are discussed elsewhere (e.g., Antler, 1987; Bloch, 1987; Kliebard, 1986; Weber, 1969, 1984). Of greatest interest here are the separate histories of childcare, nursery and kindergarten education as the cornerstones of early childhood education, and elementary education. The different histories are related to (1) the growth of the fields as professions and in different institutions and (2) the related reasons why early childhood and elementary education differed in their reliance on child development theories and psychological research.

By the early twentieth century, there were kindergartens in charitable private schools, as part of social welfare settlement house programs, and in public schools (Bloch, 1987). Day nurseries for children whose parents worked were also included in some settlement house programs as well as administered through other social welfare and private charitable groups. Nursery schools, as we know them in the United States, began during the early 1920s, frequently, although not always, as part of the growth of home economics department laboratory schools in university settings. Primary or elementary education was largely in public school settings.

The growth of the three branches of institutions most commonly associated with early childhood education today—day-care, nursery schools (now preschools), and kindergartens—were largely associated with different professional institutions at the university research and training levels. As suggested earlier, through the 1930s day-care was linked to social welfare institutions, agencies, and policies and, generally, served children from low-income families where the mother was employed. Teachers received nursery school training or on-the-job training; policy issues were debated within schools of social work as frequently as in education-related fields.

Nursery schools developed during the 1920s as a result of efforts of the Laura Spellman Rockefeller Memorial (LSRM) to build child development as a scientific discipline that could inform research, policy, and practice. The LSRM, through its leader Lawrence Frank, funded child development institutes in a variety of university settings, including Iowa, Berkeley, and Minnesota (e.g., see Antler, 1987; Schlossman, 1981; Takanishi, 1982). These institutes began as a way to provide laboratories for training young women in home economics and childcare ("scientific motherhood") and as a way to provide an easy setting in which to do experimental and scientific studies of children's development. Nursery school theory, research, and training leaned heavily on child study, and the evolving theories of child development that were promoted in these university institutes and other child development and study departments (typically based in home economics or psychology departments) or in psychiatry. Nursery schools generally served children from European-American, and middle or upper income backgrounds. While some important exceptions existed (e.g., see Antler, 1987; Bloch & Choi, 1990), continuing leadership by university-based child development institutes and researchers, funded by LSRM, pushed the field and the institutes and their associated researchers toward more "scientific" and "objective" studies of child development within nursery school contexts.

By the late 1920s, kindergartens were situated in private and public school settings (Spodek, 1980). Kindergartens and kindergarten training were split—sometimes being part of a child development department's responsibility in a university, sometimes being part of an education school's responsibility, sometimes being seen as a shared responsibility across home economics, psychology, and education. In some institutions by the 1930s, there was an attempt to consolidate at least some of the branches of education into one department; for example, Columbia's

Teachers College had a Kindergarten–Primary Education Program in the late 1920s and changed the name to the Nursery–Kindergarten–Primary Education Department in the 1930s. In more institutions, research and pedagogy concerned with 2- to 5-year-olds rested outside the school of education, while schools of education generally retained specific interest in elementary education with "add-on" interest in kindergarten education (Spodek, 1980).

The history of the different institutional affiliations that the two fields had may be an important explanation for differences between the field of elementary education and those of child development and early education in terms of their reliance on psychology and certain notions of "science." Early education as a professional group was more heavily aligned with psychology, psychiatry, home economics, and child and family studies programs at the university level than elementary education was. Freudian and other behavioral theories supported the importance of early individual and personality development in children. The institutional presence of laboratory nursery schools in, most frequently, home economics departments emphasized teaching women about families, family care, cooking, and other "family arts" as well as about scientific knowledge of child development and childrearing. Child development professionals aligned themselves, for a variety of reasons, with psychology to engage in theoretical debates on individual development and family influences, as well as to appear to be a fairly "hard" science (O'Donnell, 1985). This attempt to affiliate with the psychologial sciences and the methods of research honored within that discipline, combined with continual theoretical struggles within psychiatry, psychology, and child development, may have kept early educators' attention focused on these methods, problems, and debates.

Takanishi (1982) clearly outlines some of the debates that were held in the child development community as most turned away from G. Stanley Hall's method of child study and its strong relationship to pedagogy and policy; child development institutes and laboratory nursery schools were explicitly set up to foster objective research on children and to provide scientific evidence on children's normal development to parents and teachers.[5] While Lawrence Frank and others associated with, for example, the Bureau of Educational Research (later known as Bank Street College of Education) argued about the definition of research and its relation to practice as well as social theories related to the role of education (Antler, 1987; Takanishi, 1982), the majority of child development researchers tried to divorce themselves, as best they could, from practice or teacher-training issues. Although there was a need to train parents and nursery school teachers in laboratory nursery schools, only knowledge from the established theories and research of psychology and child development was used and given status as truth or knowledge.[6]

The Growth of Symbolic and Critical Paradigms in Educational Research

Kliebard (1986, in press) suggests that G. Stanley Hall's child study methods, included in what he calls the *developmental* approach, were eventually rejected by the field of education in favor of other models of education that were used in the struggle over the formation of elementary curriculum. These included the *social efficiency* framework of David Snedden, J. W. Charters, and Franklin W. Bobbit and a social reform or *social meliorist* framework represented by the work of Lester Ward, Harold Rugg, George Counts, and John Dewey (for detailed descriptions of the struggles within elementary curriculum formation, see Kliebard, 1986).

Thus, while child development knowledge certainly guided, and continues to guide, elementary education curriculum and pedagogy, during the first third of the twentieth century there was less reliance on developmental perspectives as the primary source of ideas about curriculum than in early childhood education (Kliebard, 1986, in press). By the 1930s, social efficiency movements within elementary and secondary education as well as social reform perspectives (social reconstructionist or social meliorist positions) had competed successfully with the developmentalists for control of the curriculum. Why early childhood education had a separate history of traditions of research and inquiry relative to the other levels of education, and why by the late 1970s these traditions had grown further apart, is an interesting question.

Within many schools of education, the remnants of social reconstructionist theories from the 1930s, through Dewey and others' work and continuing influence, kept a focus on education as social reform, especially through the continual examination of the social studies curriculum (e.g., Kliebard, 1986). During the 1960s, some social activists within elementary and secondary education turned their attention toward analysis of education's role in maintaining the status quo, or reproducing race, class, and gender differences in society; many reflected on the nonobjectivity of what was considered by many to be "objective science."

In early childhood education, social reform through programs such as Head Start also dominated discussion from the 1960s on, but issues related to which psychologically based theory of early education was best held peoples' attention. The continuing quest for how individual children and individual family units socialize the young differently dominated debate; discourse framed in individualistic terms with emphasis on families as social units rather than on larger structural groups, institutions, or forces narrowed the scope of dialogue and possibilities for other modes of analysis. As one example, until very recently, questions and discussion related to the role early education may play in maintaining or augmenting race, class, and gender inequities within the United States have been very rare; critical perspectives, in contrast, have assumed that education may serve to reproduce these differences, not to reduce them.

Summary

These various theoretical, scientific, and institutional trends in the field of early childhood education influenced the development of a strong link between early childhood teacher training and psychological— either behavioral or psychoanalytically guided—child development theories and research; early childhood education university-based faculty aligned themselves with laboratory programs and other professionals in child development for their theoretical models as well as their definitions of important knowledge and approaches to "science." In an effort to be scientific and professional, early childhood education professors appeared to emulate child psychology, varying in the constancy of their attention to early childhood education and pedagogy issues. Child development knowledge, continually based on research with largely middle-class European-American samples, was a principal source of knowledge about what to do in the curriculum, what normal children do and how they develop. While the dominant frame of research focusing on middle-class European-American children is less widespread now, the reliance on child development theories and knowledge remains the case today (see below and, for critiques of such reliance, see Kessler, 1991; Spodek, in press).

COSTS OF THE CONTINUING RELIANCE ON
EMPIRICAL-ANALYTIC PERSPECTIVES

Until very recently, the theme of individual self-help has been extremely evident in discourse at a variety of levels, but, for the purposes of this chapter, I argue that it has been especially evident at the early childhood level. A focus on individual differences in development and on family and school influences on individual development has been dominant. The perspective that social improvement results from the efforts of its individual members to "do better" is rampant and serves (whether intentional or not) to distract attention from structural analyses of the problems that help to maintain oppression and inequities in achievement. The discourse in recent reform documents, such as the *Developmentally Appropriate Curriculum* guidelines (e.g., see Bredekamp, 1987) or the National Association of State Boards of Education Task Force on Early Childhood Education's (1988) report *Right from the Start*, continues to reinforce these notions in the way attention is paid to individual development and local rather than structural level influences.

Thus one cost to the field of the continuing reliance on psychological or "child development" perspectives is the continuation of the mentality that problems and prospects are situated at the individual or family or, even, school level. With little attention to the complexity of the influences on the way, for example, groups of individuals systematically are constrained in their opportunities for development and success, we as a field continue to blame individuals. The constrained and/or narrow way in which early education research and policy has developed over time limits its ability to direct action at appropriate levels and helps to reinforce inequities that the field claims it works against.

A less serious cost of the continuing reliance on empirical–analytic methods is the loss to research of seeing things differently. Knowledge can come from many sources, and alternative ways of knowing can only add to our vision of issues, influences on development and schooling, and understanding of curriculum and pedagogy. It is useful to hear different voices tell their stories about how they experience education or schooling (e.g., Ayers, 1989); it is valuable to use a symbolic interactionist framework to examine the construction of meaning students and teachers attach to the observations researchers so often do and construe by themselves. The dominant valuing and reliance on empirical–analytic frames of reference limit our understanding of "truth" rather than providing it through the objective eyes and strategies of the researcher, as is so often claimed.

Finally, the reliance on empirical–analytic methods and frames of reference is self-reinforcing. New professionals who are brought into the field of early childhood education are typically trained by professionals who have an empirical–analytic focus and who hire new researchers (faculty members) because of their ability to do good empirical–analytically framed research. Publications and conferences are, in general, organized by these same professionals, and those with other frameworks can only hope to have a sympathetic reviewer. While these issues may seem somewhat unimportant relative to other issues mentioned above, they are important because the professionals who get into and stay in the field of early education guide the visions of the field; they define what knowledge is good and valuable and how one should construe or situate problems and actions. It is from these perspectives that I argue that we need to reconceptualize early childhood education, at the very least, to include alternative perspectives and research paradigms.

NOTES

Acknowledgments. The author acknowledges comments provided on the earlier version made by anonymous reviewers, editors for the issue and this volume, Shirley Kessler and Beth Blue Swadener, as well as the comments of Thomas Popkewitz, Chelsea Bailey, Susan Adler, Elizabeth Graue, and Robert Showalter.

1. The first conference focusing on Reconceptualizing Research in Early Childhood Education was held at the University of Wisconsin–Madison, October 3–6, 1991.

2. Research in early education that has used methods pioneered by Jean Piaget, for example, is one such obvious exception. Despite this type of exception, my argument is that the field is largely dominated by researchers using positivist or empirical-analytic paradigms and research methodologies. This chapter is particularly directed toward a critique of the dominant use of as well as the dominant belief in the truth, value, and scientific validity of research using positivist and empirical-analytic frameworks and paradigmatic assumptions over other approaches and paradigms for research. In addition, I also argue that even Piagetian-based research focuses attention toward child development to the exclusion of other macrostructural variables, for example. I do not argue exclusively for one or more alternative ways to examine issues in early childhood education, but *simply* to open up the field of inquiry to include more alternative research approaches and paradigms. In addition, I argue that early childhood education researchers' examination of individual development issues to the exclusion of other ways of lookng at ideological, cultural, economic, and political issues has narrowed our understanding of problems in the field.

3. I emphasize the word *one* here because some readers might assume that my aim is solely to critique psychologically oriented or child development oriented studies and may discount the remainder (or part) of my chapter. This is too simplistic a perception of my arguments and too simplistic a perspective on the value of psychological and child development research for the field of early education and education in general. My argument is *not* that psychological theories or research are without value, but that an *undue reliance* on the assumptions, traditions, and contributions of one field over time has had and will continue to have costs for the field of early education, scholars associated with it, and young children.

4. Dewey was an exception in the way Hall's students were influenced by Hall's ideas. While Dewey was a professor of psychology and education and was

indeed influenced by Hall, his work remained strongly tied to social philosophy and reform; his ideas about learning were not as tied to behaviorism, over time, as most of Hall's other students' work was.

5. Although self-evident by now, it is still important to remember that the concept of "normal" development based on scientific knowledge embodied clear class and culture biases; data were most frequently obtained with American children of middle-class European background who were in laboratory nursery schools. This base for much objective scientific child development information then was generalized to describe "normal" development worldwide. Similarly, the concept of providing mothers with ways to be more scientific included the notion that mothers' own knowledge about parenting and child development was inherently less truthful or knowledgeable than "scientific knowledge" and that women (mothers) needed training by experts. Many have also suggested that the movement toward scientific motherhood was related to efforts to give mothers more reasons for staying home to do women's work (see, for example, Schlossman, 1976, 1981).

6. Child development research during the 1920s and 1930s was characterized by attempts to remove stigmas of faulty science attributed to the field of child development by Hall's early methodologies; in addition, there were debates about the scientific study of the child using behavioral methodologies versus the "less" scientific but influential theories of Freud and other psychoanalytically oriented theorists, notably Erik Erikson. Anthropologically oriented child development research was couched as "culture and personality" research that frequently rested on a meshing of anthropological sites and techniques with psychoanalytic theories. While behaviorism and notions of science were also important in schools of education, social theories of Dewey and others (Kliebard, 1986) were more influential there than they were in the child development field.

REFERENCES

Anderson, G. (1989). Critical ethnography in education: Origins, current status, and new directions. *Review of Education Research, 59*(3), 249–270.

Antler, J. (1987). *Lucy Sprague Mitchell.* New Haven, CT: Yale University Press.

Apple, M. (1982). *Education and power.* Boston: Routledge and Kegan Paul.

Apple, M., & Weiss, L. (1983). *Ideology and practice in schooling.* Philadelphia: Temple University Press.

Ayers, W. (1989). *The good preschool teacher.* New York: Teachers College Press.

Ayers, W., Bloch, M., Graue, B., Grossman, C., Kessler, S., Price, G. G., Spodek, B., Swadener, B. B., & Walsh, D. (1991). *Book of abstracts.* Abstracts of presentations at the October 3–6, 1991, conference titled Reconceptualizing Research in Early Childhood Education, University of Wisconsin–Madison (Available from M. Bloch, Department of Curriculum and Instruction, 225 N. Mills St., Madison, WI 53706).

Bloch, M. N. (1987). Becoming scientific and professional: An historical perspective on the aims and effects of early education. In T. S. Popkewitz (Ed.), *The formation of the school subjects* (pp. 25-62). Basingstoke, England: Falmer.

Bloch, M. N. (1991). Critical science and the history of child development's influence on early education research. *Early Education and Development*, 2(2), 95-107.

Bloch, M. N., & Choi, S. (1990). Conceptions of play in the history of early childhood education. *Child and Youth Care Quarterly*, 19(1), 31-48.

Bowles, S., & Gintis, H. (1976). *Schooling in capitalist America*. New York: Basic Books.

Bredekamp, S. (1987). *Developmentally appropriate practice in early childhood programs serving children from birth through age 8*. Washington, DC: National Association for the Education of Young Children.

Cherryholmes, C. (1988). *Power and criticism: Poststructural investigations in education*. New York: Teachers College Press.

Ellsworth, E. (1989). Why doesn't this feel empowering? *Harvard Education Review, 59*, 297-324.

Fraser, N. (1989). *Unruly practices: Power, discourse and gender in contemporary social theory*. Minneapolis: University of Minnesota Press.

Giroux, H. (1986). Radical pedagogy and the politics of student voice. *Interchange, 17*, 48-69.

Giroux, H., & McLaren, P. (Eds.) (1989). *Critical pedagogy, the state, and cultural struggle*. Albany: State University of New York Press.

Goodson, I., & Walker, R. (1991). *Biography, education, and research*. Basingstoke, England: Falmer.

Heath, S. B. (1983). *Ways with words*. Cambridge, England: Cambridge University Press.

Kessler, S. (1991). Alternative perspectives on early childhood education. *Early Childhood Research Quarterly, 6*, 183-197.

King, N. (1982). Work and play in the classroom. *Sociology of education, 46*, 110-113.

Kliebard, H. (1986). *The struggle for the American curriculum*. London: Routledge and Kegan Paul.

Kliebard, H. (in press). 'Keeping out of nature's way': The rise and fall of child-study as the basis for the curriculum, 1880-1905. In M. N. Bloch & G. G. Price (Eds.), *Essays on the history of early childhood education*. Norwood, NJ: Ablex.

Lather, P. (1986). Research as praxis. *Harvard Education Review, 56*(3), 257-277.

Lather, P. (1991). *Getting smart: Feminist research & pedagogy with-in the post modern*. New York: Routledge and Kegan Paul.

Lubeck, S. (1985). *Sandbox society*. Basingstoke, England: Falmer.

McCarthy, C. (1988). Rethinking liberal and radical perspectives on racial inequality in schooling: Making the case for nonsynchrony. *Harvard Education Review, 58*(3), 265-277.

McCarthy, C., & Apple, M. W. (1988). Race, class, and gender in American educational research: Toward a nonsynchronous parallelist position. In L. Weiss (Ed.), *Class, race, and gender in American education* (pp. 9–39). Albany: State University of New York Press.

National Association of State Boards of Education Task Force on Early Childhood Education. (1988). *Right from the start*. Alexandria, VA: Author.

Noddings, N. (1984). *Caring.* Berkeley: University of California Press.

O'Donnell, J. M. (1985). *The origins of behaviorism: American psychology, 1870–1920.* New York: New York University Press.

Popkewitz, T. S. (1984). *Paradigm and ideology in educational research.* Basingstoke, England: Falmer.

Popkewitz, T. S. (1987). *The formation of the school subjects.* Basingstoke, England: Falmer.

Popkewitz, T. S. (1991). *Political sociology of educational reform: Power/knowledge in teaching, teacher education, and research.* New York: Teachers College Press.

Schlossman, S. (1976). Before home start: Notes toward a history of parent education in America. *Harvard Education Review, 46,* 436–467.

Schlossman, S. (1981). Philanthropy and the gospel of child development. *History of Education Quarterly,* Fall, pp. 175–199.

Sears, R. R. (1975). Your ancients revisited: A history of child development. In E. M. Hetherington (Ed.), *Review of Child Development Research, 5,* 1–73.

Spodek, B. (1980). The kindergarten: A retrospective and contemporary view. In L. Katz (Ed.), *Current topics in early education, Vol. 4* (pp. 173–191). Norwood, NJ: Ablex.

Spodek, B. (in press). Early childhood curriculum and the social definition of knowledge. In M. N. Bloch & G. G. Price (Eds.), *Essays on the history of early childhood education.* Norwood NJ: Ablex.

Swadener, E. B. (1991). Children and families "at-risk": Etiology, critique and alternative paradigms. *Educational Foundations, 4*(4), 17–39.

Swadener, E. B., & Kessler, S. A. (1991). Reconceptualizing early childhood education [Special Issue]. *Early Education and Development, 2*(2).

Takanishi, R. (1982). Early childhood education and research: The changing relationship. *Theory into Practice, 20*(2), 86–92.

Weber, E. (1969). *The kindergarten.* New York: Teachers College Press.

Weber, E. (1984). *Ideas influencing early childhood education.* New York: Teachers College Press.

Willis, P. (1977). *Learning to labor: How working class kids get working class jobs.* Lexington, MA: Heath.

CHAPTER 2

The Social Context of the Early Childhood Curriculum

Shirley A. Kessler

The increase in enrollment of 4- and 5-year-old children in educational programs in the United States in the last two decades has been dramatic. In 1970, only 28 percent of all 4-year-olds and 69 percent of all five-year-olds were enrolled in early childhood programs. However, between 1971 and 1985, when elementary and secondary school enrollment declined steadily, the percentage of 4- and 5-year-olds attending school increased substantially. By 1985, 49 percent of all 4-year-olds and 85 percent of all five-year-olds attended school in private or public settings. Of those attending school in 1985, 43 percent of 4-year-olds and 85 percent of 5-year-olds attended early childhood programs under the auspices of the public schools (National Center for Educational Statistics, 1988).

The prevalence of early childhood programs in the public schools radically alters the context of early childhood education, a context that, I believe, greatly influences what is taught and experienced in early childhood classrooms. Spodek (1982) suggested that the increase in kindergarten enrollment was related to one of the major issues facing early childhood educators today—the academic nature of the curriculum in many programs for young children. He claimed that since kindergarten education was no longer the exception, but the rule, public school educators were taking advantage of the potential of a kindergarten experience for fostering readiness for first grade and, in many instances, actually teaching in the kindergarten what used to be taught in the first-grade curriculum. He also suggested other explanations for the more academic orientation: the increased use of standardized tests and the fact that many early childhood teachers were trained in elementary, not early childhood, education. Others have pointed to public school administrators who did not have adequate knowledge of child development and who presumably pressured the kindergarten teacher to teach a more skills-oriented curriculum (Kamii, 1985), as well as to the unrealistic expectations of some first-grade teachers as further influencing the prevalence of the academic curriculum (Kessler, 1986; Smith & Shepard, 1988; Webster, 1984).

The expansion of early childhood programs into the public schools enhances the likelihood that the curriculum will be vulnerable to the same social and political influences affecting the curriculum in elementary and secondary classrooms—influences such as the faith in scientism as it applies to education, the widespread use of textbooks, federal legislation and court decisions (Eisner, 1985), and the increase in public pressure for accountability as evidenced by the widespread use of achievement testing and the current interest in the development of national goals and a national student exam (McNeil, 1991). Unfortunately, however, the heavy emphasis of early childhood research on the developing child precludes an analysis of the complexity of the school curriculum and the relationship between curriculum practice and the social and political context of the classroom and school. While there is tacit awareness among early childhood educators of the influences of the context of the curriculum, the context of particular programs has not been carefully studied. These supposed influences now need to be identified and brought to the fore of our thinking about developmentally appropriate early childhood practices.

The purpose of this chapter is to examine the context of the curriculum, in particular early childhood classrooms. I believe that by understanding the influences of contextual variables we will be better able to understand the reasons for particular practices in specific settings and act in such ways so as to effect change. Also, I believe that by taking into account contextual variables, the early childhood community will be better able to recommend desired content in the early childhood curriculum by becoming more sensitive to the relationship between the curriculum which is taught and the cultural context of classrooms and schools, as well as the vision of the future and the "good" life implied by the operational curriculum.

In this chapter, I present a framework for examining the various contexts of the early childhood curriculum and exemplify this framework by describing the curriculum in two kindergarten classrooms where I observed for four months. Furthermore, I call for the early childhood community to welcome inclusion into the public schools as a way to form alliances with groups that hold compatible philosophies of education.

THE CONTEXT OF THE EARLY CHILDHOOD CURRICULUM

One of the major purposes of schooling in any society is to socialize the young into the dominant culture; that is, to teach the knowledge, skills, values, attitudes, and beliefs that will enable individuals as adults to become productive members of society. Curriculum scholars began to examine this anthropological perspective on the purpose of schooling in the late 1960s by focusing not only on how schools taught a specific content but also on the values and norms of the dominant culture (Stevens & Wood, 1987). For example, Robert Dreeben (1968) concluded that "what was learned in school" were principles of conduct and desired norms, such as "independence" and "achievement," partially as the result of the social composition of the schools and the social relationships or roles played out in the classroom. Likewise, Philip Jackson (1968) claimed that students were socialized to be patient, docile, and "apple polishers" because schools were relatively crowded places and because teachers' roles required that they evaluate students and hold most of the power in the classroom.

Gracey's (1975) work exemplifies how kindergarten children in one classroom where he observed were socialized by the routines enforced by the teacher. Gracey concluded that the primary goal of schooling during the first semester in this kindergarten was to teach children the "student role"—"the repertoire of behaviors and attitudes regarded by educators as appropriate to children in school" (p. 84). This goal was accomplished during the first half of the school year through the teaching and learning of class routines. Those who accepted classroom discipline would be the more successful students. Children who rebelled would be labeled "deviant."

The importance of understanding the context of the early childhood curriculum cannot be overstated. As Apple and King (1977) pointed out, it was the social context of children's play in one kindergarten that determined what "play" meant. Apple and King (1977) found that children learned attitudes toward work and play by the ways in which teachers structured the school day and the classroom environment. If an activity, such as easel painting or making banana bread, was assigned by the teacher and highly specified in terms of procedures and outcome, the children labeled it "work." However, if an activity, such as alphabet bingo, were freely chosen, the children labeled it "play." In other words, the determinant of whether an activity was thought of as work or play by the children depended not on the nature of the activity itself but on the context—whether it was teacher- or student-directed.

Wilcox (1982) and Cornbleth (1990) lay out a framework for examining the context of the school curriculum, a framework that enables us to relate what is taught and experienced in programs for young children to sociological constructs that characterize the larger society. Wilcox's model is presented as a series of concentric circles: the innermost circle represents the level of the classroom; the next outer circle represents the school; subsequent outer circles represent the neighborhood, the school district, and the community. Surrounding various contexts of a particular classroom is a larger circle representing the state school system and, finally, a circle representing the culture as a whole. Wilcox claimed that each outer layer influenced the ones within but that it was possible for the inner contexts to influence the outer ones as well; in addition, she saw the various levels as interacting.

Cornbleth (1990) fleshes out Wilcox's depiction of classroom contexts by identifying components of the context at each level. To use her terminology, the "structural context" would include the shared beliefs and norms operating at a particular level, the established roles and relationships in a particular setting, and operating procedures used in a classroom, school, and/or school district. The "sociocultural context" of the curriculum is comprised of factors characteristic of the larger society: demographic, social, political, and economic conditions as well as traditions, and ideologies. Stevens and Wood (1987) define "ideology" as "the body of doctrine, myth symbol, etc. of a social movement, institution, or class" (p. 149). Elkind's (1989) reference to economic factors as in some way related to the inability of developmental theory to impact the early childhood curriculum and to encourage "appropriate practices" would be an example of what Cornbleth would call the sociocultural context of schools. King (1982) would argue that these factors all contain a political component which could be examined by focusing on such constructs as "influence," "authority," and "power" at each level.

THE STRUCTURAL CONTEXT: THE CLASSROOM

Beliefs and Norms

The beliefs and norms held by individuals and/or a community of educators comprise one component of the structural context and are realized in a particular theory of or orientation toward curriculum. Numerous orientations (Eisner, 1985) and/or conceptions of curriculum (McNeil, 1977) have been set forth: the humanistic, social reconstructionist, technologist, and academic subject curriculum. As I mentioned in the Introduction of this book, each orientation sets the parameters within which one considers the goals and content of the curriculum, the role of the teacher, and evaluation criteria. For example, beliefs about such factors as readiness for school can influence school admission practices, grouping practices, the kindergarten curriculum (see Chapter 3), and kindergarten retention practices (Smith & Shepard, 1988). In the case studies presented later in this chapter, I describe in detail how the beliefs and values held by two kindergarten teachers in the same school district differed widely and resulted in extremely different curriculum orientations.

Established Roles and Relationships

Jackson's (1968) work illustrates the way in which the established roles and relationships in a classroom teach students to be patient, to repress their desires, and to be docile in face of the teacher's authority. Because classrooms are relatively crowded places, where approximately twenty-five children and one adult spend the majority of their waking hours in closer proximity to one another than in any other common setting, children are required to repress their desires and be patient in waiting their turn for the teacher's attention. Because of the praise factor, whereby the teacher's role is to evaluate students and whereby students evaluate one another, they learn to emphasize their positive traits, sometimes in a deceitful way. Due to the teacher's power in terms of controlling the timing and pacing of lessons, the dispensing of supplies, and so forth, children learn to be docile. Jackson claimed that the "crowds," the "praise," and the "power" create a hidden curriculum which is frequently at variance with the formal curriculum expressed in school mission statements and curriculum guides. Jackson's work suggests that in order to understand the school curriculum, the social relationships within the classroom need to be identified and addressed.

Operating Procedures

Another component of the structural context of educational programs is referred to by Cornbleth (1990) as "operating procedures," which interact with a teacher's beliefs and values and his or her relationship with students and result in particular classroom practices. In Apple and King's (1977) study, for example, the teacher arranged play materials and developed the classroom schedule to correspond with her beliefs about play in the kindergarten. Rist's (1973) study in the late 1960s of an inner-city kindergarten in St. Louis also highlights the way in which teachers' values and beliefs and their relationships with students interact to create classroom procedures that result in widely differing educational experiences for students even in the same classroom. According to Rist, this kindergarten teacher formed an opinion of her students' ability based on how close they were to her ideal—a middle-class, upwardly mobile,

African-American child. She then gave different treatment to children based on these expectations, concentrating instruction on the students she expected to succeed and ignoring the students she had little hope for, whom she placed in middle- and low-achieving ability groups. The gap in achievement between the top group and the other two in terms of the amount of material covered widened as the school year progressed. Rist concluded that the differential treatment accorded these kindergarten students resulted in a castelike tracking system that insured that only those perceived as middle-class would succeed.

In sum, teachers' beliefs and norms or values interact with the roles they play in the classroom as well as their relationships with students and affect the procedures they implement to carry out their version of appropriate educational practices.

COMPARING CASES: TWO KINDERGARTENS

Two case studies that I carried out in 1985–86 exemplify the way in which structural and sociocultural contexts can influence the early childhood curriculum. Naturalistic case study methodology using qualitative and quantitative data was selected as the research method. The sites for the study were two kindergarten classes taught by two different teachers in two elementary schools, Hanover and King, in the same school system of a large Eastern city.*

For a detailed description of the procedures used for data collection and analysis, the reader is referred to the original study (Kessler, 1986). The curriculum in these kindergartens was determined by examining what was taught, the degree of separation between the content areas, and pedagogy (the major characteristics of a teacher's methods), as well as analyzing the degree of control children had over the selection, organization, and timing of school knowledge (Bernstein, 1977). Curriculum was also studied by examining evaluation methods in the two kindergartens— that is, the methods used to assess the work of a product and the grading system the teacher used.

Background Information

The District. Both Hanover and King schools were located in the Fillmore School District. At the time of this study, the district faced

---

* Pseudonyms are used throughout this description and analysis.

problems similar to those of other government agencies: fewer tax dollars, higher operating costs, and more services expected by constituents. A decline in enrollment resulted in a decrease in state aid. While overall school enrollment was decreasing, the enrollment of minority students increased: up from 7 percent in 1977 to the current level of 11 percent. Several district policies, or "operating procedures," with regard to the setting of school boundaries, the "mission" of various schools, and procedures for curriculum development had a significant impact on the curriculum in each kindergarten classroom observed.

The Schools. Hanover School was built in 1960, and during the 1985–86 school year, 309 children were enrolled. Only 3.3 percent of the student body came from families receiving Aid to Families with Dependent Children (AFDC) and/or qualifying for free lunch. Furthermore, only approximately 11 percent of the student body were children of color: black, Latino, Native American, or Asian. In the afternoon kindergarten where observations took place, there was one child of color, who had been adopted into a Caucasian family and whose exact racial background was unknown.

King School had been established five years before the onset of this study as the result of the consolidation of school districts and the closing of five schools. During the 1985–86 school year, 411 children were enrolled. In creating King, boundaries were drawn such that a majority of the school population consisted of low-income children of color. Forty-five percent of the children came from families receiving AFDC and/or qualifying for free lunches. Fifty-one percent of the student body was black, Asian, Latino, or Native American. It was believed the special needs of this population could better be met if the children were grouped in one school. Because of this belief, King teachers were given small classes and the freedom to alter the curriculum from that which had been adopted for use in the district as a whole. The primary teachers elected to implement the language experience approach to teaching reading rather than use the basal reading series adopted by the rest of the schools in the district.

Hanover School

Beliefs and Norms. The curriculum observed in the kindergarten at Hanover, the middle-class school, was representative of an academic orientation and developmentally inappropriate practices (Bredekamp, 1987). As was the case at King, the curriculum was influenced by one facet of the structural context—the teacher's beliefs and values. After one month of school, I asked the teacher, Mrs. Lang, what influenced what she taught. She explained that, although she was "never told directly," she was being influenced more toward an academic orientation. Mrs. Lang knew that most of the children in her kindergarten had attended nursery school and were ready for more difficult activities. In spite of this perception, she believed that play was still an important part of the curriculum. "The children seem happier when we have playtime," she said. "I sense they're tense if we have solid thinking for two and one-half hours."

In answer to the question about what factors she considered when planning activities, Mrs. Lang said she planned activities the children would enjoy, activities they already knew how to do, so they would not have any difficulty at the beginning of the school year doing schoolwork. Later she would work toward doing "new things." She also was concerned about meeting the expectations for first grade. She said the first-grade teachers would like all the children to finish Level 3+ in the basal reading series, but she was not sure all the children would be able to meet that goal.

When asked what was important knowledge for kindergartners to possess, besides that which was expected by first-grade teachers, she listed the following objectives in this order: sit quietly; comprehend what they are hearing; follow directions; know the letters of the alphabet as well as beginning sounds; read some words; recognize the eight basic colors and the color words, recognize numerals to 100; write numerals beyond 20, usually as far as the calendar; solve easy story problems; know how to add up to 10; and understand fractions—whole, half, fourth. Mrs. Lang also stated that there was a nationwide test given each year, which was an indication of what was expected across the United States. The socialization function of the curriculum in this kindergarten was echoed in the handout given to parents at the first open house: "Besides nurturing intellectual development and skills, the curriculum is designed to refine behavior and cultivate values."

These objectives were reflected in what was taught during the fall term at Hanover. Intellectual content was missing. Reading was clearly separate from social studies and the other content areas and was taught during reading instruction at the reading learning center. Further, the curriculum followed a basal reading series and focused on basic skills, such as visual discrimination, letter identification, and beginning sounds. In math, the content focused on counting and number recognition. Mrs. Lang's belief that she was being pressured to implement a first-grade curriculum and that the purpose of schooling was to prepare students for the next level of schooling was realized in the curriculum taught to these 5-year-olds.

Established Roles and Relationships. The predominant teaching methods employed by Mrs. Lang were modeling, direct teaching, and social reinforcement. She modeled the way to complete a task, as well as proper ways of speaking and behaving. Direct instruction was the primary means for imparting knowledge: objectives were clear, arranged in a hierarchical fashion, and directly taught to students. This teaching method created distance between the teacher and the children, wherein she was clearly the authority in selecting the curriculum that was enacted and experienced in this classroom. Furthermore, there appeared to be a relatively formal relationship between Mrs. Lang and her students. The children referred to her as "Mrs. Lang," and she always sat above them on a chair. Mrs. Lang's relationship can best be described as professional, though friendly.

Pedagogy also was analyzed by examining the degree to which children had the ability to affect the selection, organization, and timing of school knowledge. Hanover kindergartners were relatively ineffective in influencing the selection and organization of school knowledge. Children seldom asked to engage in activities, and when they did, their requests were usually denied. On the other hand, Hanover children were able to affect the curriculum by bringing things to school, which sometimes formed the focus of activity during free play. Hanover children had little opportunity to construct knowledge or understandings for themselves, since the curriculum consisted of isolated skills that were highly sequenced and since the children were taught in a rotelike fashion that emphasized the recognition of letters and numbers, rather than the construction of concepts. Hanover kindergartners were effective, however, in controlling the amount of time they would work on class tasks. Children rushed through their worksheet assignments to get to the free choice centers, and those who took more time with their work missed free play. In sum, children were relatively ineffective in affecting the selection and organization of school knowledge but were effective in affecting the timing of their endeavors.

Operating Procedures. The operating procedures at Hanover and King schools were logical outcomes of teachers' beliefs, established patterns of teacher–pupil interaction, and the roles the teachers played. At Hanover, Mrs. Lang arranged the schedule and materials to correspond to her view of the purpose of schooling in the first half of the school year.

The free choice period was scheduled, according to the teacher's plan-book, for twenty minutes each day; however, free choice typically lasted on the average about ten minutes per day. Further, the available activities were primarily of the cut-and-paste type, such as coloring and cutting out a picture of an Indian, one of the choices during free play at Hanover before Thanksgiving. In addition, the room was arranged in such a way as to clearly separate the work area (the four tables set up as learning centers) from the play area (the housekeeping corner, the loft, and table activities). Blocks were available in a box along the wall, but the setting was not conducive to children's block play, since the area was exposed to traffic, usually children on wheel toys.

Evaluation practices also contributed to the type of curriculum that predominated in each classroom and reflected the teachers' beliefs and values. At dismissal time on Fridays, Mrs. Lang would hand back all the papers the children had completed during the week. As she passed back these papers, Mrs. Lang would usually display the papers labeled "well done" and praise the child whose work that was. This was work that most nearly matched the sample she completed as she instructed children how to do an assignment. Children seemed interested in the marks on their papers and compared "grades" as the papers were returned.

King School

Beliefs and Norms. The curriculum that predominated in the kindergarten at King, the working-class school, was more characteristic of the developmental orientation and exemplified more developmentally appropriate practices (Bredekamp, 1987) than at Hanover. Early in the school year, the teacher, Kathy, said she wanted to stress thinking skills and creativity with her students. When asked what the school district expected as far as goals and objectives for kindergarten were concerned, she laughed and said she thought there were goals in mathematics, but she was not quite sure what they were. Unlike Mrs. Lang, Kathy said she felt little or no pressure to meet goals or expectations set by individuals outside her classroom. When she began teaching kindergarten, she asked two of the first-grade teachers what they expected children to be able to do when they came to first grade. One teacher said she wanted children to have had experience contributing to group discussions, to feel free to explore ideas and talk about what interested them, and to know how to get along and cooperate with others. The other teacher, however, expected them to learn how to use the bathroom and line up. It was then Kathy realized that there was no consensus among first-grade teachers as to what should be taught, so she did not bother asking the other two at

King. However, she added, she presumed first-grade teachers would want students to know "their letters" and beginning sounds, as well as be able to count and identify the numerals from 1 through 10. She also said she thought the first-grade teachers would want the children to know how to work quietly, but she was not sure she was contributing to that.

When asked how she decided to teach something, Kathy said that she thought about several things: (1) the unit or theme for the week, (2) the skill or concepts she wanted the children to experience, and (3) the students' interests. It was important to Kathy to provide opportunities for children to think about what they were doing. "I hate it when teachers give children cut-and-dried assignments to complete, which they don't really understand. They've been taught 'do this,' instead of thinking about it. Especially in math." When asked how she decided on the units she taught, Kathy said, laughing, "It's fairly arbitrary. Often it will come from some event, like a fieldtrip or an interest the children have, or one child has, that I expand upon." The idea for the current unit on animals came from Monica, the student teacher, who said she wanted to "do" an animal center. Last year the class had gone on a fieldtrip to the local historical society in the city. Kathy realized that the children had stereotypical ideas about Native Americans, so she taught a one-month unit on Native Americans to alter their perceptions. Kathy stated that prior to the start of school she would panic a bit, wondering what to teach. But, she explained, after a few weeks the children would provide her with ideas for units and lessons. Kathy was critical of the standard kindergarten curriculum based on units or themes that revolve around the time of year. "Traditional themes bore me. Like 'fall,' 'winter,' etc.," she said. "I always do a unit on dinosaurs toward the end of the year, when the children are getting restless, because they are so interested in it." Kathy saw herself as a practitioner of "open" education. She said she started reading about it as an undergraduate, and it made sense to her. "It's how the teacher views play that makes the difference in a program," she said. "Most teachers I know just have the children complete worksheets, then go and play. Naturally, the children don't take play seriously and aren't productive with it."

At King, subject areas stood in a relatively open relationship to one another and were subordinated to some main idea or theme. For example, several topics or themes unified instruction throughout the school year: "pets," "space," "important women." Reading was taught by the language experience approach, which integrates all the language arts: listening, speaking, reading, and writing. Children dictated statements that were recorded by the teacher, who then read back their statements. In this way children created an individualized reading program for themselves. Further, reading instruction often was integrated with social studies, science, and sometimes math. The underlying structure of certain disciplines, or the main ideas within a content area, were stressed more at King than at Hanover. For example, the concept of measurement was taught as children estimated, then measured with unifix cubes, the actual length of the skin that had been shed by a snake. Concepts of "fairness" and "justice" were emphasized as children studied Native Americans, aspects of the civil rights movement, and women's history. In most areas, understanding was promoted, rather than the learning of specific skills and discrete forms of knowledge.

Established Roles and Relationships. The teaching methods employed by Kathy at King also correspond more to developmentally appropriate practices. Her personal style incorporated the use of questioning techniques that focused on thinking skills and creativity, a measure of flexibility in incorporating the ideas of others into the curriculum, and a warm and personal relationship with most children in the classroom. For example, the children referred to her by her first name, and she was often observed sitting on the rug with them, participating in an activity, usually with a child in her lap or leaning on her. Children at King also seemed to be slightly more influential than children at Hanover in contributing to the selection and organization of school knowledge. For example, Kathy appeared to be sensitive to the responses of the class as a whole, particularly to their interest in an activity or event. Children's expressed interest and/or curiosity sometimes led to further instruction or experience with that topic. In addition, children had the opportunity to construct understandings for themselves. The nature of the reading curriculum, along with a focus on the major principles within a subject area and experiential learning activities, enabled children to construct understandings, such as concepts of number. However, King children had less influence over how long they would work on an activity. The children usually finished class tasks at approximately the same time. The role Kathy assumed in this kindergarten was such that she shared her power with the children by welcoming their ideas into the curriculum. She was less of an authority figure and frequently became a participant.

Operating Procedures. At King, the operating procedures likewise reflected Kathy's beliefs and values. For example, the free choice period was scheduled four times a week for thirty minutes. According to my observations, each period lasted, on the average, twenty-five minutes. The choices available to children during this time also differed in important ways: dramatic play in the housekeeping corner, block play, listening to stories and music, creative art, puzzles and games, and drawing. Here again the teacher played a different role, sharing her power by allowing children to choose from among many diverse activities so that they had opportunities to create a curriculum for themselves.

Evaluation practices at King also characterized the developmental orientation. Here children's papers were not graded. Furthermore, when good or interesting work was displayed, it was always that of children, not the teacher, and often the focus was on the creative aspects of children's completed tasks, not the extent to which children emulated the teacher's model.

Influences on the Curriculum

It seemed to be the teacher who was the major decision maker in determining the curriculum in both classrooms. Mrs. Lang saw the object of her program as that of socializing children—teaching them the skills, attitudes, and behaviors that they would need to succeed in first grade and in later years. Kathy's goal was to foster creativity and problem-solving abilities. Both teachers had opposing views of play, as well. Mrs. Lang saw play as a form of recreation—a way to replenish children's energy so they could work more. Kathy saw play as an important avenue for learning in all areas. Mrs. Lang selected activities that would be easy for the children during the fall semester, activities she thought they would enjoy because they were not difficult. Kathy selected activities based on children's interests and her perception of their needed skills. Mrs. Lang was sensitive to the indirect remarks of Lorraine Strong, the principal, that she teach a more academic curriculum and conscious of the need to meet the expectations of first-grade teachers. For the most part, Kathy ignored Harold Reinhardt, the principal at King, an attitude exemplified by her resisting and changing the discipline program he tried to implement. In addition, Kathy realized there was no consensus among first-grade teachers so their influence was minimal.

The children in the Hanover and King kindergartens differed along several dimensions: social-class background, prekindergarten experience, entry-level skill development, and end-of-year achievement. However, in neither classroom were students directly influential by asking for activities or bringing things to school. At Hanover, but not at King, children had some influence over the amount of time they would spend on class assignments. This fact contributed to their experiences, or lack thereof, in the free choice centers. At King, but not at Hanover, children had some influence over the way they organized, or constructed, knowledge. In addition, the selections they made during choice time seemed to have considerable influence on their experiences with the basic topics that unified instruction each week. In both classrooms, children's verbal behavior, such as asking questions and contributing to class discussions, seemed to influence the knowledge made available. The primary way children influenced the curriculum in both classrooms seemed to be through the teachers' impressions of their needs and interests. Because Mrs. Lang did not want any of the children to have problems in school, she taught them skills and concepts that she thought were not new to them. In addition, because she saw them as "still babies" and did not want them to be "tense," she allowed them to play for a few minutes each day. Kathy stated that children's interests were one of the three main factors she considered when planning what to teach. The dinosaur unit she taught every spring, for example, was based on the fact that this topic interested children immensely. Thus teachers' perceptions of students' needs, abilities, and interests seemed to play a major role in determining much of the curriculum in each room.

THE STRUCTURAL CONTEXT: DISTRICT AND SCHOOL ADMINISTRATIVE POLICY

Administrative policy of the school district with regard to the setting of school boundaries and busing patterns, curriculum development, and the mission of particular schools also influenced curriculum in both classrooms. The creation of school boundaries ensured that the majority of children attending Hanover would come from middle-class families and the majority of children attending King would come from working-class families. This fact partially explains the different levels of achievement of the two groups. The fact that Hanover children came to school with more knowledge of colors, shapes, the alphabet, and so forth and were able to read some words supported the assumption held by Lorraine Strong, the principal, and Mrs. Lang that they were ready for a more academically rigorous curriculum. Further, the fact that their middle-class background was similar to that of the teacher suggests that Mrs. Lang and the children's parents shared many of the same values. This could partially explain why she was thought to be the "perfect" kindergarten teacher for Hanover, according to her principal.

District policy regarding curriculum development likewise had an impact on the curriculum. The basal reading series which was developed by the curriculum committee for use in the district included activities that were formerly taught in the first grade. In addition to this curriculum, however, Mrs. Lang taught an alphabet recognition and phonics program

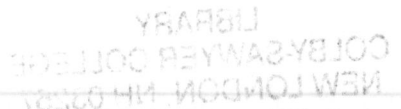

that she developed herself. Thus district policy regarding curriculum development had a major influence on what was taught but did not totally determine it in either classroom. Where the committee did not specify a textbook series to be adopted, but simply stated goals and objectives, as in the area of mathematics, teachers had more autonomy. Mrs. Lang taught the skills of counting and writing, while Kathy taught major mathematical principles, such as classification and measurement. In this case, the curriculum that resulted seemed to be influenced by the personal backgrounds, philosophy, and training of the teachers.

Finally, school district policy with regard to the mission of both schools influenced the curriculum. Lorraine Strong's mission was to "open up" Hanover to parents and community groups, and she was quite successful in doing so. For example, Hanover was selected as the site for the pilot project in education for "gifted" and "talented" students, which explained Mrs. Lang's involvement in the development of the curriculum for that project. Lessons from that curriculum were taught on Fridays when learning centers were not scheduled. The opening up of Hanover to parents led to the design and construction of not only a new playground for kindergartners but also a new playground for the elementary level pupils as well.

The mission at King was quite different. It was created to deal with the educational problems of low-income children of color. This mission influenced its status as an experimental program that led to the allocation of additional personnel and the selection of a hand-picked faculty. Further, even though Kathy frequently disagreed with Mr. Reinhardt, the principal, there seemed to be a kind of *esprit de corps* among the staff, an attitude of genuine caring and commitment to hard work in order to bring about the intellectual and social development of the students. The mission of King also influenced the school's goals. Several lessons taught by Kathy dealt specifically with the goals of fostering the ability to get along with others and an awareness and respect for the cultures of different children.

THE SOCIOCULTURAL CONTEXT

The sociocultural context (Cornbleth, 1990) of the early childhood curriculum includes the demographic, social, political, and economic conditions characteristic of the larger society, as well as its traditions and ideologies. The policies adopted by the Fillmore School District were the result of the increased number of children of color in the district and the belief in the importance of educating those individuals to succeed in white society. In 1986 a suit was filed with the Civil Rights Commission charging discrimination within the Fillmore School District because of the segregation of low-income children of color at King. The following year, the school district changed school boundaries and busing patterns to integrate King children with those at Hanover.

Court decisions and state policies are having a great deal of influence on education today, largely as the result of the current educational reform movement ushered in by the publication of *A Nation at Risk* (National Commission on Excellence in Education, 1983), as well as the fact that states now pay a higher percentage of the cost of public education than local districts. In 1988, for example, more revenues came from state sources (approximately 50 percent) than from local sources (approximately 45 percent) or from the federal government (7 percent) (National Center for Education Statistics, 1991). States exert their influence through state judges and their decisions relevant to such issues as desegregation; through the state superintendents of public instruction; through state legislators, who, for example, set up advisory committees to recommend changes in school graduation requirements; and through mandates, such as requiring state testing (Cornbleth, 1990).

State influence over public education has been most strongly felt in the area of testing student achievement (Pipho, 1991). As of 1989, twenty-four states required the reporting of test scores in some form of school district or school building report card. One significant outcome of state-mandated, criterion-referenced testing is that tests are "driving" instruction and dictating what is taught (Brooks, 1991). One first-grade teacher I know teaches her students the difference between narrative, expository, and persuasive writing because they need to know that for the third-grade state achievement test in Illinois. Unfortunately, students frequently are required to learn material for which they are not ready, simply because it is on the test (Brooks, 1991). The effects of mandated achievement tests are not only demoralizing for many teachers (Smith, 1991) but also result in a narrowing of the range of possibilities for teaching, as well as teachers' ability to tailor instruction to individual students. Furthermore, teachers' teaching methods have changed from providing opportunities for exploratory, creative experiences to teacher-centered direct instruction.

Pressure for achievement testing also is emanating from the federal level, a result of the congressionally mandated charge to the Education Commission of the States to oversee the National Assessment of Educational Progress (NAEP). Furthermore, several groups, such as the National Education Goals Panel and the New Standards Project, now favor a national examination system tied to national goals (McNeil, 1991). These initiatives have had a tremendous impact on the early childhood curriculum and must be seriously considered when explaining the prevalence of an academically oriented curriculum and when taking steps to prescribe what should be taught.

THE SOCIOLOGY OF EDUCATION: BEYOND DETERMINATION

While the above argument relative to the importance of the social context of the early childhood curriculum is vital in comprehending the way in which students are socialized in school, it must be remembered that it is possible, and probable, that what transpires in the classroom and at local levels can influence the school, the neighborhood, and even state educational policies and practices. For example, we all know that even kindergartners are capable of influencing their experience of schooling and do so on a daily basis. Gracey's (1975) observations describe vividly how the group of kindergartners he studied were very active in creating a subculture within the classroom that deliberately excluded the teacher. For example, following a trip to the zoo, Edith, the teacher in the kindergarten, attempted to engage the class in a discussion of what they saw. The children appeared to be more interested in their experiences at the "spooky house" than the teacher, and began to get excited and somewhat silly when sharing this experience with one another. The teacher did not seem to understand what the children were talking about. However, she skillfully brought the children back to the points she was trying to make. But for a few moments the children were expressing to one another an awareness and understanding not shared by the teacher. This type of thing also occurred on the playground or during playtime, and even occasionally when the children were working on seatwork, such as drawing a picture of what they saw at the zoo. Gracey concluded:

> Here the children are learning to carve out a small world of their own within the world created by adults. They very quickly learn that if they keep within permissible limits of noise and action they can play much as they please. Small groups of children formed during the year in Edith's kindergarten who played together at these times, developing semi-independent little groups in which they created their own worlds in the interstices of the adult-imposed physical and social world. (pp. 94-95)

Gracey likened these informal groups to those that develop in factories and offices, where workers and employees find "holes" in the authoritarian social structure and "create little sub-worlds that support informal, friendly, nonofficial behavior. Forming and participating in such groups seems to be as much part of the student role as it is of the role of bureaucrat" (p. 95). In studying the curriculum at Hanover and King schools, I found numerous ways in which children affected the curriculum by their verbal behavior (Kessler, 1986). Children asked questions, which were answered; contributed ideas to small and large group discussions; asked for activities; taught others; and modeled appropriate behavior.

Teachers, likewise, are no longer passive in their implementation of a mandated curriculum. While the states are gaining more control over curriculum decisions, the National Education Association (NEA) is reasserting its belief that curriculum decisions should be made by those closest to the educational process—teachers and students (McClure, 1991). This idea is currently being implemented through the NEA-sponsored Mastery In Learning (MIL) program, which was designed to develop and evaluate educational programs based on the decisions of local school faculty. Some of the individuals teaching in these programs now are ready to challenge state practices that inhibit educators at the local level in determining the appropriateness of educational practices. Teachers working together can effect change, as Smith (1991) documented when she reported that teachers in Arizona successfully lobbied the state legislature and eliminated state testing of all first-graders. She concluded that teachers have the ability to "resist" curriculum mandates by ignoring testing requirements and taking political action. In addition, an alliance of thirty-three national subject-matter groups, initially calling itself the "curriculum congress," is currently reacting to attempts to set national standards against which to compare achievement scores between states. This alliance claims such "reform" attempts are ignoring some of the key subjects normally taught in school, resulting in an "unbalanced" curriculum in schools that teach to the test (Viadero, 1991). The idea of a national curriculum is anathema to them. Thus Wilcox's (1982) assertion that individuals working at the classroom, school, and district level, as well as those in professional organizations, can exert influence on state and federal policies and practices is well supported.

CONCLUSION

The increase in enrollment of young children in the public schools will continue to rise. There will be no going back to earlier times when preschools and kindergartens were relatively isolated and autonomous.

We must examine the structural and sociocultural influences on the early childhood curriculum and the way such factors impact on what is prescribed as developmentally appropriate practices. The political context of the early childhood curriculum is particularly significant. We must learn more about the influence of state policies on the curriculum if we are to counter the current tendencies of states to impose testing policies and curriculum standards. We must learn what is being decided, how, and by whom. For example, Delpit (1988) argues that appropriate education for minority children can only be determined by members of the social groups to which they belong, and that well-meaning white liberals, who tend to emphasize informal, play-oriented practices for young children, are doing children of color a disservice. Members of nondominant cultures want their children to learn the "discourse patterns, interactional styles, and spoken and written language codes . . . [of the dominant culture] . . . so they can succeed" (p. 83)—the "codes of power" (p. 90) they need to enter institutions created by mainstream culture.

Although the incorporation of early childhood programs into the public schools makes them vulnerable to the same social and political factors that influence the curriculum at all other levels, I believe it also offers numerous possibilities for improving the early childhood curriculum. For example, because kindergarten teachers now attend the same workshops as the elementary teachers in their buildings, they have the opportunity to learn more about comparatively innovative practices, such as "process writing," whole-language approaches to literacy, cooperative learning, as well as be exposed to the current renewed interest and commitment of many educators to the goal of schooling for democracy (e.g., Wood, 1990). The incorporation of early childhood programs into the public schools also enhances the possibility for renewing the close bond between kindergarten and primary teachers that existed during the first quarter of the twentieth century (Weber, 1969). During this time kindergarten teachers were forced to abandon their "self-worshipping aloofness so characteristic of earlier days" (p. 114) to help forge a continuous experience for young children through a kindergarten–primary alliance. One result of this alliance was the influence of kindergarten practices on the first-grade curriculum, which, for a time, included child-centered, activity-oriented methods common in early childhood programs (Weber, 1969). Bredekamp (1991) agrees that the current interest in education for democratic living, for example, expressed by George Wood (1990) and others (e.g., Beyer, 1988), holds promise for creating a curriculum appropriate to children and for promoting a more democratic society.

To be influential in this debate about the early childhood curriculum, early childhood educators must break with their current isolation from elementary education and join forces with other groups sharing their philosophy of education. To find compatible affinity groups (Ellsworth, 1989), it may be necessary for early childhood educators to look outside the field of early childhood education to the work currently being done by curriculum theorists who are reexamining the potential of schooling for democracy and/or for solving social inequalities characteristic of U.S. society today. However, as Ellsworth (1989) claims, a pedagogy aimed at fostering justice between and among social groups must recognize the inability to know and make sense of the experiences of those outside one's "affinity" group.

When early childhood educators address the issue of content in future recommendations for curricula, I urge that consideration be given to the social context of the curriculum and to the relationship between what is taught in school and the structural and sociocultural factors, including issues of power and authority, as well as to visions of the future and the "good" life we imply in the curriculum we enact. We must continually study the social context of the early childhood curriculum as we ask what knowledge and whose knowledge should be incorporated into the early childhood curriculum and what political interests are served. Ultimately I believe that the early childhood curriculum should be created by different political groups based on what they perceive as important content and appropriate educational practice for their children. The issue of how local or representative of special interests these groups should be is a matter of serious debate. Reducing the isolation of the early childhood community has the potential of influencing the interest groups opposing what it views as sound early childhood educational practices; it also has the potential for contributing to curriculum scholarship and practice aimed at creating a more just society.

REFERENCES

Apple, M. W., & King, N. A. (1977). What do schools teach? *Curriculum Inquiry,* 6, 341–357.

Bernstein, B. (1977). *Class, codes and control: Vol. 3. Towards a theory of educational transmissions* (2nd edition). Boston: Routledge and Kegan Paul.

Beyer, L. (1988). Schooling for the culture of democracy. In L. E. Beyer & M. W. Apple, *The curriculum: Problems, politics and possibilities* (pp. 21–238). Albany: State University of New York Press.

Bredekamp, S. (Ed.). (1987). *Developmentally appropriate practice in early childhood programs serving children from birth through age 8.* Washington, DC: National Association for the Education of Young Children.

Bredekamp, S. (1991). Redeveloping early childhood education: A response to Kessler. *Early Childhood Research Quarterly, 6,* 199–209.

Brooks, M. G. (1991). Centralized curriculum: Effects on the local school level. In M. F. Klein (Ed.), *The politics of curriculum decision-making* (pp. 151–166). Albany: State University of New York Press.

Cornbleth, C. (1990). *Curriculum in context.* New York: Falmer.

Delpit, L. D. (1988). The silenced dialogue: Power and pedagogy in educating other people's children. *Harvard Education Review, 58,* 78–95.

Dreeben, R. (1968). *On what is learned in school.* Reading, MA: Addison-Wesley.

Eisner, E. W. (1985). *The educational imagination.* New York: Macmillan.

Elkind, D. (1989). Developmentally appropriate practice: Philosophical and practical limitations. *Phi Delta Kappan, 71,* 113–117.

Ellsworth, E. (1989). Why doesn't this feel empowering? *Harvard Educational Review, 59,* 297–324.

Gracey, H. (1975). Learning the student role: Kindergarten as academic bootcamp. In H. Stub (Ed.), *The sociology of education: A source book* (pp. 82–95). Homewood, IL: Dorsey Press.

Jackson, P. (1968). *Life in classrooms.* New York: Holt, Rinehart and Winston.

Kamii, C. (1985). Leading primary education toward excellence: Beyond worksheets and drill. *Young Children, 40,* 3–9.

Kessler, S. A. (1986). *The child's effect on the kindergarten curriculum.* Unpublished doctoral dissertation, University of Wisconsin–Madison.

Kessler, S A. (1991). Alternative perspectives on early childhood education. *Early Childhood Research Quarterly, 6,* 183–197.

McClure, R. M. (1991). Centralized curriculum decision making: The view from the organized teaching profession. In M. F. Klein (Ed.), *The politics of curriculum decision-making* (pp. 198–209). Albany: State University of New York Press.

McNeil, J. (1977). *Curriculum: A comprehensive introduction.* Boston: Little, Brown.

McNeil, J. (1991). New exam system debated. *Update, 33,* 1, 4–6.

National Center for Education Statistics. (1988). *Digest of education statistics 1988.* Washington, DC: U.S. Government Printing Office.

National Center for Education Statistics. (1991). *Digest of education statistics 1990.* Washington, DC: U.S. Government Printing Office.

National Commission on Excellence in Education. (1983). *A nation at risk.* Washington, DC: U.S. Government Printing Office.

Pipho, C. (1991). Contralizing curriculum at the state level. In M. F. Klein (Ed.), *The politics of curriculum decision-making* (pp. 67–97). Albany: State University of New York Press.

Rist, R. (1973). *The urban school: A factory for failure.* Cambridge, MA: MIT Press.

Smith, M. L. (1991). Put to the test: The effects of external testing on teachers. *Educational Researcher, 20,* 8–11.

Smith, M. L., & Shepard, L. A. (1988). Kindergarten readiness and retention: A qualitative study of teachers' beliefs and practices. *American Educational Research Journal*, *25*, 307–333.

Spodek, B. (1982). The kindergarten: A retrospective and contemporary view. In L. Katz (Ed.), *Current topics in early childhood education* (Vol. 4)(pp. 173–191). Norwood, NJ: Ablex.

Stevens, E., Jr., & Wood, G. H. (1987). *Justice, ideology, and education: An introduction to the social foundations of education.* New York: Random House.

Viadero, D. (1991, September 4). Alliance formed to push curriculum to front of reform agenda. *Education Week*, p. 14.

Weber, E. (1969). *The kindergarten: Its encounter with educational thought in America.* New York: Teachers College Press.

Webster, N. K. (1984). The 5's and 6's go to school revisited. *Childhood Education*, *60*, 325–330.

Wilcox, K. (1982). Differential socialization in the classroom: Implications for equal opportunity. In G. Spindler (Ed.), *Doing the ethnography of schooling: Educational anthropology in action* (pp. 166–187). Albany: State University of New York Press.

Wood, G. H. (1990). Teaching for democracy. *Educational Leadership, 47*, 32–37.

CHAPTER 3

The Impact of Context on
the Play of Young Children

Nancy R. King

A focus on context is relatively rare among educators who study children's play. In fact, the field of education as a whole does not have a long tradition of attention to context variables. Typically, educational research measures the skills of children and tests the efficacy of discrete teaching and learning strategies. This focus on the individual tends to narrow the range of variables considered. Recently, researchers have recognized variables such as race, class, and gender as salient. These particular variables, however, continue to emphasize the characteristics of particular individuals, and the full array of context variables continue to be largely ignored in the research literature.

Context variables suffer the same neglect in the field of early childhood education. Here, developmental perspectives dominate, and although family constellations and childrearing practices may, at times, be considered, much of the literature focuses on describing the growth and development of young children as a record of the processes of maturation. If context variables are considered, only those with a direct, immediate, and obvious influence on the child are studied with care.

Nowhere is this lack of interest in context variables more evident than in the study of children's play. Play activity creates a context of its own and may seem, therefore, to be uncontaminated by external context variables. Part of the importance of play in the lives of children (and in the lives of adults!) is that play permits a certain independence from reality; contexts and individual characteristics can be ignored and surmounted. Timid children can become giants or lions, older siblings can become babies, quiet children can run and shout, and obedient children can create mischief.

Educational researchers believe that play activity permits them to observe the child at his or her most natural. Consequently, they usually observe play in order to describe and understand developmental patterns

43

and to compare the progress of particular children to developmental standards. In spite of the apparent independence of play behaviors, I find researchers' neglect of context variables particularly misguided in the area of play research.

Before considering play behavior, in particular, I want to emphasize that no behavior has meaning apart from the context in which it occurs. For example, shouting and cheering may be appropriate at a baseball game, but such behavior is considered inappropriate in the library. Similarly, reading a book in the library is different from reading a book at the baseball game. Although the actual behaviors are identical, the meanings are different because the contexts are different. Context, then, is the source of the meanings of all human behavior, and context variables must be investigated if we hope to achieve an understanding of any human interaction. This is particularly true in the area of play, where the very definition requires attention to aspects of the context.

DEFINITIONS OF PLAY

In spite of their lack of sensitivity to the rules of public behavior in nonplay settings (see, for example, Zinsser, 1987), young children are fully aware that an activity can be defined as play only with reference to the contexts in which it occurs. This became clear in a study of children's play in the elementary school in which children were asked to categorize their daily classroom activities as either work or play (King, 1987). The responses of the kindergartners were remarkably consistent and revealed a sophisticated analysis of the classroom environment. The children categorized most of their classroom activities as work; work included such apparently different activities as listening to a story, resting at their places, painting papier-mâché sculptures, and lining up to leave the classroom. Fewer activities were defined as play, and, again, the list includes a diverse set of activities including building with blocks, listening to a record, and coloring pictures. The children enjoyed their play activities but took as much pleasure in the activities they described as work. Pleasure, then, was not a criterion that differentiated between work and play in kindergarten.

For kindergartners, the criteria differentiating between work and play depend entirely on the social context. Examination of this context reveals the two characteristics of play that sharply differentiate it from work. First, play is always voluntary. All activities assigned by teachers were always labeled work by the children; only activities the children chose for themselves were called play. Second, work activities are standardized and closely supervised by the teacher. The more aspects of an activity to come under the child's control, the more likely the child was to label the activity play. If the child freely chose the activity and the materials, and if the child controlled the course of events and the duration of his or her involvement, the activity was considered play by all kindergartners.

Although most of the kindergartners spoke enthusiastically about most of the classroom activities they labeled work, they spoke more energetically and spontaneously about their play activities. While they believe that play has no important educational function, kindergarten children believe it is an important part of the school day.

These findings indicate that children's play, as defined by kindergartners, cannot be used to serve the goals of the school. When teachers incorporate play activities into the kindergarten curriculum, the children redefine such activities as work. Much of the activity that an adult observer may identify as play, then, may not be play from the children's perspective. Children who seem to be playing in kindergarten may, in fact, be children who are enjoying their work.

The impact of the setting on the children's definitions of play emphasizes the fact that these definitions are socially constructed in particular contexts. These contexts may be subtle or obvious, common or particular, recognized or not. Whatever the circumstances, it is clear that contexts are a source of information vital to understanding children's play in school.

CLASSROOM CONTEXTS

The contexts that most obviously influence children's school play are those found in the classroom itself. While these contexts have been inadequately studied by educational researchers, in general, and researchers of children's play, in particular, teachers and other practitioners have always taken classroom contexts into consideration when planning learning experiences for young children. Even teachers, however, may not realize the extent to which classroom contexts shape children's play in school. There are at least four classroom contexts that have a profound impact on classroom play.

Physical Context

The first, the physical context of the classroom itself, includes a spatial dimension and a temporal dimension. The physical objects in the classroom have long been recognized as essential components of the early childhood curriculum. The furniture, equipment, and materials available to the children shape their activities. While children's use of materials does vary based on each child's interests, previous experiences, and immediate goals, there is a consistency in the behaviors objects elicit Renninger, 1989). In general, more versatile materials are more likely to elicit complex improvisation during play (McLoyd, 1986).

The arrangement of the materials in the classroom also has an impact on children's play. Ordinarily early childhood classrooms have well-defined spaces for play, and the size and arrangement of these play spaces influence children's activities. For example, the size of the block corner will determine both the nature of the construction activities and the number of children who can use the blocks simultaneously.

The importance of the selection and organization of the physical objects is matched by the importance of the organization of time in educational settings. The length of play periods has a significant influence on the cognitive and social levels of children's play. Researchers focusing on the social and cognitive characteristics of children's play have found that more play occurs during longer play periods; specifically, more group play and more constructive play occurs. (Christie, Johnsen, & Peckover, 1988).

Personal Context

The second important classroom context that has an impact on children's play is the personal context. Each individual child has particular characteristics, aptitudes, interests, skills, and attitudes that contribute to the nature of classroom events. There is both a stable psychological context and a daily psychological context to be considered. At a simple level, this can be seen in the fact that an activity that is exciting for one child may be frightening for another or an activity that captivates the attention of a child on one day may be of no interest whatsoever on another.

Children also bring their personal histories to bear on classroom events. Their autobiographies as children of particular families with particular demographic characteristics influence their approaches to play, their familiarity with play materials, and their preferences for play activities. Gender, for example, is a demographic characteristic that has been shown to have an impact on the play of young children in that each sex has a distinctive play style (Deaux & Major, 1987; Liss, 1986; Maccoby, 1988; Maccoby & Jacklin, 1987). Children's games can also reveal subtle aspects of their ethnic culture and family situation (Farrer, 1977).

Social Context

When all of the classroom participants come together, the third important classroom context is created: the social context. Elements of the social context include the organization of human relations, peer-group friendship networks, and the exercise of power and authority in the classroom. The social context enhances classroom play by enabling children to participate in a wide variety of activities that require guidance by adults or the participation of peers. The social context also sets limitations and imposes restraints in the classroom (Jackson & Wolfson, 1971). The number of children in the peer group, the race and sex of those involved, and the age of participants all influence the dynamic of the social context and, consequently, the nature of play.

The larger social context includes the teacher and other adults present in the classroom. Their influence on play in which they do not participate should not be overlooked. The rules governing classroom conduct as well as the implicit expectations concerning interpersonal etiquette provide a structure even when the teacher is not present personally. Although the influence may be subtle and indirect, the larger social context of the classroom always influences the immediate social context of the play event.

Curricular Context

The final classroom context that influences school play is the curricular context. In many classrooms that emphasize the early mastery of academic material and rely on direct instruction to the entire class, the time for play may be brief. Further, play activities may not be valued by the teacher as important contributors to school success. These circumstances obviously have an impact on the children's school play.

The way in which specific lessons are organized is also an important influence on the way children organize their play. For example, in one kindergarten classroom where the children spent extended periods of time at assigned seats at long tables, no child was observed to sit at the tables during "free play." Additionally, the content of academic lessons as well as unplanned classroom events affect play themes and behaviors.

In summary, classroom play is never, simply, the free expression of children. It is always shaped in one direction or another by several classroom contexts. These classroom contexts do not necessarily work together to achieve common goals. The messages they convey may, in fact, produce considerable contradiction and discomfort for classroom participants.

To some extent, the teacher controls classroom contexts and can use them to shape play in one direction or another. Those contexts that distort the expression of play tendencies considered to be healthy are more likely to be noticed by adults, but the contexts that promote play that is considered expressive and creative are no less coercive.

THE HISTORICAL CONTEXT

There are other relevant contexts that have a less direct but no less profound impact on children's play. Their impact is heightened by the fact that they are often ignored; in some cases, educators may be unaware of the part they play in shaping classroom events or may discount the importance or possibility of controlling their influence. The historical context, for example, has an impact on play in the classroom but may be entirely unnoticed by teachers and others who believe that current attitudes toward play are obvious and natural. In fact, however, the nature of play in today's classrooms has a great deal to do with attitudes toward play in the past.

In colonial America, adults encouraged children to give up play for work and study because they believed that play was frivolous and led to moral laxity and sloth. These views persisted, and a textbook published in 1839 warned children as follows:

> If you waste your schoolboy years in indolence and play . . . in all probability, you will not be successful in any business in which you may engage, and you will live and die in poverty and obscurity. (Abbott, 1839, p. 12)

By the late nineteenth century, attitudes toward play were not so clear-cut. Some adults failed to see the importance of play, but they tolerated the playfulness of young children because the young continued to play in spite of adult efforts to prevent their doing so. Other adults saw children's play as a natural and charming expression of naive innocence, innate curiosity, and zest for life.

It is possible to trace the changes in adult attitudes toward play in the first half of this century by examining the stories in elementary school basal readers (King, 1991). These stories depict acceptable attitudes toward play as the spontaneous thoughts and activities of young children themselves. Throughout this time period, young children are shown playing; they are most often involved in physical activity such as running, jumping, and playing tag, although they also play guessing games, sing songs, read books, and listen to stories. At the turn of the century, children run through grassy fields and play loosely organized games. Adults are involved in children's play as co-participants; for example, Mother picks flowers with the children and Father takes his turn sledding down the hill. In the 1920s, the children continue to play in neighborhood settings, but some of their play is planned with the help of adults. For example, numerous stories of neighborhood circuses, plays, and pageants suddenly appear; these events are often quite complicated, and some include sophisticated costumes and elaborate refreshments.

In the 1930s stories about playground activities introduce highly organized play to the readers. Playground activities are organized in space in that they occur in designated, bounded areas and organized in time in that activities are tightly scheduled and children are expected to move quickly from one to another. Playground play, then, stands in striking contrast to the informal play of children at the turn of the century.

Children's play also assumes an increasingly impersonal quality over the first half of this century. Before 1920 children play with siblings, with neighborhood friends, and with their parents and other adult relatives. Their play activities are produced spontaneously by their immediate daily experiences. By 1930, however, children play with strangers; specifically, they play with playground directors and with children they meet for the first time on the playground. The activities on the playground also have an impersonal quality in that they are planned by others and provided for large groups of children simultaneously.

At the turn of the century, while play is always depicted as appropriate for the young, it is rarely extolled; children who avoid play are occasionally admired, and children who play before completing their chores are admonished. The readers also include, however, a small number of stories that encourage children to play outdoors and that indicate that laughing and playing can restore physical health.

By the 1940s, play emerges as an important component of life, and the readers become considerably more approving in their attitudes toward play activity. Simultaneously, however, the stipulations about where, when, and for whom play is appropriate grow in number, and play is justified and evaluated with increasing frequency from 1900 to 1950. While the play of babies and young children is accepted as natural and appropriate throughout this time period, by 1940 the play of older children and adults is usually justified. Two major justifications appear frequently. First, the readers point out that children at play are learning or practicing skills they will use as adults. Girls pretend they are grown women when they clean the play house, for example, and boys are encouraged to play airplane in order to prepare to be aviators.

The second major justification of play points to the restorative power of play activities and the importance of play for health. As already pointed out, early in the century there are occasional comments concerning the relationship between play and physical health. By 1940, the importance of play for health is extended to include mental health, and the restorative power of play as a respite from work is introduced.

Thus readers published from 1900 to 1950 stress with increasing frequency and emphasis that play should have a purpose. The goals of play are linked not only to personal satisfactions but to good citizenship as well. The opportunities to learn and practice social and physical skills turn the play of the young into a preparation for adulthood. The rest and relaxation play provides is valued because it permits the player to return to his or her work with renewed vigor and concentration.

Current attitudes toward play are an extension of these historical trends. Play is usually seen as a natural activity of both children and adults. However, educators today justify classroom play by stressing the contribution of play to the cognitive, psychological, and social development of young children (Isenberg & Quisenberry, 1988). Play is also used in classrooms to motivate children to participate in academic lessons and to reward them for their accomplishments and efforts regarding schoolwork. This instrumental view of play often precludes the close observation of classroom play and obscures the actual play episodes and their meaning to the children.

As attitudes toward play changed from rejection to idealization and justification, adults also sought to control children's play. The goal has been to create environments and situations in which children will produce only "good" play and to focus upon and study good play and laud its relationship to school success and socialization. This tendency also has historical antecedents. The "good" play depicted in the basal readers may have had little to do with the actual play of real children at the time. For example, a survey of children's street play in New York City in 1905 showed that the two most popular activities were playing with fire and gambling (Chase, 1905). Needless to say, such play is never seen in the readers or tolerated in the classroom.

Brian Sutton-Smith (1986) is a play researcher who warns the educational community about what he perceives as a continuing tendency to paint an unduly rosy picture of play and its place in human life. He points out that whereas play can be free, joyous, and flexible, it can also include danger, cruelty, and conformity. Adults may view "good" play as natural to childhood and "bad" play as an indication of pathology, immaturity, or social disintegration.

Noting the influence of past attitudes toward play on our current attitudes also reveals that the characterization of good play in the past changed in response to the pressure of societal forces at the time. The urbanization and industrialization this country underwent from 1900 to 1950 is reflected in the impersonalization and organization of children's play. By midcentury play is depicted in a mode designed to help socialize children to the demands of work settings in the city. Play is expected to be productive and to involve concentrated effort and energetic activity. Children are expected to be highly motivated to participate in play activities scheduled and organized by others. Thus it is possible to show historically that the social and economic contexts of a given time shape children's play. As these conditions change, so do the parameters of acceptable play.

SOCIETAL CONTEXTS

If past societal forces shaped attitudes toward and possibilities for play, there is no reason to assume that present societal forces are less potent. Still, the influence of societal contexts may be difficult to apprehend and their impact on children's play may be difficult to assess. Nonetheless, they have an immense impact on the lives of children and on the nature of children's play.

Play Under Extreme Circumstances

As ever, it is easier to recognize indirect, subtle, or overly familiar influences when they make us uncomfortable or when they occur in circumstances so extreme that they cannot be overlooked. Unfortunately, we have such an example in the play of young children during the Holocaust. This example is instructive because the social circumstances are so harsh that their impact cannot be ignored. Children's Holocaust experiences demonstrate that the contexts salient to an understanding of children's play are not limited to the immediate setting of the play event.

Play in the Holocaust, though created by small children, was shaped by conditions dictated by the Nazis. As George Eisen shows in his book *Children and Play in the Holocaust* (1988), children used their play to provide a counterbalance to their immediate social reality. The children's games and activities helped them "assimilate the horrors on their own terms and accommodate their psychic universe to the environment"

(p. 81). In their play, children developed a response that nurtured and encouraged their desire to survive.

Every play activity was an act of defiance and resistance to the reality of the ghetto or the concentration camp. Any moment snatched from the grim surroundings and devoted to an activity that created camaraderie and laughter defied the determination of the Nazis to kill all Jewish children. At times the children also used their play in a conscious fashion to express their disdain for their oppressors. Eisen tells of one incident, for example, when a group of ghetto children showered a visiting Nazi official with exaggerated and consequently ludicrous homage.

This play was not merely symbolic resistance. By providing the children with a way to cope with daily life, play provided a genuine resistance to the Nazi's determination to subjugate and defeat the children's will to live. Play, then, registered the children's opposition to their oppression, helped them adjust to the extreme situation in which they found themselves, and demonstrated their determination to survive and their willful optimism in the face of tyranny and death.

The internal context of play was also influenced by the reality of life in the Holocaust. Many children's games reenacted atrocities and dramatized the hardships of ghetto life. Children in one ghetto were observed playing a game based on their experiences smuggling food past concentration camp guards; another of their games reenacted the mass execution of the Vilna Jews in Ponary. Without toys, bits of wood and rags became precious playthings; without time, children played with great intensity. In the face of the moral deterioration around them, the moral content of their games deteriorated, and death became a prominent theme in their games. The coercive impact of the setting, then, was obvious as it intruded on the children's play. Games and pastimes reflected the immediate conditions of the children's lives and the constricted future planned for them even as these play activities provided an avenue of response and coping.

Ultimately, of course, play had no impact on the fate of the children. Jewish adults were rarely able to protect their children from the Nazis, and the respite from reality provided by play was short-lived and ephemeral. Although play enhanced the survival of the spirit, it was no match for the determination of the Nazis or the brutality of their regime.

Children's play in the Holocaust forces us to recognize the impact of societal contexts on the play of children. Although the impact of context may not always be so clear and undeniable, there is every reason to believe that children's play under ordinary circumstances is also influenced by the societal contexts in which it is embedded.

Play in School

Play in school is particularly susceptible to societal influences because the school is an institution that expresses cultural themes and values. The socioeconomic, political, ideological, and cultural contexts that have an impact on classroom play are fundamental, subtle, and difficult to disclose. The influence of ideology and culture, for example, may seem so indirect, pervasive, and immutable that it deserves little attention from educators who work daily in early childhood classrooms. Yet, when one considers specific examples of the intrusion of ideological messages into children's play, it is clear that teachers do respond, whether knowingly or unknowingly, to their influence. The social organization of schools, the allocation of educational resources, and the content of specific lessons, for example, are, in part, responses to societal messages and ideological positions. Studying educational practices while ignoring the societal contexts that support them, therefore, leads to distortion and an overemphasis on the school's power and autonomy. On the other hand, it is equally erroneous to assume that educational practices are nothing more than responses to societal demands.

There are several ways to bring societal contexts into focus and to make their impact on classroom life and classroom play more apparent. Cross-cultural studies create an understanding of our own cultural context by comparing it to the cultural contexts of others. A recent investigation of preschool practice in Japan, China, and the United States, for example, reveals notions of child development and appropriate practice that are clearly tied to the cultural milieu (Tobin, Wu, & Davidson, 1989). Cross-cultural studies of children's play are equally revealing, as are studies of the play of immigrant children. In these studies it becomes clear that the cultural context exerts an indirect influence on play because the child's family acts as a "mediating link between the transmission of culture and emergent patterns of play" (Slaughter & Dombrowski, 1989, p. 304).

One of the most salient characteristics of the family, social class, exerts a strong influence on children's play. All too often, however, studies of the impact of class on the play of young children focus strictly on describing the ways in which the play of lower-class children fails to match the play of middle- or upper-class children. Economic, environmental, parental, or cultural deprivation is then cited as the cause, and the school is encouraged to intervene in order to help the lower-class child play well. While this approach may not be wrong, it fails to explore the class context thoroughly before moving on to programmatic solutions.

John D'Amato (1989), on the other hand, in his study of children's play among low-income Hawaiian second-graders, explores carefully both the larger cultural milieu, as it is expressed in the children's games of rivalry, and the social context the children themselves create during play. Games of rivalry are often volatile, and the ability to hold them within the bounds of playfulness requires a sophistication the children must acquire to prevent their games' deteriorating into actual conflict. The children D'Amato studied valued friendliness and peer solidarity; they also valued "toughness," standing up for oneself, and responding to an affront. The children achieved standing in their peer cohort by handling confrontation so as to maintain a reputation for toughness. Consequently they sought opportunities in the classroom and on the playground to create games of contention. They competed for opportunities to sit next to the teacher, for turns to speak in class, and for positions at the beginning and end of the line. The children joked, teased, developed contests, and used games at recess to test their peer-group status. Their school experience, then, included affronts, challenges, and disputes on a daily basis.

A detailed look at the boys' social structure reveals the ways in which they attempted to "win peer acceptance and regard without simultaneously offending peers and provoking conflict" (p. 255). The boys established three groups: a group that was not tough and two rival groups of tough boys. The latter groups were typified as fighting gangs, although confrontations between them were extremely rare. Membership in a gang validated the boys' claims to toughness, while a sensible avoidance of their enemies permitted them to avoid conflict. Establishing the other gang members as enemies also enhanced solidarity among members of the same gang. "Ultimately, the gangs were much more about friendship than fighting. It was less the case that the boys of the gangs had banded together in order to fight off enemies than that they had used the idea of enemies as a pretext for creating and sustaining friendship" (p. 272).

The social structure established by these boys and their focus on rivalry and competition is related to the children's social class and cultural context. Restricted economic and social mobility among lower-class Hawaiians has resulted in social structures that emphasize contention and rivalry for status. Thus societal "themes of social structure, interaction, and self-presentation . . . are at least partly responsible for Hawaiian children's rivalrous peer dynamics" (p. 278).

War Play

In this example of the play of young Hawaiian boys, it is not difficult to discern the influence of societal contexts on children's school play. This influence is also apparent in classrooms where teachers observe play episodes in which children dramatize drug deals and police raids. Similarly, children's interest in war toys and war games is linked to multiple contexts, although there are those who explain children's penchant for war games simply as a developmental stage. Play, they explain, is an important vehicle for learning, and war play provides children with the opportunity to create situations in which they learn to express and control aggressive tendencies. Developmentalists note that the power and adventure of war play is particularly attractive and exciting to boys and boys' indulgence in such play is a healthy manifestation of a particular stage in their growth.

While the developmental perspective is not wrong, it is extremely limited in that it fails to recognize other contexts that encourage war play among children. War play is the children's expression of a major theme that is prominent in many aspects of popular culture. Although there are numerous groups advocating peaceful solutions to all conflicts, there is also an avid interest in war in this country. Books and movies, for example, display a fascination with war and weaponry; histories idealize wartime and the lives of soldiers, while fantasies about the future often included awesome weapons and catastrophic warfare. In current accounts, the technological superiority of our military is extolled, and a great patriotic pride is evident in tales of our powerful weapons.

A fascination with war is also evident in the portrayal of nuclear weapons. These images are not based on science or fact; rather they have a mythical quality. The nuclear bomb is associated in popular culture with mad scientists, evolution gone awry, destructive monsters, and flying saucers. The symbol of the *mushroom*-shaped cloud associates the bomb with a mystical image of poison and death. In addition, the typical symbol of the atom itself as a ringed nucleus is scientifically meaningless. Rather it is a folk symbol, a mandala that indicates a spiritual rather than a scientific quest (Weart, 1988).

This fascination with war includes the tendency to vilify other cultures as our enemies and to depict them as depraved aliens, quite unlike ourselves. This is, of course, necessary in order to maintain distrust and to justify the use of lethal weapons against them. This tendency also extends to elements of our own culture, as in, for example, the war imagery used in "campaigns" to "combat" drug use.

One reason that war themes have such a profound impact on children's play is the commercialization currently surrounding this aspect of the cultural context. The proliferation of violent cartoons on television is one example. During the Reagan administration, many of the regulations designed to control children's television were canceled, and television producers responded by including more violent cartoons and commercials during hours when young children are likely to be watching. Many of the commercial products featured are war toys such as "action figures" based on cartoon characters, complete with armed vehicles and weapons. A combination of advertising and peer pressure keeps the market for these war toys strong, encouraging and supporting war play among children. That this situation is tolerated is a clear indication that the themes and activities associated with war play are acceptable to most adults.

There are striking differences between the sexes with regard to their use of war toys. It is boys who are likely to want war toys; girls continue to prefer dolls and toys that have to do with domestic activity and personal grooming (Lawson, 1989). Since girls do not ordinarily choose to play war even when provided with war toys, the toy itself cannot be said to determine children's play behaviors. Similarly, banning war toys from the classroom does not eliminate the desire of most boys to reenact war themes in their play.

While the themes of war play may concern physical violence, most war play is not actually aggressive. The play episodes may focus on destruction and mayhem, but the peer interaction is likely to be friendly and cooperative. In fact, children must cooperate in order to sustain their sociodramatic play; actual aggression and interpersonal conflict destroys the game, and the play disintegrates into squabbling. For the most part, then, and in the minds of most children, war play is not a display of direct aggression. Many children who describe war as terrible and who make thoughtful arguments against the use of violence nonetheless enjoy the fun and excitement of war play (Wegener-Spöhring, 1989).

A close look at early childhood educators' dislike of war play reveals that it may have less to do with their dislike of violence, aggression, and weaponry and more to do with their desire to promote an ideal form of play. While there are teachers and other adults who discourage children from including any violent themes in their play, recent scholarship concerning war play distinguishes between a good game of war and a bad game of war (Carlsson-Paige & Levin, 1987).

In a good game of war there is no direct or real aggression. Any apparently aggressive act is strictly make-believe and does not interrupt the friendly cooperation among the playmates. Disagreements or conflicts that occur during play are solved in a way that maintains the play group and extends the play event. Thus the first characteristic of a good game of war is that it does not confuse pretend aggression with actual aggression and that it does not deteriorate into actual conflict.

The second major characteristic of good war play is that it includes the creative elaboration of play themes. Bad war play is simply the endless reenactment of scenarios from television cartoons using toy figures depicting the main characters. The children accept their roles passively; the relationships among characters are static, and the play event is an aimless rehashing of old material. In contrast, good war play includes novel play themes developed by the children in the course of their play. When children play a good game of war, they develop and elaborate the play themes; roles evolve and relationships are negotiated. The children learn and practice cooperation, communication, and compromise even as they act out episodes of murder and mayhem.

Teachers have a variety of reactions when they observe war play in their classrooms. There are teachers who tolerate all war play, including the rote reenactment of violent scenarios. Other teachers ban war play and reject both the violent themes and the ways in which children include these themes in their play. Some teachers, following advice to be found in recent research reports, differentiate between good war play and bad war play and intervene in bad war play (Carlsson-Paige & Levin, 1987). In order to facilitate good war play, it is recommended that teachers ban commercial war toys and that play themes avoid cartoon scenarios. Intervention is for the purpose of shaping the classroom context so that the children's developmental needs are protected. The influence of the larger societal context is thus mitigated, while the themes and messages it includes are accepted.

Although good war play may be responsive to the developmental needs of young children, it is no less influenced by the cultural context than is bad war play. In both cases, societal messages influence the content and the form of children's play and force teachers to shape classroom contexts in response.

The example of war play is vivid and therefore particularly instructive. It is more difficult to see the ways in which societal contexts influence play when the results appear benign or are welcome. There is no reason, however, to believe that these more palatable influences are any less coercive.

CONCLUSION

As George Eisen (1988) points out, one reason that adults provide play settings for children is that it brings the adults themselves satisfaction and joy to do so. Adults are affirmed in their roles as nurturers by the fact that they can provide opportunities and settings for children that permit the children to freely express themselves in play. When we see them at play, we confirm our ability to keep our children safe to indulge their innocent pastimes and to provide for their growth and development. Thus the play of children is an important source of satisfaction to adults—in particular, to teachers of young children.

Classrooms filled with bright, healthy, energetic children busily occupied in meaningful play activities are a source of pride to early childhood educators. The children's play, under the teacher's guidance, is elicited, indulged, examined, and adored as much for the pleasure it brings the teacher and other adults as for the pleasure it is assumed to bring children. It is not so much that this supportive classroom context provides children with the opportunity to reenact life's enigmas; we know from studies of play in the Holocaust that nearly any context will provide such an opportunity. Rather, I believe adults delight in the play of young children in such nurturing settings because it gives them the luxury of seeing children as life's little philosophers. We must not forget, however, that although the play appears benign and spontaneous, the societal contexts that influence and the classroom contexts that elicit this play are compelling, structured, and directive.

A full understanding of the contexts influencing children's play is necessary to an understanding of play in school. The impact of societal influences, the demands of the institution in general, and the constraints of the classroom in particular all help to shape the children's play. School play, then, cannot be taken as simply a measure of the children's developmental ability. It is, rather, a product of multiple, embedded, and mutually reactive contexts and influences.

It is particularly important and difficult to keep this in mind when thinking about play. Play is, after all, about the deconstruction of and the escape from contexts; in fact, one of play's major purposes is to make context irrelevant. In this way young children become daring heroes in spite of their youth and inexperience: children fly in spaceships although no such travel opportunities exist; and they conquer dragons and monsters in spite of their fears and weaknesses. Nonetheless, even as they create opportunities to ignore real contexts, these contexts intrude upon and shape the children's play. Consequently, adults cannot adequately understand children's play until we recognize and account for the influence of context.

The play literature is slowly coming to grips with the importance of context. In a recent study of classroom play, for example, Christie and Johnsen (1989) stated that their findings were attributable to "an interaction of context variables, particularly the effects of play materials and teacher attitudes toward play, and social class differences" (p. 323). Further, they found that, of these variables, "setting variables may be relatively more powerful than social class differences in terms of influencing play patterns, at least in school situations" (p. 324). Christie and Johnsen conclude by pointing out, "A key to interpreting these findings may be that play that occurs in academic settings is not really free play; the play observed in our study was constrained by several factors including the materials available and the expectation of the adult staff" (p. 325). In school, classroom contexts may overcome developmental trends and impose quiet task-oriented play in service to the goals of the setting.

As researchers become more aware of the importance of context variables, they must also realize that the research undertaking itself is embedded in multiple contexts. Researchers bring ideological preferences and particular attitudes toward children, play, and research to their work. For example, Sutton-Smith and Magee (1989) found that the definition of aggressive play is clearly related to the perspective of the observer when they asked several people to categorize the activity on a videotape of play fighting. The child involved called it playing; the teacher called it fighting; college males called it playing; and college females called it fighting. In a similar study, participants watched fourteen videotaped incidents of children's free play. Again, they disagreed on what was play and what was aggression. Differences were related to the viewer's gender, whether or not the viewer had engaged in war toy play, and whether or not the viewer had worked in a preschool (Connor, 1989).

Further, the research community imposes standards and norms that constrain researchers, impose procedures, and limit the ways in which findings can be communicated. In order to be considered legitimate and noteworthy, research must follow the pattern approved by the research community. While most researchers function comfortably within the acceptable parameters, this context does impose limitations and constraints on research activity. There are also analytic contexts that influence the research activity after the data has been collected (Lubeck, 1988). Theories and assumptions about the social world and the purposes of research have a powerful impact on the nature of research findings and their uses.

Finally, an awareness of context variables and the multiple ways in which they shape classroom play create both an added opportunity and an extra measure of responsibility for early childhood educators. Teachers who are aware of societal messages are able to mitigate their impact on classroom life; and teachers who understand the ways in which classroom contexts inhibit some play behaviors and inspire others can design learning environments that educate and encourage children through play.

REFERENCES

Abbott, J. S. C. (1939). *The school-boy or a guide for youth to truth and duty*. Boston: Crocker and Brewster.

Carlsson-Paige, N., & Levin, D. E. (1987). *The war play dilemma*. New York: Teachers College Press.

Chase, J. (1905). Street games of New York City. *Pedagogical Seminary, 12*, 503–504.

Christie, J. F., & Johnsen, E. P. (1989). The constraints of settings on children's play. *Play and Culture, 2*, 317–327.

Christie, J. F., Johnsen, E. P., & Peckover, R. B. (1988). The effects of play period duration on children's play patterns. *Journal of Research in Childhood Education, 3*, 123–137.

Connor, K. (1989). Aggression: Is it in the eye of the beholder? *Play and Culture, 2*, 213–217.

D'Amato, J. J. (1989). Rivalry as a game of relationships: The social structure created by the boys of a Hawaiian primary school class. In M. N. Bloch & A. D. Pellegrini (Eds.), *The ecological context of children's play* (pp. 245–281). Norwood, NJ: Ablex.

Deaux, K., & Major, B. (1987). Putting gender into context: An interactive model of gender-related behavior. *Psychological Review, 94*, 369–389.

Eisen, G. (1988). *Children and play in the Holocaust: Games among the shadows*. Amherst: University of Massachusetts Press.

Farrer, C. (1977). Play and inter-ethnic communication. In D. Lancy & A. Tindall (Eds.), *The study of play: Problems and prospects* (pp. 98–104). West Point, NY: Leisure Press.

Isenberg, J., & Quisenberry, N. L. (1988). Play: A necessity for all children. *Childhood Education, 65*, 138–145.

Jackson, P. W., & Wolfson, B. J. (1971). Varieties of constraint in a nursery school. In M. Silberman (Ed.), *The experience of schooling* (pp. 148–161). New York: Holt, Rinehart and Winston.

King, N. R. (1987). Elementary school play: Theory and research. In J. H. Block & N. R. King (Eds.), *School play* (pp. 143–165). New York: Garland.

King, N. R. (1991). See baby play: Play as depicted in basal readers, 1900–1950. *Play and Culture, 4*, 100–108.

Lawson, C. (1989, June 15). Toys: Girls still apply makeup, boys fight wars. *New York Times*, pp. C1, C10.

Liss, M. B. (1986). Play of boys and girls. In G. Fein & M. Rivkin (Eds.), *The young child at play* (pp. 127–139). Washington, DC: National Associated for the Education of Young Children.

Lubeck, S. (1988). Nested contexts. In L. Weis (Ed.), *Class, race and gender in American education* (pp. 43–62). Albany: State University of New York Press.

Maccoby, E. E. (1988). Gender as a social category. *Developmental Psychology, 24*, 755–765.

Maccoby, E. E., & Jacklin, C. N. (1987). Gender segregation in childhood. In E. H. Reese (Ed.), *Advances in child development and behavior* (pp. 239-287). New York: Academic Press.

McLoyd, L. (1986). Scaffolds or shackles? The role of toys in preschool children's pretend play. In G. Fein & M. Rivkin (Eds.), *The young child at play* (pp. 63-77). Washington, DC: National Association for the Education of Young Children.

Renninger, K. A. (1989). Individual patterns in children's play interests. In L. Winegar (Ed.), *Social interaction and the development of children's understanding* (pp. 147-172). Norwood, NJ: Ablex.

Slaughter, D. T., & Dombrowski, J. (1989). Cultural continuities and discontinuities: Impact on social and pretend play. In M. N. Bloch & A. D. Pellegrini (Eds.), *The ecological context of children's play* (pp. 282-310). Norwood, NJ: Ablex.

Sutton-Smith, B. (1986). The spirit of play. In G. Fein & M. Rivkin (Eds.), *The young child at play* (pp. 3-15). Washington, DC: National Association for the Education of Young Children.

Sutton-Smith, B., & Magee, M. A. (1989). Reversible childhood. *Play and Culture*, 2, 52-63.

Tobin, J. J., Wu, D. H. Y., & Davidson, D. H. (1989). *Preschoolers in three cultures: Japan, China, and the United States*. New Haven, CT: Yale University Press.

Weart, S. R. (1988). *Nuclear fear: A history of images*. Cambridge, MA: Harvard University Press.

Wegener-Spöhring, G. (1989). War toys and aggressive games. *Play and Culture*, 2, 35-47.

Zinsser, C. (1987). Playing around: Children's play under constraint. In G. A. Fine (Ed.), *Meaningful play, playful meaning* (pp. 75-84). Champaign, IL: Human Kinetics Publishers.

CHAPTER 4

Meanings of Readiness and the Kindergarten Experience

M. Elizabeth Graue

Discussions of kindergarten education often seem to tumble across the idea of readiness for school. That is not surprising; kindergarten programs often have readiness screenings, reading readiness, readiness programs, readiness teachers, readiness workbooks, readiness scores. Teachers think about readiness as they sort children, plan instruction, evaluate progress, and make summative judgments (Graue, in press; Smith & Shepard, 1988; Walsh, 1989). Policy makers debate the perfect school entrance age to ensure that children will be ready when they start school (Graue & Shepard, in press). Assessment programs are set up to determine whether children are ready for their kindergarten or first-grade year and to evaluate the efficacy of preschool programs (Meisels, 1985; National Education Goals Panel, 1991). And many parents search for a way to decide if their child is ready, from a check of the school entrance date to a complex comparison with the children of neighbors and friends (Graue, 1991).

Regardless of who talks about readiness, it is almost always portrayed as a characteristic of an individual child that comes about in the process of growth and development. It is usually depicted as some combination of cognitive, psychomotor, and social-emotional development that should be present in balance and congruent with the child's chronological age. From this perspective, questions of readiness are related to the characteristics of ready children (Cameron & Wilson, 1990; National Education Goals Panel, 1991; Uphoff & Gilmore, 1986), prediction of readiness at some later point (Wood, Powell, & Knight, 1984), treatments to enhance readiness (Shepard & Smith, 1988), and the psychometric properties of readiness assessment instruments (Ellwein,

This chapter is adapted from M. E. Graue, *Ready for What?: Constructing Meanings of Readiness for Kindergarten* (in press). Used by permission of SUNY Press.

Walsh, Eads, & Miller, 1991). Readiness is seen as a stable, measurable capacity that can be used by professionals to make educational decisions, especially those related to instruction and placement. We should be able to see readiness in children, quantify it, and provide placements that will increase readiness if there is a problem.

The confidence in this conception of readiness has been shaken of late as a variety of critics question the utility of readiness-as-a-child-characteristic for reasons as varied as problems related to the technical properties of instruments used to assess it (Meisels, 1987; Shepard, 1990) and its incompatibility with guidelines for "developmentally appropriate practice" (National Association for the Education of Young Children, 1990; Willer & Bredekamp, 1990). Here, I concur with this movement for the reexamination of the readiness idea but choose to study it from a very different perspective than is usually taken in the early childhood literature. Rather than conceiving of readiness as a developmental characteristic of individual children, this work examines readiness from a social and cultural perspective. It moves the focus from attributes of young children to contextual forces that shape early school experience. To explore this change, I examine commonly held models of readiness, tracing them to the analytical traditions from which they have developed. I discuss problems (both philosophically and pragmatically) with these conceptions and posit an alternative to the current psychologically based view of readiness. As an illustration of an application of this perspective, I present data from an ethnographic study of the meaning of readiness in two communities.

CURRENT CONCEPTIONS OF READINESS

Current conceptions of readiness for school share a legacy of psychological thought that has permeated the child development/early childhood education field in the twentieth century (Bloch, 1991). These views focus on individual children and the influences of biology, families, and prekindergarten experience on differences in their growth and development. Readiness from this perspective is tied to development, and readiness problems are seen as synonymous with developmental delay. Work on readiness typically examines the characteristics of children who might fail in the early school years; age, test results, and performance after extra-year experience are the usual foci for such studies.

Despite a common disciplinary tradition, the proposed mechanisms of readiness vary greatly, echoing the debates about how children learn that have enlivened the field for decades. For some, readiness is related to biological development, something that grows as the child develops and matures. This orientation to readiness, exemplified by those affiliated with the Gesell Institute, is premised on the concept of physical or social maturation, which can be developed only with the passage of time. Lack of readiness is related to an underdeveloped organism, which will be damaged if challenged by tasks that are posed at a higher developmental level. Teachers and parents are admonished to wait if there is a concern about readiness, to give the *gift of time* (Eisenhart & Graue, 1990; Kagan, 1990; Shepard & Smith, 1988; Weber, 1984).

For others, readiness is a matter of environmental stimulation. Readiness is developed when children have experiences that prepare them for school life. Mismatch between experience and task requirements is the source of readiness problems and can be remedied by providing instruction in specific skills. A skilled teacher is the key in remediation of readiness difficulties; she or he is responsible for accurate assessment and instructional strategies for targeted deficiencies. Behavioral analysis, DISTAR (Direct Instruction System for Teaching Arithmetic and Reading), and the Early Prevention of School Failure program are examples of the environmental readiness approach (see Peck, McCaig, and Sapp, 1988, for a discussion of direct instruction programs).[1]

These views of readiness are oriented to individual children, their growth and development. They are premised on a sequential view of development, variations of building-block or stage theory in which children accumulate readiness. Implicit in this view is the idea that children must have a certain amount of readiness to benefit from school experience, that deficiencies in one dimension of readiness makes success highly unlikely.

This notion of readiness as sequentially developed and related to universal and invariant stages of child life has been brought into question in relation to the views of development on which it is based. In work that examined assumptions about development, Walsh (1991) proposed two key points that make stagelike, universal views of development problematic. First, the conception of invariant stages that are predictable and necessary has not been consistently borne out in empirical work. What may seem like a unitary process is characterized by more exceptions than regularities. We are reminded that development is jagged, uneven, and not nearly as uniform as the stage charts in many child development textbooks would have us believe.

Second, the focus on individual children making sense of the world alone does not attend to the way that social context *mediates* a child's experience. Interactions with others and with materials do not occur in a vacuum; they are part of the sociohistorical fabric of life and carry with them the meanings that have been constructed in a context. Contrasting this view and the dominant psychological conception of the child, Walsh places the child in new relationship to the world at large: "Development is seen as occurring in the social context, as moving from outside the child to inside the child, rather than from the inside out. The child is seen not as creating the world but as socially recreating it" (1991, p. 116). In this view, the child is active in the developmental process that occurs through the social mediation of the context of the home, the school, and the community. Rather than a biological push from inside the child or responses to stimuli from the environment, physical growth and social resources work together to frame the mechanism and our understandings of the developmental process. This is different from the maturational or environmental approach to child development, in which the child is relatively passive in the process of developing expertise. It also departs from Piagetian views of development, in which the child constructs knowledge individually in interactions with materials. The resources available in a child's environment, including the people, materials, and ideas, provide opportunities for growth and interaction that actually shape development.

Jipson (1991) has added to the argument against the hierarchical view of development from the perspective of the knowledge and behavior privileged in these orientations. Jipson contends that the developmental theory on which much of current early childhood practice is based is founded on a very specific *cultural*, rather than *scientific*, base. That cultural base is European-American and middle class and is tied to the child behaviors that are fostered by that cultural group and the characteristics and abilities prized by their teachers.

Shifting to more practical concerns, the area of readiness assessment provides little more than confusion if one is trying to understand the construct. Readiness tests vary from instruments to help teachers make day-to-day instructional decisions to those designed to help be a first step in a diagnostic process for children with special needs (Meisels, 1987). Unfortunately, these tests are often misused, given their purpose (Meisels, 1987), and their content represents outmoded models of cognitive development (Stallman & Pearson, 1990). None of the current instruments is sufficiently accurate to predict whether a child will have later problems in school (Ellwein et al., 1991; Shepard, 1990). Many developmental screening tests used for determining extra-year placements are so much like intelligence tests that they could be said to be testing IQ rather than readiness (Shepard, 1990). Perhaps the assessment problems go beyond technical issues of norms and sampling. Could it be that the construct, as currently understood, simply does not exist?

Finally, at the level of practice, the actions taken by people in relation to ideas about readiness are too diverse to indicate that a single view of readiness exists. In the United States, children generally begin school at age 5; in Sweden, they are not believed to be ready until they reach the age of 7 (Engel, 1989). In one school district, the kindergarten entrance date is December 15; in another it is July 1. In some communities, large numbers of children have had their kindergarten entry delayed by a year. This practice, called "academic redshirting," is particularly popular for middle-class boys with summer birthdays (Shepard, Graue, & Catto, 1989).[2] This is often parent-initiated, a voluntary exclusion from school based on judgments of readiness. In other places, virtually all children enter school as soon as they are legally eligible. Elsewhere, children with readiness deficits are given extended school experiences, involving more time in school so they can catch up with their more ready peers. One school sets up extra-year programs before or after the kindergarten year (called developmental kindergartens or transitional first grades), another retains children in grade, and the third passes those children on with the hope that next year's teacher can do what needs to be done to help in the educational process (Graue, in press; Smith & Shepard, 1988; Walsh, Ellwein, Eads, & Miller, 1991).

AN ALTERNATIVE CONCEPTUALIZATION

Considering the underlying theories of development, the conceptions of readiness, the assessment problems, and the practices that relate to readiness, it is striking how they are oriented to individuals and how they ignore the social and cultural forces that shape the educational experience for children, their families, and teachers. How could we enrich our understanding of readiness if we shifted our thinking away from the view that readiness is a universal child characteristic that can be identified and measured? Could we approach the problem of readiness from a social and cultural perspective and know more?

Given the lack of success we have had in trying to utilize a psychological view of readiness, I suggest that a shift in perspective is not only warranted but required. It makes more sense to think about readiness as an *idea* that is more or less shared in a setting. Rather than existing as a physical fact and carried around by individual children, conceptions of readiness are constructed in social interaction as parents, teachers, and others interested in the education of young children cope with the resources and constraints of their environments. These views represent negotiations and historical arrangements, including ideas about how children grow and what it means to be a good parent or teacher. They are complex and simultaneously very personal and public. Ideas about readiness, developed by the adults and used as a way to understand children, shape the interactions between children and adults in and out of school.

Thinking about readiness in this way has not been suggested without precedent. Encountering the murkiness of traditional research on readiness, some researchers have begun to rethink readiness. Smith and Shepard (1988) studied readiness as a set of beliefs that teachers hold about children and education. They found that beliefs about readiness varied along a dimension of nature–nurture and that these beliefs influenced such practices as retention in grade. Further, they noted that beliefs about readiness tended to be shared among people in a setting.

In addition, work that examined kindergarten enrollment patterns suggested that ideas about when to enter a child into school, which can be taken as orientations to readiness, were locally defined. Analyzing the age distributions of over 31,000 kindergartners in seventeen school districts, it was found that the proportion of children held out of school (redshirted) varied from 0 to 70 percent (Shepard, Graue, & Catto, 1989). These variations indicated that school communities defined informal rules about when children should be enrolled in school, and in many cases these rules were more important than the legal entrance age.

This work on retention and readiness set the stage for an examination of readiness as a contextual issue that frames the educational process in local settings. The study discussed in this chapter approached readiness as a *socially constructed meaning* rather than a child characteristic. As such, it departs from the traditional psychological view of readiness and addresses the problem from an interpretive frame. It is different from earlier work because it is founded on the assumption that ideas like readiness are developed at a social and cultural level rather than on the level of the individual. Salient issues from this perspective include the negotiated process of construct development as well as the implications for practice that come out of various constellations of definition.

Moving consideration of readiness from differences between individual children to the social context in which the characteristics are given meaning required a different theoretical framework. One of the main points that guided the development of the theoretical framework for this study was the idea that meaning is socially constructed and constituted. According to Erickson (1982), the social context does more than *mediate* learning; it provides the pieces that form what is learned. Therefore ideas can be seen as socially constituted because they come out of the contextual arrangements that arise in a setting. In addition, contexts are built or constructed by people in interaction—people in interaction do the work and thus become part of the meaning of the context itself (Mehan, 1980).

This orientation has been highlighted in the research community of late with the recent English translations of the work of Vygotsky. At the most general level, Vygotsky's work could be described as an examination of human mental functioning within its social context. More specifically, Wertsch and Toma (1990) have described it as a "sociocultural approach to mediated action," which asserts that mental life cannot be abstracted from the cultural, historical, and institutional context in which it occurs. Using this perspective, the normal focus on individual mental functioning is turned on its head. Instead, attention is given to the sociocultural context in which individuals act. In the study of the construction of the meaning of readiness, the focus becomes the ways in which communities work to develop an understanding of readiness; that is, examining the social and institutional forces that shape it. Of secondary interest is the way that individuals internalize that meaning and use it in their lives.

For the specific purposes of this study, an important point in Vygotsky's work is the notion that higher mental functions, such as ideas, have origins that are social. Vygotsky (1978) explained this clearly when he said, "the social dimension of consciousness is primary in time and fact. The individual dimension of consciousness is derivative and secondary" (p. 30, quoted in Wertsch, 1985). Using this model for the construction of meaning, ideas of readiness are negotiated at the level of the group first, among participants in a setting. This socially constructed meaning could then be used by individuals such as parents and teachers as they make decisions for children.

In this chapter, I focus on the *social* process through which members of communities develop a local meaning of readiness. Attention is on the process by which various audiences defined and enacted meanings of readiness in their experience, highlighting what Geertz (1981) has called *interpretations*, the meanings attached to institutions, actions, images, utterances, events, and customs of a group. In the context of readiness, they could be seen as having elements that are formal and elements that are local. The formal elements are derived from child development theory through academic discourse; they are the ideas learned about children in educational psychology and child development courses. The local elements are generated in particular communities, neighborhoods, schools, and families; they have repercussions for individual children and their education. This work describes local interpretations in two communities, those ideas shared by members of a community that shape educational practice. They include ideas about child growth and development, the purpose of kindergarten education, and what it means to be a good parent or teacher. As parents and teachers participate in the kindergarten experience, social interpretations of readiness focus the images about children and their ability. These interpretations put limits on the actions that are deemed reasonable for parents and teachers, forming the foundation for evaluations about what a ready child might be.

STUDYING READINESS

The data presented here come from a larger study of the meaning of readiness in three communities in the same school district (Graue, in press). Schools were chosen that had different orientations to readiness in terms of the enrollment and promotion practices in the early grades. This was based on the assumption that decisions about whether to enroll, redshirt, or retain a child were based on beliefs about how children develop readiness. Due to space limitations, I discuss the social interpretation of readiness that was constructed in only two of the three communities. Two schools were chosen to examine what have been called middle-class practices related to readiness, such as academic redshirting, in the context of a school with a diverse population. Norwood and Rochester provided an opportunity to think about that situation.[3] Table 4.1 provides information about some of the salient school characteristics for the two communities discussed here.

These schools were the sites for a participant observation study that examined the ways in which social interpretations of readiness developed in local settings. Multiple data sources were used to weave together an

Table 4.1 School Characteristics

School & Teacher	Socioeconomic status	Ethnicity	Academic Redshirting	Retention
Norwood Mrs. Sunden	Middle class in a middle class community	Primarily Anglo students in a homogeneous ethnic school	Popular (14%)	Infrequent in kindergarten but popular at grade one (12%)
Rochester Mrs. Ramirez	Working class students in mixed SES school community	Primarily Hispanic students in mixed ethnic community	Popular among middle class (22%), not among working class (0%)	Infrequent (3%)

understanding of how community members thought about and enacted meanings of readiness as they participated in the kindergarten experience. Information from the school at large was gathered to understand a broad view of the community meaning of readiness and was contrasted with its enactment in a single classroom. Once a week during the fall and several times during the spring semester, I worked as a teacher aide in Mrs. Sunden's and Mrs. Ramirez' kindergarten classrooms. By taking on the role of aide, I became part of the school community and was included in the day-to-day lives of these teachers. Fieldnotes of my visits were provided to the teachers and their comments on the notes were included as data. Monthly interviews outside of classtime focused on my emerging understanding of the meaning of readiness. Documents such as lesson plans, school and classroom letters, and worksheets were collected throughout the school year.

In addition to understanding the instructional instantiation of readiness, I examined how parents developed understandings of readiness for school. Parents, selected from each school at large (five or six per school), were interviewed in the month preceding the start of school. At the end of the first quarter of school, a different group of parents from each of the study classrooms was interviewed at the time of parent–teacher conferences. These interviews focused on what parents were thinking about as their children approached and entered their first public school experience, with interiews lasting from fifteen to forty-five minutes.

Analysis of these data (interviews, fieldnotes, and documents) was an ongoing process throughout the project and included both themes that were suggested by the theoretical framework used to frame the study and themes that arose during its course. An important aspect in the analysis portion of this work was the development of vignettes, an ethnographic analysis technique that aims to capture a complex scene in a special moment of time (Van Maanen, 1988). Vignettes provide an opportunity for the researcher to encapsulate a theme in the story of an event or situation. In developing these vignettes, quotes were pulled from interviews and fieldnotes and woven into a story that represented a salient theme in each context. As the vignettes were developed, the participating teachers read them and gave feedback about their representativeness and salience to the portrayal of school life in their community.

In addition to their analysis purposes, vignettes are used to transport readers into the fieldwork situation; "not to tell readers what to think of an experience but to show them the experience from beginning to end and thus draw them immediately into the story to work out its problems and puzzles as they unfold" (Van Maanen, 1988, p. 103). The vignettes are included here to illustrate the social processes that undergird the social interpretations of readiness, to present data in a context that preserves their highly personal nature, and to help the reader enter the field. Following each vignette, I examine the salient themes of social interpretations in each setting through analysis of interview, participant observation, and document-analysis data.

Interpretations at Norwood: Communicating Meanings of Readiness

"BUT IS HE READY?"

The hallway is bright and decorated with nursery characters. It's too cold to stand outside, so a group of mothers huddle next to the classroom doorway. Waiting to pick their children up from the morning preschool session, they talk about the hottest topic of the day—kindergarten enrollment.

"Well, how old is he?"

"Gary'll be 5 in August—he's a full month older than the deadline," Anne replies with a puzzled look on her face. She is standing against the wall with the other women gathered around her.

"But that'll make him one of the youngest in his—"

"And do you know what they do in kindergarten now?"

"Isn't it pretty much like preschool, with more kids?"

"No way," Kristin, a tall blond woman in jeans and a hand-painted sweatshirt, says laughing. "Do you remember what we did in kindergarten? Some clay, some paint, snack and rest, right? At Norwood, they need to know their name, they have to know their phone number, they have to know all this stuff. *Before* they can be in kindergarten!" The five women shake their heads collectively in frustration.

"Sounds like before you can even start, you have to know how to read and stuff like that."

"But Gary knows how to write his name, he knows his colors and most of his shapes—"

"Have you talked to Sandy [his teacher] about it?"

"Well, she did mention that she thought he was a little young. But I figured that by September he'd be ready."

For the first time this morning, Jean speaks, looking very serious. "I just know that with our oldest, I had to make the same kind of decision—he knew a lot but was a summer birthday. We went ahead and put him in and I've always regretted it. I think that he would have had a lot easier time if we had just waited. . . . He was smart enough to go. That isn't the issue. It's more a thing of attention span, being able to sit long enough to listen to what they tell you. Feeling more secure about what you are doing. You really have an edge if you are a few months older, especially at this age . . . It's one of those things you can't go back and change. Pushing them just doesn't seem worth it when you can let them be on the top by waiting an extra year."

The door opens and a gaggle of 4- and 5-year-olds tumble out of the yellow classroom. They are raucous and full of news from their morning in school. Some are clutching easel paintings, others wear colored macaroni necklaces. Gary's mother looks at him with new eyes, comparing him to his classmates.

"Maybe he isn't ready . . ." she thinks to herself.

Norwood was a bedroom community of professionals working in nearby cities; it provided a setting for families to raise children with all the advantages that middle-class life could afford. Children were involved in out-of-home activities from toddlerhood; it was through these activities that parents were drawn into a social network of carpools, volunteering, and preschool news. As they participated, many of the stay-at-home mothers became acquainted with the expectations and normative nature of the child's preschool experience; they learned to think of their children in comparison to their peers.

One of the most pervasive themes that came out of my interactions in the Norwood community was illustrated in the vignette: the social network that joined the parents of preschoolers provided much information about the rules for parental behavior and keyed them in to issues of readiness. There was a lively communication process in this community, evidenced by the fact that nine of eleven parents interviewed in the course of this study spoke of discussions they had had with their peers about the upcoming kindergarten experience and related expectations. They told of the pressure they felt from their friends and neighbors to compare their child to the Norwood norm of readiness, which was anchored by a maturational approach. Adam's mother told me that she had been shaken by the nonstop flow of advice she had received about whether to send her son to school in September:

I've been trying and trying to decide whether to put him into school—he just turned 5 and seems to be in really good shape, but everybody says that I shouldn't send him until next year. They say I'll be doing him a disservice. I was really worried so we had him tested. . . . and she ended up saying he was fine. Still, everybody says that I'm wrong and that he'd better wait. He's little for his age and they say especially later, that being so little will be a problem. The big thing is sports, that he'll be too little.

Good parents attended to issues of readiness as defined by the Norwood community. One of the most important aspects of readiness was related to age; nine of eleven parents spoke of age as a readiness indicator. Children with summer birthdays, particularly boys, were seen to be readiness risks.[4] One of the best ways that they could help children succeed was to put them at the top of the age distribution, which they related to the top of the ability distribution. Many stories were told of people who knew someone, like Jean in the vignette, who regretted the mistake of putting a "young" boy in school. Jean had a son in Mrs. Sunden's class, and she was greatly relieved that Michael was a January birthday so that his age was not a concern.

This orientation to age was promulgated in the community at the preschool level. Alyson's mother, whose first child was beginning school in the fall at the age of not-quite-5, was worried about her daughter being the youngest in her class. She had already experienced sorting by age in her daughter's preschool, where children clearly past the entrance age were given a more academic program:

I don't know if she'll be one of the youngest kids in the class—the other kids will have already been 5. The preschool she goes to—they have a prekindergarten class and she didn't get to go in that because she wasn't 4 yet; she wasn't ready to go into that. . . . The kids in the prekindergarten class were learning to write their name and doing a lot with markers and the kids in Alyson's class, they did mostly things with buttons and beads.

Although the word *readiness* was never introduced by the researcher in these interviews, eight of eleven parents brought it up themselves when asked to think about their child's kindergarten experience. In addition to the age component, parents spoke of worrying about their child's social readiness, a way of behaving that indicated that she or he was mature enough to be in school. Talk of maturity or social readiness came up with nine of the Norwood parents. Alice, Greg, and Rick's mothers talked about this social type of readiness in relation to their children, who had been redshirted the year before:

Last year he would have been starting out with cold feet,
which emotionally—maybe he just wasn't quite ready.
Whereas now, I think that he is real ready. [Greg]
I'm a little apprehensive. I'm not sure he is socially ready; he's
just not interested in school. [Rick]
I think that she is mature enough now. Last year she could
have gone to school—she'll be 6 in September. We waited the
extra year because we felt that she really wasn't ready. . . . I
think I just watched her, how she interacted with other children. [Alice]

Interestingly, none of the parents appeared to be concerned about their
child's academic readiness; they all felt that their children had all of the
cognitive skills needed to succeed.

What was it about Norwood that had the parents so attuned to fitting
their child into the school structure? The school community had a history
of developing alternative arrangements for children who did not fit
Norwood performance standards. Based on a maturational model of
readiness, the school trained a number of teachers in the Gesellian model
of early education and implemented transitional programs between
grades. They had a developmental kindergarten and a transitional first
grade, placing children on the basis of Gesell screening at the start of the
school year.[5] These special programs were less structured, and many
children spent an extra year as they made their way from kindergarten
through first grade. Mrs. Sunden had been the teacher for the developmental kindergarten, and she described it this way:

The teachers really wanted it because they could see the kids
that were younger having problems in the second and third
grade. A lot of them were too young to catch up. It was really
difficult for them. . . . I had a lot of them—they were too
young. They just wanted to lay on the floor, and I had a little
girl who had her blanket. They liked to play in the water.

After four years, parents pressured the school to disband the program. Mrs. Sunden noted sadly that, "The parents were not supportive
of it at all. I think it was OK until they said their child needed to be in
it." Without the special programs, the readiness concerns did not go
away, however. Instead, the system adjusted. Parents selectively delayed
kindergarten entry; in Mrs. Sunden's classroom 41 percent of the boys
were a year older than they should have been for kindergarten. In
addition, first-graders were often recommended to repeat. In the year

before my work at Norwood, the first-grade teachers suggested retention for almost one-quarter of the first-graders, and half of those ultimately stayed back.

One of the most interesting aspects of the social meaning of readiness at Norwood related to the informal power structure in place at the school. The first-grade teachers had a very strong influence over the primary program. They felt that it was their job to guide the less experienced kindergarten staff in program development, and Mrs. Sunden often alluded to stinging barbs that came her way in meetings and in the teachers' lounge:

> We've heard about things in the past where we've heard them say, "These kids don't know how to write their name." And we told them, "We teach them how to write their name." We do the best we can do and then they get what they get when they get to first grade, and if they have a problem with what we are doing, we want to know about it. We don't want to hear about it via the lounge.

To try to bridge the kindergarten–first-grade communication gap, the kindergarten teachers asked for a meeting between the two groups. During that meeting, the first grade teachers complained vehemently about the skills their children took from kindergarten; the following is an example of comments made by first-grade teachers during a rapid-fire discussion in that staff meeting:

> Alice: I don't have any readers. There aren't any stars except for two from out of state. There just seem to be more on the low end.
> Jean: The kids don't know their color words!
> Alice: Or they write their name in all capitals.
> Milly: And they don't know the alphabet names. They say things like "BA" for B. We're not saying that you don't teach these things. You are just trying to do too many things and they are not ready.

All three kindergarten teachers interpreted these comments as criticisms of their work the previous year. They had sent on children who were low in skills, and apparently that had been a mistake. They began to look at this year's students in a new way, trying to figure out whether individual students would be able to make it in the fiercely academic program the following year. Mrs. Sunden sounded as if her heart was going to break as she described what her children experience when they leave her class to go on to first grade:

> First grade at Norwood is very academic and I think their ex-
> pectations are way too high, and they put too much pressure
> on the kids, and I really feel sorry for them. That's one con-
> cern I have about sending my kindergartners to first grade.
> . . . I've been in the workroom and I know what kinds of
> things they do. . . . They just do worksheets. They have five
> or six worksheets sitting on their table when the kids walk in.

One of the strategies that became increasingly popular was implicit
encouragement for parents to hold their children out of school. What
better way to increase readiness than to provide a whole year to grow?

The theme of kindergarten at Norwood was getting ready—there
was a chorus of parental voices worrying about whether their child was
ready for kindergarten, punctuated by Mrs Sunden's focus on getting the
children ready for first grade. What is interesting about all of this is that,
by most standards, the children in Norwood were those who would be
least likely to be seen as readiness risks. Coming into school with a rich
base of quality preschool experience and many material advantages, they
had strong parental support for their education and were well prepared
for their kindergarten year. The children in Mrs. Sunden's class were
bigger, more mature, and more experienced on a number of dimensions
than students in the other classrooms I studied. The expectations for their
performance were extremely high, and the school seemed caught in a
system of ever-increasing standards. As children were held out of school,
the focus came to rest on an older, more mature group level. Children in
this setting were put at-risk by a normative system that prized the oldest
students in a group. Expectation shifted upward, the child with an August
or September birthday seemed quite young compared to a 6-year-old
with three years of preschool. It seemed that Norwood parents were not
only involved in this escalation but were in some ways producing it by
their interventions. Their teachers, too, played a role in this curriculum
shift as they oriented instruction to the more able group. These interventions came out of a comparative and maturational view of readiness.

Interpretations at Rochester: Translating and Constructing a New Meaning of Readiness

"AND THEN THERE ARE MY KIDS . . ."

Standing in the hall, Mrs. Ramirez watches one of the half-day
kindergarten classes walk to the library. In two neat lines, they
move quietly behind Mrs. Jones. Chuckling, Mrs. Ramirez com-

pares them with her class. They are getting better, but for some reason their lines seem to undulate with lives of their own.

At the classroom door, she sends her class out to recess. They tumble out of the room, heading for the playground equipment. Again she thinks how different the two sets of children are. "In the other kindergarten, children come in who are reading. They have all those basic kindergarten skills and are ready to go on. And their parents are asking, 'You know, my child is reading, so what are you going to do for my child?'

"And then there are my kids. They are here because they are behind. They don't know their address, they don't know their phone number, they don't know colors. Forget numbers and letters, that's just like a world away. And their parents are different. They say things like, 'Well, I didn't know that I was supposed to talk to my child about colors. I didn't know that reading was important to them.' They come to my classroom with a wide range of experiences. . . . However, they are not the experiences that the public school system values. A lot of them are bilingual . . . they have traveled. They go to Mexico annually. And that means that they are out of school for maybe two or three weeks. And in the public school system, there is nothing that draws on all of the experiences that they have. So they come back and it's like, 'OK, that's really nice that you did that, but we're in school here, and this is what you need to go to school. So can you repeat this story? Now I'm going to do some design and I want you to copy it.' And that could be really irrelevant to the child, but that's what we judge them on. For some of these kids, you might say that they are not ready to be in school. What this child needs is another year at home. But then you look at home and say, 'Nope! That's OK. What this child needs is to be in school.' Because at home there is nothing happening."

Rochester Elementary joined groups of people with diverse interests, experiences, and resources to participate in the educational process. At the top of the hill overlooking the school were the homes of Anglo professionals with lifestyles much like the Norwood families. At the bottom of the hill were tract homes (often rented) and apartments of working-class families of both Anglo and Hispanic heritage. The parents worked in nearby factories, and their children spent the years before school in day-care homes. A third group, bused in from the Clarendon Elementary area, were recent Mexican immigrants (both legal and illegal) whose first language was Spanish and who were having their first experience with school. Their parents had factory and service jobs, and many lived in subsidized housing. Together, these groups formed a school community with vastly different expectations and orientations to the public schools. These differences are vital to understanding how the meanings of readiness were constructed at Rochester, because they resulted in applying *multiple* meanings and standards to these disparate groups so that children might avoid failure.

The interviews completed before the start of school were exclusively from the Anglo population; since the Hispanic parents, for the most part, did not preregister their children in the spring, they were not part of the district database. The themes that emerged were much like those at Norwood: age and readiness were constant concerns for the five parents with whom I talked. Four of five spoke of age and holding out; Nathan's mother's comments were typical of this group:

> Well, when we put him in preschool—he's an August birth-
> day—we always knew that would be a question. . . . He's also
> big for his age, so he looks older than he is, so sometimes
> people expect him to act one way when he is actually acting
> the way he should for his age. I talked to [his preschool
> teacher] and she said that she knows that there were some
> kids that shouldn't start when they are a borderline birthday,
> but felt that Nathan could. But when I talked to her at the
> end . . . she agreed that it would be better if he waited.

The concern for age and consideration of whether to hold children out could be seen in the practices in place at Rochester. Two of the five parents interviewed had redshirted their children the year before, and it was estimated that 22 percent of the male kindergartners had been held out overall.

In earlier times, this middle-class Anglo group had anchored the expectations at Rochester Elementary. These parents were active as volunteers in the classrooms, and they provided a variety of goods and services. They also made demands on their children's teachers, expecting programming responsive to children with advanced skills. Mrs. Ramirez described them this way: "They're the ones that are fortunate enough to be able to be the mother helpers, to be in the classroom, they're probably the ones that are in the PTO. . . . [They are] more involved. . . . And their expectations are higher."

Changing demographics and attendance boundaries recently broadened the Rochester school population and presented challenges that required rethinking of the programming and standards that were the foundations of the educational program. Increasingly children came to kindergarten without the skills and experiences that were expected by the middle-class teachers at Rochester. As Mrs. Ramirez explained:

> We were getting a large number of children coming in not
> ready for kindergarten. They were unprepared as far as our
> expectations. And consequently, since they came in lower,
> they left kindergarten a little bit lower. So you could feel the
> ripple effect all the way through. There was concern among
> the kindergarten and first-grade teachers . . . the kindergarten
> teachers were saying, "They come in, you've got the ones here
> who can read and then you have the ones who don't know
> their name. It's too hard. We don't know how to deal with this
> span. It's too difficult."

Out of this gap the extended-day kindergarten program was born. At the beginning of school all children went through a readiness screening, and those who lacked kindergarten skills were placed in special classes that included a longer school day and more instructional support. Mrs. Ramirez' class was a bilingual, extended-day classroom, with students who were primarily Spanish speakers who had not attended preschool. All of her students entered school as soon as they were legally eligible; that is, none of them were redshirted. Their entrance to Rochester was marked by a label of unready, often based on the fact that their primary language was Spanish. In most cases, they were placed in Mrs. Ramirez' classroom on the basis of their language even before they were screened.

As the Rochester school community found a place for the children in Mrs Ramirez' class, several issues arose that framed their understanding and expectations. First, these children were seen as unready. Mrs. Ramirez' students did not have the skills, experiences, or abilities that the school felt were necessary to make them successful in school. The deficits and the label of "unready" that came with them were linked to the school's assessment that they were culturally different. There was a mismatch between the school's understanding of the lives and experiences of a child who would do well in school and the lives that Mrs. Ramirez' children experienced. They looked different from their Anglo peers, they spoke a different language, they came to school with a different background. As Mrs. Ramirez said in the vignette, these children had incredibly rich lives that included regular travel to a foreign country. These attributes were seen as barriers to school success rather than enrichments because they often disrupted the traditional school calendar. In many ways, they were so far away from the typical middle-class Rochester kindergartner that the school developed an entirely new meaning of readiness for these children. This is evident in the expectations for Mrs. Ramirez' class versus the half-day kindergartners at Rochester. This is how she described them:

> [The half-day teachers] say, "You know, our expectations are just so different." And they *are* different. For one of the other kindergarten teachers, they may have this child that they consider very low, a very good candidate for retention. And if they were in my classroom, I wouldn't even *dream* of retaining them. Because they would be in the middle. Because I would have five that would be much lower than they were.

The parents with whom Mrs. Ramirez worked were different from the rest of the Rochester parents as well. Most of them were first-generation Mexican-Americans whose primary language was Spanish. Their memories of school were unpleasant for the most part, and they did not feel comfortable in the school when their children started kindergarten. According to Mrs. Ramirez:

> They don't like it, a lot of them. They will say things like, "Well, I hated school and those teachers and they made me feel like this . . ." And they're the ones who are real hard to get to. Their attitude will really make a difference. [I tell them] "Your child is going to want to be like you." So if dad didn't like school, I want to be like dad. "Yeah, I hate school and school stinks."

In addition to their discomfort in the school setting, they had limited access to the school resources because they did not speak English. At the beginning of the year, they were dependent on Mrs. Ramirez to translate the school experience for them. Participation in most school-based activities was low (one-third took part in homework activities and one-half attended fall parent–teacher conferences), and Mrs. Ramirez found that her biggest challenge was getting families involved in education as defined at Rochester.

Unlike the Norwood parents who anticipated the upcoming year in fine-tuned detail, these parents did not have a well-defined set of expectations for their children's kindergarten year. Mrs. Ramirez explained that:

> When I look at my parents, most of them haven't been thinking about what do I need to do to get my child ready for

school? And so they say, "Well, now you're 5 and so now you go to school. And at school is where you're going to learn all these different things." . . . It's not that they're not concerned. And it's not that they don't want success for their child. But it's just really that they see it as the school's job. "Here's my child, now you teach him."

This theme was echoed when I talked with Pedro's parents in November:[6] "Well in our minds he was ready . . . we had spoken to him about school; that is, we had told him he would learn how to write, how to count—everything." These parents focused their attention on wanting their children to like school, and according to Mrs. Ramirez, they did not put forward any agenda on what should be done during the kindergarten year. They were hopeful that their children would do well in kindergarten and focused mainly on concerns about how language differences would affect their child's school progress. This is how Berta's mother approached the kindergarten experience: "I don't know English, but Spanish—I teach her what I know and she learns it very well."

Because of their cultural separation from the Rochester school community, Mrs. Ramirez' parents did not negotiate for their children in the same manner as other Rochester (or Norwood) parents. They assumed that their child was going to school and that education would occur there. It was up to Mrs. Ramirez to show them the ropes of the school as an institution over the course of the academic year. For the children in Mrs. Ramirez' class, the idea of readiness was constructed in the context of cultural difference. It was framed in terms of a widening gap that existed between the Anglo children who were the former point of reference and the Hispanic children who now challenged the system to meet their needs.

Two systems of readiness were in place at Rochester, one for the middle-class clientele and a second, newly emerging conception for the children who were seen to be at-risk for later school failure. These two systems ran in parallel, and it was assumed that the children in Mrs. Ramirez' class would stay together as a group because of their language needs. In fact, in the year following this study, Mrs. Ramirez went with her students when they passed on to first grade as the school tried new staffing patterns.

It is interesting to consider the future of the children in Mrs. Ramirez' class, given their separate status in the school. The way that the school community worked to meet the needs of diverse learners was to resort to a kind of segregation by readiness level. When Mrs. Ramirez' children were considered in comparison to the half-day kindergartners at Rochester, many of whom had been redshirted, they would appear to have serious deficits. It is reasonable to suggest that the practice of redshirting exacerbated the judgment of deficit that came with their entry to school. Whether the development of new standards and definitions will work to their advantage or serve to further remove them from the educational process can only be seen as they make their way through school.

Mrs. Ramirez recognized that in other settings (even within the school), professionals might look at her students, invoke an immaturity label, and recommend redshirting. According to the maturational approach, children would develop more readiness with time. This is based on the assumption, however, that what was happening in the intervening year would enhance the skills a child brought to school. It was premised on an image of a middle-class child who attended preschool or whose home environment developed the specific characteristics teachers value. But those were not the children Mrs. Ramirez welcomed into her classroom. As she said in the vignette, "You might say that they are not ready to be in school. What this child needs is another year at home. But then you look at home and say, 'Nope! That's OK. What this child needs is to be in school.' Because at home there is nothing happening." Her students could not wait for time to provide readiness; time would only widen the gap. Her children *needed* to be in school to receive the stimulation and experience that will make them more like their peers. That was the key to readiness for her students: closing the gap that came out of their cultural difference, different views of readiness for different groups of children.

IMPLICATIONS OF VARIOUS INTERPRETATIONS OF READINESS

The descriptions of the kindergartens at Norwood and Rochester show that these communities had different interpretations of readiness. To a great extent, these interpretations were shared within a local context; the members of the community constructed them together, and their ideas were more alike than they were different. In a school with a homogeneous population, it was possible to examine the developing meaning of readiness from almost a wide-angle perspective; it was applied equally across groups. With a more diverse group, it was necessary to move in closer, focusing first on the school in general and then moving in to examine a single classroom.

In the course of this study, several dimensions emerged as important to the meanings of readiness at Norwood and Rochester. Table 4.2 summarizes their characteristics. Included in this table is the contrast of the

Table 4.2 Dimensions of Readiness at Norwood and Rochester

| | Norwood | Rochester | |
		1/2 day classes	Bilingual program
Readiness	Maturational approach. Seen as a prerequisite to success in kindergarten.	Maturational approach. Prerequisite to kindergarten.	Environmental approach. Language & cultural difference transformed the meaning of the ready child.
Institutional arrangements	Formal extra-year programs disbanded under parental resistance but were now informally in place through academic redshirting & 1st grade retention.	Much redshirting and little retention at any grade level.	Children entered when age-eligible & were placed in a special class because of readiness level. The school made the decision that these children were not ready. Most stayed together in grade one.
Children	Most had several years of preschool experience, A large number of the boys were overage. As a group, scored too high on the district readiness screening instrument to be eligible for special services.	Most had preschool experience and many were overage. Were identified as ready according to the district test.	Many were recent immigrants to the U.S.; few had gone to preschool. Many placed in the extended-day program even before they had been screened.
Parents	Highly involved in educational process from preschool. They gathered information from their peers and felt pressure to make decisions about child's readiness.	Involved as volunteers.	Initially disconnected from school, they were dependent on Mrs. Ramirez to translate the kindergarten experience. They did not make educational decisions for their children; that was the school's job.
Professional relations	Strong boundaries between grade levels. Mrs. Sunden worried that she might send an unready child to the academic first grade program and that she would be criticized by the first grade teachers.	Little contact with the extended day program.	Mrs. Ramirez worked from special curriculum and standards for her students. Closing the gap was the goal for her program; she did not attend to the grade level goals set for the 1/2 day students.

half-day programs and Mrs. Ramirez' extended-day bilingual program, based on August parent interviews and Mrs. Ramirez' reflections.

The power that participants had in each setting vis-à-vis the kindergarten experience was bound to the way that readiness was understood and the actions that were possible within a system. At Rochester, the school determined that Mrs. Ramirez' children were not ready, and the strategies related to how to deal with readiness problems. The staff did, however, adapt programming to meet the needs of children whose parents did not participate in practices such as academic redshirting. These parents did not have access to the social knowledge base that would make redshirting a potential strategy as their children entered school. They were involved to the extent that they supported the school's work, but they did not work to advance any particular agenda on their children's or their own behalf beyond wanting them to get a good start. To the school, their participation seemed more like nonparticipation in the context of the other Rochester parents, who were involved in educational issues for their children. Mrs. Ramirez worked to close the gap between her students and their age peers, widening the educational process to help parents become a part of the school community. An inclusive but separate educational experience was the result for the children in the bilingual, extended-day kindergarten program at Rochester.

At first glance, the parents at Norwood would appear to be very powerful in both the construction of the meaning of readiness and in the progress of their children's education. They had access to social knowledge and the savvy to intervene in educational processes to help their children advance. They negotiated for their children with their peers and educational professionals, advancing a personal agenda that maximized success. In an interesting way, they were prisoners of their own actions, contributing to an ever-escalating system of expectations that identified more and more children to be at-risk for failure. Given the social constraints that made only certain actions possible, their options were actually quite limited unless they wanted to fly in the face of a potent community force. This factor was an influence on Mrs. Sunden as well, as she constantly toed the line dictated by the first-grade teachers. Worry for her students and her professional reputation shaped the kindergarten program, so that getting ready for first grade became the goal.

The themes that emerged from this study are strikingly parallel to Lareau's (1989) work on social class and parental involvement in education. Comparing working-class and upper-middle-class communities, Lareau found vast differences in parental resources available to affect their children's school experience and their attribution of responsibility for educational intervention and success. In the working-class community there was separation between home life and the school. Parents were supportive but took a hands-off attitude toward the educational process. This was easily a description of Mrs. Ramirez' families; they cared about school but did not feel it was their job to educate their children. In contrast, the upper-middle-class families that Lareau studied were strongly connected to the school; they not only prepared their child academically but also intervened when problems arose. These patterns are vividly portrayed at both Norwood and Rochester, where middle-class parents had information and perceived power to make decisions about their children. In her analysis of the way that social class frames interinstitutional linkages, Lareau points to the fact that social class provides cultural capital (such as language and knowledge of how to navigate their way with educational professionals) that can be used in interactions with the school as an institution. This capital provided the middle-class children with a home advantage as they went through school.

Considering the unequal power that parents had to enter into their children's education is compelling when readiness is framed from a social, rather than psychological, perspective. Obviously, Mrs. Ramirez' students were different from the middle-class children at Norwood and Rochester. They came to school with different experiences, language, and culture than their agemates. But it could be argued that the *meaning* of the difference, the shape it was given in the educational experience, was formed in the context of differential access to the cultural capital these families had available and could use in the school setting. Their separation from the institution vested power in the school to determine that their children were not ready and segregated them from their agemates so that a special instructional program worked to close the gap. This appearance of separation was amplified by the connected relations that existed between the school and the middle-class families at Rochester. When readiness is a comparative social system, deficits are more glaring when one group participates in practices that gives them a performance advantage, no matter how temporary.

In some ways, the power the middle-class parents had in both schools is indicative of what Lareau called the "dark side of parent involvement." In their search for an optimal early school experience for their children, the parents at Norwood, in particular, developed a strong set of informal rules for the parent community. These included searching out and sharing information about school programs and expectations, comparing child skill, and delaying school entry. As they worked to gain an academic advantage for their children, a sorting mechanism resulted in which both parents and teachers looked for the ready child. The youngest children in the group were always seen to be at-risk and often pulled out, with a slightly older, seemingly more able set of children as a result. What would normally seem to be a plus for the teachers may actually have contributed to the contentious relationship between the kindergarten and first-grade staff—rather than providing a more homogeneous group, it appeared that the sorting practice increased differences.

In the process of describing the construction of the meaning of readiness, it was interesting to see how the story swirls around the adults in each setting. The children, about whom the discussions and policies and practices revolved, seem to fade into the background as the picture develops. The ideas and beliefs of the parents and professional staff were such intense factors in this process; the innate characteristics of children seem to be a secondary concern. This is not to say that there were not differences among children that played into readiness decisions. Children are different, but it was the meanings that the adults gave to those differences, the factors they emphasized and the educational implications attached to them, that were the most salient aspects of the local conception of readiness. Certainly children were active participants in their kindergarten experience, but the argument here is that the meaning of readiness became a resource/constraint that affected their educational program. In other words, it is the *meaning* of readiness rather than basic child characteristics that helps us understand the interactions of teachers, parents, and students.

In pursuing a study of the meaning of readiness, the expressed purpose was to view it from a social and cultural perspective. This view was useful throughout the study, helping me to understand the actions of those who shared a context. The coherence of the community meanings of readiness shaped the kindergarten experience, and in many ways it can be seen as a lens. As participants in these kindergarten contexts interacted to build an educational environment, ideas about readiness helped people focus on children in specific ways and the images of children were formed by it. Who was ready for school, why they might be ready or not, and appropriate instructional practices did not come from a measurable characteristic called readiness; it came out of the ideas and tradition in the local context. The image of children was built from the outside inward.

This view of readiness is especially important in an educational context in which one of the national education goals states that "By the year 2000, all children in America will start school ready to learn." (National Governors Association, 1990, p. 3). How do we work toward such a goal when readiness is not something that we can measure in individual children? How is it that we can address the concept of readiness when it is more a matter of shared meaning than of psychological construct? Some have suggested completely discarding readiness as a concept; it would be nice if it were that easy. Deeply held and connected to ideas about child development and the purposes of education and parenting, ideas of readiness are too complex to contemplate throwing away like yesterday's newspaper. Change will require discussions among the academic, policy, teaching, and parent communities directed to understanding the contextual nature of readiness.

Kagan (1990) has posited some steps that we might take in implementation. She suggests that we move from attending to readiness for school, which is a limiting concept that has been used as a gate to keep children out of school. Instead, our new conceptualization should focus on readiness for learning and should include two principles for its development: equity and individualization. From this perspective, we would work to maximize the chances of all children from the time they enter our world, rather than waiting until they came knocking on the kindergarten door. Once they reached school age, the issue would be the readiness of school people to work with individual children rather than whether individual children would fit into the existing school program. It is a shift in responsibility for readiness from the child to society at large. It puts the burden on parents, teachers, and policy makers to make sure that children have all the opportunities they deserve regardless of their relative ages, language, skills, or family background. This approach will require fundamental changes in the way we organize early education, breaking down some longstanding structural arrangements that have worked to reinforce the idea of homogeneous groupings and the need for lockstep performance standards related to the average 5-year-old. It would move us to reexamine the community pressures that escalated the curriculum and standards at Norwood and to rethink the separate track that was developed for the children in Mrs. Ramirez' class at Rochester. In time, exclusionary methods of testing, sorting, and labeling by readiness level could be processes we forget as bad educational practice.

NOTES

Acknowledgments: I would like to thank Ellen Ansell, Marianne Bloch, Shirley Kessler, and Beth Blue Swadener for their help in developing the ideas in this chapter.

1. A third group could be identified in the early childhood community in relation to the discourse of readiness. For those who see themselves as constructivists or developmental-interactionists, readiness is an idea that does not fit their

conceptions of the mechanism of growth and development (DeVries & Kohlberg, 1987). Because learning is a process of active construction by children, readiness as a threshold is not an issue. In his work with early childhood teachers, Walsh (1991) found very few practitioners who held this view in its pure form; others often combined the developmental label with elements of the maturationist perspective.

2. "Academic redshirting" is a term derived from athletics. When a team redshirts players, they sit out a year to allow an additional period of growth and development, increasing their power on the playing field. The year that they sit out is not counted against their eligibility, and in their last year of playing they are older than most of their teammates.

3. All names of people and places are pseudonyms.

4. It is interesting that when school entrance dates were clustered around December 1, those concerned about readiness talked about fall birthdays. With September and October 1 being more prominent, the focus is on the summer birthday as a readiness problem.

5. This was a very different model from that used at Rochester. According to district guidelines, the students at Norwood would not qualify for the extended day program. The basis for identification for these programs was developmental immaturity, not skill problems.

6. Interviews with six of the parents from Mrs. Ramirez' class were scheduled, but only three were completed. This fit in with the overall fall conference attendance rate of 50 percent. Because I do not speak Spanish, these conversations were facilitated with the aid of an interpreter.

REFERENCES

Bloch, M. N. (1991). Critical science and the history of child development's influence on early education research. *Early Education and Development*, 2(2), 95–108.

Cameron, M. B., & Wilson, B. J. (1990). The effects of chronological age, gender and delay of entry on academic achievement and retention: Implications for academic redshirting. *Psychology in the Schools, 27,* 260–263.

DeVries, R., & Kohlberg, L. (1987). *Constructivist early education: Overview and comparison with other programs.* Washington, DC: National Association for the Education of Young Children.

Eisenhart, M. A., & Graue, M. E. (1990). Socially constructed readiness for school. *International Journal for Qualitative Studies in Education, 3(3),* 253–269.

Ellwein, M. C., Walsh, D. J., Eads, G. M., & Miller, A. K. (1991). Using readiness tests to route kindergarten students: The snarled intersection of psychometrics, policy, and practice. *Educational Evaluation and Policy Analysis, 13(2),* 159–175.

Engel, P. (1989, June). *Assessment of kindergarten readiness for first grade: Policies and practices of industrialized nations.* Paper presented at the 1989 Annual Assessment Conference, Education Commission of the States, Boulder, CO.

Erickson, F. (1982). Taught cognitive learning in its immediate environments: A neglected topic in the anthropology of education. *Anthropology & Education Quarterly, 13*(2), 149–180.

Geertz, C. (1981). Interpretive anthropology. In H. Applebaum (Ed.), *Perspectives in cultural anthropology* (pp. 520–524). Albany: State University of New York Press.

Graue, M. E. (1991, April). *Construction of community and the meaning of being a parent.* Paper presented at the annual meeting of the American Educational Research Association, Chicago.

Graue, M. E. (in press). *Ready for what? Constructing meanings of readiness for kindergarten.* Albany: State University of New York Press.

Graue, M. E., & Shepard, L. A. (in press). School entrance age. In L. R. Williams & D. P. Fromberg (Eds.), *Encyclopedia of Early Childhood Education.* New York: Garland.

Jipson, J. (1991). Developmentally appropriate practice; Culture, curriculum, connections. *Early Education and Development, 2*(2), 120–136.

Kagan, S. L. (1990). Readiness 2000: Rethinking rhetoric and responsibility. *Phi Delta Kappan, 72,* 272–279.

Lareau, A. (1989). *Home advantage: Social class and parental intervention in elementary education.* London: Falmer.

Mehan, H. (1980). The competent student. *Anthropology and Education Quarterly, 11*(3), 131–152.

Meisels, S. J. (1985). *Developmental screening in early childhood: A guide.* Washington, DC: National Association for the Education of Young Children.

Meisels, S. J. (1987). Uses and abuses of developmental screening and school readiness testing. *Young Children, 42*(2), 4–9.

National Association for the Education of Young Children. (1990). NAEYC position statement on school readiness. *Young Children, 46*(1), 21–23.

National Education Goals Panel. (1991). *Measuring progress toward the national education goals: Potential indicators and measurement strategies.* Washington, DC: Author.

National Governors' Association. (1990). *National education goals.* Washington, DC: Author.

Peck, J. T., McCaig, G., & Sapp, M. E. (1988). *Kindergarten policies: What is best for children?* Washington, DC: National Association for the Education of Young Children.

Shepard, L. A. (1990). Readiness testing in local school districts: An analysis of backdoor policies. *Journal of Educational Policy, 5,* 159–179.

Shepard, L. A., Graue, M. E., & Catto, S. F. (1989, March). *Delayed entry into kindergarten and escalation of academic demands.* Paper presented at the annual meeting of the American Educational Research Association, San Francisco.

Shepard, L. A., & Smith, M. L. (1988). Escalating academic demand in kindergarten: Counterproductive policies. *The Elementary School Journal*, 89(2), 135–145.

Smith, M. L. & Shepard, L. A. (1988). Kindergarten readiness and retention: A qualitative study of teachers' beliefs and practices. *American Educational Research Journal*, 25(3), 307–333.

Stallman, A. C., & Pearson, P. D. (1990). Formal measure of early literacy. In L. M. Morrow & J. K. Smith (Eds.), *Assessment for instruction in early literacy* (pp. 6–44). Englewood Cliffs, NJ: Prentice-Hall.

Uphoff, J. K., & Gilmore, J. E. (1986). *Summer children: Ready or not for school.* Middletown, OH: J & J Publishing.

Van Maanen, J. (1988). *Tales of the field: On writing ethnography.* Chicago: University of Chicago Press.

Vygotsky, L. S. (1978). *Mind in society.* Cambridge, MA: Harvard University Press.

Walsh, D. J. (1989). Changes in kindergarten: Why here? Why now? *Early Childhood Research Quarterly*, 4(3), 377–391.

Walsh, D. J. (1991). Extending the discourse on developmental appropriateness: A developmental perspective. *Early Education and Development*, 2(2), 109–119.

Walsh, D. J., Ellwein, M. C., Eads, G. M., & Miller, A. K. (1991). Knocking on kindergarten's door; Who gets in? Who's kept out? *Early Childhood Research Quarterly*, 6(1), 89–100.

Weber, E. (1984). *Ideas influencing early childhood education.* New York: Teachers College Press.

Wertsch, J. V. (1985). *Vygotsky and the social formation of mind.* Cambridge, MA: Harvard University Press.

Wertsch, J. V., & Toma, C. (1990, March). *Discourse and learning in the classroom: A sociocultural approach.* Presentation made at the University of Georgia Visiting Lecturer Series on "Constructivism in Education."

Willer, B., & Bredekamp, S. (1990). Redefining readiness: An essential requisite for educational reform. *Young Children*, 45(5), 22–24.

Wood, C., Powell, S., & Knight, R. C. (1984). Predicting school readiness: The validity of developmental age. *Journal of Learning Disabilities*, 17, 8–11.

PART II

CRITICAL AND FEMINIST PERSPECTIVES ON EARLY CHILDHOOD EDUCATION

The chapters in this section address the significant issues of interests, voice, and pedagogy in research and practice in the early childhood curriculum. In Chapter 5 Susan Jungck and J. Dan Marshall outline the relationship between critical theory and curriculum by focusing on "interests." Jungck and Marshall begin by drawing upon Miller and Seller's (1985) distinctions among curriculum as transmission, transaction, and transformation; the relationship between these "overarching curriculum metaorientations"; and Habermas's (1971) analysis of the relationship between forms of knowing and human interests (technical, practical, and emancipatory). Jungck and Marshall recast the debate between those advocating an academic versus developmental orientation toward curriculum by focusing the discussion on the intentions of those enacting the curriculum.

Chapter 6 represents one of the major strands of "reconceptualist" curriculum scholarship: feminist perspectives on the school curriculum and teachers' lives. Janet Miller uses teacher–researcher collaboration and autobiography to illuminate the socially constructed nature of assumptions about the role of the early childhood teacher, and the relationship between those assumptions and the political realities of particular educational contexts. Through dialogue journaling and an ongoing teacher–researcher "support group," Miller and Georgette Neville Vosseler, a first-grade teacher, reflect on their embeddedness in a myriad of similar and conflicting relationships that constitute theirs and others' expectations of teaching as women's work.

In Chapter 7 Valerie Polakow looks at the "implicit curriculum" (or implicit meanings and underlying ideology) of family, motherhood, childhood, and "children at risk." Within a Western European and American social and cultural context, Polakow names many often unacknowledged sources of physical, psychological, social, and economic oppression, including internalized oppression, on mothers and children. Unlike other historical and critical treatments of early childhood in this volume, Polakow utilizes a post-structuralist feminist analysis, based, in part, on the work of Foucault, which analyzes the body as the site of power and control over women and children as embedded in a "biopower" of discursive practices. Through her analysis and use of narratives of mothers and children "on the edges" of the dominant society, Polakow makes vivid an "antichild discourse of care," rife with contradictions, which makes problematic much of the prevailing rhetoric and policy discourse (in the United States and elsewhere) on children and families. This chapter frames issues that must be addressed in any reconceptualization of the early childhood curriculum.

In Chapter 8 Janice Jipson describes the enactment of a feminist form of pedagogy, where the curriculum in a graduate seminar in early childhood education emerged out of the areas of interests of the participants and where dialogue journaling was employed to facilitate participants' personal connection with content. Using interpretive analysis, Jipson makes problematic several of her initial assumptions about the course, drawing heavily from the journals of her students in this seminar on women and children in the workplace.

REFERENCES

Habermas, J. (1971). *Knowledge and human interests*. Boston: Beacon Press.
Miller, J. P., & Seller, J. (1985). *Curriculum perspectives and practice*. New York: Longman.

CHAPTER 5

Curricular Perspectives on One Great Debate

Susan Jungck
J. Dan Marshall

As curriculum generalists we are fortunate to write about early childhood education; the occasion represents another opportunity for dialogue and sharing across subdivisions in education. What follows is an introduction to perspectives in curriculum theory, particularly drawn from current reconceptualist and critical work, which we find helpful when reconsidering what goes on within educational environments. Specifically, we offer a set of ideas suggesting the interests represented in various curriculum conceptualizations that we intend to serve as an introductory framework for the critically oriented chapters that follow.

Throughout the past three decades curriculum workers have pushed their field well beyond its traditional intellectual boundaries and enabled educators to break free from more than half a century of attention to curriculum as a technical plan for reaching some predetermined and measurable outcomes (see, e.g., Klohr, 1980; Miller, 1978). Contemporary curriculum workers, through a growing array of perspectives, strive to understand and alter the complex interrelationships among and between those who participate in the formal educational enterprise (see, e.g., Pinar, 1988). Recognizing that the curriculum is fundamentally a normative and value-based process, this growing body of work reflects the importance of combining knowledge with deliberative action, or praxis, and goes well beyond curriculum development itself (see, e.g., Beyer & Apple, 1988; Sears & Marshall, 1990).

CONCEPTUALIZING CURRICULUM:
TRANSMISSION, TRANSACTION, AND TRANSFORMATION

Over the years, curriculum generalists have developed several conceptual ways of understanding the epistemological relationships between knowledge and curriculum. Known variously as conceptions, paradigms, or orientations, these categorization schemes are quite consistent among the most popular curriculum textbooks (e.g., Eisner, 1985; Giroux, Penna, & Pinar, 1981; McNeil, 1985; Miller, 1983; Miller & Seller, 1985; Saylor, Alexander, & Lewis, 1981; Schubert, 1986; Zais, 1976). They serve as a way to distinguish and illustrate the nature of knowledge and the intentionality represented in the curriculum (Jungck & Marshall, 1988). In the broadest sense, curricularists typically describe three overarching curriculum metaorientations: curriculum as transmission, transaction, and transformation (Miller & Seller, 1985).

Within the transmission framework, knowledge is clearly and carefully defined, prescribed, and measured as a commodity or "product." The intention is to have students successfully achieve predetermined "ends," and the process of assuring this is largely a technical one. As Miller & Seller (1985) point out:

> This orientation stresses mastery of traditional school subjects through traditional teacher methodologies, particularly textbook learning; . . . acquisition by students of basic skills and certain cultural values and mores that are necessary in order to function in society; . . . and the application of mechanistic views of human behavior to curriculum planning, whereby student skills are developed through specific instructional strategies. . . . In this position, there is primarily one way movement to convey to students certain skills, knowledge, and values. The philosophical–scientific paradigm for this position is an atomistic view of nature in which reality is seen in terms of separate, isolated building blocks. (pp. 5–6)

The sorts of curricula represented by this transmission position range from purely behavioral to planned programs that incorporate "scope and sequence, interpretation and balance of subject matter, motivational devices, teaching techniques, and anything else that can be planned in advance" (Schubert, 1986, p. 27). These understandings of curriculum are the most longstanding and commonplace among school personnel in general and curriculum workers in particular.

The curricular orientation identified as transaction has both "means" and "ends" as its focus. Here, knowledge is seen as constructed and reconstructed by those participating in the teaching–learning act. The curriculum is thus conceptualized as a transactional process enabling meaning and understanding to occur. The individual

> is seen as rational and capable of intelligent problem solving. Education is viewed as dialogue between the student and the curriculum in which

the students reconstruct knowledge through the dialogue process. The central elements in the transaction position are an emphasis on curriculum strategies that facilitate problem solving; . . . application of problem solving skills within social contexts in general and within the democratic process; . . . and the development of cognitive skills within the academic disciplines. . . . The philosophical-scientific paradigm for the transaction position is the scientific method. (Miller & Seller, 1985, pp. 6-7)

The curricula here focus on providing meaningful student experiences. In Schubert's (1986) words:

Education or pedagogy is not pursued by service delivery systems; rather, human beings communicate through attempts to reveal that which lies deep within them and speaks through them, connecting their beings to that of existence itself. (p. 182)

A third orientation, transformation, reflects those conceptions of curriculum in which knowledge is constructed through but goes beyond processes of inquiry into the realm of encouraging personal and social change. Guided at all times by visions of equity and justice, curricula representing this position value

teaching students skills that promote personal and social transformation; . . . a vision of social change, . . . and the attribution of a spiritual dimension to the environment. . . . The paradigm . . . is an ecologically interdependent conception of nature that emphasizes the interrelatedness of phenomena. (Miller & Seller, 1985, p. 8)

Curricula that represent this position reflect the belief that

meaning and virtue desired by practical interests can only be pursued if pedagogy goes beyond the interaction to provide for socioeconomic equity and justice. Thus, [this position] combines inquiry and action in an attempt to realize and expose that which is oppressive and dominating. (Schubert, 1986, p. 182)

Although necessarily oversimplified here, the above conceptual frameworks can serve as a backdrop for viewing the present debate within the field of early childhood education typically dichotomized as the "academic" versus the "developmentally appropriate" curriculum. Those in the academic camp argue for a curriculum that will provide young children with knowledge and skills necessary for a successful transition into their subsequent years of schooling, while those in the developmentally appropriate camp argue for a curriculum that recognizes and addresses the wide range of children's personal and social needs.

With respect to curriculum paradigms or metaorientations, the academic side in this debate emphasizes a view of curriculum as the transmission of a product, in which preexisting knowledge and skills are taught in the most efficient and effective ways so that children can arrive at the appropriate "ends" on time and intact. From this view, the concept of readiness means preparing the child for the next academic hurdle. On the other hand, the developmentally appropriate camp values the process of children's growth and believes that children are better suited for the academic demands of schooling when they have been encouraged to develop strong, positive personal and social images and a curiosity for understanding the world around them. This approach to curriculum fits comfortably within the curriculum as transaction and process orientation noted above. Readiness, when used in this conceptual context, focuses on understanding a child's abilities and providing for meaningful experiences within situationally relevant contexts.

As in most such debates, we can find some who argue that the good intentions (e.g., self-esteem or process focus) highlighted by one camp (i.e., developmentally appropriate curriculum) can also characterize the other (Bullock, 1989; Greenberg, 1990)—or at least that they need not be mutually exclusive (Spodek, 1989). Others argue that the two camps, and what they represent, will always be mutually exclusive (Smith, 1990). For us, the more fundamental issue in this or any such curriculum debate is the one that addresses the nature of the *interests* or *intentionality* of those responsible for bringing life to any form of curriculum.

CURRICULUM INTERESTS AND ACTIONS

We noted earlier that reconceptualized curriculum thought and work considers all curriculum to be normative praxis—a value-oriented combination of knowledge and action. In this light, curriculum—however constituted with whatever beliefs and intentions—knows no life until it is acted upon. Thus, in the realm of schooling as we know it, the curriculum gets constructed by teachers and students. Their interests and intentions must be illuminated, understood, and respected in any debate or discussion of appropriate curriculum.

In *Knowledge and Human Interests*, Habermas (1971) presents a social theory that is useful in understanding various human interests. In brief, Habermas introduces three types of human interests: technical (work accomplishment), practical (communication), and praxis (emancipation). Our work-related interests, he claims, are technical and rational in nature and seek knowledge that will enable us to predict and control. Our communicative–practical interests, those that seek deeper and shared understandings, stimulate different types of knowledge and ways of knowing. For example, in promoting this interest human beings have developed and valued more hermeneutical, interpretative, and aesthetic approaches to understanding, interpreting and communicating. And we can hold more socially critical interests, which are generated by our desires for change and emancipation from the ideological and structural constraints perpetuating the inequalities characterizing our day-to-day lives.

Teachers' and students' actions are also driven by various interests and intentions. So before we debate curriculum on levels of outward appearances and behaviors that typify educational programs (such as academic versus developmentally appropriate curriculum), it is important for us to know more about the interests and intentions that drive the individuals who enact the curriculum. For as Grundy (1987) reminds us, "Both knowledge and action as they interact in educational practice are determined by a particular interest" (p. 10). Adopting Habermas's interests framework allows us to better understand the importance of teachers' and students' interests in any discussion of curriculum. Although space limitations prevent us from providing an appropriately thorough discussion of the ideas of Habermas (1971, 1973, 1979), we encourage readers to investigate these ideas in general and their relationship to the field of curriculum in particular (see, e.g., Bernstein, 1976; Giroux, 1980; Hultgren, 1982; Schubert, 1986). The following brief summary draws heavily from Grundy's (1987) recent work.

Habermas's work–technical interest is product- and control-centered and largely reflects those interests that value curriculum as transmission. Skill is central, and knowledge of "how" and "what" to do is sought to achieve improved actions for better outcomes. The success of one's actions is determined by the measurement and documentation of improvement; the good of one's actions is determined by the extent of efficiency and effectiveness achieved.

Habermas's communicative–practical interest is engagement- and process-centered; it largely reflects those interests that reflect curriculum as transaction. Judgment is central. In contrast to those with a technical interest for whom important knowledge is that which is manifested in generalizable ideas and productlike ideas, important knowledge for those with communicative–practical interests is that which facilitates shared attitudes or levels of understanding. Success here would be determined, for example, by the meaningfulness students and teachers generate from the curriculum, for meaning-making results in worthwhile outcomes. The good of one's actions is arrived at through reflection and determined by the continual development of wisdom and prudence (which arises when practical judgment, not technique, is primary).

Habermas's emancipatory interest relates to our earlier discussion of transformative curriculum; it is liberation-centered and recognizes worthwhile knowledge as that which is authentic and both personal and social—critical knowledge, reflectively assimilated and tested for authenticity in light of both theory and practice. For those who hold this interest, critique is central. In contrast to mere psychological change, the emancipatory interest is concerned with social change and contains both a critical social perspective and a desire for action designed to change the school's (or society's) organization or structure. As an example, the success of one's actions here would be determined by the extent to which students and teachers develop an ability to struggle and take risks in light of their developing critical social consciousness. The good of one's actions is judged in light of one's efforts "towards a deliberate reorientation of the power relationships intrinsic in the pedagogical situation" (Grundy, 1987, p. 140).

Clearly, the previously described broad metaorientations to curriculum knowledge (transmission, transaction, and transformation) coincide with Habermas's knowledge- and action-oriented interests (work–technical, communication–practical, and emancipatory). It should be readily apparent that those with a particular interest who plan and design curricula will favor programs that serve those interests. Although our schools have struggled with these curriculum orientations and interests throughout their recent history (Kliebard, 1986), technical interests and transmission-oriented curricula have prevailed. This can be attributed, in part, to our inattention to the deeply embedded nature and implications of human interests themselves.

Returning to our discussion of the debate over academic versus developmentally appropriate early childhood curricula, we can now begin to see the importance of a focus on interests. Those who support a more academic curriculum for young children do so in large part because they hold technical interests; that is, they genuinely believe that generalizable academic–school knowledge is the most appropriate "end" for all children, and that efficient and effective ways to transmit that knowledge exist and should be employed. In their minds, the more technical and objective the knowledge we can develop about children (through testing and empirical research), the better able we are to help them achieve (through early intervention programs, special services, and so forth). Schools and learning are viewed through rational models that implicitly value prediction and control.

On the other hand, those who champion developmentally appropriate curricula do so because they believe with equal fervor that early childhood is the critical period for children to develop personal and social identities, attitudes, habits, and skills while being introduced to the wonder and joy of knowing and understanding the world around them. Their goal is to understand the child; the more practical their work with young children is, the better able they are to know and make good pedagogical decisions concerning cognitive, affective, and psychomotor growth environments and practices (which will increase children's likelihood of becoming successful beings—even academically successful students). Understanding and accommodating the child is a central value here.

In practice, however, these perspectives and beliefs can look quite different in light of one's curriculum interests. Teachers of young children who work within academically oriented programs easily and frequently resist and short-circuit such curricula because their actual interests are more ones of understanding and accommodating than the technical ones of predicting and controlling. Although they may espouse the goal of preparing their young charges to succeed next year in kindergarten or second grade, these teachers have simply never believed that there exists some formula to control this, nor would they accept that such a formula could have predictive power with every child (or category of child) given similar circumstances. Teachers like these learn by doing and upon reflection.

Likewise, we know there are teachers who argue vehemently for developmentally appropriate curricula yet hold fundamental interests that subvert those programs. Such teachers go to great lengths to test and group children in order to carefully assess where they "belong" developmentally, then look to others for the most appropriate materials and strategies to use with the children so that they might develop to their fullest potential (to be determined by one standard measure or another). In other words, technical interests can dominate the intentions and practices of those who profess to be developmentally oriented advocates.

THE INDIVISIBILITY OF CURRICULUM INTERESTS AND ACTION

We believe that it is possible and desirable to break out of the traditional dichotomous understanding of curriculum as "ends" and "means." More importantly, in light of our discussion above, the debate over academic versus developmentally appropriate early childhood curricula should not be limited to the nature of curriculum knowledge and structure alone, but must include a critical analysis of the values inherent in any orientation to curriculum as well as *the intentions and interests of those who will enact the curriculum.*

In light of our discussion of the overarching metaorientations to curriculum and their correlated interests, we believe that most curriculum discussions need to become more complicated. Due to what Bullough, Goldstein, and Holt (1984) refer to as an excess of "technocratic-mindedness," educators have for too long been insufficiently critically minded. When curriculum is viewed as transmission and technical interests predominate, we see an overreliance on the development of organizational schemes that label ("at-risk"), track (developmental kindergartens), and intimidate (through excessive testing and psychometric imperialism) children. Developmentalists who value technical interests may endorse similar practices. The interests that guide such practices have most to do with maintaining, controlling, and accounting for the organizational and political requirements of schools; illuminating them, however, helps us little in understanding how children experience schooling. It is important to critically analyze technocratic-mindedness if we wish to address some of the social conditions that make individuals appear so different and enter so "disadvantaged" that these sorting and measuring schemes are deemed necessary in the first place.

Teachers whose curricular intentions are transformative and whose interests are emancipatory struggle to create environments that are enabling, democratic, and just. They inevitably build and sustain these in a variety of ways. Some will emphasize academics and skills, some will have what they call developmentally appropriate curriculum, and others will defy simple categorization. However, the impact of their curricula will be directly related to how and why they do what they do, how conscious they are of their interests, and the extent to which they create opportunities for themselves and their students to actively engage and affect their shared experience.

CONCLUSION

We have tried in this chapter to introduce some of the essence and challenge of reconceptualized curriculum thought in a way that relates to discussions within early childhood education. We have recast one debate regarding the most appropriate form of early childhood curriculum because it represents a perennial one within the general field of curriculum. We have recast it, choosing to underscore the importance of considering the interests that underlie any curriculum. In doing so, we hope to have shown that contemporary curriculum workers view such discussions through varied new lenses and bring a diversity to curriculum studies that "holds great promise, enriches the debate about curriculum, proposes intriguing ways to grapple with the complexity of the field, and emphasizes the fundamental importance of curriculum theory, research, and practice" (Klein, 1990, p. 13).

In his book *The Good Preschool Teacher*, Ayers's (1989) concluding passage serves us well here:

> And so we return to the good preschool teacher. We see a person who chooses and creates her teaching in a world not of her own choosing. We see a person who lives and works with ambiguity—who engages the questions in a world of uncertainty. And we see a kaleidoscope of possibility, for there are endless good preschool teachers, each grounded in a real situation, a living context; each caring, dreaming of a world where people care more, and working to make that more-caring world come to be. (p. 141)

Many contemporary curriculum workers embrace visions of a similar world. Perhaps in recognizing the complexity of such a world we are moving closer to it?

REFERENCES

Ayers, W. (1989). *The good preschool teacher*. New York: Teachers College Press.

Bernstein, R. J. (1976). *The restructuring of social and political thought*. Philadelphia: University of Pennsylvania Press.

Beyer, L. E., & Apple, M. W. (1988). *The curriculum: Problems, politics and possibilities*. Albany: State University of New York Press.

Bullock, J. R. (1989). Processes or products: What's important for your children? *Early Childhood Development and Care, 47*, 159-163.

Bullough, R. V., Goldstein, S. L., & Holt, L. (1984). *Human interests in the curriculum*. New York: Teachers College Press.

Eisner, E. W. (1985). *The educational imagination* (2nd ed.). New York: Macmillan.

Giroux, H. A. (1980). Critical theory and rationality in citizenship education. *Curriculum Inquiry, 10*(4), 329-366.

Giroux, H. A., Penna, A. N., & Pinar, W. F. (Eds.). (1981). *Curriculum & instruction*. Berkeley, CA: McCutchan.

Greenberg, P. (1990). Ideas that work for young children. *Young Children, 45*(2), 70–80.

Grundy, S. (1987). *Curriculum: Product or praxis?* London: Falmer.

Habermas, J. (1971). *Knowledge and human interests.* Boston: Beacon.

Habermas, J. (1973). *Theory and practice.* Boston: Beacon.

Habermas, J. (1979). *Communication and the evolution of society.* Boston: Beacon.

Hultgren, F. H. (1982). *Reflecting on the meaning of curriculum through a hermeneutic interpretation of student-teaching experiences in home economics.* Unpublished doctoral dissertation, Pennsylvania State University. University Park.

Jungck, S., & Marshall, J. D. (1988, April). *Teachers and curriculum discourse.* Paper presented at the annual meeting of the American Educational Research Association, New Orleans.

Klein, M. F. (1990). Approaches to curriculum theory and practice. In J. T. Sears & J. D. Marshall (Eds.), *Teaching and thinking about curriculum* (pp. 3–14). New York: Teachers College Press.

Kliebard, H. M. (1986). *The struggle for the American curriculum—1893–1958.* Boston: Routledge and Kegan Paul.

Klohr, P. R. (1980). The curriculum field: Gritty or ragged? *Curriculum Perspectives, 1*(1), 1–7.

McNeil, J. D. (1985). *Curriculum: A comprehensive introduction* (3rd ed.). Boston: Little, Brown.

Miller, J. L. (1978). Curriculum theory: A recent history. *Journal of Curriculum Theorizing, 1*(1), 28–43.

Miller, J. P. (1983). *The educational spectrum: Orientations to curriculum.* New York: Longman.

Miller, J. P., & Seller, J. (1985). *Curriculum perspectives and practice.* New York: Longman.

Pinar, W. F. (Ed.). (1988). *Contemporary curriculum discourses.* Scottsdale, AZ: Gorsuch Scarisbrick.

Saylor, J. G., Alexander, W. M., & Lewis, A. J. (1981). *Curriculum planning for better teaching and learning* (4th ed.). New York: Holt, Rinehart and Winston.

Schubert, W. H. (1986). *Curriculum: Perspectives, paradigm and possibility.* New York: Macmillan.

Sears, J. T., & Marshall, J. D. (Eds.). (1990). *Teaching and thinking about curriculum.* New York: Teachers College Press.

Smith, K. E. (1990). Developmentally appropriate education or the Hunter teacher assessment model: Mutually incompatible alternatives. *Young Children, 45*(2), 12–13.

Spodek, B. (1989). *Early childhood education in America: Consistencies and contradictions.* ERIC Document Reproduction Service No. ED 313 101.

Zais, R. S. (1976). *Curriculum.* New York: Harper & Row.

CHAPTER 6

Teachers, Autobiography, and Curriculum
Critical and Feminist Perspectives

Janet L. Miller

As I gently opened the door and slipped into the classroom, I immediately and ironically felt overwhelmed by the diminutive school desks and chairs that framed, yet did not contain, the undulating movements of twenty first-graders. I quickly sought the familiarity and comfort of the teacher's calm gaze above the small swells of activity, and I began to tread slowly to her through the children's inquiring glances and sometimes gestured hellos. "Who are you?" asked one girl, tugging on my skirt and then brushing her red hair from her eyes to clear her upturned stare. "Yes, who are you?" chimed the others.

And I thought to myself, quickly, "Gosh, in these unfamiliar waters, I'm not sure!"

I was entering this first-grade classroom at the invitation of the teacher, with whom I had been working in an inservice program on the writing process. As a university teacher, I was committed to spending a portion of my time in the schools, working directly with other teachers and students. Although I teach graduate courses in curriculum theory and qualitative research, my inservice commitments most often focus on aspects of the writing process. This reflects my preparation and experiences as a high school English teacher, as well as my ongoing interest in writing process as congruent with aspects of autobiographical methods and intentions developed within the reconceptualization of the curriculum field.

Thus I attempt to integrate theoretical tenets of both writing process and autobiography as I work with teachers to excavate, reflect on, and analyze underlying assumptions, expectations, and constructions of our daily work. Such self-reflexive processes are necessary, I believe, in order also to view our educational roles through critical lenses that enable us to focus on social, historical, and political forces that shape and influence our personal assumptions about teaching. Situating autobiographical narratives and analyses of our own teaching practices, assumptions, and expectations within these larger contexts might enable us, then, "to break with submergence, to transform" (Greene, 1986, p. 429).

As I waded through this sea of first-graders, however, my only thought was to land safely at the teacher's desk without ignoring or floating past any of these children's outstretched hands. I was overwhelmed not only by my lack of experience with early childhood contexts but also by the ways in which the children's immediate and spontaneous responses triggered expectations in myself to respond in kind. In one brief voyage from one side of this every-inch decorated classroom to the other, I felt the pull of social and historical constructions of early childhood educator as nurturer, mother, caretaker, as well as facilitator, captain, guide. And I wondered how this teacher, and every other early childhood teacher, dealt with the problematic and often contradictory tensions that such embedded constructions could create within conceptions and enactments of teaching and curriculum.

Since that first-grade initiation, I have worked with a number of teachers who are interested in utilizing critical, feminist, and autobiographical perspectives to investigate the intertwined social, historical, and personal assumptions that frame and guide their roles as early childhood educators. Here, in sketching some possibilities that such perspectives have created, in particular, for one first-grade teacher, Georgette, and myself as teacher–researchers, I specifically want to explore some contradictory aspects of teacher–nurturer that tend to reify early childhood education, especially, as "women's work." Such work is historically grounded in social expectations and schooling structures that rely on women's accustomed roles as subservient, genteel, and docile replicators of the status quo.

At the same time, I want to examine ways in which my role as a female academic is imbued with some of the same stereotypic characteristics as that of early childhood educator, thus contributing to a sense of fragmentation within my professional life. For, as a woman teaching in the university, I too feel the pull of internalized expectations for myself *either* as distanced "expert" and "conveyor of knowledge" *or* as nurturer and caretaker of my students' needs and interests.

Thus I want to describe how Georgette and I are struggling, within the context of an ongoing six-year collaboration with four other classroom teachers, to both nurture and teach in ways that acknowledge our own sense of authority as dedicated, knowledgeable, questioning, and caring educators. We are trying to understand these possibilities as "both/and" rather than "either/or" constructions.

These attempts reflect similar grapplings with a variety of issues that have emerged within the context of our six years together as a teacher-researcher collaborative. Within our teacher–researcher group, we have explored, and continue to examine, tensions as well as possibilities in our attempts to effect collaborative and critically oriented research relationships among university and classroom teachers. Initial examples and narratives of those explorations during our first three years together now appear in book form (Miller, 1990).

Part of our work, as represented in that publication as well as in our continuing collaborative ventures, involves explorations and critiques of the very notions of "collaboration" and of "emancipatory teaching and research." We continue in our attempts to examine, to critique, and to enact these concepts within our group as well as within our daily educational settings. Another part of our work together, then, is a constant confrontation, both collectively and individually, of the difficulties inherent in such enactments, given the ways in which we have internalized socially constructed versions of our roles as classroom and university teachers. These internalizations often reflect assumed hierarchies within our relationships to one another as well as within the structures of schooling, within the precepts of educational research, and within the very constructions of teaching that frame and guide our practices.

Embedded within those assumptions, then, are particular versions of teaching that have created dichotomous expectations for ourselves: we still often assume, for example, given prevalent social constructions of "teacher," that we must be "experts" as well as "transmitters" of others' creations of knowledge in particular subject areas and pedagogical practices. While these constructions do not necessarily restrict our abilities also to be "caring teachers" in relationships with our students, colleagues, and other members of our educational communities, they do tend to emphasize prescriptive, hierarchical, and end-product orientations to teaching and learning. For women and men who teach, and who also wish to attend to contexts and processes that acknowledge the multiple positions, needs, and contexts of ourselves and our students, these expectations sometimes lead to contradictory stances within our particular educational settings. And both Georgette and I continue to discover that, for women who teach, these expectations can also lead to reification of stereotypic and essentialized notions of women teachers as only caretakers and nurturers rather than as nurturers *and* creators *and* examiners, with our students, of our own as well as others' knowledges and practices.

Georgette and I continue these explorations and discoveries within the contexts and processes of our teacher–researcher group. We have found the group to be supportive in terms of our confrontations with deeply embedded assumptions about our work as teachers. In addition, the processes in which our group participates encourage us in our attempts to challenge and to change both those assumptions and those structures that tend to reinforce oppressive and inequitable relationships within educational contexts. Our collaborative processes include regular meetings and discussions, dialogue journal writing to one another, and individual journal writing as ways of situating analyses of our particular educational autobiographies within the social, historical, and political contexts in which we teach and do research. And we particularly are influenced by autobiographical, critical, and feminist perspectives that continue to evolve in the work of curriculum theorists associated with the reconceptualization of the field. As I share shifting connections and discrepancies in contexts, positions, assumptions, and expectations between Georgette, as early childhood educator, and myself, as university teacher, I also will attempt to illuminate some of those perspectives and influences.

DAILY LIVES: CONTRADICTIONS AND POSSIBILITIES IN THE WORK OF WOMEN WHO TEACH

The First-Grade Teacher

Georgette[1] has described her journey through our collaborative attempts thus far as one of "becoming vocal." As a first-grade teacher, she continues to struggle, perhaps more than anyone else in our group, with the ways in which historical and social constructions of teaching as "women's work" have framed and contained her own expectations for herself as early childhood educator. Through autobiographical musings as well as through dialogue in our group meetings, Georgette enables us all to confront the difficulties embedded in constructions of our work that are not our shapings but which we have internalized as our own. For Georgette, functioning as a socially constructed nurturer in the first-grade classroom and yet working to conceive of herself as a teacher grounded in her own sense of authority, these dichotomous pulls remain the focus of her autobiographically situated inquiries within our teacher–researcher collaborative.

Georgette and I both are attempting to explore the nature and possible forms of our own "authority" in ways that do not reinforce or replicate unequal power relationships inherent in predominant interpretations of that particular concept. We find support for such explorations in the work of many feminist curriculum theorists. For example, in arguing that our attachments ought to give point to our work, and that those attachments are most often overtly expressed in the nurturing and domestic realms of our experience, Jo Anne Pagano (1988a, 1988b, 1990) illuminates the connectedness between public and private domains that history and culture have separated and reified as gender-role specific. She argues that, for women who teach, there need be no conflict between nurturance and authority if women can acknowledge, critique, and work to move through the power of masculinist totalizing discourses. Such discourses often portray worlds through one set of lenses, lenses typically worn and created by white males. These lenses often condense multiple realities into one unitary vision, thus distorting or even eliminating the experiences and expressions of many who see and live in those worlds differently. Pagano argues that women must work to excavate and to claim the sources of our own authority. We must do this not only by challenging unequal power relationships inherent in those totalizing discourses, with their oppositional constructions of research and practice, emotion and intellect, public and private, for example, but also by contextualizing such challenges within our daily teaching lives.

Thus Georgette continues to address the possibilities and difficulties of claiming the sources of her own "authority" within the contexts of our research group and the elementary school in which she teaches. And she does so most directly by grappling with the sources and enactments of her internalizations of early childhood education as a premier site of "women's work," work essentialized by many as the embodiment of women's "innate, natural" tendencies to nurture, to caretake, to guide the young, as well as to perform those acts in unquestioning ways.

Georgette's willingness to tackle her underlying assumptions about herself as early childhood educator, with all of those accompanying assumptions about nurturing and mothering as aspects of this particular arena of "women's work," also provides us all with challenges to confront our own assumptions. In addition, her grapplings with those assumptions within our group context provide vivid exemplification of contradictory feelings that such excavations often elicit.

For example, even though Georgette had participated in several of our group's public discussions and presentations of our collaborative inquiries, she had decided not to attend a conference in which we would be sharing our ongoing work. She explained that she felt too great a discrepancy between the active questioning that such a gathering encouraged and the passive, submissive atmosphere that permeated the elementary school where she taught.

In particular, Georgette was wrestling with the ways in which our collaborative raises questions about "Who decides?" in all arenas of daily school activity and the ways in which the particular administrative group in her elementary school did not welcome such a question. Georgette knew that our conference presentation and discussion would focus on just such discrepancies, for we all were attempting, in this fifth year of our ongoing work, to move much of our group questioning and reflecting and critiquing into our individual educational settings. And she knew, too, having previously attended this particular conference, that audience discussion would be lively, challenging, and extensive on such issues of power and control. Georgette felt, at this particular juncture in our collaborative ventures, that returning to her controlled environment after such active and lively exchange would pose too great a discrepancy within her. She was struggling, at that point, to remain in the teaching profession itself, let alone our collaborative research group.

Georgette had talked with our group about her decision to not attend the conference, and she wrote:

> I know that I have changed as a result of our work together, changed from an accepting, docile teacher, to a questioning, challenging person. . . . With this comes the realization that some people with whom I work are uneasy and uncomfortable around me. Perhaps I've become the unexpected and others are unsure how to "handle" me. For me, "handle" means suppress, control, or keep me in my place. I know that it is my thinking that offends them. I am in turmoil, struggling to exist and not be made quiet again. So to go to the presentation would be to deliberately depress myself. The emotional impact would be too hard for me. I work in a world so far removed from what we do here in our group, and certainly even further removed from what we do at the conference. The differences are too intense, too large for me to try and merge at this time.

We went to the conference without Georgette, and her absence was a presence. After our presentation, in which we relayed Georgette's reasons for not attending, many in the audience talked with us about similar tensions that such critically oriented questions raise for themselves as educators.

Georgette's particular struggle to reposition herself within her elementary school as both a caring, nurturing teacher and a questioning, challenging educator reflects many educators' difficulties not only with hierarchies of schooling but also with the gender-specified roles that we are expected to play within those hierarchies. Georgette had noted that much of her uneasiness had to do, at that point, with acting and speaking in ways that belied her "good girl" upbringing and professional preparation as an early childhood educator.

Another of Georgette's writings about our group's discussions and reflections and their influences on her daily work portrays her willingness to extend and to push against theoretical and concrete boundaries of her work as a female first-grade teacher. She wrote on February 8, 1991:

> I've been thinking. . . . Autobiographical work should be as truthful a record as possible, recording things as they are at a particular time in one's life. Therefore, after consideration, I feel it important now to eliminate the protection that an alias provides and write as myself. This is contrary to what we, the group, felt at the time of the book's publication. However, I feel that even in this small way, I can begin to give credence and respect to the elementary teacher within me, and in turn, to other elementary teachers who struggle to be heard as teacher–researchers.
>
> Being aware of such questions as "Who decides?" and "In whose interest is it decided?" has made it difficult for me to accept any statement at face value by either administrator or teacher, male or female. This can have an isolating effect on one's life at work in an elementary school. These questions, though not always vocalized, are thought of, causing an uneasiness within me whenever someone else's assumptions or expectations are put forth as "truth" or "mandatory reality." For me, as part of a twenty-three-female, three-male teaching staff, the ideas of elementary teacher as nurturer, caretaker may be part of this forced "mandatory reality" put upon me (or us) by the male-oriented hierarchy.
>
> To illustrate this point, I recall several faculty meetings when the principal of the school compared the teaching staff to a "family." This was meant as a compliment, a positive thing. However, I resented the use of this term, and I can remember thinking to myself, "I don't want to be part of his family." As I thought about my reaction to this term, I began to realize that the word "family" is a loaded comparison, filled with expectations (different for each of us), assumptions, and emotions.

Further comments were made at meetings, again using the term "family," such as "We've always functioned as a family." Is that the principal's way of saying, "OK. I see something I don't like, it's not good. So do something about this, behave again like you're supposed to." It seems that this remark was made to generate some kind of guilt—since no one wants to be labeled a "disfunctional family."

The use of the word "family" in the elementary school setting may be a deliberate choice in order to continue the idea of elementary school teacher as nurturer and caretaker. Does such a comparison allow this present thinking to be perpetuated at this educational level? Does this solidify the principal's decision-making status, with classroom teachers, mostly females, remaining in a role of only emotional supplier?

How does the principal use this term? Is he the father image, and we, the teachers, his children? Are the teachers "the mothers" to the students? What results does the principal want or expect now that we've been labeled "family." Has he the right to make such emotional demands on his faculty? What can I do about this? What action can I take? What choices can I make? Right now, my choice of action is to question, internally, for the most part, "Whose reality is this?" and "Why should it be mine?"

Thus Georgette shares the ongoing discrepancies that she feels between being a participant in our group's questioning processes and being a first-grade teacher, who, as she notes, is not used to asking or being expected to ask questions. However, she chooses to continue to question the languages of administrative and teaching relationships and practices, for example, as containing, replicating, and reifying authoritative discourse, unequal relations of power and authority, and particular gender-specified and identified roles within those relations. As Georgette raises questions about her particular teaching situation within such framings, she also challenges me to confront my own discrepancies in the processes and articulations of my work. As she noted in a recent meeting of our group, "It's not easier to feel like you must ask the questions now, but you must, because you can't go back after this kind of work together."

The University Teacher

Georgette's identification of her situational discrepancies as lodged in historical and social constructions of early childhood educators, who perform the nurturing and unquestioning work of women, has enabled me to confront and to attempt to dislodge similar constructions within my own educational arena.

Thus, although Georgette and I do not share similar educational contexts, the similarities in our expectations and in our underlying assumptions about ourselves as women and as teachers continue to intersect. Our long-term examinations of those assumptions and expectations as reflections of socially and historically constructed and situated conceptions of teaching as "women's work" are framed by our evolving understandings of ourselves within the processes of our research collaborative. At the same time, those examinations have led to our emerging understandings of the difficulties and dangers of essentializing all women's experiences in education as similar to our own.

In exploring our similarities to and our differences with one another as well as other women who teach, then, I think that Georgette's willingness to grapple with discrepancies and contradictory feelings about herself as woman teacher has encouraged me to examine the sources and nature of the many contradictions that characterize my work as a woman academic.

For example, Georgette's struggles have provided me with incentives for parallel analyses of my own expectations and internalizations of caretaker and responsible leader roles within our research group. These internalizations reflect in many ways similar conceptions of myself as woman and as teacher that Georgette confronts.

Those conceptions reflect my early and unquestioning acceptance of myself as nurturer, caretaker not only of students but also of others', rather than my own, sources of authority and knowledge creation. These enactments of educator predominated in my early teaching experiences and in my understandings of curriculum as evidence of others' knowledges, even though I chose secondary and university teaching rather than elementary or early childhood teaching contexts. In the mid-1960s, when I began my teaching career, the scripts for women teachers were similar, regardless of the instructional level.

Thus much of my present work continues to focus on the excavations of those assumptions that continue to encapsulate and to limit understandings of my own possibilities. For me, those possibilities include being both nurturer and authority. I want to be, with my students, an explorer and a creator of knowledges. I also want to be a participant in relationships that enable us to examine and to forge ever-emerging new knowledges about ourselves and our worlds. This work is situated within feminist and autobiographical approaches within the reconceptualization of the curriculum field.

RECONCEPTUALIZATION:
AUTOBIOGRAPHICAL AND FEMINIST PERSPECTIVES

In the late 1960s and early 1970s, a disparate yet concerned group of scholars who were dissatisfied with the prescriptive and positivist orientations of curriculum work in the United States began to analyze, critique, and reconceptualize the field.[2] Although curriculum was relatively young as a field of study, having emerged during the 1920s in response to school administrators' needs within burgeoning school bureaucracies, it quickly had assimilated the characteristics of the field of education in general. Thus emphasis in curriculum theory and development from the 1920s through the 1960s was on linear and sequential constructions of teaching and learning, with curriculum conceptualized as "content" or "course of study," as information that could be dispensed by teachers, received by students at predetermined, developmentally appropriate stages, and then returned to the teacher in measurable, testable, and standardized forms.

The classic question "What knowledge is of the most worth?" supposedly undergirded curriculum designers' and developers' work during those years. However, accompanying critical and, later, post-modern questions about the very processes and forms of knowledge production only began to emerge with the coalescence of the curriculum movement known as reconceptualization. These questions included

> Whose knowledges are of the most worth?
> What is legitimated as knowledge? And how?
> What are the conditions that structure the production of knowledge?
> How do I experience knowledge?
> Who can construct knowledge?
> Who decides?
> In whose interest is this decided?

Contributing to the reconceptualization of the curriculum field were existential and phenomenological studies of the school and of curriculum, especially from the point of view of the individual, as well as Neo-Marxist studies that focused upon school and curriculum as preeminently political realities. From these two often divergent perspectives emerged a focus on knowledge as occurring in the experience of situation, in contexts of daily lives, a focus that child-centered educators have been arguing for decades.

Autobiography was, and continues to be, a predominant mode utilized by some working within the reconceptualized field as one way in which to examine such contextualized knowledges (Pinar, 1981; Pinar & Grumet, 1976). Autobiographical work attempts to acknowledge, and to examine as knowledge, the interwoven relationships among one's educational experience, one's contextualizations of that experience within sociopolitical worlds, and one's constructions of curriculum as both reflecting and creating those worlds.

Autobiographical work, particularly from feminist perspectives, encourages individuals to review those relationships within larger contexts of language and of power and authority that frame every teaching practice and curricular creation or choice. In those reviewings, many have begun to reconceptualize teaching, learning, and curriculum as processes that are informed, influenced, and shaped by particular historical and social forces as well as by unique individual perspectives and interactions. Such reconceptualized versions of teaching, learning, and curriculum can move us, I believe, from mechanistic, developmental, skill-oriented, end-product emphases in education, into reciprocal yet constantly shifting relationships with our students, with contents, and with ourselves as teachers.

Within these contextualized realms, feminists working in the early years of the reconceptualization utilized autobiography as means by which to acknowledge and include women's experiences into existing curriculum structures (Krall, 1981, 1988; Mitrano, 1981; Wallenstein, 1979). However, as they worked to expand conceptions of women's voices and women's stories, reconceptualist feminists also were challenging the very processes and intentions of knowledge construction and legitimation, even as they insisted on inclusions of women's experiences and contributions within disciplines and on their representations in all areas of curriculum (Grumet, 1988a; Lather, 1984; Miller, 1986, Reiniger, 1988).

As the reconceptualization continued to influence and to change conceptions of curriculum, feminist curriculum theorists began to further explore and question such constructs as subjectivity, gender, and identity in order to also question tests of knowledge legitimation. They began to challenge the power relations inherent in constructions of the very disciplines in which they initially had demanded inclusion (Grumet, 1981; Lather, 1989). And they began to explode the research methodologies that have historically constrained that which can be said to be known as well as the ways by which it is known (Lather, 1986; Roman & Apple, 1990).

Via a refinement of autobiographical methods as well as modification of Neo-Marxist and socialist feminist perspectives, curriculum feminists began to explicate concepts of self in relation to shifting interpersonal and political contexts. Multiple and contradictory conceptions of self emerged, as curriculum feminists worked to develop pedagogical perspectives and research methods that could encourage all teachers and students to understand the particularity and contingency of their knowledges and practices (Britzman, 1991; Ellsworth, 1989; Lather, 1991).

As feminist curriculum scholarship continues to mature, then, autobiography has become one means of "rewriting the self in relation to shifting interpersonal and political contexts" (Martin & Mohanty, 1986, p. 208). As curriculum feminists' evolving scholarship vividly demonstrates, autobiography can be a means by which individuals can draw their own portraits and create multiple accounts of their educational experiences, perspectives, assumptions, and situations. Those multiple accounts point to the complexity of experience that any one story necessarily reduces (Brodkey, 1987, 1989); to the necessities and difficulties inherent in individuals voicing their different experiences of the same processes and events (Lewis & Simon, 1986); to the different stories that individuals construct that both represent and create their particular historical and social situations; and to the possibilities for individuals not only to discover evidence of external forces that have diminished them but also to recover their own possibilities (Grumet, 1988a).

Thus, in working to resist the compartmentalization and isolation promoted by dichotomous constructions of the world, feminist curriculum theorists also now are working to create new forms of curriculum scholarship and research that acknowledge and restructure the ways in which knowledge comes to form in human relationships:

> Feminist scholars work to bring together domains of experience and understanding that history and culture have kept apart. For what it means to teach and to learn is related to what it means to be male or female and to our experience of reproduction and nurturance, domesticity, sexuality, nature, knowledge and politics. (Grumet, 1988b, p. 538)

MULTIPLE CONTEXTS

I have been working and struggling, as a participant in the reconceptualization since its formal inception, to both incorporate and extend feminist critiques and analyses in my own practice as well as in my work with teachers in graduate classrooms and inservice contexts (Miller, 1983, 1986, 1987). However, even as I waded through those waves of first-graders on that important inservice day more than five years ago, and even as I continue to excavate assumptions with Georgette and others in our teacher–researcher group, I often feel the still dominant dichotomous pull between "teacher as nurturer" and "teacher as expert" within myself. And, as I began my inservice work in that first-grade classroom, and as I continue my collaborative research with our group, I know that my own work must continue to focus on the sources and expressions of those apparent contradictions inherent in my role as woman academic.

As a woman teaching in academe, I have often been posited, as have my male colleagues, as "the expert," especially in inservice contexts with teachers. As I worked to resist that construction and, instead, to forge collaborative relationships with teachers and with students at the university and in schools, I also experienced expectations, from others as well as myself, to nurture, to guide those students and teachers in ways that often were not expected of my male counterparts. I felt the tensions embedded in my attempts to forge collaborative rather than hierarchically imposed "expert" relationships with students and classroom teachers and, at the same time, to pursue the authority of my own educational experiences and knowledges. And I felt those same tensions again as I met those twenty first-graders on that important initial inservice day and, in another context, as I listened to Georgette explain why she could not attend the curriculum theory conference.

Even before these particular encounters, I had been employing autobiography as a method within research, writing, and teaching contexts in attempts to make explicit my internalizations of others' expectations of me as woman teacher (Miller, 1983). As I grappled with excavations of those assumptions, especially as they reflected my complicit acceptance and enactments of myself as teacher–nurturer–caretaker, I also began to confront the self-alienation that such heretofore unexamined assumptions had spawned. I began working to understand Pagano's claim that there need be no conflict between nurturance and my own, not others', sources of authority, and I began to identify those sources in the relationships I established in collaborative work with teachers.

At this point, I wanted to preserve the nurturant capacities that I believe frame the generation of knowledges and identities and, at the same time, to apply critical and feminist perspectives to the normative and essentialist constructions of woman teacher as nurturer. I thus became interested in the possibilities and concurrent contradictions emerging in feminist teachers' attempts to develop collaborative and dialogical relationships with students and colleagues as ways of challenging and working through what Pagano calls the power of masculinist totalizing discourses.

Academic configurations of research, especially in the field of education, are replete with such totalizing, generalizing, and encapsulating

discourses. I felt that emerging feminist conceptions of research processes and methodologies might be a particular area in which I could attempt my own challenges and my own investigations into the sources and
forms of my own authority as teacher and researcher. Because feminist
conceptions concentrate on the relational aspects of researcher and researched, in particular, I joined with five classroom teachers, including
Georgette, to investigate possibilities of integrating critical and feminist
conceptions of research, curriculum, and teaching into standard enactments of teacher-as-researcher.

Working together now for six years, we *have* begun to challenge
underlying power relationships and totalizing discourses that often characterize even inquiry that supposes to be collaborative and reciprocal.
And, in our work together, as Georgette and I so vividly demonstrate, we
have come to understand that finding our own voices as teachers and
creating spaces for collaborative and critical inquiries about schooling are
not definitive, boundaried events but rather are constantly emerging and
contradictory processes.

For example, Georgette's pain, situated in the discrepancy between
the questioning that our work together elicited and the schooling structures that repressed or discouraged such questioning, heightened my
ongoing concerns about the ways in which my own intentions and interests in our research collaborative might be imposing on Georgette's as
well as the others' own needs and desires in this work.

Thus initial framings of my worries about imposition within our
collaboration and my contradictory feelings of responsibility as academic
researcher who *should* know the forms and directions of our work together are being reframed. These reframings are made possible not just
by my own continuing excavations of assumptions in these areas, but also
by the group members' own varying versions of potential contradictions
and discrepancies in their own educational work.

So, even though others in the group also now chronicle our group's
collaborative research attempts, through dialogue journaling and through
some coauthored writing, I still struggle with issues embedded in attempts to decenter my authorial voice as the one in charge of both the
group's processes of collaboration and the researching of those processes.
Even though the chronicle of our first three years together, in book form,
reflects each group member's participation in the construction and re-
viewing and revisioning of this representation of our work together, I still
grapple with the ways in which that text is my version of our group's
interactions and movements. And I worry about the ways in which my
writing, my curriculum and feminist discourses, construct and are constructed as partial, interested, and academically positioned perspectives

of our work together. I struggle with the ways in which my critiques of collaboration and empowerment as potential forms of both teacher-proof administrative maneuverings *and* "critical" catchphrases—important more for their promises of liberation than for their power to actually help teachers transform their practices and workplaces, for example—are caught up in the very processes and mechanisms and languages that I am analyzing.

Thus Georgette's reluctance to participate in what I had accepted as *appropriate* academic forums for the sharing and questioning of our work enabled me to confront the ways in which I had internalized, so deeply, others' constructions of scholarly representations of research. By her willingness to point to the discrepancies and difficulties inherent not only in collaboration between university and classroom teachers but also in the ways and forms in which we might share the processes of that collaboration, Georgette also drew my attention to social and historical constructions of each of our teacher–researcher roles. And she vividly exemplified her discrepancies with their accompanying prescriptions for viable participation in educational communities. In sharing those discrepancies, she also highlighted the embedded issues of hierarchy and power relations that such discrepancies revealed.

By extension, her reluctance to participate in academic forums that signaled, for her, the relative lack of autonomy as well as time and space in which to consider and reflect on our collaborative issues also pointed to my unexamined acceptance, bolstered by the appearance of relative autonomy in choice of research directions and methods, of the sanctioned forms and arenas for scholarly research and writing. This unquestioning acceptance mirrored those issues of compliance and complicity that had characterized my entry into the teaching profession and that still undergirded to some extent my conceptions of university teaching and research, even as I had been working to disrupt and dislodge those conceptions as potentially reifying hierarchical and oppressive relationships.

Given Georgette's illumination of such discrepancies that emerged from our collaborative work, I had to consider again the ways in which my conceptions of our work, centered in critical and feminist explorations of transformative versions of teaching, research, and curriculum, still carried the potential of impositional tendencies embedded in traditional university researcher roles. I now also had to consider the potential of my own compliance with others' conceptions of appropriate academic forms and forums for our work. Such compliance denied my own as well as other group members' capacities to generate new forms and forums for the reporting and sharing of our collaborative work.

In effect, I had to consider the ways in which I still carried vestiges of myself as "good girl" teacher and researcher, now willing to attempt fresh and challenging forms of collaborative research and of dialogical and reciprocal pedagogy, but still hesitant to report such attempts in forms that defied or challenged socially sanctioned constructions of research reporting and writing within the academy. Thus, in the published book, while I had attempted to describe my roles as member of the collaborative and as narrator in self-reflexive ways, and while I wrote from the collective discussions and choices of journal entries that we wanted to share in order to tell our stories, I also felt compelled to include what I now call the "bookend" chapters. These chapters in the book, the first and the epilogue, more so than the other chapters, contain examples of traditional academic writing—that is, referenced and researched and inscribed in Chicago style—as well as my constant attempts at self-reflexivity within the writing and the research. I now see that writing, even as unorthodox as it appears next to much of what is reported as educational research, as reflecting my ambivalences and discrepancies in moving beyond accepted and traditional research and writing norms.

And so, Georgette and the others continue, in thir willingness to question me and to share in their own discrepancies and contradictions, to challenge, to push, to extend my theoretical perspectives into new forms of writing, research, and collaboration. We want those evolving and shifting forms to honor autobiographical and self-reflexive stances by extending the boundaries of such work to include collaborative as well as individual possibilities, discrepancies, and contradictions.

Thus we are attempting to understand Pagano's claim that there need be no conflict between nurturance and authority by sharing our particular pedagogical and research stories. We now know, at the same time, that others' educational experiences and assumptions may not contain and reflect situations, assumptions, or expectations that our stories reveal. And so we share multiple and often repetitious versions of our stories within those critical frames that encourage us to question our similarities and our differences, even as we continue to grapple with seemingly ever-emerging manifestations of assumptions we often feel we have already excavated. As we move through our sixth year together of collaborative inquiries, we are aware of the reciprocal relationships that we have forged among ourselves, among our theories and practices, and among our research, teaching, and curriculum processes. And, through those reciprocal relationships, we have begun to understand that excavations and examinations of assumptions do not eradicate their constant and habitual influences on our educational experiences.

And so we share, too, not only to challenge our internalizations and heretofore unquestioning acceptances of those assumptions and expectations but also to participate in the forging of new possibilities for ourselves as educators, engaged in the relational processes of teaching, learning, and curricular creation. For Georgette and me, those challenges still center around our emerging understandings and questionings about what it means to be women who teach, women who simultaneously value and yet question the very attributes of nurturer and caretaker with which we have identified and have been identified since our own early childhoods. The extent to which we grapple with our still-evident and deeply felt contradictions about nurturance and the sources and manifestations of our own authority reflects our multilayered assumptions about the very constructions of gender, of identity, and of their relationships and influences on our resulting constructions of our roles as women teachers.

Within the contexts of our collaborative research group, the excavations of those assumptions, the individual and collective reflections that we share around those assumptions, and the resulting actions that we are able to take in our daily educational lives are evidence of the strength and support that autobiographical perspectives and processes can provide to critical inquiries on teaching, research, and curriculum. We continue to share, to re-view, and to add new versions of our stories in order that we might enable ourselves and others to see through and beyond specific situations in order to envision new educational possibilities for ourselves and our students.

Thus autobiographical work that focuses not only on individuals' narrations of their educational experiences but also on the historical contexts and social situations in which they construct those experiences and remembrances encourages educators to integrate similar processes into their conceptions of teaching and learning. The early childhood educator who engages in self-reflexive and critical analyses of her or his own educational biography might also approach teaching with similar intents, recognizing social and historical constructions of the early childhood classroom as perhaps representing particular discourses that maintain as isolated, solitary, and segmented the learning and teaching processes and interactions of children and teachers.

As I gingerly approached those first-graders a few years ago, I could not deny the immediacy of their presence and of their gentle invitation to jump in—to further submerge myself in the turbulent and vigorous waves of their questions and their answers, their declarations of personhood and of connectedness to one another and to their emerging worlds. I am grateful for their invitation—for my resulting plunge has allowed me and those educators with whom I work to explore the depths of our own relations to one another, to those whom we teach, and to our own and others' constructions and possible reconstructions of educational worlds.

NOTES

1. I am grateful for Georgette Neville Vosseler's enduring commitment to our research processes and for her willingness to share her insights and reflections here. Georgette, a first-grade teacher in a small school district on Long Island, New York, is a member of our ongoing collaborative and has been an early childhood educator for fourteen years. It is to her that this piece is dedicated.

2. For comprehensive surveys of the emergence, development, and integration of reconceptualist perspectives in the curriculum field, see Pinar (1974, 1975, 1988). Also, *The Journal of Curriculum Theorizing* (now *JCT: An Interdisciplinary Journal of Curriculum Studies*), a journal devoted to curriculum history, criticism, and theory, has, since its inception in 1978, represented various aspects and perspectives of the reconceptualist movement. The Bergamo Conference on Curriculum Theory and Classroom Practice, an annual conference sponsored by *JCT*, also provides a national forum for curriculum debate, dialogue, and sharing of myriad curriculum conceptions and perspectives.

REFERENCES

Britzman, D. P. (1991). *Practice makes practice: A critical study of learning to teach.* Albany: State University of New York Press.

Brodkey, L. (1987). Writing critical ethnographic narratives. *Anthropology and Education Quarterly, 18,* 67–76.

Brodkey, L. (1989). On the subjects of class and gender in "The literacy letters." *College English, 51,* 125–141.

Ellsworth, E. (1989). Why doesn't this feel empowering? Working through the repressive myths of critical pedagogy. *Harvard Educational Review, 59,* 297–324.

Greene, M. (1986). In search of a critical pedagogy. *Harvard Educational Review, 56,* 427–441.

Grumet, M. R. (1981). Pedagogy for patriarchy: The feminization of teaching. *Interchange, 12,* 165–184.

Grumet, M. R. (1988a). *Bitter milk: Women and teaching.* Amherst: University of Massachusetts Press.

Grumet, M. R. (1988b). Women and teaching: Homeless at home. In W. F. Pinar (Ed.), *Contemporary curriculum discourses* (pp. 531–539). Scottsdale, AZ: Gorsuch Scarisbrick.

Krall, F. R. (1981). Navajo tapestry: A curriculum for ethno-ecological perspectives. *The Journal of Curriculum Theorizing, 3*(2), 165–208.

Krall, F. R. (1988). From the inside out: Personal history as educational research. *Educational Theory, 38*, 467–479.

Lather, P. (1984). Critical theory, curricular transformation, and feminist mainstreaming. *Journal of Education, 166*, 49–62.

Lather, P. (1986). Research as praxis. *Harvard Educational Review, 56*, 257–277.

Lather, P. (1989). Postmodernism and the politics of enlightenment. *Educational Foundations, 3*, 7–28.

Lather, P. (1991). *Getting smart: Feminist research and pedagogy with/in the postmodern.* New York: Routledge.

Lewis, M., & Simon, R. I. (1986). A discourse not intended for her: Learning and teaching within patriarchy. *Harvard Educational Review, 56*, 457–472.

Martin, B., & Mohanty, C. (1986). Feminist politics: What's home got to do with it? In T. deLauretis (Ed.), *Feminist studies, critical studies* (pp. 191–212). Bloomington: Indiana University Press.

Miller, J. L. (1983, Summer). The resistance of women academics: An autobiographical account. *The Journal of Educational Equity and Leadership, 3, 2,* 101–109.

Miller, J. L. (1986). Women as teachers: Enlarging conversations on issues of gender and self-concept. *Journal of Curriculum and Supervision, 1*, 111–121.

Miller, J. L. (1987). Teachers' emerging texts: The empowering potential of writing inservice. In J. Smyth (Ed.), *Educating teachers: Changing the nature of pedagogical knowledge* (pp. 193–206). London: Falmer.

Miller, J. L. (1990). *Creating spaces and finding voices: Teachers collaborating for empowerment.* Albany: State University of New York Press.

Mitrano, B. S. (1981). Feminism and curriculum theory: Implications for teacher education. *The Journal of Curriculum Theorizing, 3*, 5–85.

Pagano, J. (1988a). The claim of philia. In W. F. Pinar (Ed.), *Contemporary curriculum discourses* (pp. 514–530). Scottsdale, AZ: Gorsuch Scarisbrick.

Pagano, J. (1988b). Teaching women. *Educational Theory, 38*, 321–339.

Pagano, J. (1990). *Exiles and community: Teaching in the patriarchal wilderness.* Albany: State University of New York Press.

Pinar, W. F. (Ed.). (1974). *Heightened consciousness, cultural revolution, and curriculum theory.* Berkeley, CA: McCutchan.

Pinar, W. F. (Ed.). (1975). *Curriculum theorizing: The reconceptualists.* Berkeley, CA: McCutchan.

Pinar, W. F. (1981). "Whole, bright, deep with understanding": Issues in qualitative research and autobiographical method. *Journal of Curriculum Studies, 13*, 173–188.

Pinar, W. F. (Ed.). (1988). *Contemporary curriculum discourses.* Scottsdale, AZ: Gorsuch Scarisbrick.

Pinar, W. F., & Grumet, M. R. (1976). *Toward a poor curriculum.* Dubuque, IA: Kendall/Hunt.

Reiniger, M. (1988, Fall). Traces of misogyny in women's schooling: Autobiographical search for gyn/ecology. *The Journal of Curriculum Theorizing, 8*, 7–89.

Roman, L. G., & Apple, M. W. (1990). Is naturalism a move away from positivism? Materialist and feminist approaches to subjectivity in ethnographic research. In E. W. Eisner & A. Peshkin (Eds.), *Qualitative inquiry in education: The continuing debate* (pp. 38–73). New York: Teachers College Press.

Wallenstein, S. (1979). *The reflexive method in curriculum theory: An autobiographical case study*. Unpublished doctoral dissertation, University of Rochester, Rochester, New York.

CHAPTER 7

Deconstructing the Discourse of Care
Young Children in the Shadows of Democracy

Valerie Polakow

But the young, young children, O my
brothers,
They are weeping bitterly!
They are weeping in the playtime of the
others,
In the country of the free.

(Elizabeth Barrett Browning, *The Cry of the Children*)

This chapter is about young children, not in the mines and factories of nineteenth-century industrial England but rather in the last decade of the twentieth century in the United States. They, too, are weeping; weeping in the playtime of others, suffering in the shadows of affluence, lacking the freedom to develop in the country of the free. This chapter is also about their mothers; poor mothers who inhabit the profoundly unequal and undemocratic landscape that the feminization of poverty and the growing infantilization of poverty have created in the United States.

Poor mothers and their children give rise to another discourse—a discourse of otherness. They living out there in the unnamed landscapes, are placeless, inhabiting other lifeworlds. Out of this otherness we constitute a discourse of concealment and invisibility that forms a construct of social-psychological pathology corroborated by an educational discourse of deficiency and remediation. The theme of *otherness* is reframed as an individual problem in need of redress, not a structured practice em-

This chapter is based exclusively on material from V. Polakow, *Lives on the Edge: Single Mothers and Their Children in the Other America* (University of Chicago Press, forthcoming). Reprinted by permission of The University of Chicago.

bedded in a discourse of exclusion and inequality. Both the ideology of care and the discourse of otherness are addressed in this chapter in order to deconstruct prevailing patriarchal and monocultural assumptions about the nature of care, attachment, and early development. The discourse of care holds particularly pernicious outcomes for poor children, whose otherness removes them from the "normal" paradigms of development.

The problems of single parenthood, minimum-wage destitution, and the undeclared war on the poor, including restricted or no access to health care, childcare, or educational opportunities, along with a swelling tide of homelessness, have created an invisible class of children as our single most disadvantaged group. One out of four young children (age 3 and under) in the United States is being raised in poverty. The most extreme forms of this poverty are found in the economic injustice experienced by black and Hispanic families.

In attempting to analyze the discourse of care in which the lives of both women and young children are embedded, and in prising apart those assumptions and taken-for-granted meanings upon which our own constructions of identity rest, we see how our ways of seeing and norms of thought about care go to the heart of our own anthropology of self. To speak a discourse of motherhood and childhood is also to speak a shadow discourse—of domestic ideology, of specific family frames, of patriarchy, and of the spatialization of power. In the case of women and children, it is also to link power and the site of control, the body, to a social history of surveillance, classification, and regulation embedded in a "biopower" of discursive practices—those anonymous historical configurations that shape our discourse and action. (Foucault, 1977). The relationships between early childhood development theory, child poverty, and single parenthood intersect at a critical point in our social and educational history. As economic injustice, class stratification, racism, and gender converge in classrooms, at-risk children and their mothers are constructed and the social pathology of poverty is frequently recast as individual developmental disability.

Hence in this chapter I argue that the historical discourse of development and current developmentally appropriate practice need to be challenged. We need to examine our historical assumptions about motherhood and the family, as well as the monocultural and class-biased frames into which we attempt to mold economically disadvantaged and culturally diverse young children. A language of existential entitlement needs to be constructed as part of a reconceptualized theory and practice of early childhood.

THE HISTORICAL SPACE OF THE FAMILY AND CHILDHOOD

In order to deconstruct development theory it is necessary to disassemble the concept of care and trace its formation as indivisibly tied to mother as the central reproducer of a healthy child—biologically, emotionally, and intellectually. It is also instructive to examine the social-historical records of the family and childhood. We see that the social space of childhood has undergone dramatic historic shifts, which stand as evidence for the post-structuralist arguments against the "incredulity of metanarratives" (Lyotard, 1989, p. *xxiv*). Such metanarratives, which encompass fixed enduring images of mother love, of nuclear family units, and of childhood as a distinctive universal stage with age-specific characteristics, are part of a persistent mythology that has promoted concepts of family dysfunctionality and deficiency; yet this metanarrative is neither historically accurate, culturally nuanced, nor inclusive of class diversity. Childhood is not and never has been a timeless, unchanging developmental essence; rather it is an economic and cultural construction, rooted in prevailing historical and contemporary images of class, culture, and gender. Family, too, is a contingent social category; as both divine and secular construct it has been produced and reproduced by theologians and social scientists alike, as the stable "natural order" from which all diversity of form and resultant pathology diverge.

A Eurocentric Legacy

When we explore the changing meanings of childhood and the family within the Western Eurocentric tradition, the spaces in which women and children have been placed are revealing; for the stories of their lives, lived under surveillance and regulated by religion and the state, all bear witness to the biopower of patriarchy. Questions of attachment and love, indifference and abandonment are entwined with the public and private faces of the family, whether these are mirrored in the opacity of the little commonwealth of Puritan New England (Demos, 1970) or the invisibility of the disposable "tour" of nineteenth-century France (Fuchs, 1984).

We know that until late in the Middle Ages there was no linguistic term to describe what we now know as the nuclear unit. As Mitterauer and Sieder (1982) point out, even until the eighteenth century the German *Familie* based on the French *famille*, which in turn was taken from the Latin *familia*, referred to the household unit as "hearth," comprising blood relations, maid- and manservants, and their respective children—

all connected together as a domestic community in which ties of kin played a secondary role to the household functions performed by the domestic unit.

In tracing the changes from a society based on a familial domestic economy in which women shared in economic production to an industrial one in which the family unit no longer formed the basis for the organization of labor and production, we see that the social form of the family structure during industrialization underwent dramatic shifts. As the separation of the workplace from the dwelling place became institutionalized, a sentimental rather than functional image was ascribed to the family, emphasizing blood ties and the exclusivity of the parent–child bonds.

Hence, if we consider the case of France in the late eighteenth century, brimming with postrevolutionary fervor, sparkling with the enlightened romanticism of Rousseau's images of childhood, we see a clear illustration of the modern sentimental sense of the family emerging in the bourgeois and aristocratic strata and spreading in concentric circles to other classes, reaching the proletariat during the nineteenth century. It was also during this same period of enlightened romanticism that the privileged ideal of the "noble savage" became a far cry removed from the grim realities of a destitute childhood. Such glaring contradictions in the treatment of children were clearly visible as France began to wrestle with its "social question": how to dispose of its unwanted destitute pauper children, who, it was feared, would grow up to form the "dangerous classes." Abandonment of newborn children constituted an integral facet of French society, where, for example, as Fuchs (1984) documents through archival records, one-quarter of all newborns, and fully one-half of illegitimate newborns, were abandoned each year during the early nineteenth century at the Paris Foundling Hospital. These abandonments were institutionalized through the "tour" for poor mothers. The "tour" was a revolving cylindrical box, built into the walls of hospices and foundling hospitals, in which mothers placed their babies; thus "the tour was deaf, dumb and blind" (Fuchs, 1984, p. 23) and guaranteed invisibility and anonymity to desperate pauper mothers. In essence, it centralized child abandonment and regulated the process by which the state took control of pauper children and fashioned them into useful capital for the state. When this controversial practice was discontinued, state policy took a new turn—the displacement of babies to wetnurses in the countryside.

Wetnurses had been a common feature of young children's lives, even during the eighteenth century. In 1780, one year after the French Revolution, a Paris Lieutenant noted that of the 21,000 babies born in Paris that year, 19,000 were sent away to wetnurses outside the city

(Badinter, 1981, p. *xix*). The wetnurse later became an institutional norm for all social classes, legitimating the desertion of infants and young children for an average period of two to four years. This raises questions about maternal indifference, as well as the meaning of mother love and the meaning of family as a sentimentalized construct. In reality this was a world in which the young had very little place. Thus when assumptions about the durability of mother–child bonding in "traditional" families are made, and the historical necessity of the mother–child couplet is seen as rooted in tradition and ascribed the status of a natural law, we need to question the meaning of such meanings. As Laslett reminds us, in our recent past family membership was always "evanescent, family relationships brief, intermittent and presumably unstable" (cited in Mitterauer & Sieder, 1982, p. *ix*).

The social historical records of childhood are sparse—biographies, diary accounts, police records, physician journals; except for these, children are strangely absent from our written records. In fact Phillipe Ariès' (1962) seminal work on *Centuries of Childhood* throws into question the notion of any constructed social space for childhood prior to the Enlightenment. Early infancy was recognized as infants were customarily disposed of through the agency of the wetnurse. This was followed by a period of miniature adulthood in which children and adults shared the same world, a world, for example, in which sexual play was common; for a terrain of psychological and developmental space did not exist. Plumb (1972) argues similarly, seeing children as victims of time, of place, of a brutality and indifference that characterized much of the premodern world. It was rare to see children portrayed as children, in either art or literature, before the Enlightenment, when a new sensibility began to emerge. DeMause (1974), depicting the historical child, claims that "the history of childhood is a nightmare from which we have only recently begun to awaken" (p. 1) and that the further back in history we delve, the worse the levels of brutality, abandonment, abuse, and terror.

These accounts are strongly disputed in the work of Linda Pollock (1983), whose studies of diaries and autobiographical accounts of the literate bourgeoisie and the nobility from the sixteenth to nineteenth centuries reveal nuances that do display a limited sensibility toward children; but they, too, unveil a pervasive punitive and regulation discourse. In some ways children represented not only the condition of otherness but also the enormity of a dangerous and risky burden of caretaking, which increased by devastating odds in proportion to the poverty of the mother.

We see, too, how the exposure and abandonment of the child was integrally linked to the subjugation of woman s body and her position in the social order. Both women and children were properties of men, and the public acceptance of male ownership of the *body space* of both women and children created multiple life themes: maternal indifference and shattered bonds; maternal nurturance and ideals of mother love; the bearing and rearing of a child as unwelcome burden; and the wielding of maternal power within patriarchal subjugation. These themes wove their ways through the fabric of family forms, and through it all the economic position of woman as mother was pivotal. As Fuchs (1984) points out, abandonment was often "a radical solution to the social, psychological, and above all economic pressures the women faced" (p. 277).

Badinter (1981) argues that the male invention of motherhood was successful among middle-class women in late eighteenth-century France, promoted by Rousseau's conception of marriage, which accorded the husband companionate control over the domestic world as wife became a devotee of husband and child. In *Emile* (Rousseau, 1762/1964), for example, Sophie is raised to fulfill the desires of Emile and his children and woman as mother gains status and responsibility within the family as a "sentimental nest" is born. As Badinter points out, it was certainly no accident that the women who heeded such arguments for the "new mother" were middle class, since they saw in this role the opportunity for an increase in social status and an emancipation that aristocratic women were not seeking. The new mother now had local power and swiftly gained domestic credibility, becoming the ally of the physician as medical institutions began to create a pediatric science—in short, mother became the "holy domestic monarch" (Badinter, 1981, p. 189).

Yet poor mothers were the last to benefit from the new mother image. More than ever, wives of artisans and of proletarians had to get rid of their children in order to bring in a second income—even the destitute peasant women sent their own children away, as they received the city children for wetnursing or went to live in the homes of the affluent "new mothers" to wetnurse their babies. It is instructive to read physicians' accounts in the middle of the nineteenth century, where, for example, Drs. Monot and Brochard express indignation over the abominable conditions to which children sent out to wetnurses were subjected; but both concur that "poor women with no choice but to work cannot do otherwise" (cited in Badinter, 1981, p. 192). While French philanthropists tried to improve the conditions of the children, no effort was made to improve the destitute and appalling conditions of the wetnursing women—who continued to sell their breasts, if not their bodies, in order to survive. And babies died in startling numbers: of 20,000 infants sent from Paris to Nogent-le-Rotrou during the 1850s, only 5,000 survived due to lack of care and supervision (Badinter, 1981).

This window into eighteenth- and nineteenth-century France is illuminating because it throws into sharp and finely etched relief the enduring myths and multiple meanings of motherhood and mother love. Clearly some mothers throughout history have loved their children, but clearly many have not. Badinter states, "It was not so much because children died like flies that mothers showed so little interest in them, but rather because mothers showed so little interest that the children died in such great numbers" (p. 60). Many of these mothers were wealthy aristocrats and educated bourgeoisie. It is noteworthy, too, that fathers as parents were hardly featured in the discourse of the time.

Children represented the forces of both burden and disorder when life was harsh and lived on the edge of survival. When religion and the state controlled one's body, one's sociality, and one's civil society, there was little psychological space for the development of compassion. Neither was the mother of privilege free from the burdens of her own subjugation and surveillance in the social and political structures that effaced her as a public voice and increasingly placed and bound her to the interior world.

On the one hand, Rousseau's (1762/1964) image of the male child as a free developing self offered a passionate critique of a brutal history of childhood and posed Emile as the natural prototype. On the other hand, girls were not to receive the same education or freedom; rather "woman is formed to please and to live in subjection" (p. 218). The task of mother was to assist the pedagogue in guiding children toward their differential inclinations and protecting them against the unnatural corrupting forces of the time. Pestalozzi (1801/1898), also writing in the late 1700s, paid homage to the lofty sentiments that characterized an early pedagogy of compassion, which integrally tied the child's union with a righteous mother and the Divine to an activity-based nature education that began to see unfolding developmental change as a significant theme. Froebel (1887/1900), who began developing the founding principles of the kindergarten in the 1830s, argued similarly for the development of the intellect and a selfhood through the cultivation of the inner connections, where self-activity was to unfold the forces of natural development.

In these pedagogical philosophers we see a developing sensibility toward childhood, but the sensibility is tied to the construction of the new mother, of mother love as a natural law, modeled on Rousseau's Sophie, who displays the ideal feminine nature of both devotion and sacrifice. Here biology has become destiny, and mother alone becomes the primary force for health or pathology.

But the most contradictory aspect of the discourse of mother–child love, and the elevation of mother to a domestic pedestal during this period, is the plight of thousands of poor babies dying in foundling hospitals, thousands of young children laboring and dying in the factories and the mines, on estates, and sent out to the colonies as indentured servants at 7 or 8 years old. The class-structured consciousness that was pervasive then is not much different now, although we have invented new forms of talk to explain why some children's and some mothers' lives matter more than others. Dickens (1867/1975) tells us, as he begins the tale of Oliver Twist, the story of one mother's life and death, a life that speaks for other grim fates of countless women in the poorhouse. Oliver's mother, before giving birth, is brought dying to the poorhouse infirmary, having been found "lying in the street. She had walked some distance, for her shoes were worn to pieces; but where she came from, or where she was going to, nobody knows" (p. 17). Or cared. Mother and child alone, as always, destitute and "badged." In our post-modern decade, we can predict Oliver will be labeled ADD, EI, and probably LD[1]—an at-risk casualty of a dysfunctional, single-parent, destitute family—one of the 50 percent of single-parent families living in poverty, grubbing for food stamps, humiliated by the regulatory apparatus of a public assistance bureaucracy that vitiates dignity and keeps *them* out there away from *us*.

As these contradictions are revealed in terms of our current discourse about family, mother love, and attachment theory, it is necessary to deconstruct those embedded forms of psychosocial knowledge that drive public policy and create a two-tiered world of care for children.

Attachment and the Ideology of Care

If we trace the growing sensibility toward childhood and the formation of the new mother image through modern times and we look at development through the frame of Freud's nineteenth-century Vienna, we see that within Freud's (1916/1935) patriarchal image of the family, woman emerged desexualized, suffering from her Electra complex, yet a vital force for the psychosexual development of her child's healthy ego. Infant-mother bonding continues to echo through the discourse of attachment theory. For Anna Freud (1945/1974), and for both Spitz (1945) and Bowlby(1969), the "normal" development of object relations through the healthy formation of the ego was crucial. Object relations theory is rooted in a stable fixed image of a patriarchal family. While Freud was iconoclastic in his discourse about sexual drives and repression, his model of a Victorian family remained conventional and bourgeois. Perhaps that is why he reversed his seduction theory and committed what Jeffrey Masson (1984) has termed the "assault on truth"; for if hysterical women were made so by actual molestation rather than fantasy, the edifice of family and the structures of staged psychosexual development were threatened with collapse. Current data on child sexual abuse indicate that one in four girls and one in seven boys will encounter an experience of sexual abuse prior to their eighteenth birthday (Crewdson, 1988). Freud's Vienna was, in all probability, not markedly different. As Wolff's (1988) study of child abuse in Vienna in 1899 documents, "The world of 1899, however, barely recognized the concept of child abuse, and a powerful Victorian sentimental ideal of the loving family made it hard to believe that parents brutalized their children" (p. 4).

Hence family, mother love, and stage theory norms, when deconstructed, reveal sets of discursive practices that speak to power, regulation, and the silencing of distorted relations within a class- and gender-stratified social structure. This is our development theory heritage—a complicit participation in the naming of pathology as normality.

Erikson (1950), while expanding Freud's theory beyond the deterministic psychosexual markers of early childhood, also predicated his psychosocial stages on the resolution of developmental crises initiated by the fundamental trust versus mistrust duality, where mother as attachment persona is central. Helene Deutsch (1944), writing in the 1940s, argued persuasively to a ready academic and lay public for the necessary sublimation of woman's desires and aspirations through motherhood. Yet it was Bowlby's (1951) widely read and disseminated studies of infant attachment and loss that shaped much of post-World War II attachment discourse. For Bowlby (1951) the mental health of both mothers and children was based on a stable, enduring intimate relationship buttressed by a joint dependency on fathers as financial providers ensuring that their wives would be enabled to

> devote themselves unrestrictedly to the care of the infant and toddler (p. 13). . . . Just as the baby needs to feel that he belongs to his mother, the mother needs to feel that she belongs to her child. . . . This provision of constant attention day and night, seven days a week and 365 in the year, is possible only for a woman who derives profound satisfaction from seeing her child grow from babyhood, through the many phases of childhood, to become an independent man or woman and knows it is her care which has made it possible. (p. 67).

In this way, Bowlby constitutes the mother–child attachment couplet in suffocating images of reciprocal development, in which bonding is recast as mother bondage. Mental health can only be assured by exclusive maternal care conducted within a patriarchal family structure in which the strict division of male–female roles forms part of the natural order. Other family forms and home settings become landscapes of pathology.

Bowlby also cautions against any form of institutional care, arguing that even "bad home" environments are better than good institutions. (Such claims assume particular irony when we consider the alarming statistics on child physical and sexual abuse mentioned earlier, which document that the majority of these cases occur within families.)

Mary Ainsworth's studies, following in the tradition of Bowlby, elevated attachment behavior to a functional scientific model of healthy infant adaptation through her famous stranger-situation experiments, which measured the degree of attachment to mother under controlled laboratory conditions (Ainsworth & Bell, 1970). This experiment and its findings of separation anxiety augmented the ahistorical and often hysterical assumptions about the natural laws of attachment, which were illuminated to fullest advantage in the silhouettes of suburbia.

It is interesting to recall the social conditions and cultural practices in Europe, as well as in this country, in which this construct of child-inextricably-tied-to-mother gradually gained such dominance. As Badinter (1981) has pointed out in her analysis of bourgeois motherhood in eighteenth- and nineteenth-century France, maternal love mythologized as biological female instinct has never been an unquestionable constant; rather historical decoding reveals its contingency on social and political mores. In fact, during this period in France children were an annoyance and hindrance for bourgeois women, and breastfeeding was perceived as a "ridiculous and disgusting habit." Women of rank were supported by doctors in choosing social obligations over care, for "nothing was less fashionable than to seem to love one's children too much and to give up one's precious time for them" (Badinter, 1981, p. 71). While at all times some mothers—aristocratic, bourgeois, and poor—have loved their children, this construct of mother love as biological and innate has served to legitimate conceptions of womanhood and motherhood that have dominated women's lives and cast sweeping shadows over public and private landscapes in which family texts are written.

Chodorow (1978) argues that mothering and the reproduction of mothering is neither a product of biology nor intentional role training but rather a product of "social structurally induced psychological processes" (p. 7) that constitute personality and sex differences in early childhood. Hence children reach adulthood with distinctive and gendered conceptions of identity and experience self, and social-self, definitions of mothering and fathering that are layered with the discursive practices of one's biography. It is woman who must reproduce attachment as a social form, and woman-as-mother who finds her identity in such psychological formation and incorporation.

In this country, in the late 1940s and early 1950s, attachment, mother–child bonding, and the Norman Rockwell vision of middle America's home and hearth were promoted. But what happened in 1945? The end of World War II marked the end of a strange era in this country's history—a brief moment in which 4.7 million new women had entered the workforce (many of them married and over the age of 35), with 3.5 million women taking jobs they would otherwise not have taken and often being paid "man-sized wages" (Kessler-Harris, 1982). Furthermore, in 1942, $4 million in federal government funds went to local communities to assist in the building of childcare centers to house the babies and young children of mothers who joined the workforce. But in 1945, the women were sent home, displaced by returning veterans, and in 1946 federal childcare funds were terminated and 100,000 children were threatened with eviction as childcare centers were forced to close (Hewlett, 1987). The GI Bill, with low-cost mortgages for the single-family home, and the Highway Act of 1944 contributed to the swell of suburbia and domestic isolation of which Levittown (built in 1946) is but one visible symbol. Economic strategies to keep women out of the workplace, buttressed by the developmental–attachment arguments for the healthy growth of children, placed pathology in the laps of insufficiently bonded infants and insufficiently identified and sublimated mothers; once again the mother–child couplet was at center stage.

In this way we can trace how the exclusion of women from public space returns us to The Home as a domestic site of confinement, the boundary of private and public space, the concrete site of woman's inner space, the terrain for her production of a well-developed child. It was here that the private space between mother and child also became the object of the scientific gaze, and here, too, that the child became the product object of mother's labor—a double internment. As woman's placelessness in public life was sealed by domestic ideology, so, too, were the practices of family life.

While the image of family as "haven in a heartless world" is central to our cultural consciousness, the patterns of family life that lie behind closed doors, fenced facades, and manicured lawns, and also behind roach-infested tenements, are often sites of abuse and fear, of violence and humiliation—of family as hell, "of breeding grounds of hatred," and of a pervasive poisonous pedagogy "used to condition a child at an early age not to become aware of what is really being done to him or her" (Miller, 1983, p. 9). For as Alice Miller dramatically argues in her existential analytic reconstruction of child case studies, our own childrearing practices are often a revengeful biography of our own childhoods—sites in which hidden cruelty and violence are the countertext to attachment and bonding and nurturance.

Punishment and the Subjugation of the Body

> Break the will, if you would not damn the child . . . make him do as he is bid . . . if you whip him ten times running to effect it (Wesley, cited in Newson & Newson, 1974, p. 56).

John and Elizabeth Newson (1974), in attempting to analyze the cultural aspects of childrearing in the English-speaking world over the last two centuries, argue that the evangelical movement, despite its minority status, cast a moral net over pedagogy, with its mission being to conquer the will of children as early as possible, a necessary foundation for a religious education. This deity-centered pedagogy saw the subjugation of the body as the pathway to the proper formation of mind.

While the discourse changed in the early part of the twentieth century to one of regulation and medicalization, the conquest of the body and domestication of the mind became a critical pedagogical imperative for the early months and years of a child's life. Thus the construction of childhood and the formation of an obedient and docile child took many forms, forms in which the body of the child became the site where the most intimate social practices became linked to the exercise of parental and pedagogical power. Foucault's (1977) analysis of the discourse of power as a subjugation and regulation of the body finds its analogue in the text of childhood punishment under the guise of education—in short an emblematic poisonous pedagogy of "for your own good" as articulated by Miller (1983) and earlier Rutschky (1977). This theme of power and regulation, through the subjugation of the body of the child, forms a discourse aimed at creating "docile bodies" or, to quote Sulzer, an eighteenth-century German pedagogue, "one of the advantages of these early years is that force and compulsion can be used. Over the years children forget everything that happened to them in early childhood. If their wills can be broken at this time, they will never remember that they had a will" (quoted in Miller, 1983, p. 13).

Greven (1991), in exploring the apocalyptic impulse in American Protestantism, questions the meaning and impact of physical punishment on the private and public aspects of American culture and character and suggests that "physical punishment of children appears to be one of the subjects in America that are still profoundly disturbing, because they are too deeply rooted in our individual and our collective psyches to be confronted directly" (p. 4). Physical punishment is still widely accepted as an acceptable form of parental discipline and is still permitted within public schools in many states as an acceptable method of control. Such legalized assaults on children in families and schools are only determined abusive when severe injuries and bodily harm result.

Hence, in discussing dominant cultural motifs in the construction of motherhood and childhood, we find that a deconstructionist perspective reveals patterns of power, control, brutality, and indifference to the sensibilities of children despite a growing development discourse about the cultivation of childhood as a separate state to be tended and nurtured. We also find that the progressivist myth of childhood improving with each successive century (DeMause, 1974) is disputed by Plumb (1972), Demos (1986), and child advocacy historians such as Greven (1991), who point out how the discourse of concealment has operated with such efficiency and continued the assault on young lives. Educational discourse has succeeded in eclipsing such dominant realities.

The horrors of destitution and the brutality of homelessness have also been successfully concealed and neutralized by an anesthetic language of scientific categories. Mainstream educational texts deal with these issues under special categories, such as "at-risk" or "special needs" children. In this way we obscure once again the dominant role that abuse and poverty continue to play in the everyday lives of children. In the case of poor children, these forms of abuse multiply in all realms of existence, as every form of viable existence is systematically stripped from childhood, and by extension from motherhood.

AN ANTICHILD IDEOLOGY OF CARE

In the 1990s, despite the dramatic demographic shifts and the increasing infusion of mothers into the labor force, taking care of children is still seen as a private and predominantly female responsibility, with no public obligations. The U.S. "pro-family" policy, a facade for the hegemony of domestic ideology, has effectively constrained the development of social policies, and until the 1988 presidential elections, childcare was not an urgent priority agenda. The Act for Better Child Care, in its original form, never became legislative reality; but in the 101st Congress, four years of intensive lobbying by child advocacy organizations finally resulted in the first comprehensive childcare legislation, which will offer minimal assistance to low-income children through the Child Care and Development Block Grant of $2.5 billion to improve childcare affordability, accessibility, and quality. However, the United States continues to lag behind both Western industrialized and former Eastern bloc countries in providing maternity leave and prenatal benefits to mothers, childcare for their children, and health insurance. Over 51 percent of preschool-age children have mothers in the workforce, yet a grave shortage of high-quality, accessible, and affordable childcare continues to exist. Over 12.6 million children are now living below the poverty line, accounting for a child poverty rate of 19.6 percent. Among children living in female-headed households, more than 51 percent are poor. A single mother with only one child working full time at minimum wage all year cannot earn enough to escape poverty. Recent estimates from the Children's Defense Fund (1991) indicate that these poverty statistics are rising, not diminishing. In addition, the rising number of children without any health insurance (currently one in six), the high infant mortality rate, and the record number of nonimmunized children in urban inner cities—approaching 50 percent (Children's Defense Fund, 1991)—point to a brutal public policy neglect of poor children and, by extension, of their single mothers.

The chronic lack of available and affordable childcare creates a double-edged sword for such mothers, who cannot enter the labor force without full-time childcare and who cannot escape poverty by remaining on welfare. For those who do find childcare, minimum-wage employment continues to guarantee poverty and little or no entitlement to health benefits. This reflects a fundamental failure to implement public and economic policy that assumes the entitlement of children to care and the entitlement of mothers to work and earn a viable wage, to detach themselves from the deterministic mother–child couplet of attachment, and to forge independent lives with autonomous relationships with their children.

Ironically, it is the "talk" of our developers, our contemporary successors to attachment theory, whose words continue to be used and abused to promote the image of a stable, enduring nuclear family unit (see Belsky, 1986; Belsky & Ravine, 1988) with a stay-at-home mother who is seen as having an entitlement to neither an independent wage-earner existence nor to state support as a working mother. Yet current Department of Labor statistics indicate that 50 percent of all American children during the 1990s will spend part of their childhood in a single-parent household and fewer than 10 percent will live in a two-parent traditional nuclear unit, with a wage-earner father and a stay-at-home mother. Hence the failure to recognize diverse family forms and the visible reality of the working and single mothers' desperate need for care contribute in no small measure to the feminization of poverty and the lack of public policy affirmation of women's place, rather than placelessness, in public life and public labor.

It is ironic, too, that childcare has not, until the past decade, been a top agenda item of mainstream feminist organizations, nor have maternity benefits—another instance in which the push for individual rights has resulted in the neglect of children and the casualty of a social feminism. In the arena of childbearing, childrearing, and childcare, feminists in this country, in contrast to social feminists in Western Europe, have, until recently, been strangely reticent to push for the rights of working mothers, who do require differential treatment, such as the right to child sick-leave days and the recognition that childbirth and early infant care are dramatic turning points in one's biography. For while attachment is not, and should not, be the all encompassing hegemonic psychoanalytic configuration that shapes the future worlds of mothers and their children, those early human moments that unfold in the weeks after birth deserve recognition—not as a deterministic, psychosocial marker of the future but as a critical existential space for the development of a relationship that promotes a bonding free of the bondage of poverty. Hence mothering—for in most cases it *is* still mothers who take major responsibility for their children—deserves recognition as a crucial phase of developmental and economic vulnerability. When a public policy support structure is brutally deficient, the daily consequence is a society that casts off its children while perpetuating a double "blaming the victim" syndrome. Mothers are blamed for their inability to care for their children; children are blamed for their lack of care and are constituted as a new category, those "at-risk." The ideology of care thus serves to promote mother–child *attachment* as a private and individual reality, while simultaneously legitimating a public policy of *detachment and nonresponsibility* toward such private and individual realities.

In the following section I examine the consequences of this ideology of care as I turn to brief narratives of daily life as experienced by mothers from diverse worlds who share in common critical child care needs.

Lives Outside

Several brief fragments of interviews conducted with mothers over an eighteen-month period are presented here.[2] These mothers' stories make visible the consequences of an antichild ideology, as it takes a particularly pernicious form in a society where health, housing, and the care of children is not seen as a public responsibility or a guaranteed entitlement. Taking care of children is a private family matter, and when the parent is female, single, and poor, such private responsibility is made precarious by public neglect.

Linda became pregnant at 17, in her junior year of high
school, where she was a competent student with a B grade
point average. Due to restrictions on Medicaid abortions, she
was told she was ineligible for funding and carried the baby
to term, dropping out of school in the second semester of her
junior year. Lamar was born in August and is now almost two
months old. When interviewed, Linda, who is black and poor,
expresses her bitterness and sense of defeat: "I had to drop
out 'cos my school didn't have no baby program and now I
got no diploma and a baby who don't quit bothering me."
Linda is currently living with her aunt and baby in a small
one-bedroom apartment in a housing project, saying, "I didn't
want to live with my mother no more—with all the drugs and
stuff and her on welfare and me never going nowhere in my
life." She also describes her difficulties with the welfare bureaucracy and how she has tried to get a job, "but there just
ain't no folks who can take care of Lamar—first my aunt, now
her back's so bad she's laid up half the time . . . the money
they give me [Department of Social Services] that don't even
pay the rent, and the daycare won't take babies and besides—
it costs more than the apartment each month—how'm I gonna
pay that money . . . so here I am a B student but brains don't
help you if you poor and pregnant . . . now I got no diploma
and a baby who won't quit crying . . . how'm I gonna get my
education and a job if nobody gonna help me with him?"

Linda's struggle and sense of desertion is a common experience
among poor teenage mothers, whose children constitute the fastest growing group of the new poor—members of a new "infantilization" of
poverty trend in which both mothers and children stand on the margins
of a social structure—with little or no health care, no childcare, and very
few opportunities to build a future. Listen to Joyce's story, which echoes
the struggles of Linda but from a different vantage point.

Joyce is on AFDC, a white single mother of three, whose husband, a laid-off auto worker, left her four years ago when she
was pregnant with their third child. She wants to go to a community college and enter a nursing program. However, she
has no childcare for her 3- and 4-year-old sons. Her oldest
child, a daughter, is in first grade. "AFDC keeps you a pris-
oner—they give you so little money I don't know how I can
keep food in this house and a roof over their heads and win-

ter coats to buy and Sam needs new boots . . . I want off welfare, it's bad for my kids and bad for me—right now they
control me and keep me down and I need my self-respect . . .
I want to go to school so bad and get a decent job. Right now
the only jobs I can get are $4.25 an hour and who's going to
take care of the kids? Both boys are on the Head Start wait
list, but even if those spaces open up, who will sit for them in
the afternoons and on Fridays? And how'm I going to get
home in time for the bus that drops off the kids, and if you
aren't home the teachers tell the social worker you not taking
care of your kids right.

The struggles that Joyce encounters are part of the theme of despera-
tion voiced by so many other mothers on welfare. Junne (1988), in
analyzing the predicaments of female school dropouts who later completed their GED diplomas, points out that to be eligible for aid one must
be destitute. In describing his interviews with black women on welfare
and their struggles for higher education, he demonstrates how public
assistance is actually punitive assistance. As one informant remarks:

I was told recently that since I am in College my food stamps would be
cut. . . . Why cut my food stamps when I'm trying to get off [welfare]?
I have to go to school to get off and you're going to cut my food stamps
so I can't eat? (p. 154)

The main source of public assistance for poor families, primarily
single-mother-headed households, is Aid to Families with Dependent
Children (AFDC), but benefits are so low that they leave families in
destitution. In 1990 the median state's maximum AFDC benefit for a
family of three was $367 per month—45 percent of the federal poverty
level. In five states it was only $200 per month. In addition, benefits have
not kept pace with inflation and housing costs have skyrocketed, so that
in thirty-nine states the fair market rent exceeds by two or three times the
entire AFDC grant for a family of three. Food stamp allowances, available to most AFDC families, were cut drastically during the Reagan
administration and remain too low to meet basic nutritional needs, so that
millions of young children are currently estimated to be hungry (Children's Defense Fund, 1991).

Hence poor mothers and their children live contingent lives, on the
edges, always one step away from the desperate void of homelessness. As
one Michigan mother of three, recovering from the trauma of recent
homelessness and a new round of AFDC cuts told me, "The governor is

cutting our benefits *and* people's property taxes—so more people will be homeless and then they'll blame us after they make us homeless!" Toni Morrison, portraying the experience of homelessness, poignantly reminds us in *The Bluest Eye* (1972) how this is "the real terror of life": "There is a difference between being put *out* and being put out *doors*. If you are put out, you go somewhere else; if you are outdoors, there is no place to go. The distinction was subtle but final" (p. 18).

As we move from the fictional world of Pecola and Cholly Breed-love, we hear the themes of "the real terror of life" echoing once more in the voice of Clare, pregnant with her fourth child, homeless for over a year, and the victim of two cutoffs of food stamps and Medicaid by her assistance worker because she had failed to file forms by the due date:

> It's a terrible feeling to know you can't take care of your
> kids—to just feel so desperate that there is no place left to go.
> For us there was no place to go after my mother threw us
> out—that's when I reported her for beating up my son—we
> lived in the back of a truck for a while and then the trailer
> and then DSS put us in a motel and everyday we had to look
> for apartments, but how do you find something for $300 that
> has three bedrooms in this area—they wouldn't let us rent a
> two-bedroom and all this time the assistance workers shrug
> and say that's your problem!

These brief narratives are part of the ongoing stories of lives *outside*, the stories of women and children that lend vivid actuality to the lives that lie behind the cold public face of poverty statistics.

The At-Risk Discourse

Every at-risk child in our early childhood classrooms is a potential victim of such public indifference, of our disenfranchisement of the poor—a witness to our failure to provide entitlements for all children. We can no longer afford the liberal complacency or conservative victim blaming that continues to frame our social and educational agendas. Early childhood theory and practice has a scarred and stratified history of exclusion, and the two-tiered system of childcare merely reflects the instrumentality that pervades our treatment of poor young children—a mirror image of how we treat their parents, in particular their mothers. Poor children, it appears, are only deserving of public money if early intervention has demonstrable economic payoffs. They matter instrumentally, not existentially. Funding for early intervention programs for poor children is premised on cost-benefit accountability, but fee-based centers do not have to develop a rationale to provide a place for children to play and to learn. In the absence of a national childcare system, poor children go to Head Start and other public preschool programs if eligible for an at-risk designation, which tickets them for entry to a compensatory or pre-primary special education program. Thus access to an early educational program also guarantees economic and racial segregation in a two-tiered system of childcare, ensuring that young children experience educational segregation in their earliest years and poor children enter not as little persons, but as at-risk cases. Yet while we, as early child educators, speak a discourse of developmentally appropriate practice (Bredekamp, 1987), many of the practices we promote in our teacher-training institutions and professional accreditation agencies are grounded in regulation and compliance, forming part of the development discourse described earlier.

Furthermore, much of the language of developmental appropriateness contains embedded monocultural and class-based assumptions of order, specific behavioral norms and styles, and a taken-for-granted daily life that excludes the overriding impact of poverty and homelessness as an ongoing life theme in young children's lives. One of the dominant motifs in many compensatory education programs is an inflexible set of structured choices; it is assumed that at-risk children need extra doses of order medication and training in activities that focus on sequence, seriation, and recognition because their lives are seen to be so disordered and chaotic. Consider the following observation gathered from a Head Start preschool classroom designed to serve a population of poor, predominantly minority children designated as at-risk.

> All twenty-five children were seated in the circle and listened to the story about "Curious George," whose unchecked curiosity led him into troublesome encounters and untold dangers. While the teacher read to the children, Timmy lay down and took a truck out of his pants pocket. "Timmy, sit up please and pay attention—and we don't bring our toys from home into class," said Teacher B. Following the circle time, the children were instructed to move from the rug to their seats, and they were given worksheets to fill in, matching pictures of objects with corresponding activities. After completing worksheets they were permitted playtime. Playtime involved a choice of games on the rug, cutting/pasting/blockbuilding, or bookcorner. Both the painting easel and housekeeping corner "are closed today as you were too noisy yesterday and some children moved the blocks into the housekeeping area."

Timmy, an inveterate squirmer in circles, was described as "having difficulty staying on-task," where staying on-task involved compliance to a rigidly structured set of routines devoid of child-initiated expressive activity. When Timmy was observed off-task on another occasion, he was using different blocks and shapes to make a "Sears Tower" instead of performing a sorting/classification activity, thereby initiating a set of actions that fell outside of the behavior to be observed on today's checklist.

In such classrooms, specific activities happen within strictly defined temporal and spatial frames. Violation of the norms creates nonnormative or deviant behavior and is occasion for concern about the child's ability to stay "on-task" and his or her social maturity and readiness. Boundaries between activity areas are strictly maintained, so the possibility of building a house with blocks in the housekeeping area violated the strict demarcation of objects rule, which is an implicit norm of the classroom. The rhetoric of developmentally appropriate practice is reduced in such classrooms to a set of implicit spatial norms. Children's activities are controlled, kept under surveillance, and creative or divergent expression is perceived as an act against the normative order.

Another visit to a state-funded public preschool program, serving at-risk children, yielded some disturbing observations. Many of the children in this program were destitute and had experienced persistent episodes of homelessness.

As I enter the room, the white teacher tells me, "These kids are real problems—I don't know if I can work here much longer." The children receive breakfast, a snack, and lunch at the program, which runs four mornings a week. I notice that four of the children seem to have insatiable appetites, constantly asking for seconds and thirds. A snack is being served, and the teacher aide (who is black) is preparing graham crackers and peanut butter with two child helpers. The remaining sixteen 4-year-olds are required to sit with their arms folded in silence as the snack is passed around. I notice that the teacher twice reprimands Greg for comments that the snack "looks real yummy!" Since Greg talked out of turn, he is passed over and has to wait for his snack until the kids at the table behind him receive theirs. Greg begins to protest "gimme mine—no fair—gimme," and he grabs at the tray. Teacher Peggy grabs Greg and wipes his runny nose with a look of distaste and takes him to the time-out chair. At this point, Greg is alternately sobbing and yelling "no fair" and is

forced to sit on the chair for fifteen minutes as he hungrily
looks at the others eating. The teacher comes over to tell me
this is part of their "classroom management plan" with Greg,
since "food is what he really cares about."

Here Greg is stripped of his human dignity and reduced to the
mechanistic behavioral training modification schedules reminiscent of
Watson's notorious experiments with Albert and the white rat. This becomes even more problematic when we realize how an early intervention
program, operating on a "deficit/deprivation" model, is found to be
perpetuating such practices toward poor and minority children. While
this incident was certainly the most disturbing, I observed several such
programs using food as a reinforcement. The fact that in several districts
public preschool teachers openly displayed their prejudice toward poor
and minority children and their families is another pointer to the promoting of deficit perceptions of small children in classrooms, which, in itself,
fits well within the larger regulation discourse and practices of discrimination toward the poor. It is assumed *they* are there because of individual
failure—mothers without husbands, families without breadwinners, abusive and neglectful parenting, spongers off welfare, problem children,
future criminals—*not* because of the structurally induced poverty of the
American economic system or a pernicious public policy that directly
constructs such patterned inequalities.

Teachers do not live above their culture, nor do human service
professionals. All of these microcosmic practices in classrooms embody
macrocosmic traces. They also implicate the forms, goals, and organization of teacher-training institutions, which by and large have also failed to
confront the overriding impact of poverty in the lives of young children
and families. Such educational institutions in turn become sites for the
reproduction and dissemination of regulated and leveled lives—and in
the case of poor children, remediated and corrected lives. In both cases
the child is constituted as the inferiorized other—and the more visible
one's otherness status, the more in need of regulation and remediation
one becomes.

These practices of regulation and enforced compliance become particularly disturbing when food is used as a reinforcement with hungry
children, when behavior modification programs abuse the child through
an exploitation of his or her poverty. This example is not an unusual
occurrence; other classroom observations of at-risk children gathered
during 1990 in Michigan are also illustrative of these practices. They
merely mirror the general public attitudes of callous disregard for the
poorest members of our society—from Learnfare programs in Wisconsin

to similar programs proposed in Michigan, where a family's welfare benefits (usually single-mother households) would be cut if any children drop out of school.

These attitudes and sensibilities toward poor children and their families do not escape early childhood educators; we are not immune to the ravages of prejudice and discrimination that have permeated all our educational institutions. Labeling certainly plays its part in constructing pathology out of differences and implicating all those of us who fail to rethink the destructive implications of our ideologies toward women and children in poverty. It is we who need to restructure—both our ways of seeing and our ways of practicing our educative responsibilities.

ANOTHER WAY OF SEEING

In order to change the discourse, Greene (1988) argues that we need "to develop the capacity to surpass the given, to look at things as if they could be otherwise" (p. 3). But in asking how things could be otherwise, we need to look at the walls that barricade and begin to deconstruct the practices and ideologies that constrain and restrain the entitlement of children to a viable future. There are both macro- and microsocial spaces that need to open, a searching for the many roads hitherto not taken; for things could be otherwise in a transformed social and economic infrastructure that nurtures its youngest members rather than destroys their existential possibilities. As early childhood educators we need to become aware of the context and meaning of the lives of children in poverty, destitution, and homelessness. We need to recognize that the lack of entitlement to health care, housing, nutrition, and childcare create stressed and powerless lives; that the problems that are often diagnosed as emotional impairments and learning disabilities are very real reactions to concrete conditions of want. As Maslow pointed out years ago in his hierarchy of needs, at the base of the pyramid lie physiological and safety needs; belonging, self-esteem, and self-actualization emerge when these basic needs are met. At the present time fully 25 percent of our youngest children have not experienced those two fundamental levels. Hence stressed and desperate households, living on the edges of contingency, experience enormous powerlessness. Young children, too, experience the powerlessness of poverty One of the most important shifts that need to occur in our early childhood programs is a move away from regulation and compliance toward an existential perspective that promotes autonomy and empowerment.

Education for compliance merely mirrors the endless subjugation that poor people are subjected to at the hands of innumerable public assistance bureaucracies. We also need to begin looking at what the child can do and likes to do, rather than what the child cannot do. The standardized assessment and screening instruments that are still in use in early childhood and early elementary settings create deficiency constructs because the child's prior knowledge is not valued for what it is, but for what it should be. Shaping and molding the child to fit monocultural institutional norms does not promote autonomy or build on the child's strengths.

In studying the emerging reports on homeless children, particularly the study done by Bank Street College of Education (Molnar, 1988), we see how conventional assessments do not assess the child's strengths and often miscue researchers. For example, homeless children do not readily respond to play invitations, and observers report how such children will frequently choose food over play; they quote the responses of 4- and 5-year-olds, who, when asked what they liked most about a summer preschool, enthusiastically responded "snack" and "rest" (p. 79). Such children's strengths are often masked by behaviors that are considered inappropriate in classroom settings. Children who pace and run constantly are not necessarily hyperactive; they are cooped up living in one room in cramped and often dirty conditions and need space to move. Such children often need far more flexible programs that adapt to their needs for movement, for food, and for rest and where the curriculum and the teachers are tuned to the child's lived world.

Both space and time structures need to shift. Children who live without possessions and private spaces very often need both an object and a private hidden space where they can be alone. I have observed homeless and destitute children investing enormous concentration and energy in creating their own private bounded spaces: tents, forts, block structures. Such activities preoccupy all preschoolers, but for children without houses and rooms to call their own, these objects assume a greater significance and are loaded with meanings that need to be respected, not violated because of the exigencies of a time schedule.

While children whose worlds have been destabilized need the stability and security of routines, these routines need to be tuned to the child, not the management agendas of teachers. Furthermore, educators need to focus on creating autonomy-promoting landscapes where children's divergent choices and initiatives are respected and their voices listened to. As Tim, a third-grader, says, "They think 'cos I haven't got no home that I haven't got nothing inside me—they won't play with me, they won't even be buddies when we go on trips and no kids will be my friend."

As educators, we can hear Tim and help other children hear him, too; but that requires restructuring our classrooms so that no child is marginalized by lack of concern or lack of sensitive intervention. Confronting marginalization is not easy in the classroom; but our task as educators is also to create the possibility of a future for all children. The classroom is the first outside world that the child inhabits; and a landscape that promotes autonomy and promise can shift the powerlessness of poverty. It is possible to begin to address, on a microscale, the small local worlds of our childrens' dailyness, so that we may develop ways of seeing that promote a vision of children as competent rather than impaired and deficient, as resilient and often remarkable survivors of the social pathology of poverty.

In this chapter I have argued that a deconstructed theory of early childhood needs to move beyond the class- and gender-based ideologies of attachment, the family, and motherhood to a critical and dialectical understanding of development in poverty. This implies a restructuring of our own sensibilities, a move away from a blaming-the-victim orientation to a promotion of a vision of entitlement that supports mothers and their children in maintaining viable lives of dignity and autonomy. We need to develop ways of viewing poverty not as a self-created condition of deficiency but as an unjust social and economic policy that can be eradicated and should not be accorded the status of a natural law. Poverty is no child's entitlement; and no child should be disenfranchised and disempowered by this injustice. A language of existential entitlement needs to be constructed as part of a reconceptualized theory and practice of early childhood. Early childhood educators have a critical front-line role to play in forging a new and concrete praxis, for

> We may have reached a moment in our history when teaching and learning, if they are to happen meaningfully, must happen on the verge. Confronting a void, confronting nothingness, we may be able to empower the young to create and recreate a common world—and in cherishing it, in renewing it, discover what it signifies to be free. (Greene, 1988, p. 23)

NOTES

Acknowledgments. I wish to thank my research assistant, Joshua Cohen, for his able assistance in the preparation of this manuscript; Ton Beekman for his challenging comments and scholarly critique, particularly on the historical and ideology sections; and Jerry Weiser for his insightful review of the manuscript and the invaluable dialogue about the ideas developed in this chapter.

1. ADD: Attention deficit disorder; EI: Emotionally impaired; LD: Learning disabled.

2. All names used here are fictitious, and all identifying characteristics have been changed to protect the identity of my informants.

REFERENCES

Ainsworth, M., & Bell, S. (1970). Attachment, exploration and separation: Illustrated by the behavior of one-year olds in a strange situation. *Child Development, 41,* 49–67.

Ariès, P. (1962). *Centuries of Childhood.* New York: Vintage.

Badinter, E. (1981). *The myth of motherhood: An historical view of the maternal instinct.* London: Souvenir.

Barrett Browning, E. (1900). The cry of the children. In H. W. Preston (Ed.), *The comeplete poetical works of Mrs. Browning* (pp. 126–127). Boston: Houghton Miflin.

Belsky, J. (1986). Infant day care: A cause for concern? *Zero to Three, 6,* 1–7.

Belsky, J., & Rovine, M. J. (1988). Nonmaternal care in the first year of life and the security of infant-care attachment. *Child Development, 59,* 157–167.

Bowlby, J. (1951). *Maternal care and mental health.* Geneva: World Health Organization.

Bowlby, J. (1969). *Attachment and loss* (Vol. 1). London: Hogarth.

Bredekamp, S. (Ed.). (1987). *Developmentally appropriate practices in early childhood programs serving children from birth through age 8.* Washington, DC: National Association for the Education of Young Children.

Children's Defense Fund. (1991). *The state of America's children, 1991.* Washington, DC: Author.

Chodorow, N. (1978). *The reproduction of mothering.* Berkeley: University of California Press.

Crewdson, J. (1988). *By silence betrayed: Sexual abuse of children in America.* Boston: Little, Brown.

DeMause, L. (Ed.). (1974). *The history of childhood.* New York: Psychohistory Press.

Demos, J. (1970). *A little commonwealth: Family life in a Plymouth colony.* New York: Oxford University Press.

Demos, J. (1986). *Past present, and personal.* New York: Oxford University Press.

Deutsch, H. (1944). *The psychology of women: A psychoanalytic interpretation.* New York: Grune & Stratton.

Dickens, C. (1867/1975). *Oliver Twist.* New York: Vintage.

Erikson, E. (1950). *Childhood and society.* New York: Norton.

Foucault, M. (1977). *Discipline and punish: The birth of the prison*. New York: Pantheon.

Freud, A. (1974). *Infants without families*. London: Hogarth. (Original work published 1945)

Freud, S. (1935). *A general introduction to psychoanalysis*. New York: Livewright. (Original work published 1916)

Froebel, F. (1900). *Education of man*. New York: D. Appleton and Company. (Original work published 1887)

Fuchs, R. (1984). *Abandoned children*. Albany: State University of New York Press.

Greene, M. (1988). *The dialectic of freedom*. New York: Teachers College Press.

Greven, P. (1991). *Spare the child*. New York: Knopf.

Hewlett, S. (1987). *A lesser life*. New York: Warner.

Junne, G. H. (1988). *The GED college graduate: A profile of Detroit-area community college graduates who were high school dropouts*. Unpublished doctoral dissertation, University of Michigan, Ann Arbor.

Kessler-Harris, A. (1982). *Out to work: A history of wage earning women in the United States*. New York: Oxford University Press.

Laslett, P. (1965). *The world we have lost*. New York: Scribner.

Lyotard, J. F. (1989). *The Postmodern condition: A report on knowledge*. Minneapolis University of Minnesota Press.

Masson, J. M. (1984). *The assault on truth*. New York: Farrar, Strauss & Giroux.

Miller, A. (1983). *For your own good*. New York: Farrar, Strauss & Giroux.

Mitterauer, M., & Sieder, R. (1982). *The European family*. Chicago: University of Chicago Press.

Molnar, J. (1988). *Home is where the heart is: The crisis of homeless children and families in New York City*. New York: Bank Street College of Education.

Morrison, T. (1972). *The bluest eye*. New York: Pocket Books.

Newson, E., & Newson, J. (1974). Cultural aspects of childrearing in the English-speaking world. In M. Richards (Ed.), *The integration of a child into a social world*. London: Cambridge University Press.

Pestalozzi, J. (1898). *How Gertrude teaches her children*. New York: Bardeen. (Original work published 1801)

Plumb, J. H. (1972). *In the light of history*. London: Penguin.

Pollock, L. (1983). *Forgotten children*. Cambridge, England: Cambridge University Press.

Rousseau, J. J. (1964). *Emile*. New York: Barrons. (Original work published 1762)

Rutschky, K. (1977). *Schwarze Padagogik*. Frankfurt: Ullstein.

Spitz, R. (1945). *Hospitalism: An inquiry into the genesis of psychiatric conditions in early childhood*. International Universities Press.

Wesley, J. (1872). *Works*. London: Wesleyan Conference Office.

Wolff, L. (1988). *Postcards from the end of the World: Child abuse in Freud's Vienna*. New York. Atheneum.

CHAPTER 8

The Emergent Curriculum
Contextualizing a Feminist Perspective

Janice A. Jipson

Monday, 4:00 P.M. I sit at my computer, crafting the sentences that will weave the strands of this paper together—
looking at the clear sky through the pine trees in the loft window—thinking—it is probably the last nice day of the year—
the rainy season will probably start before I get back—poor
me. The phone rings. My secretary. I don't have to pick up
Emmie at the lake at 6:00; she got a ride. I plunge back into
my project, energized by the reprieve from maternal duty. I
don't think about how I'll now miss the chance to drive
through the country on the last nice day of the year. (From
my journal)

Women and children in the workplace—not usually, in my experience. Children or the workplace competing for mom, more likely. I
reflect on the irony of the distance achieved as I sit at my computer,
writing about teaching a class on women and children in the workplace—
my children safely in the workplace of someone else. Several months
later I recorded:

I sit on hotel room bed in a distant city. Last night I had
called home. My 4-year-old Erik said, "Mommy, I need you
to come home now." I explain that I have to "deliver a
paper." What does that mean when you're 4? Erik delivers
papers to me all the time. Little scraps with pictures and notes
saying, "Stop working now" or "Please come down. I don't
want you to stay up there this late."

How can I convey this absurdity—my talking about trying to create
nurturing, connected environments for my students just as the day-care
teacher is right now trying to do for my son. My dad asks, "Aren't you

149

taking Erik to Ohio with you? How can you leave him at home?" How can I bring him here?—this is a workplace for grownups, not kids. I begin with this question: How can I bring my experience as woman, with workplace and child, to my class and to you?

The writing shared here is part of my ongoing reflection on my experiences and those of my students as teachers and learners working to create responsive classroom contexts. The course chosen for this study was a graduate seminar, *Issues in Early Childhood Education: Women and Children in the Workplace*, which was developed through a grant from the Center for the Study of Women in Society at the University of Oregon and offered during the spring term of 1989. This chapter portrays the continually emerging curriculum as it responded to the growing power and involvement of the participants. It also shares the stories of the participants as we live as mothers, with children, in the workplace.

The seminar had an agenda. I wanted to provide my students with opportunities to explore contemporary social issues surrounding women and children and to focus on their experiences as they related to changing patterns in the involvement of women in work outside the home, the increased use of day-care for infants and young children, and the exploitation of women both as the consumers and providers of childcare. I wanted them to connect with one another and with me around our shared experiences as mothers and teachers.

A dynamic curriculum emerged through our participation as seminar members in the continual reexamination and reconstruction of personal power, temporal and positional space, and interpersonal relationships, both within the context of the seminar and in a consideration of issues related to the roles of women and children. These issues soon focused on questions concerning the role of women and children in European-American society and on our personal roles as caregivers. From its original objective of examining the changing roles of women and children in the workplace, the seminar evolved to a consideration of our personal experiences as women and children.

The study reported here actually emerged as I planned the seminar and planned how I would teach the course from a feminist perspective. I saw the highly personal nature of the topic as presenting an ideal opportunity to explore the creation of an interactive and collegial college classroom environment. I also saw the seminar as providing an opportunity for participants to examine the meaning of these issues in terms of both their work and their personal lives. As early childhood educators we would, I hoped, identify our personal roles in perpetuating the inequalities that exist for women and children in our culture. Finally, I saw the seminar as an opportunity to enact a methodology based upon relational and connected forms of knowing.

Feminist conceptions of knowing and teaching have emerged over the past decade to offer educators alternatives to traditional models and theories (Gilligan, 1982; Grumet, 1988; Ruddick, 1989). These models of pedagogy have been very validating to me as I struggled to affirm my own teaching. Shrewsbury (1987) discusses what education might become if teachers and students were to "integrate the skills of critical thinking with respect for and ability to work with others" and begin to think in ways that "enhance the integrity and wholeness of the person and the person's connections with others" (p. 7). Belenky, Clinchy, Goldberger, and Tarule (1986) have proposed a model, based on a maternal metaphor, that they call "connected teaching." Proudfoot (1989) has developed a "relational education" model that also addresses many of these concerns from a multicultural perspective.

Relational education focuses on the relationships that exist between teachers and students in classrooms. It emphasizes nurturing relationships based upon commitment and caring and affirms the interconnectedness of people, ideas, and experiences. In my exploration of relational education, I reflected on my role as a teacher-educator in developing integrated curricula and a responsive classroom and in encouraging multiple ways of knowing. I decided to plan the seminar based upon an emergent curriculum, one which I believed would validate the relationships between participants through their active involvement in its creation. I determined that the methodology of teaching the seminar would emerge in connection with the content that I had planned. I also decided to use the seminar as an opportunity to study my own teaching.

Du Bois (1983) has recommended that research methodology be informed by and reveal the perceptions that actually derive from women's experience, grounded in their own classrooms. By situating this study in the seminar, I hoped to explore how a relational education model might be enacted. By using student and teacher journal writing as the primary data source, I hoped also to examine the role of personal narrative in the research process.

THE PROCESS

The curriculum for this seminar emerged through the interests of and collaboration among seminar members. As part of the process of planning the seminar, I created the following set of topics and readings to provide an initial context for further construction of the curriculum:

The Changing Roles of Women, Mothers, and Children
The Valuing of Women and Children in European-American Societies
The Disappearance of Childhood
The Feminization of Poverty
The Institutionalization of Childcare
Cultural Transmission and Childcare
Social Policy and Change

From this list of topics, I determined, the students would select those having the most significance to them. I felt the choice of topics would provoke dialogue, debate, reflections, and change. The nature of the topics themselves and the informal seminar discussion format I had anticipated would, I hoped, provide a personal, challenging, and highly meaningful context for the participants, most of whom were teachers and mothers who continued to go to school or work as they raised their children. My personal investment in these issues would also be reflected in my teaching, I believed.

Eighteen graduate students registered for the seminar. In addition to seven students earning master's degrees in early childhood education, the topic also attracted master's and doctoral students from elementary and secondary education, public policy, and music. Among the participants were fifteen women—nearly all mothers, stepmothers, or grandmothers and ranging in age from about 22 to 63 years—and three men, who were 40 to 50 years of age. Most participants had had day-care or public school teaching experience, and several had been longtime teachers and administrators in the public schools. The seminar was culturally diverse, including international students from Taiwan, Peru, and Canada as well as Native American, European-American, and Japanese-American students.

Students were asked to engage in dialogue journal writing and, thus, share their reflections on the topics as well as to respond to the ongoing experiences within the seminar. In addition, the journals provided an opportunity for personal reactions to the readings and classroom activities and for relating the readings to personal experiences as parents, children, and teachers. Participants shared their journals with me after class, shared them with one another, or both.

Group presentations on one of the central issues identified for the seminar were also required. Each group was to review the readings for one seminar session, meeting outside of class and planning and facilitating activities and discussion for that session. Each student was also required to write a paper analyzing the ideas and information discussed during his or her small-group presentation, including a personal position statement on one central theme related to the chosen topic.

NARRATIVES AND REFLECTIONS

At the first seminar meeting, I presented my hopes for the course and the expectations I had of the students. I initiated a discussion of the syllabus, asking students to choose which topics were of greatest interest to them for their small-group work. Five topics were selected, and I agreed to be responsible for including the others. I presented an introduction to the first topic, the changing roles of women and children during the past century. I asked participants to reflect on the stories they had heard from their mothers and grandmothers as well as on their own experiences. We discussed what each of our childhoods had been like. I tried to share my experiences as a mother and a teacher and my apprehension about beginning a new class.

Finally, I asked them to form small groups to plan for individual sessions. The scurry to sign up for groups was difficult for me. Several students who had been together in previous classes formed a group and immediately began to discuss what they wanted to do. They "knew" what I expected and had done cooperative learning activities before. The others approached one another. I watched several women assume a caretaking responsibility for some of the international students in the seminar and tried to refrain from taking an active role as teacher.

The second seminar session focused on the valuing of women and children in European-American society. We discussed assigned readings from Christopher Lasch (1979), Shulamith Firestone (1970), and David Elkind (1981). We began the journals. Participants once again shared personal stories about their childhoods and their current lives as teachers and parents. The seminar so far had been fairly traditional, with me, as teacher, directing the discussion and urging them to read and write in their journals.

Beginning with the third week, group projects were presented to the class. Several student journal entries are presented below for each session to illustrate what happened during the session and to provide insight into the actual experiences of the students in the group projects. Fictitious names have been assigned to all students quoted in the following excerpts.

Group 1: The Roles of Women

The first group included advanced-level graduate students, many of whom had participated in other, similar courses. The group began by asking the other seminar participants to produce collages from popular magazines and present them to the larger group and then to discuss the issues raised. This activity was initially met with resistance and irritation from many of the students, who either were unsure of what to do or who questioned the purpose of the activity. Students concluded the class by writing in their journals about how they had felt about the activity. Some of their responses are reported below.

Jane, a middle-aged mother of three returning to school after many years of clerical work, described the small-group experience and the importance of the makeup of the group. She recalled a participant expressing anger, not at the readings but at what was evoked within her. Jane felt the woman's honesty allowed the others to be open and exchange personal growth. She portrayed her group as "limited in attitudes, academic background, and language." The group's decoupage analysis of media images of women was characterized as "meager and embarrassing." She suggested that the "education students" had an advantage over those majoring in other fields and that some class members needed help in understanding what to do.

Bill, an elementary school principal in his fifties who had been "almost required" to take this class by his advisor, reacted:

> As this was my first experience with a learning activity of this type, and not being an art person, I was a little reluctant to be involved in this project. Since magazines were our primary source for our collage, it limited the eventual outcome of the project. Magazines are in general for middle- or upper-class audiences. The poor have little time or finances to be able to afford these items. . . . They put an emotional, as well as financial, burden on people who believe that these magazines portray how people should live.

Other students also discussed how their images were limited by the contents of the magazines. They were frustrated by being unable to include more "positive" and "independent" roles for women, which they believed were underrepresented in the magazines and newspapers provided. They expressed much dismay at the stereotypic images that they seemed to be noticing for the first time. The class, I thought to myself, was off to a good beginning.

Group 2: The Roles of Mothers

The next week we analyzed the roles of mothers, using a brainstorming strategy and cooperative learning activities. The presenting group seemed to sense the discomfort of some participants during the past week and presented a more teacher-directed seminar based on discussion of the readings. Again, some students struggled to participate fully and understand what was "meant" by the activity. Their journal entries at the end of class revealed their reactions to the experiences. In writing in her journal about her small-group project, Betty said:

We had some difficulty getting started. We had not previously worked together and did not know each other's background and culture. I felt some members did not feel supported in a secure domain when examining the issues. The safe space occurs when people have had the time and activities that facilitate this process.

Net, an experienced teacher in her fifties and one of the planners of the second group session, wrote:

Small groups seem to be very productive. Some people feel more comfortable sharing, and it lowers the level of concern. My group was very interesting because of personal dynamics . . . and was very verbal. Betty, however, had a different experience . . . and felt she had to prompt and lead her group.

Sue also discussed her reactions to the evening in her journal: "I very much enjoy the small group personal sharing of viewpoints. It is always a wonderful learning experience to find out more about myself as I listen to people speak about themselves."

At first I thought this week had not gone as well as the previous week. But, as I reflected on the evening, I decided that it was good that we were beginning to become uncomfortable and were realizing how serious and personal the issues were. Although most of the participants in the seminar were mothers, the discussion had forced the men and women who had no children to look at their relationships with women who were mothers.

Group 3: The Feminization of Poverty

A noticeable change in the tone of the seminar occurred the next week as students became more comfortable with each other. Perhaps it was the reading about homeless families or perhaps it was because the class was feeling more comfortable after their struggle to define themselves in terms of the concepts of woman and mother.

The third group examined women and poverty as portrayed through movies and through a presentation by several Head Start families. The movie portraits ranged from Scarlett O'Hara saying, "I'm never going to be hungry again," in *Gone with the Wind*, to a documentary featuring Mother Theresa and her family of humanity. The final film clip of young girls on the streets of Portland was a jarring reminder of the poverty of our time.

Betty responded to the presentation of film clips in her journal: "The group projected . . . not only a European-American perspective but also a minority perspective. I saw central women figures take charge of their families' plight by giving it direction either emotionally or financially."

Tom, a single elementary school teacher, also wrote about the women in his journal: "The film clips were . . . mind-boggling. . . . It's amazing how men and women respond differently to poverty: the strength and powerlessness of the females, the power and weakness of the males."

Several students commented on the visit by the Head Start parents. Dawn, an elementary teacher, reflected in her journal on the size of the room and inability of the group to create a sense of intimacy. "The physical setting was a problem during the visit with the Head Start women. However, it felt like an atmosphere in which personal safety through distance was important."

Anna also wrote of her feelings about the guest speakers. "When I walked into class, I saw three strangers, women, who seemed 'out of place,' looking haggard . . . and based on looks and clothes . . . poor." She addressed her reluctance to analyze once again the sources of inequality in women's lives.

Jane expressed a more ideological reaction in her journal as she inquired about the political dimensions of poverty and then went on to write of her need to work to support her family:

> Why has . . . government consistently devalued and undercut the . . . economic status of women at home? Where is the legitimization of women's "traditional" contribution in the bureaucratic framework of family, parental computations, and economic remunerations? And my work. . . . has placed a great deal more marital stress on us. . . . One of us is usually with the children, but we're rarely together alone.

I, like the students, was taken up with the seriousness of the issues. Each class seemed to be emerging with its own focus as we considered the topic of the day. Poverty had been a particularly difficult topic to view from the perspective of the mother. Many of the students had worked with poor children and recalled having tended to blame the parents for the conditions of the children's lives. The discussion based on social inequity seemed to remind them that the "cause" was not so clear-cut.

Group 4: The Institution of Childcare

The fourth group looked at issues related to childcare. One participant led a large-group discussion of an excerpt from Oprah Winfrey's television talk show on inadequate and hazardous day-care. Two others presented a puppet show suggesting that we were "playing" with children's lives in deciding about childcare placement. A fourth shared a multimedia presentation that he had put together, comparing the institution of day-care to a prison. Four parents who were also childcare professionals joined us as guests and discussed their personal "solutions" to the childcare dilemma. Our guest presented slides of parents and children in Third World countries. Once again, the impact of the seminar was intense.

Jeff, a single male teacher who created the multimedia presentation on prisons, reflected in his journal on the institution of day-care and the ambivalence parents experience in leaving their children:

> My mind flashed. Stealing time. That could be the crime that our children being sent off to childcare had committed. I expected that some of my audience would find the comparison inappropriate, since they felt they were sending their child to such places because they had to work, they had no choice.

Jeff also wrote about how his idea of comparing a childcare facility to a prison was received: "It was a pleasant, indeed encouraging, feeling that my idea was met with more than just approval but delight . . . that I would undertake such an approach."

Net wrote in her journal:

> Each speaker had very strong convictions about what they saw as important for themselves and their children. I guess I was surprised that Kay [one of the parent guests] did not put her child with her in the same program. I realized how little I know about the world.

Tom also wrote of the impact of day-care on both children and parents:

> Children suffer in situations created by adults. I was moved especially by the slides and by the dilemma posed by our guests, Kay and Beth, regarding their own children and their roles as day-care teachers. I'd like to bring my kids to work, sometimes at least . . . the presentations, ways of knowing continue to be powerful—real life, . . . people, . . . stories. . . . The alternative ways of expression allow for validation.

Anna also reflected on the childcare issues in her journal: "Women are made to feel guilty for putting their kids in day-care centers. Why? Why in the hell aren't men made to feel guilty every morning when they walk out the door?"

When the seminar ended, I wrote in my journal: "This topic has touched many of us in a deep and personal way. Again, the class seemed to reach an awareness of the complexity of the childcare issue, that it was not just about finding quality programs."

Group 5: Social Policy and Change

As if sensing the need to release some of the emotional pressure and look toward the future, the final small group examined social policy and change through the messages of the popular press and music. They concluded their session with information about legislation related to workplace issues and childcare and provided us with the opportunity to "write to a congressperson." A group of teenagers and their babies from the local New Mothers Program also joined us for an hour to talk about their experiences.

Dawn again reflected in her journal on the lack of intimacy in the environment:

> The group from the New Mothers Program was real . . . young women with living, breathing, crawling, squalling, tumbling children—in a class focused on women and children—I loved it. I wanted more of an opportunity to get closer to them.

And Jane ended her journal by writing:

> The cumulative effect of . . . exposure to notions of redistributing wealth, reconstructing . . . societal values . . . [and] structure. . . . What are the strategies one uses for change? Or-

ganizing a parent coalition seems possible. . . . Political advocacy seems the only avenue for effective change.

The vibrant and hopeful attitudes of the young women who had joined us seemed to surprise many members of the class. One student commented, "They seemed to not yet have been beaten down by the culture in which we live."

At the end of the term, participants wrote of the effect that the seminar had on them personally. As relationships between participants developed and as trust grew, the personal experiences of individuals were allowed to emerge, each person responding to the issues of the class in his or her own way. Chen wrote of her 18-month-old daughter she had left in Taiwan with her own parents as she pursued her Ph.D. (In August she brought her visiting baby to see me.) Jane reflected on an international student at her day-care co-op who is concerned that her son will become "Americanized, too soft" and will suffer when he returns to Korea and appears "different" from others in his culture. Jane then wrote of her own sons, who have become "tough" and "survivors" in the same day-care environment.

FINAL CONSIDERATIONS

Several core themes emerged from the journal entries, in addition to those focused around the identified issues of the seminar. Control and relationships were described by several participants as important issues within both the content and the activities of the seminar. They were, one wrote, "two aspects of the same process." Linda spoke of the difficulties of being a single parent for most of her teenagers' lives and the way in which control issues were sorted out through their relationships with one another. Net told of her courageous mother-in-law, raising a family without any of the traditional support systems and providing a model for the rest of the family as to what a woman could do.

The negotiation of position and power within the class, initially seen as privileging the more advanced students, appeared to change as a sense of community developed and participants became involved in cooperative inquiry and planning groups. A valuing of being connected to and caring about one another was apparent. The growing respect they had for one another was evidenced by the seriousness with which they engaged in each discussion and activity. Participants brought their personal lives, interests, and experiences to the class, sharing them with one another and valuing and acknowledging the differing perspectives of the others. By the end of the term, the initial hesitations about talking about oneself had virtually disappeared.

The fifteen women and three men in the seminar struggled to react in their journals to the sometimes angry and insistent reactions some participants had to the issues of gender. Jane described her observation of how she felt men in the class reacted to "feminist rhetoric" as "more walls and less dialogue." She added that both men and women were responsible for perpetuating nonempathetic and exclusive "solutions." She suggested that "we have not yet learned to like ourselves. Mutual respect is an extension of self-respect."

The empowerment of "students" and "teacher" by the process was characterized by a participant as an equalizing of opportunities for participation, regardless of whether one was a "high talker," a "non-native English speaker," or a "grandmother." In examining their personal and collectively constructed beliefs and in sharing them with one another, several European-American participants mentioned a growing sense of cultural understanding between themselves and international students and North American minority students in the class. Consideration of shared issues had allowed them to acknowledge their shared beliefs and experiences.

As the class ended I was left with a feeling of sadness for all of the problems that had gone unanswered, that were unanswerable. The curriculum that had emerged far exceeded my plans and expectations. At the same time, however, I was disappointed in my inability to engage every student in the process of constructing their own learning. The reality of those individuals who see themselves powerlessly sitting at the margins, unable to make the space their own, was distressing; I began to plan yet another course, another chance to explore such issues with everyone's voice represented.

The creation of this teaching and learning community did not end with the last week of the term. Many of the original participants continued to work with me in a summer seminar on Research in Early Childhood Education: Feminist Methodology. Four from the original group continued to meet as a biweekly study group, discussing issues related to teaching and research, such as imposition, the appropriation and ownership of ideas, and relationships. The dialogue continues.

REFERENCES

Belenky, M. F., Clinchy, B. M., Goldberger, N. R., & Tarule, J. M. (1986). *Women's ways of knowing: The development of self, voice and mind*. New York: Basic.

Du Bois, B. (1983). Passionate scholarship: Notes on values, knowing, and method in feminist social science. In G. Bowles & R. Duelli-Klein (Eds.), *Theories of women's studies* (pp. 105–116). Boston: Routledge and Kegan Paul.

Elkind, D. (1981). *The hurried child: Growing up too fast, too soon.* Reading, MA: Addison-Wesley.

Firestone, S. (1970). *The dialectic of sex: The case for feminist revolution.* New York: Bantam.

Gilligan, C. (1982). *In a different voice: Psychological theory and women's development.* Cambridge, MA: Harvard University Press.

Grumet, M. (1988). *Bitter milk: Women and teaching.* Amherst: University of Massachusetts Press.

Lasch, C. (1979). *The culture of narcissism: American life in an age of diminishing expectations.* New York: Warner.

Proudfoot, R. (1989). *Relational education.* Unpublished manuscript.

Ruddick, S. (1989). *Maternal thinking: Toward a politics of peace.* Boston: Beacon.

Shrewsbury, C. (1987). What is feminist pedagogy? *Women's Studies Quarterly, 15*(3 & 4), 6–14.

PART III

ISSUES OF CULTURAL AND LINGUISTIC PLURALISM

The chapters in this section place issues of culture, language, race, ethnicity, and class in the foreground of a reconceptualization of the early childhood curriculum. Authors raise wide-ranging issues through stories, narratives, policy implications, and possibilities for early Afrocentric education.

In Chapter 9 Mary Louise Gomez tells of the silenced stories of children and adults from diverse cultural, linguistic, and economic backgrounds. She explores the outcomes of such silences and the effects of differentiated reading and writing curricula on children's learning and school achievement. Gomez draws from multiple layers of research and experience to suggest a multicultural, social reconstructionist framework in which "teachers can work to break silences." She also offers a vision and related guidelines for early childhood teachers, who, in partnership with their students, can "build new stories of classroom life." Gomez creates a multi-faceted vision of the future of early childhood curriculum: a future in which teachers and students construct responsive relationships and learn from each other.

In Chapter 10 Lourdes Diaz Soto and Jocelyn Smrekar present important historical, political, and conceptual background information on bilingual early childhood education issues, as well as the stories of Latino and Native American children and families. This chapter serves as a bridge between a broader reconceptualization of the early childhood curriculum and the specific needs, as well as strengths and contributions, of young native speakers and their families. The proliferation of English-only immersion programs for young native speakers is critiqued by Soto and Smrekar as problematic on several fronts.

Chapter 11 by Janice Hale provides an overview of the Visions for Children (Afrocentric) early childhood program, including its formal curriculum and a number of related critical issues in the education of young African-American children. This chapter also presents data from the Phase Three evaluation on this unique program. Like Lisa Delpit

(1988), Jawanza Kunjufa (1984, 1987), Asa Hilliard (1990), Molefi Asante (1987, 1988), and other advocates of Afrocentric education, Janice Hale addresses the cultural background, learning styles, and particular needs of young African-American children. Hale also addresses the need for such bicultural children to learn the "codes of power" (Delpit, 1988) in order to be academically successful in dominant-culture schools and other institutions. Thus, this chapter includes test score data and emphasizes the longer-term outcomes of a culturecentric, pre-academic early childhood program and curriculum. In doing so, Janice Hale offers an important reconceptualization of the early childhood curriculum as one which should be quite consciously adapted to the specific cultural backgrounds, traditions, and values of the learners—in this case, young African-American children, in order to "succeed." The importance of cultural relevance and identity, self esteem, and academic achievement are emphasized throughout this chapter.

REFERENCES

Asante, M. (1987). *The Afrocentric idea*. Philadelphia: Temple University Press.

Asante, M. (1988). *Afrocentricity*. Trenton, NJ: Africa World Press.

Delpit, L. D. (1988). The silenced dialogue: Power and pedagogy in educating other people's children. *Harvard Education Review, 58*, 280–298.

Hilliard, A. G., Payton-Stewart, L., & Williams, L. O. (Eds.). (1990). *Infusion of African and African American content in the school curriculum*. Morristown, NJ: Aaron Press.

Kunjufa, J. (1984). *Developing positive self-image and discipline in black children*. Chicago: African-American Images.

Kunjufa, J. (1987). *Lessons from history: A celebration in blackness*. Chicago: African-American Images.

CHAPTER 9

Breaking Silences
Building New Stories of Classroom Life Through Teacher Transformation

Mary Louise Gomez

My intentions in the pages that follow are fourfold: (1) to tell of the silenced stories that characterize the experiences of so many persons disparate in race, class, gender, and language background in the United States; (2) to explore the outcomes of such silences on diverse pupils' learning and achievement in school; (3) to suggest a multicultural, social reconstructionist framework in which teachers can work to break silences; and (4) to offer guidelines for the development of teaching practices with which early childhood teachers can, as partners with their students, build new stories of classroom life. I suggest that such story-making is one means for monocultural teachers of writing—from the earliest years of schooling on through the grades—to become multicultural teachers of their diverse student populations. Together, listening to one another's stories, I believe teachers and students can construct responsive relationships that can open the insights of each to the other. Further, these partnerships can help students develop the skills necessary to effectively share their ideas in writing with others and to fashion that content in authentic and vivid ways.

Among the vignettes of teaching I share in this chapter are those of intermediate grade elementary teachers who have confronted the challenges of teaching diverse learners and, in so doing, have confronted their own preconceptions and misconceptions regarding these children's abilities to learn and to achieve. While some might suggest that using the stories of fifth- and sixth-grade teachers to make these points has little application to teachers of younger children, I argue that the rethinking of what it means to learn and to teach contravenes traditional boundaries of early childhood, middle school, and secondary teaching. In this text, aimed at *reconceptualizing* early childhood curriculum and instruction, it seems especially timely for teachers of students from varied ages and grades to reconsider what we can learn from and share with one another.

Silence can be a plan rigorously executed.
                                    —Adrienne Rich (1978, p. 16)

In her recent text *Writing a Woman's Life* (1988), Carolyn Heilbrun marks 1970, the year Nancy Milford's biography of Zelda Fitzgerald was published, as the beginning of a new era for women's biographies. In her story of Zelda Fitzgerald's life, Milford demonstrates F. Scott Fitzgerald's presumptive claim to his wife as an artistic property, thus rendering her storyless and ultimately, mad—a woman without a narrative of her own. Likewise, Heilbrun notes 1973 as the watershed year for women's autobiographies. For it was then that May Sarton's second volume of work about her life appeared. Just as Milford had cast new images of the roles the Fitzgeralds had played to one another, Sarton recast *our* visions of *her* life in her second book about it. In this work Sarton deliberately corrects the idealized, romantic version of her life, a version which she had written earlier (1968), a version devoid of the pain and loneliness she had actually experienced. Heilbrun uses Milford's new vision of Zelda—as victim rather than victimizer—and Sarton's recast version of her own days as the point of departure for analyses of the sugar-coated visions of women's lives that were, until so recently, prevalent in biography and autobiography.

Just as Zelda Fitzgerald, May Sarton, and countless other women have experienced the silencing of their stories, so, too, argues Toni Morrison (1989), have the narratives of blacks been appropriated in fiction published in the United States. Morrison points out that black characters and other characters of color have been present in renowned U.S. authors' work since our nation's inception. Yet Morrison posits that people of color have largely been used in these stories to heighten the contrasts between *their* moral, social, and political behavior and the more desirable and admirable behaviors of whites. In these cases, and in those of other persons of diverse cultural, ethnic, and language backgrounds, the right to present one's story has been preempted or denied altogether.

A parallel set of silences exists today in U.S. public schooling, where the color of one's skin and the socioeconomic status of one's family often determine the rights of children to write their own stories. Numerous studies (e.g., Cole & Griffin, 1987; Nystrand & Gamoran, 1988; Taylor & Dorsey-Gaines, 1988) document the differentiation—by color, class, and perceived ability—of the literacy curriculum of U.S. learners. Put simply, the darker one's skin, the poorer one's family, the greater the distance of one's language from "standard American English," and the lower one's perceived ability, the more likely that a child will pass his or her days in school working on decontextualized skills and drills and the less likely he or she will be offered opportunities to read and write meaningful texts. Despite our knowledge of such disparities and our growing understandings of the importance of holistic experiences in reading and creating text for learners' literacy development, children on the margins of the U.S. social and economic order continue to be taught in ways that narrow their opportunities to write their own stories.

Such silencing occurs in ways disparate in method yet homogeneous in their detrimental outcomes. For many Native American peoples forcibly educated in boarding schools across the United States in the nineteenth and twentieth centuries, the silencing came in the form of physical punishment for the use of their native tongues. So, too, Latino students in a Florida middle school I visited in 1989 were forbidden personal conversations in Spanish at school—as their monolingual English teacher explained, "This prevents talk which we [teachers] do not understand." For these angry teenagers with whom I spoke and for thousands of Native American students across this country, communication during school time was limited to the language of those in charge of school, regardless of the facility of the students in communicating in that language. The implicit message is clear: "if you talk like us, you are more like us, and that makes us more comfortable," or, as U.S. Indian Commissioner of Education J. D. C. Atkins said in 1887, "nothing so surely and perfectly stamps upon an individual a national characteristic as language" (quoted in Adams, 1990, p. 169).

For others, such as Jamaican author Michelle Cliff (1988), this silencing did not spring from forbidden tongues but from a learned "split consciousness," ways of thinking about herself that heightened those qualities of mind, body, and voice that matched those of her teachers and diminished those that were uniquely Jamaican. Cliff explains her dilemma in this way:

> My dissertation was produced at the Warburg Institute, University of London, and was responsible for giving me an intellectual belief in myself that I had not had before, at the same time rendering me speechless about who I am. At least I believed in the young woman who wrote the dissertation—still, I wondered who she was and where she had come from. I could speak fluently, but I could not reveal. (p. 57)

Christian Niera (1990), a black Harvard University undergraduate, provides an additional example of silencing that occurs when teachers fail to acknowledge those whom they teach or attend only to those qualities of persons most like their own. Poised between two worlds, that of his family's home in the housing projects and that of the ivy-walled campus, Niera speaks eloquently of becoming a raceless, faceless person in the eyes of his Harvard classmates and faculty. Once admitted to the prestigious institution as a token of his race, he was without a story, a presence with an unacknowledged present or past.

Finally, another sort of silencing occurs when teachers unaccustomed to working with students unlike themselves ascribe negative meanings to their students' unfamiliar behavior. Imani Perry (1990), a black teenager, writes of this phenomena:

> Black and Hispanic students have less of a chance at building strong relationships with any teachers because their appearance and behavior may be considered offensive to the middle-class White teachers. These students show signs of what White teachers, and some teachers of color, consider disrespect, and they do not get the nurturing relationships that develop respect and dedication. They are considered less intelligent, as can be seen in the proportion of Blacks and Hispanics in upper-level classes. There is less of a teacher-student contact with "underachievers" because the teachers have less of a vested interest. (p. 7)

So, Perry believes, a self-perpetuating cycle is developed, a cycle feeding on misperceptions, on the failure to acknowledge, understand, and act on that which students bring to school.

As Denny Taylor and Catherine Dorsey-Gaines (1988) have documented in their longitudinal study of the lives of young, low-income learners of color, such silencing begins as soon as children enter schools. There, children of color, those who are poor, those of non-English language backgrounds, and others labeled "different" struggle to succeed in classrooms where their lives and experiences are represented neither in their reading materials nor in the posters and pictures hung on classroom walls; nor are their experiences and lives taken into account in the activities and assignments they are asked to complete in school. Even as young children, learners living outside that which *has been* mainstream U.S. culture must read, write, and speak about often unfamiliar topics while they conform to foreign behavioral norms.

In 1987, a colleague, B. Robert Tabachnick, and I decided to address such problems countless children face through the development of an alternative teacher education program designed to better prepare elementary teachers to work with diverse student populations. Developed in collaboration with local school district teachers and administrators, the program focuses particularly on preparing preservice elementary teachers (who at the University of Wisconsin–Madison, like their peers around the nation, are primarily middle class and white) to more effectively teach low-income children of color. Since 1987, two cohorts of teachers from our program have graduated from the university. Data we have collected on their development as multicultural teachers lead me to support the arguments of Perry and of Taylor and Dorsey-Gaines: the first response of many teachers and other school personnel to *difference* as it is manifested in children is to ascribe this to some flaw in the children or their family.[1]

Students enrolled in our program conduct three field experiences—two nine-week practica and a twenty-week student teaching experience. The first practicum generally occurs in the second semester of their junior year, when they are studying literacy teaching and learning. The second one occurs the next semester, when they study the teaching and learning of mathematics, science, and social studies. With each field experience, we co-lead, with the school-based supervisors of the field experiences, a weekly seminar.

Early in their field experiences, the preservice teachers enrolled in our program tend to talk in seminars about what they see as the different behaviors of poor children, children of color, and others unlike *them*. They see these behaviors as challenges to their understanding of how students should behave and learn and achieve, and most often they ascribe these differences to the perceived pathology of the children and the children's families and neighborhoods. In these early practica, the prospective teachers fail to see that difference does not need to translate into problems or that *their own behavior and their responses* to children play significant roles in their students' relations with others and in the children's learning and achievement in school. The coursework, conversations, and experiences we provide these new teachers in the weeks that follow are designed specifically to disrupt such notions of deficiency as well as to supply the teachers with instructional strategies that draw together home and school life. Later in this chapter I tell the story of how one of these new teachers began to rethink his practice while enrolled in our program.

Unfamiliarity and discomfort with others, such as that which our new teachers experienced, can breed a terrible silence, one based on the belief that there is something wrong with students that prevents their success and precludes their story-making, effectively denying their learning. Today in the United States, the challenges of breaking silences for disenfranchised learners extends beyond the moral and ethical grounds for such work to the demographic reality of the U.S. population. We live in a society in which people of color, people living in poverty, and those with language backgrounds other than English will soon represent half of our population. Such great numbers of diverse learners and their families cannot be ignored.

> Let's begin by saying we are living through a very dangerous time. . . . We are living in a revolutionary situation, no matter how unpopular that word has become in this country.
>
> —James Baldwin (1988, p. 3)

As we approach a new century, the numbers of learners of color, students living in poverty, and children of language backgrounds other than English are growing (Center for Education Statistics, 1987a, 1987b, 1989; Romero, Mercado, & Vasquez-Faria, 1987). Hodgkinson (1985) estimates that the nonwhite school population will rise from 24 percent of the total in 1976 to 30 to 40 percent in the year 2000. Further, Hodgkinson (1991) estimates that by the year 2010, 50 percent of the total population of the following states (as well as the District of Columbia) will be people of color: California, Florida, Hawaii, Illinois, Louisiana, Maryland, Mississippi, New Jersey, New Mexico, New York, South Carolina, and Texas. Across the United States, the population with a non-English language background is expected to grow to nearly 40 million in the next decade. Many children of color and those of non-English language backgrounds also live in poverty; while 25 percent of their white and English-speaking counterparts live in low-income families, 50 percent of blacks and 40 percent of Latino children are poor (Strong, 1989).

Our schools currently silence and fail these children at alarming rates. For example, one source estimates that of students enrolled as sophomores in public secondary schools in 1980, 12.2 percent of whites had dropped out by the autumn of 1982 while 17 percent of blacks, 18 percent of Latinos, and 29.2 percent of Native Americans had dropped out (Wheelock & Dorman, 1989). These students' failures cannot be attributed solely to their school experiences, since complex cultural and economic webs bind people and their options. Yet schools and teachers must stop acting in silent collusion with other societal forces if we are to cease the tide of failure of diverse learners in our nation.

Changes in teaching practices are required, yet it is unrealistic to think that educational change at any level of schooling will be conducted by teachers whose skin color, social class, or language background matches that of the learners whom they will teach. Currently, the majority of U.S. teachers at every level of schooling, kindergarten through college, are whites with limited knowledge of languages beyond English, and at the preschool and elementary school levels, the majority of teachers are middle-class females (Center for Education Statistics, 1987a, 1987b, 1989; Georgiades, 1988). Changes in classroom practices in U.S. primary education, then, must be carried out by middle-class, white women with little inclination to teach or live near people unlike themselves (American Association of Colleges of Teacher Education, 1987).

Researchers and policy makers (e.g., Carnegie Task Force on Teaching as a Profession, 1986; Goodlad, 1990; Holmes Group, 1986) calling for the reform of teacher education have mandated that we rethink all of the experiences in which we engage such preservice teachers. I concur that changes in preservice teacher education coursework and field experiences are required in order for teachers to be better prepared to teach those unlike themselves. Yet the transformation of both thinking and practice required of teachers—if they are to be effective educators of greater numbers of children—transcends categories of preservice and inservice education. The sort of alterations in perspectives and in practice that are required to create a more equitable, pluralistic school culture are not necessarily achieved through teachers' participation in what we traditionally conceive as the boundaries of a "program of teacher education," nor are such changes likely to derive from implementation of prepackaged curricula. Further, it is unlikely that teachers can develop new ways of thinking and acting for change by working in daily isolation with batches of students. These changes in schooling and in the larger arena of U.S. life mandate both individual and collective analyses and activities not bounded by traditional notions of when one becomes a teacher or how one lives that role.

A call for such transformation derives from a multicultural and social reconstructionist model, a framework mandating that teachers become engaged in:

1. Self-reflection about the role of cultural identity in one's personal development of literacy
2. Examination of the activities of classroom life as situated in a larger sociocultural milieu
3. Collaboration with others for thinking and action

Kenneth Zeichner and B. Robert Tabachnick (1991) argue that the central concern of multicultural, social reconstructionist teaching is "how teachers' actions maintain and/or disrupt the status quo in schooling and in society in general" (p. 8). Further, they believe that key to such teachers' practice is its democratic and emancipatory impulse; close scrutiny of instances of inequality, inequity, and injustice; and working with others for reform. Teachers who draw on a multicultural, social reconstructionist model for teaching are engaged in continual cycles of challenging their beliefs—about what it means to know, to teach, and to learn—as well as cycles of challenging their actions as they play out those beliefs in the classroom. In the following section I explore how cultural identity provides the lenses through which we view others and how, left unexamined, these cultural lenses become blinders, narrowing the possibilities of our understandings of and interactions with people different from ourselves. I argue that multicultural, social reconstructionist teachers must explore their own cultural identity and its role in their successes and failures in teaching children different from themselves.

> The further away the teacher from the child's cultural or temperamental background the more likely it is that the wrong questions will be asked. The child instinctively knows the questions are inappropriate, but soon figures out that *he* must be the one who is inappropriate. Thus, he begins the energy-consuming task of trying to cover up his differences.
> —Vivian Paley (1989, p. *xiv*)

Cultural identity, writes Bernardo Ferdman (1990), is based on an individual's relation to a group's core values, those which are most distinguishing to the group and form the heart of

> those behaviors, beliefs, values, and norms that a person considers to define himself or herself socially as a member of a particular ethnic group—and the values placed on those features in relation to those of other groups. . . . Via his or her cultural identity, the individual answers the question, "What is the appropriate way for someone like me, for someone having my ethnicity, to interpret and to behave in the world?" (p. 194)

In other words, the Spanish of Latino teenagers in Florida, the behaviors of the black students of whom Perry speaks, and the consciousness of a Jamaican noted by Cliff are marks of one's particular cultural identity that teachers must confront and acknowledge in their daily practice. Especially for those who teach writing, questioning the role cultural identity plays in the acquisition of written literacy is imperative, since the purposes for which writing is conducted, the audiences to whom it is aimed, the form and intentions of the assignments given and the evaluation of that work can either honor or deny the lived experiences of those we teach.

For many teachers, confronting the role cultural identity plays in one's school learning and achievement poses dilemmas. As Vivian Paley writes in her book *White Teacher* (1989), to be blind to color or other distinguishing characteristics of one's students has been the "essence of the creed" for many teachers (p. 9). Indeed, a call to those common qualities of our humanity as "sisters" and "brothers" under the skin was a rallying cry of the civil rights movement in the United States. For many U.S. residents, one way to make connections with people unlike themselves has been to think about people of color or people of non-English language backgrounds as "just like me" with the exception of dark skin or difficult-to-understand English.

While these sentiments once may have appeared egalitarian and worthy, such beliefs now appear to support an assimilationist perspective, one that Ferdman (1990) believes "emphasizes the dysfunctionality of differences and the maintenance of the dominant culture, and so demands that subordinate groups acculturate" (p. 183) or, alternately, supports a "melting pot" perspective, one in which a new culture is formed through a hodgepodge of elements from the differing contributing groups. One potential outcome of such thinking about the cultural identity of ourselves in relation to those we teach is the denial of differences.

Unfortunately, such denial often results in frustration and anger on the part of the teacher as the strategies and materials he or she used effectively in the past fail to engage or foster the achievement of the new population of learners in the classroom. For students, such misunderstandings lead to alienation followed by failure as they understand their lack of "fit" with the teacher's expectations. Yet even in the face of such problems of teaching and learning, many teachers persist in ignoring the role cultural identity plays, particularly in literacy learning, in their classrooms.

Roger Schank (1990), an artificial-intelligence researcher, explains our human penchant for the maintenance of such beliefs long past the time they are useful or yield positive outcomes in light of the scripts he believes we unconsciously use to guide our behavior. Schank believes these scripts are "a set of expectations about what will happen next in a well understood situation" (p. 7). These allow us to behave in ways that do not call for thinking or new actions but rather are automatic responses to activities or situations in which we have participated before. Such scripts make our lives easier because we have to think less. Schank explains, "You don't have to figure out every time you enter a restaurant how to convince someone to feed you. All you really have to know is the restaurant script and your part in the script" (p. 7). As teachers, we, too, can use old scripts; these ground the teaching and curriculum choices we make in working with people unlike ourselves; they are choices that no longer work yet cause us to blame our students when they fail to play their proper role in our expectations.

Schank believes that people must work especially hard to attend to the anomalies in their daily experiences; that, rather than dismiss these as rare occasions of script failure, or of the failure of other players—in this case students—to properly conduct themselves, people need more often to call into question the scripts by which they live. How might we as teachers rethink the assumptions, the comfortable scripts, upon which we base our actions? Next, I explore the consequences of taking into account the cultural identity of those whom we teach in U.S. classrooms. I have three stories to tell that appear useful in answering the question of how, as teachers, we might rethink our assumptions about ourselves and others. Each story focuses on a teacher. The first is a story of a preservice teacher, Mark Burns.[2] The second is of a novice teacher, Barbara Lewis, whom I have been studying this year in a project designed to understand the impact of portfolio assessment on elementary teachers' work and on their understandings of students' learning and achievement.[3] The third is my retelling of the story of an experienced teacher, Vivian Paley, as she examines her beliefs and teaching practices with preschool children whose race and ethnicity differ from her own.

> We can learn from the stories of others, but only if what
> we hear relates strongly to something we already knew.
> We can learn from these stories to the extent that they
> have caused us to rethink our own stories. But mostly we
> learn from a reexamination of our own stories.
> —Roger Schank (1990, p. 83)

In the stories that follow, the teachers are working with a number of diverse learners for the first time and examining, through collaboration with others, the scripts that ground their teaching and the outcomes these have on diverse students' lives. These stories are, in part, stories of the transformation of teachers. I begin with Mark Burns, a working-class, white student from rural Wisconsin, who enrolled at the university to complete a degree abandoned a decade earlier because he lacked the money to continue his studies. In the interim years, Mr. Burns had been a field operations manager for a large restaurant chain, where his job was to make ineffective franchises work more efficiently and profitably. In order to turn these failing businesses around, he had learned to look beyond an individual's race, ethnicity, or language background and view the person as a worker in a system that was flawed in its execution. Mr. Burns tried to make everyone's work routines conform to those proven effective in the business. He accomplished this in a pleasant, kind way; and usually, over a period of weeks or sometimes months, he was able to put the franchise back on track and moved on to solve the next problem.

Through these experiences, Mr. Burns developed scripts that told him where routines broke down; he discovered he could retrain or cajole people into following the routines laid out by the company, or that he could make slight modifications to the routines that worked better for the particular needs of a restaurant or its workers. Yet in these endeavors, the roles for the workers and the management, as well as the procedures that the company had laid out as appropriate ways to behave, remained intact. Mr. Burns brought these scripts from the business world to teacher education and drew on them to make sense of the experiences he was having in his teacher education program.

For example, in his first semester in the program, Mr. Burns tutored low-skilled, alienated black middle school boys as part of his noncredit school of education requirements in order to learn about people unlike himself. As we talked in our weekly seminar about the various volunteer and practicum classroom experiences in which the prospective teachers were engaged, it became clear that Mr. Burns viewed his tutees as "colorless." To him, these students were like the restaurant workers with whom he had formerly worked; they needed "retooling" to better learn or adjust their behaviors to those required for the system—in this case, the classroom—in order to succeed. Mr. Burns believed the boys he tutored needed to memorize the parts of speech, learn the procedures for writing a report, and follow more carefully the routines laid out to learn their spelling lists for the week. Once these were incorporated into the student's repertoire of knowledge or skills in English, he believed the student's problem was solved, and a new boy replaced the old at Mr. Burns's after-school tutorial table.

Mr. Burns saw the problems of the restaurant workers and of the black adolescents he tutored as derived from individual's failures to fit into legitimate, existing systems of business and school. Mr. Burns had been a successful restaurant manager; no one had questioned the scripts he had developed for his successful troubleshooting of unprofitable restaurants. Yet his membership in a cohort group of prospective teachers that met weekly to discuss issues related to teaching culturally and socioeconomically diverse learners required just such questioning. Long, intense discussions within and outside of class about the role cultural identity plays in one's success in and response to school culminated one week in Mr. Burns's angrily denouncing the point of view that one's color, race, or language background influenced either his behavior as a teacher or students' opportunities to learn and achieve success in school. He insisted that the children with whom he worked were like *anyone's* children and deserved the *same* help *his* future children would merit.

Mr. Burns failed to acknowledge that the long line of low-skilled, angry, and disillusioned black males placed by their teachers on a list to work with him were representative of any phenomenon but that of individual students who had failed to "tune in" to their teachers. It was not until this one week, in which he confronted his peers and teacher educators (concerning the role of cultural identity in one's learning and achievement in school), a week in which a visiting black scholar also matter-of-factly told the group that a "colorfree" point of view was a racist one, that Mr. Burns *began* to rethink his position. Originally he had believed that these young black males were deficient in skills simply because they had missed the intent of a lesson or had not worked hard enough to acquire the information freely offered to all; over the subsequent months, Mark Burns began to rethink these ideas. While he had denied the role of race and culture in students' learning in our program seminars and in interviews conducted in February and May 1990, in late September of the same year, Mr. Burns told me:

> I have always based my teaching on an individual basis. I said
> this last semester, and I saw this on the videotape I watched
> [of multicultural teacher-educators], that you just can't say,
> and I said this last year, "I don't see color when you go into a
> classroom"—and you have to. Each person *has* a history.

Mr. Burns began to see the roles that schools as institutions play in setting routines and expectations that do not match the home routines, language patterns, and expectations—the cultural identity—of many of the learners whom they are supposed to serve.

The opportunity to engage in honest, lively, ongoing debate—to reexamine the scripts by which he had lived—within a community of persons concerned with teaching diverse learners appears to have been critical for the transformation of Mark Burns's thinking about teaching people unlike himself. So, too, have such ongoing opportunities for talk been important for Barbara Lewis, a novice fifth-grade teacher in whose classroom I have observed for a year. Ms. Lewis completed a master's degree with teacher certification at another midwestern university last year and moved to Madison, Wisconsin, so that her spouse could also pursue graduate work in his field. Barbara Lewis is white, 29 years old, and earned her bachelor's degree in English some years ago.

Like Mark Burns, Ms. Lewis is from a working-class family and experienced financial burdens as she paid her own way through college. I met Barbara Lewis in her second month of full-time teaching when she agreed to allow me to observe her classroom as she used portfolios to teach reading and writing. As my weeks of observation passed, it became clear that she was a gifted teacher of the subject. Having learned about a process approach to teaching writing during her master's degree program, Ms. Lewis implemented a writing workshop in her fifth-grade class of diverse learners.[4] This group included four black children, one of whom, Simon, had recently been homeless; two Hmong children of limited English proficiency whose families had recently emigrated to the United States from Southeast Asia; and many students who lived with a single parent or who traveled during the week between two divorced parents living within a few blocks of each other. Over half of Ms. Lewis's children lived in poverty.

The scripts that Ms. Lewis used to guide her teaching of this class were informed by both the theories she had learned in her teacher-education courses and by her prior experiences as a child growing up in circumstances similar to those in which her students now lived. In a fall interview, Ms. Lewis explained her expectations that all of her students, regardless of race, ethnicity, language background, or socioeconomic status, could work effectively in the cycles of writing, peer response, editing, and publishing she offered. She gave an example of Crystal, an elfin 11-year-old with masses of teased blonde hair and heavily madeup eyes.

> Lots of teachers might not have high goals for Crystal. She doesn't always come to school, and she isn't working at grade level. But I really think she can be a writer, a good writer. I know her life is hard. She lives alone with her dad and a 16-year-old sister and lots of times if I call, even fairly late at night, he is not home. Maybe he's at work, he has two jobs; I don't know. I do know that if Crystal and I try, she can be a writer. I lived alone with my dad when I was a kid and I know how hard it is. I really have to think up more strategies to help her.

Ms. Lewis's early personal experiences with poverty helped her make connections with the children she taught. Like Crystal, she knew the difficulties of living only with one's father; like Justin, another student, she knew about life as a foster child. Yet, as the weeks passed and we continued to talk about her teaching, Ms. Lewis recognized that she knew little about the experiences and needs others of her students brought to school. She began to question, for example, whether the writing workshop, with its freedom to move about and talk with others, benefited Simon, a black child, and Pao, a Hmong boy, as much as it did Crystal.

Together, we began to track how both boys used the freedom of the workshop to avoid writing. We watched as Simon used the option to work in the adjacent library to move in and out of the classroom from three to ten times in any given hour. While he always carried a pencil and paper, Simon rarely landed anywhere long enough to write more than a few words. Rather, he used the workshop time to dance, twirl, leap, and stroll among his classmates, moving restlessly to rhythms often expressed in drumbeats on desktops or recitations of rap music. Through these activities, Simon avoided confronting his inability to write more than simple sentences.

Ms. Lewis noticed that Pao, too, used the opportunities of the workshop—to talk to peers about writing or to write collaboratively—to *only* tell or talk about stories. We watched as he changed the individuals with whom he worked several times during the winter, moving from collaboration with a group of white boys to partnerships, first with another white boy and then with a black male classmate. By taking advantage of Ms. Lewis's invitation to work with peers, Pao orchestrated activities that precluded his composing in the English language, a language he was still learning to speak as well as write. Ms. Lewis explained:

> I figured my teaching was good for everybody, that the
> workshop I had put together benefits all kids. Little did I
> know! How could I have thought that? I guess before, I
> thought so much about having high expectations for every-
> body, about having a sort of democracy. I have always as-
> sumed that everybody benefited. But, as I watched Simon
> and Pao this winter, I began to understand that the teaching
> that benefited Peter and Jack and Lauren and the others did
> not equally benefit Simon and Pao.

As she closely observed Simon's and Pao's behavior, Ms. Lewis began to see that what she had purposefully developed as equal opportunities to learn were differently benefiting children in her classroom. As one means of providing more equitable instruction, she decided to meet individually with Simon and Pao to set daily goals for class performance. For herself, she set two goals: first, to continue close monitoring of Simon's and Pao's progress and second, to continue exploring the ways in which her teaching enhanced or denied the skills and experiences that all children brought to her classroom. The scripts by which Barbara lived and taught enabled her to see beyond the children's immediate difficulties to their future promise. Therefore she took steps in the winter of her first year of teaching to insure that her future practice would be more equitable for her diverse students.

Just as Ms. Lewis closely examined her teaching over her first year in the classroom, Vivian Paley (1989) also confronted the scripts that had guided her interactions with children a decade ago, when her class first included a number of black children. She had long been a successful teacher of white and Asian children when she began to note the anomalies in her expectations and goals for the learning of black students. For example, Paley noted her need for the black children to behave better than the whites and Asians. Further, she saw the ways in which she generalized about black children's behaviors as representative of their racial group as opposed to her ready acceptance of her white and Asian students' individuality. Paley also realized that the feelings she had about her own alien status as a Jewish child in elementary school did not transfer to her interactions with children who also recognized themselves as outsiders. She writes:

> They [our teachers] insisted we were all just children, which meant we were all Gentile children since that was the only kind of child they thought about or talked about. The more my parents provided me with roots in my own culture, the more I felt my differences from the culture of the school. Failing to be recognized as a Jew, and knowing I was not a Gentile, I did not know what I was at school. (p. 12)

Paley began to see that, although she, too, felt an outsider at school, she reinforced those very feelings of alienation in her black kindergarten students. For example, when a white child told a black one that her skin was the color of chocolate pudding or that she should sit at a "black" chair, Paley felt confused. She responded to what she saw as unkind actions, such as the refusal to sit next to someone black, and pointedly told the white child such behavior was unacceptable. Yet she initially avoided the very mention of color in her classroom, failing to acknowledge one of the fundamental differences that marked the black children in her room.

Increasingly uncomfortable with her actions, Paley began to track the dissonance between her stated ideals and her daily practice. She used a method of journal-type recordkeeping she had begun years earlier to "re-search" her teaching. Through the writing and rereading of her journals, Paley listened more carefully to her own teaching. She became increasingly disturbed at the anomalies in her scripts and began to ask questions of others whom she trusted, a black student teacher and a longtime friend who was a music teacher in her school. They answered her honestly, and Paley used their responses to further test the gaps that existed between her ideals and her practice.

Like Mark Burns and Barbara Lewis, Vivian Paley learned to think about the broader sociocultural context in which she, her classroom, and school were situated. Also like them, she learned to consider children's needs, learning, and achievements as marks of their individuality as well as outcomes related to a shared cultural identity, a set of some common experiences, beliefs, values, and behaviors. The stories of Vivian Paley, Barbara Lewis, and Mark Burns demonstrate both the power of self-reflection about the role of cultural identity in teaching and learning and the power of community in helping teachers question the silences we have constructed in our classrooms, silences that replicate the world outside of school for so many individuals.

> Children need to be able to create public and private text worlds with continual opportunities to use their expressive abilities to generate new meanings and maintain personal and shared interpretations of the social, technical, and aesthetic uses of literacy. It would be hard to dispute that, in most of our schools, few such opportunities exist.
> —Denny Taylor and Catherine Dorsey-Gaines
> (1988, p. 201)

What can teachers of young children learn from the stories of others who are not teaching children of the same age or grade? What do these stories of white teachers' reflections about their work tell about breaking silences and building stories? First, I argue that transforming one's thinking about teaching people unlike oneself in race, class, ethnicity, or language background crosses traditional barriers separating teachers' concerns. Regardless of the age of children one teaches, the subject matter in which we are schooled, our status as novice or expert, or our *own* cultural identity, we benefit from rethinking our practice in relation to "others"—whomever they may be. Second, while only the story of Barbara Lewis shows a teacher whose instruction in story writing changed as a result of her self-reflection and collaboration, all three narratives show how teachers' thinking about their work with children was transformed. Before silences can be broken and new stories of classroom life can be written, the scripts that ground and guide our activities with all children must undergo careful consideration.

Teaching that gives voice to silence requires that as we test our assumptions about learning and learners, we also examine our teaching in light of recent developments in writing theory. Martin Nystrand (1990a) argues, for example, for a conceptual shift away from dichotomous idealist theories of meaning (meaning resides in the reader) and formalist theories of text (meaning resides in the text) toward a social-interactive theory of writing. This model is one that focuses on meaning as a

> social construct negotiated by writer and reader through the medium of text, which uniquely configures their respective purposes. The limits of text meaning are determined not only by objective properties of text and not only by the readers' cognition, but by reciprocity between writers and their readers which binds the writer's intention, the reader's cognition, and properties of text in the enterprise of text meaning. In other words, meaning is between writer and reader. (p. 78)

Nystrand posits that in such a model, text is viewed as the medium of communication that bridges writer and reader purposes and interests and "underscores the quintessential mutuality of written communication" (p. 82).

A social-interactive model of writing places the creation of text in a central role linking the writer and the reader and holds the potential to bridge worlds of home and school for all children. The pedagogical implications of this model challenge predominant practices of teaching writing to diverse learners in the United States today. Generally, these focus on students' deficits and deny the immediate, lived experiences of children through drill in tedious, acontextual exercises on the pieces of language. On the other hand, a social-interactive model of writing, bound to multicultural social reconstructionist visions of teaching, points teachers to classroom activities that focus on the skills, experiences, and interests that diverse learners bring to school. Most important, these point teachers to engaging all students in actual writing for genuine purposes.

Among the pedagogical implications of a social-interactive model of writing are fifteen key factors associated with effective writing instruction as detailed in a text titled *Language Diversity and Writing Instruction* (Farr & Daniels, 1986):

1. Teachers who understand and appreciate the basic linguistic competence that students bring with them to school, and who therefore have positive expectations for students' achievement in writing
2. Regular and substantial practice in writing, aimed at developing fluency
3. The opportunity to write for real, personally significant purposes
4. Experience in writing for a wide range of audiences, both inside and outside school
5. Rich and continuous reading experience, including both published literature of acknowledged merit and the work of peers and instructors
6. Exposure to models of writing in process and writers at work, including both teachers and classmates
7. Instruction in the processes of writing; that is, learning to work at a given task in appropriate phases, including prewriting, drafting, and revising
8. Collaborative activities for students that provide ideas for writing and guidance for revising works in progress
9. One-to-one writing conferences with the teacher
10. Direct instruction in specific strategies and techniques for writing
11. Reduced instruction in grammatical terminology and related drills, with increased use of sentence-combining activities
12. Teaching of writing mechanics and grammar in the context of students' actual compositions, rather than in separate drills and exercises
13. Moderate marking of surface structural errors, focusing on sets of patterns of related errors
14. Flexible and cumulative evaluation of student writing that stresses revision and is sensitive to variations in subject, audience, and purpose
15. Practicing and using writing as a tool in all subjects in the curriculum, not just in English

Although authors Marcia Farr and Harvey Daniels originally suggested these as guides for the teaching of middle and secondary school students of diverse language heritages, they transfer, with modest alteration, to teaching writing to young learners of varied race, ethnic, cultural, and language backgrounds. Integral to these factors is a fundamental belief in the power of shared, written communication between student-writers, all of whom have something to say, and teacher-readers eager to practice what Mary Kitagawa (1989) has called "akapen", the nurturing reading of another's work with a primary goal of understanding the writer's intent.

These practices also respond to recent calls from researchers (e.g., Florio-Ruane & Dunn, 1987; Graves, 1986; Nystrand, 1990a, 1990b) to recognize student-writers as both individuals trying to communicate their intentions and as members of discourse communities with distinct, shared purposes and language. These researchers comment that the relationships of student-writers to their teacher and to their peers influence students' feelings about the meaningfulness of their work, their motivation to write, and the quality of their work.

The writing teacher's role becomes one of "initiating and sustaining appropriate writing activities and arranging for feedback" (Nystrand, 1990b, p. 155), or as Denny Taylor (1991) defines it:

> Our task as educators is to use [our] understandings to support and enhance children's learning opportunities, guiding them in both direct and indirect ways as they develop personal understandings of literacy that are socially constructed and individually situated in the practical accomplishments of their everyday lives. (p. 186)

Implicit in teaching this way is the opportunity for both student-writers and teacher-readers to become transformed in their understandings of one another.

Nurturing teachers of writing assist children in becoming, Lisa Delpit (1988) suggests, "authentic chroniclers of their own experiences" (p. 297). Nurturing teachers of writing assist children in what Christina Baldwin (1977) calls finding one's place; that is, developing a sense of self that takes into account societal expectations for the development of academic literacy skills, but reframes these in the context of what the learner brings from home and community.

One recent example of such nurturing teaching comes from *Literacy con Cariño* (Hayes, Bahruth, & Kessler, 1991), the story of one elementary school teacher who realized that teaching from textbooks failed to provide the educational success required by the children of migrant workers whom he taught. In this book, Robert Bahruth and his colleagues tell how, in his second year of teaching in a poor, rural southern Texas community, he led a class of bilingual fifth-graders who ranged in age from 10 to 16. At the beginning of the year, only one of the children had a reported grade-level reading achievement higher than that of second grade; she read, by standardized measures, at a fourth-grade level. Many of the children were unable to read or write at all—in either Spanish or English.

As one means of linking home and school, Bahruth used dialogue journals with his class; the students wrote—in English and in Spanish—about their interests, fears, and hopes, and he responded with encouragement, support, and information.[5] These were a focal point of his literacy curriculum. Daily the children wrote, and daily he responded. As they did so, their skills in spelling, punctuation, and English grammar grew. As the year went on, they published anthologies of stories about themselves, *Autobiographies of Not Yet Famous Persons*, wrote about trips they took together, and investigated natural and social science phenomena that interested them. Central to Bahruth's curriculum were the children, their lives, and their interests. In this environment, the students flourished.

Their learning and achievement, as documented by both their work products (published books, reports, stories, and poems) and by school-administered standardized tests, increased. Yet the heart of Bahruth's program did not emphasize correct spelling, punctuation, and grammar; rather it highlighted the significance of students' communicating their ideas to others with whom they wished to communicate. In writing for real purposes and genuine audiences, the students' motivation to learn also increased—their collective attendance rates improved from 65 percent in the prior year to 98 percent—as they participated in a community of learners. This story of Robert Bahruth's class is but one of many one could tell where teachers have taken risks and joined their students in exploring and linking what Paulo Freire (Freire & Macedo, 1987) has called "the word and the world." It is a striking story, however, because these were "the children of August," migrant children, students for whom others had abandoned hope of teaching, since their lives and their families matched neither school expectations nor traditional school calendars.

In leading classes of young writers of diverse backgrounds and experiences, teachers like Robert Bahruth make opportunities for themselves, children, and colleagues to listen closely to one another, to hear the ways in which they are different and those in which they are the same. Regardless of the ages, grade levels, or writing skills of their students, they work as partners with them and with their colleagues to acknowledge, treasure, build upon, enhance, and analyze the ways cultural identity creates perspectives on the multiple worlds in which we live. In partnership, listening to and learning from one another, they participate in breaking the literal and metaphorical silences that characterize the experiences of so many people diverse in race, gender, ethnicity, social class, and language background in our country.

In so doing, they provide themselves with greater opportunities to reconsider the scripts by which they have lived and taught, scripts that may no longer work as they teach persons different from themselves.

They provide themselves, their students, and their colleagues with opportunities to be transformed—opportunities to question, to consider anew who we believe we are and who we wish to be, to consider as James Baldwin (1988) suggested that "if I am not what I've been told I am, then it means that you're not what you thought you were either!" (p. 8). They write actual and metaphorical new stories of classroom life, stories with themes of democracy, justice, equity, and fidelity, stories in which many voices are heard and honored.

NOTES

1. The experimental teacher education program I co-direct with my colleague, B. Robert Tabachnick, at the University of Wisconsin–Madison is designed to better prepare prospective elementary school teachers to increase the learning and achievement of low-income children of color. It contains four components unique to the "regular" program of elementary education at the university: (1) the students remain in a cohort group throughout the four-semester professional sequence of courses and field experiences in the program; (2) the students receive heightened attention to the promise and problems of low-income children of color in their courses and in the seminars in which they concurrently enroll with their field experiences; (3) the prospective teachers conduct all field experiences, including twenty weeks of student teaching, in one of two elementary schools in the Madison district (both have a nearly 50 percent enrollment of poor children of color, most of whom are black); and (4) all supervision of the students' field experiences is conducted by one of two "instructional resource teachers" based in the two buildings, experienced Madison teachers who work half-time in the schools as multicultural resource teachers and half-time as supervisors of the cohort of prospective teachers.

2. The names of the teachers, Mark Burns and Barbara Lewis, and the names of all of the children mentioned here are pseudonyms. Data for the section of this paper discussing Mark Burns were collected through five semistructured, audiotaped interviews and multiple observations of Mr. Burns's classroom teaching conducted over the three semesters of the program.

3. After serving as a university representative on the Madison (Wisconsin) Metropolitan School District Portfolio Committee from 1988 to 1991, I approached the district with the idea of observing the implementation of the guidelines for development of elementary students' language arts portfolios, which this committee had developed. In collaboration with my colleagues Marianne Bloch and Beth Graue, and with the assistance of two doctoral students, Janice Schenk and Julie Kailin, we observed eleven elementary teachers in grades 1–5 as they implemented literacy portfolios in their classrooms. Observations were conducted from October through June 1990–91, and interviews with the teachers and their building principals were conducted in the late fall and at the close of the school year. The section

of this chapter concerning Barbara Lewis's work draws on over forty occasions of classroom observation I conducted as a part of this project (each observation lasted from one to two-and-a-half hours; these were conducted approximately twice a week for the school year) and three structured, audiotaped interviews (ranging from one-and-a-half to two hours in length).

4. A writing workshop approach is based on the work of researchers and teachers Nancie Atwell (1987), Lucy Calkins (1986), and Donald Graves (1986). Teachers who use this model lead their classes in recursive cycles of drafting, revising, editing, and publishing.

5. Teachers who conduct written dialogues with their classes respond to their students' writing in various ways: some respond only to the content of their students' writing and do not focus on the mechanics, grammar, or spelling of the work; others respond *primarily* to the content of the students' writing, yet attempt to use in their responses the correct spellings or mechanics or grammar of language with which students have evidenced problems in their work. Many teachers of young children now use written dialogues between themselves and their students to enhance children's literacy learning, yet these do not always take place in journals. Such dialogues are carried out in various ways: on individual pieces of paper where child and teacher write to one another about the student's drawing (L. Pils, personal communication, November 2, 1991); in a notebook where kindergarten students' take turns writing to one another about a stuffed animal and their out-of-school interactions with their families (Durst, 1988); or through written conversations conducted between a kindergarten teacher and his or her children on a writing "bulletin board" (Martinez, Cheyney, McBroom, Hemmeter, & Teale, 1989).

REFERENCES

Adams, D. (1990). Fundamental considerations: The deep meaning of Native American schooling. In N. M. Hidalgo, C. L. McDowell, & E. V. Siddle (Eds.), *Facing racism in education* (pp. 162–188). Cambridge, MA: Harvard College.

American Association of Colleges of Teacher Education. (1987). *Teacher education enrollment survey, fall 1987*. Washington, DC: Author.

Atwell, N. M. (1987). *In the middle*. Upper Montclair, NJ: Boynton/Cook.

Baldwin, C. (1977). *One to one: Self-understanding through journal writing*. New York: M. Evans.

Baldwin, J. (1988). A talk to teachers. In R. Simonson & S. Walker (Eds.), *The Graywolf annual five: Multicultural literacy* (pp. 3–12). Saint Paul, MI: Graywolf Press.

Calkins, L. M. (1986). *The art of teaching writing*. Portsmouth, NH: Heinemann.

Carnegie Task Force on Teaching as a Profession. (1986). *A nation prepared: Teachers for the 21st century*. New York: Carnegie Forum on Education and the Economy.

Center for Education Statistics. (1987a). *The condition of education*. Washington, DC: U.S. Government Printing Office.

Center for Education Statistics. (1987b). *Digest of education statistics.* Washington, DC: U.S. Government Printing Office.

Center for Education Statistics. (1989). *Digest of education statistics.* Washington, DC: U.S. Government Printing Office.

Cliff, M. (1988). A journey into speech. In R. Simonson & S. Walker (Eds.), *The Graywolf annual five: Multicultural literacy* (pp. 57-62). Saint Paul, MI: Graywolf Press.

Cole, M., & Griffin, P. (1987). *Contextual factors in education: Improving science and mathematics education for minorities and women.* Madison: Wisconsin Center for Education Research.

Delpit, L. (1988). The silenced dialogue: Power and pedagogy in educating other people's children. *Harvard Educational Review, 58*(3), 280-298.

Durst, S. S. (1988). Oscar's journal. In T. Newkirk & N. Atwell (Eds.), *Understanding writing: Ways of observing, learning, and teaching* (pp. 23-30). Portsmouth, NH: Heinemann.

Farr, M., & Daniels, H. (1986). *Language diversity and writing instruction.* New York, NY: ERIC Clearinghouse on Urban Education, Institute on Urban and Minority Education, Teachers College, Columbia University; Urbana, IL: ERIC Clearinghouse on Reading and Communication Skills, National Council of Teachers of English.

Ferdman, B. (1990). Literacy and cultural identity. *Harvard Educational Review, 60*(2), 181-204.

Florio-Ruane, S., & Dunn, S. (1987). Teaching writing: Some perennial questions and some possible answers. In V. Richardson-Koehler (Ed.), *Educator's handbook: A research perspective* (pp. 50-83). White Plains, NY: Longman.

Freire, P., & Macedo, D. (1987). *Literacy: Reading the word and the world.* South Hadley, MA: Bergin & Garvey.

Georgiades, W. (1988). A new America for the third millennium. In D. E. Orlosky (Ed.), *Society, schools, and teacher preparation* (pp. 25-30). Washington, DC: ERIC Clearinghouse on Teacher Education.

Goodlad, J. (1990). *Teachers for our nation's schools.* San Francisco: Jossey-Bass.

Graves, D. (1986). *Writing: Teachers and children at work.* Portsmouth, NH: Heinemann.

Hayes, C. W., Bahruth, R., & Kessler, C. (1991). *Literacy con carino.* Portsmouth, NH: Heinemann.

Heilbrun, C. (1988). *Writing a woman's life.* New York: Ballantine.

Hodgkinson, H. L. (1985). *All one system: Demographics of education—kindergarten through graduate school.* Washington, DC: Institute for Educational Leadership.

Hodgkinson, H. L. (1991, April 10). Remarks made on a video teleconference. *Who's missing from the classroom? The need for minority teachers.* Washington, DC: American Association of Colleges of Teacher Education and the ERIC Clearinghouse on Teacher Education.

Holmes Group. (1986). *Tomorrow's teachers: A report from the Holmes Group.* East Lansing, MI: Author.

Kitagawa, M. M. (1989). Letting ourselves be taught. In D. M. Johnson & D. H.

Roen (Eds.), *Richness in writing: Empowering ESL students* (pp. 70-83). White Plains, NY: Longman.

Martinez, M. G., Cheyney, M., McBroom, C., Hemmeter, A., & Teale, W. H. (1989). No-risk kindergarten literacy environments for at-risk children. In J. B. Allen & J. M. Mason (Eds.), *Risk makers, risk takers, risk breakers* (pp. 93-124). Portsmouth, NH: Heinemann.

Milford, N. (1970). *Zelda.* New York: Harper & Row.

Morrison, T. (1989). Unspeakable things unspoken: The Afro-American presence in American literature. *Michigan Quarterly Review, 28*(1), 1-34.

Niera, C. (1990). Building 360. In N. M. Hidalgo, C. L. McDowell, & E. V. Siddle (Eds.), *Facing racism in education* (pp. 9-14). Cambridge, MA: Harvard College.

Nystrand, M. (1990a). A social-interactive model of teaching writing. *Written Communication, 6*(1), 66-85.

Nystrand, M. (1990b). On teaching writing as a verb rather than as a noun: Research on writing for high school teachers. In G. Hawisher & A. Soter (Eds.), *On literacy and its teaching: Issues in English education* (pp. 144-158). Albany: State University of New York Press.

Nystrand, M., & Gamoran, A. (1988). *A study of instruction as discourse.* Madison: National Center for Research on Effective Secondary Schools, University of Wisconsin-Madison.

Paley, V. (1989). *White teacher.* Cambridge, MA: Harvard University Press.

Perry, I. (1990). A black student's reflection on public and private schools. In N. M. Hidalgo, C. L. McDowell, & E. V. Siddle (Eds.), *Facing racism in education* (pp. 4-8). Cambridge, MA: Harvard College.

Rich, A. (1978). Cartographies of silence. *The dream of a common language: Poems 1974-1977* (pp. 16-20). New York: Norton.

Romero, M., Mercado, M., & Vasquez-Faria, J. A. (1987). Students of limited English proficiency. In V. Richardson-Koehler (Ed.), *Educator's handbook: A research perspective* (pp. 348-369). White Plains, NY: Longman.

Sarton, M. (1968). *Plant dreaming deep.* New York: Norton.

Sarton, M. (1973). *Journal of a solitude.* New York: Norton.

Schank, R. C. (1990). *Tell me a story: A new look at real and artificial memory.* New York: Scribner's.

Strong, L. A. (1989). The best kids they have. *Educational Leadership, 46*(5), 2.

Taylor, D. (1991). *Learning denied.* Portsmouth, NH: Heinemann.

Taylor, D., & Dorsey-Gaines, C. (1988). *Growing up literate: Learning from inner-city families.* Portsmouth, NH: Heinemann.

Wheelock, A., & Dorman, G. (1989). *Before it's too late.* Boston: Massachusetts Advocacy Council.

Zeichner, K. M., & Tabachnick, B. R. (1991). Reflections on reflective teaching. In B. R. Tabachnick & K. M. Zeichner (Eds.), *Inquiry-oriented practices in teacher education* (pp. 1-17). London: Falmer.

CHAPTER 10

The Politics of Early
Bilingual Education

Lourdes Diaz Soto
Jocelynn L. Smrekar

Devaluing young children's language and culture is an educational practice raising serious ethical concerns. Current English-immersion practices are neither child-centered nor developmentally appropriate for young learners. What constitutes optimal practices for young native speakers is at the heart of innovative curricular reform. Enhancing and protecting young children's native linguistic and native cultural attributes are the salient features of the "best practice" for young bilingual learners. If the intent is to serve the needs of young learners, families, and society, then the ecological context needs to reflect innovative language policies reflecting a historically democratic and potentially pluralistic society. Educators intent on reconceptualizing early childhood education can be instrumental in pioneering empirically based and developmentally sound programs. The issue of advocacy on behalf of linguistically and culturally diverse young learners will be ongoing and will be met by resistance from assimilationists and English-only advocates. Early childhood educators, researchers, policy makers, and legislators can be assured that their collaborative efforts on behalf of diversity can only enhance the educational benefits and the future of a proud nation.

Well-intentioned educators can impart misinformation to families by encouraging English-only communications. A phrase that we have heard repeatedly from Hispanic families in Pennsylvania is "La missy nos dijo" ("The teacher told us"). Indeed, the advice given by educators to these families, who value and respect professionals, might as well be the law of the land. Interference calling for English-only practices can affect family language use among parents, elders, and children. Consider these examples of "La missy nos dijo" advice imparted to parents of bilingual kindergartners in an urban Pennsylvania setting. The Colon family relates, "The teacher told us that we should speak only English at home;

189

that way Juanito will do better in school. Grandmother tries not to speak to Juanito so that she will not confuse him." In the Colon family the intergenerational lines of communication have been affected by the "La missy nos dijo" advice. The Diaz family reports, "Grisella is going to be left back in kindergarten this year. The teacher said that she cannot make it in first grade. She said, 'I warned you to only speak English to Grisella.'" The Diaz family received advice and a "warning" to speak only English.

Large-scale documentation of how families have been affected is available from the NABE No-Cost Study[1] (Wong Fillmore et al., 1991). It is evident that the intergenerational lines of communication continue to be affected by present policies and practices (Wong Fillmore, 1991a). Wong Fillmore (1991b) presents the following:

> Breakdowns in family communication sometimes figure in tragic events. After our study was completed, a news story provided a terrifying epilogue to the situation we have sought to warn the public about. In Sacramento, California, four Vietnamese youths took over a store, holding customers and staff hostage for nearly eight hours. The police at first brought in a Thai interpreter, since the boys didn't appear to be speaking Chinese or Vietnamese. They were speaking their version of English.
>
> The siege ended with six people killed, including three of the gunmen, and eleven wounded. Three of the gunmen were brothers. Their parents said in an interview later that they had not been able to communicate well with their sons in years. The boys spoke little Vietnamese—at the level of three-year-olds, their mother said. They had abandoned Vietnamese years ago. The mother said her boys were in a "middle world"—caught between their family and the larger society. This was communicated through an interpreter since the parents speak little English. (p. 34)

The psychological price native speakers pay for shedding language, customs, traditions, and values may include a dysfunctional society. A tremendous price is being paid by culturally and linguistically diverse families, as well as by our nation as a whole. It is crucial that early childhood educators, policy makers, and parents gain knowledge about optimal practices affecting young bilingual learners. The trust families place in professionals is indicative of the need to impart well-informed advice.

Should educators have the right to advise families on home language use? Will schools continue the proliferation of English-immersion programs currently affecting most young native speakers? The important communicative function of language is relayed by Sotomayor (1977):

> Language is the intermediary of ideas, which allows people not only to think in that language, but also to think through the vehicle of language itself. Thus, it is a creative force molding one's thoughts and inevitably influencing behavior. . . . Language is also a cohesive force that promotes a sense of belonging and solidarity. . . . The sense of belonging, vital to the development of self-concept, becomes blurred if one's language, cultural patterns, and ethnic experiences are not reflected and supported, but given a negative connotation. (p. 196)

Our present society needs to gain understandings of the meanings of languages and cultures for young children and families. Traditions and avenues of communication are preserved within family systems through language.

Reed, a former Crow educator and linguist, states, regarding his Native American language, "My lexicon is my way of life." He goes on to say, "Culture is expressed by the language, and my language is tied up with the culture" (quoted in Crawford, 1987, p. 45). Underwood (1981) states that without language it is impossible to refer to a common past and that language is a major link with our ancestors, who spoke with the same words we use.

RESEARCH EVIDENCE

Empirical evidence clearly indicates that there are a variety of misconceptions about how young children acquire a second language (Soto, 1991a) and that there are distinct cognitive and social advantages to being bilingual (Soto, 1991b). The idea of encouraging English-immersion programs for young learners is not an empirically sound one, nor is it beneficial to our society. The empirical research evidence initiated by Peal and Lambert's (1962) landmark study continues to uphold the notion that bilingualism is an asset for learners. A brighter and more positive view of bilingualism was ushered in by this study, which found intellectual advantages to include mental flexibility, superiority in concept formation, and a more diverse set of mental abilities. The St. Lambert Project (Lambert & Tucker, 1972) dramatically confirmed Peal and Lambert's work. Additional evidence was provided by Ianco-Worrall (1972), who found children raised bilingually to be more attentive to semantic relationships than monolinguals; Ben-Zeev (1977), who documented bilingual children's superior awareness of linguistic rules and structures; and Cummins's (1978) investigation, which indicated bilingual children's metalinguistic awareness.

Additional evidence of the positive effects of bilingualism on cognitive performance has been documented by Torrance, Wu, and Alliotti (1970), who measured divergent thinking and creativity; Cummins and Gulutsen (1974), Bain (1974), and Liedtke and Nelson (1968), who studied concept formation; Duncan and DeAvila (1979), who studied Piagetian conservation and field independence; Bain and Yu (1980), who investigated the ability to mentor cognitive performance; Hakuta, Ferdman, and Diaz (1986), who note the contributions of second-language proficiency to a variety of cognitive measures, including the Raven Progressive Matrices; and Hakuta (1986), who found advanced bilinguals to have the advantage of cognitive flexibility and divergent thinking.

The importance of enhancing native-language competence to assure optimal second language learning continues to be evidenced by the following:

1. The Carpinteria Preschool in California, whose native-language instruction afforded young learners an opportunity to outscore comparison groups on standardized test measures such as the Bilingual Syntax Measure, the School Readiness Inventory, and California Achievement Tests (Keatinge, 1984; Krashen & Biber, 1988) (Additional preschools have initiated early native-language instruction in spite of tremendous political opposition.)
2. Research by Skutnabb-Kangas (1977) and Cummins (1977) calling for threshold levels of linguistic competence in order to avoid cognitive deficits and ensure the potential cognitive benefits of becoming bilingual
3. Ethnographic studies noting that culturally responsive classroom environments work well with culturally and linguistically diverse young learners (Au & Jordan, 1981; Macias, 1987; Moll, 1987; Phillips, 1972)
4. Head Start evidence indicating that bilingual preschool curricula are effective for both Spanish- and English-preferring young children (Arenas, 1980; Juarez & Associates, 1980)
5. Research indicating that children in bilingual programs outperform children in nonbilingual programs, regardless of language used for testing (Willig, 1985)
6. NABE's No-Cost Study (Wong Fillmore et al., 1991) describing a large data set of culturally and linguistically diverse families who have been affected by current educational policies
7. Soto's (1991c, 1991d) studies indicating that families of successful higher-achieving young learners (according to school criteria) rely on home native language instruction to a greater extent than comparison families (The evidence points to the idea that threshold levels of native

language competence will provide a "linguistic immunization" assuring school success for young learners.)

8. Existing reviews of bilingual research evidence (Crawford, 1989; Hakuta, 1986; Soto, 1991a) that continue to document the cognitive, academic, and social advantages of bilingualism for young learners

The research evidence clearly indicates that bilingualism can no longer be viewed as a deficit. The current political impetus for early English-immersion programs cannot be substantiated by existing bilingual education research or by second-language-learning research. The questions we need to ask in light of current strong documentation include: Who stands to benefit from existing English-only policies? How long will the personal language and cultural expressions of learners, families, communities, and our nation be suppressed?

HISTORICAL DATA

The shift from the non-English language to English without the maintenance of native culture and language can be likened to the loss of a valuable national resource. All non-English languages used in the United States will die out eventually according to Fishman (1966). In immigrant groups the second generation has generally given up the language of their parents, especially if the language is associated with poverty and ignorance.

Most non-native English speakers know how to speak English. One in eight Americans comes from a minority-language background, yet in a 1976 survey, 98 percent of the respondents said they spoke English well or very well (Crawford, 1989). Ninety-eight percent of Hispanic immigrants stated they believed their children must learn to speak perfect English in order to succeed. In the same survey, only 94 percent of the Anglo parents stated their children should learn English perfectly. Minority-language speakers know that the lack of English proficiency is a barrier to education and employment, in effect restricting one's economic potential. "There is a clear relationship between job success and linguistic capability and an even clearer relationship between job access and language" (Crandall, 1981, p. 15).

It is interesting to note that nowhere in the U.S. Constitution did the founding fathers of the United States establish English as the official language. This has always been a multilingual country, with people immigrating here from every corner of the earth. The United States was open to immigration from all countries without restrictions during the first hundred years of its existence. Linguistic diversity was the norm when the men who wrote the Constitution (many of whom were German-English bilinguals themselves) carefully omitted any reference to an official language. Public and private use of languages other than English was accepted, with English becoming the lingua franca of the United States through custom and practice (Daniels, 1990).

There were three peaks of immigration from 1825 to 1925 (Frick, 1990). The first peak, between 1830 and 1854, was composed of Irish, German, Swedish, Norwegian, Sicilian, and Neapolitan ethnic groups. From 1880 to 1900, the railroad era, Chinese immigrated in vast numbers, while large eastern and southern European immigration occurred from 1900 to 1925. The large number of European immigrants established language islands where education and everyday communication in and outside the home occurred in the mother tongue (Kim, Lee, & Kim, 1981).

Each time immigration peaked, eruptions of hostile feelings toward immigrants occurred. "Know-nothingism" was a policy in the 1850s that prohibited bilingual education, with differences in language becoming a contentious public issue. During the third wave, Theodore Roosevelt, for example, proclaimed that there was room for only one language in America, and that language was English (Daniels, 1990).

Immigration has not been the sole source of linguistic diversity in the United States. Colonization and annexation have integrated French speakers in Louisiana, Spanish speakers in the Southwest and Puerto Rico, as well as speakers of hundreds of Native American languages. Each time a non-English-speaking territory was added to the United States, it was not permitted statehood status until the majority of the population became English speakers.

Historically, native-speaking children are more likely to sink than to swim in our nation's English-speaking classrooms. In 1908, for example, 13 percent of immigrant children were enrolled in high school compared to 32 percent of children with native-born parents (Crawford, 1989). Disproportionately high dropout rates for Puerto Ricans, Mexican-Americans, Asian-Americans, and Native Americans persisted through the 1960s. Currently, Waggoner (1988) notes that minority-language youth are 1.5 times more likely to drop out prior to completing high school than are native English-speaking students.

The Bilingual Education Act of 1968 marked the first time that bilingual education was endorsed as a national policy. The lawmakers felt that the schools' neglect of native-speaking children needed to be rectified. Policy in this era was also set by the *Lau* vs. *Nichols* Supreme Court decision, which made random assignment of limited-English-proficient children to "sink-or-swim" classrooms illegal (Crawford, 1989).

In the 1980s and 1990s the language policy debate has centered on amending the U.S. Constitution to declare English as the official language. The issue of an English-language amendment has been fraught with racism and misunderstandings about the role of language in a democratic nation. Bilingual educational curricular policies have aroused passions of political power and social status without regard to child and family benefits.

As of mid-1990 the following sixteen states had passed some version of an official-English law (dates in parentheses):

Arizona (1988)	Kentucky (1984)
Arkansas (1987)	Mississippi (1987)
California (1986)	Nebraska (1923)
Colorado (1988)	North Carolina (1987)
Georgia (1986)	North Dakota (1987)
Florida (1988)	South Carolina (1987)
Illinois (1969)	Tennessee (1984)
Indiana (1984)	Virginia (1981)

Only Hawaii and Louisiana have passed laws giving legal status to multiple languages (Daniels, 1990).

Young children in our nation are expected to shed native language and cultural knowledge at an early age, yet it is acceptable for secondary students to learn a foreign language. Efforts to assimilate whole community groups have created not national unity but rather ethnic divisiveness and educational gate-keeping outcomes. If only 4 percent of Americans speak no English (Crawford, 1989) and linguistic assimilation continues to increase, why must we "hot house" young culturally and linguistically diverse learners in English-immersion programs?

LINGUISTIC ASSIMILATION

The maintenance of native languages by immigrant groups has not been successful in our nation (Guitart, 1976). The United States has "developed one of the most efficient patterns of linguistic assimilation in the world" over the last two centuries (Daniels, 1990, p. 3). Non-English-speaking immigrant families arriving in the United States have usually shifted from being speakers of their native language to a bilingual stage, and then to being monolingual English speakers within three generations, according to Guitart. Veltman (1978) notes that the shift from native language to English may occur in just two generations.

Linguistic assimilation has been accelerating according to demographic research cited by Crawford (1989). European immigrants, such as the 9 million Germans and 10 million French who had come to this country by 1910, were not successful in maintaining their language; their culture experienced a continuous decline in the absence of their mother tongue (Fishman, 1966). The large numbers of European immigrants made it possible for them to establish language islands where education and everyday communication both in and outside the home took place in their mother tongue. Language devotees of these groups once hoped to maintain the ethnic traits of the old country by teaching their children the culture and mother tongue of the homeland in parochial and public schools in the community, by books and newspapers in their language, and by forming organizations for language and culture maintenance. "Neither the education of their children in the parochial schools, nostalgic sentiment, patriotism, nor ethnic pride, however, could stop the gradual, but powerful, force of the erosion of the immigrants' old linguistic and cultural system" (Kim et al., 1981, p. 75); by the third generation, the language and culture of the parents and grandparents were no longer behavioral traits of the children. Permanent maintenance of a non-English mother tongue appears to be an unrealistic goal even in the "well-bounded ethnic community" according to Kim and colleagues. There is tremendous pressure from within and from without on young immigrants and second-generation children to learn and use English.

The United States is a multilingual nation according to the U.S. Census Bureau. In 1970 about 15 percent of the total population reported their mother tongue as other than English (U.S. Bureau of the Census, 1973). In the 1980 Census roughly 9 percent of the population gave their mother tongue as other than English (U.S. Bureau of the Census, 1984). This represents a drop of 6 percent in ten years of the number of people claiming a mother tongue other than English. Perhaps this illustrates a growing reluctance to acknowledge that one's native language is other than English due to the increasingly negative political attitude toward minority languages.

Taking a look at some of the many languages that have been lost, let us consider the Native American languages. The federal government has wavered between limited support to Native American mores and cultural genocide against them, including language destruction (Spitzer, 1985). The government expected Native Americans to absorb American culture. Some groups found it easy and others found it difficult. Assimilation was most formidable for the Hurons, Houmas, Pawnees, and Papagayos.

Today there are 289 tribes living on 286 reservations in 26 states (Medicine, 1980). There are 207 different Native American languages and language dialects, but they are dying out on most reservations. The majority of the languages lack functional alphabets and are primarily preserved by the older generations. Forty-nine languages have less than ten speakers all aged 50 or over. Six languages have 10,000 speakers of all ages. Fluency in the 152 other Native American languages is somewhere in between these two extremes (Chafe, 1962; cited in Medicine, 1980).

Only a small fraction of Native American children speak ancestral tongues. English is often the predominant language in Native American homes (Crawford, 1989). In a study done among Navajos in Utah, Arizona, and New Mexico, it was found that most schoolchildren spoke very little Navajo (Howard, 1988). Until recently Native American children were likely to suffer harsh punishment for speaking in their native tongues. For example, in the 1950s the Crow language was still being banned in Montana schools, and children were disciplined for speaking Crow (Crawford, 1987).

German was another of the immigrant languages widely used in American schools in the eighteenth and nineteenth centuries, especially in parochial schools in Wisconsin, Ohio, Pennsylvania, Missouri, Minnesota, and the Dakotas. Beginning in about 1830 and continuing for six decades, five million German people settled in the United States, especially in the Midwest (Perlman, 1990). By 1900 there were 600,000 or about 4 percent of American school children receiving their education partially or totally in the German language (Crawford, 1989). Subtly, in the 1880's there had begun a gradual decline of the German language, as several states began to pass anti-bilingual education legislation. At first some of the teachers involved could not even speak English and enforcement of the English instruction laws was weak. However, by the turn of the twentieth century, German-American communities were assimilated and Americanized. By World War I there was a complete collapse of the German language due to increasing anti-German sentiment aroused by the war (Perlman 1990).

The Chinese people in the United States today are predominantly first-generation immigrants (Sung, 1979). The Chinese had been excluded from entering this country by the Chinese Exclusion Act of 1882, roughly coinciding with their peak of immigration during the railroad era. It was not until 1965 that significant numbers of Chinese were afforded entrance. The most common form of communication for Chinese immigrants is Mandarin, but there are diverse dialects among the world's most populous people.

Ninety-nine percent of Koreans living in Los Angeles, New York, and San Francisco, of principally middle-class or professional backgrounds, attempt to maintain their home language (Kim et al., 1981). The tradi-

tional Korean family is a supportive environment for language maintenance, and having an extended family in the home, especially grandparents, is one factor that helps maintain the Korean language. "A large
proportion of second generation Koreans who understand and speak
Korean are from such families" (Kim et al., 1981, p. 30).

Hispanics, who are the largest linguistically diverse group in the
United States, are comprised of mainly Mexican-Americans and Puerto
Ricans. Hispanics became U.S. citizens either through annexation of
territories or as spoils of war. In New Mexico in the nineteenth and early
part of the twentieth centuries, education in most public schools was
conducted entirely in Spanish, or, later, in Spanish and English (Perlman,
1990). Successful maintenance of the Spanish language today in the
Southwest is largely due to the constant influx of new Mexican immigrants and to the geographic proximity to Mexico. This makes it possible
for Mexican-Americans to have frequent contact with their homeland
(Glazer, 1966, cited in Kim et al., 1981).

The Jones Act of 1917 afforded citizenship to Puerto Ricans, and the
island maintains a commonwealth status. Frequent migrations from island to mainland affect the language use of young Puerto Rican learners.
In 1990 Puerto Rico passed a Spanish-language amendment initiated as a
result of reaction to interference by English-only lobbyists during the late
1980s. Younger Puerto Ricans of the third generation prefer to use English, but when adolescents enter young adult roles they increase the use
of Spanish (CENTRO, 1980).

POLICY ISSUES

Policy makers may appear to be more distant from a child's everyday experience, yet the impact of macro decision making can have far-
reaching effects on the lives of children, families, schools, communities,
and society as a whole. Figure 10.1 illustrates the intersection of language
among the ecological domains, as the players interact and communicate
within the social context. The visible and invisible language policies of
our nation continue to affect the intersections among children, families,
schools, and communities. The messages young children receive and
impart are governed by rules chosen by adults. The language nest provided for our youngest learners has been dominated more by political
rhetoric and power struggles than by empirical evidence.

The more powerful voices have silenced the needs of our youngest
learners by encouraging the association of native language with poverty,
powerlessness, and immigration. The end result has been the loss of

Figure 10.1 Language Use Among the Ecological Domains

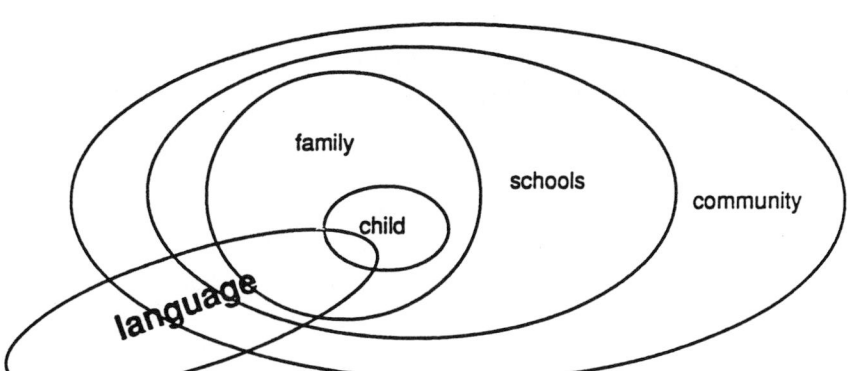

language capital for young children, families, and entire communities. Our schools have not listened to expert empirical evidence; instead, an assimilationist perspective has driven the language curriculum among the ecological domains. How much of a price are we willing to pay when such policies continue to impart social inequality? How long will linguistically diverse families be silenced and marginalized?

Our concern as a nation should center around whether we want to retain or obliterate languages. The urgency of the issue cannot be overstated, since it is our youngest learners who continue to be affected by language loss. The experiences of our Native American communities highlight the fact that language loss is very real. Traditional languages handed down by elders have been lost with the advent of interference by assimilationists. The Carlisle School in Pennsylvania stands as a reminder of how young children and families were separated and militarized for the sake of assimilation. Native American children were separated from their families and transported in railroad cars for the purpose of receiving a military education. The tragedy includes the loss of language, the loss of culture, and the loss of life.

Americans seem to have felt threatened each time a new wave of immigrants arrived or non-English-language speakers became part of the U.S. population. Americans have historically been afraid that newcomers are in some way subversive. In reality, there is no evidence that using language other than English has ever caused political fragmentation in the United States (Judd, 1990).

CONCLUSION

In this chapter we have examined the political issues affecting second-language learning of young children and made a case against the increased proliferation of English-only immersion programs for young native speakers by examining existing empirical evidence, describing our nation's continued loss of languages, and raising educational ethical concerns.

The problem lies in the fact that the optimal educational needs of young native speakers are not being met. In spite of interest by early childhood educators and policy makers regarding bilingual programmatic and curricular issues, English-only continues to drive daily instruction. In spite of the fact that politics is a part of all decisions about the curriculum, historically it has been difficult to separate political debates from bilingual policy issues. The inherent danger in allowing politics and power struggles to drive the language learning curriculum is that the voices of children, families, and communities are being silenced. The emotionally embedded decision making has affected policies without regard to empirical evidence and the young child's best interest.

Recent public sentiment in our nation has tended to link monolingual English-only with patriotism, leading to an isolationist perspective limiting global collaborative capabilities. Culturally and linguistically diverse young learners across the nation afford possibilities for the inclusion of a kaleidoscope of enriching language and cultural learnings. Can we afford to encourage a sanitized curriculum in the midst of diversity and global international concerns? It can be argued that the truly "patriotic" option was set forth by the nation's founders, who accepted bilingualism by publishing official documents in English, French, and German, including the *Artikel des Bundes und der immerwahrenden Eintracht zwischen den Staaten*, or Articles of Confederation (Crawford, 1989).

The responsibility for the education of linguistically and culturally diverse young learners rests within the societal contexts of homes, schools, and communities. The ongoing implicit and explicit curriculum and instruction is imparted by adults whose world views have been affected by a host of experiences, events, and personal attributes. Young children depend on decisions made by educators, parents, and policy makers for their educational and social well-being.

Each one of the players, immersed within the ecological context of a child's world, has a particular role as a mediator, facilitator, or caregiver. The role of parents and teachers as caretakers is particularly salient regarding the everyday interactions and decisions affecting young children. Parenting and teaching roles are currently merging and emerging so that interactions within the domains pose both challenges and opportunities for the parent–teacher–child triad.

NOTE

1. The NABE No-Cost Study was conducted by over 300 volunteers from the National Association for Bilingual Education (NABE), who interviewed 1,100 families across the nation.

REFERENCES

Arenas, S. (1980, May/June). Innovations in bilingual/multicultural curriculum development. *Children Today*. Washington, DC: U.S. Government Printing Office.

Au, K., & Jordan, C. (1981). Teaching reading to Hawaiian children: Finding a culturally appropriate solution. In H. T. Trueba & G. P. Guthrie (Eds.), *Culture and the bilingual classroom: Studies in classroom ethnography* (pp. 139-152). Cambridge, MA: Newbury House.

Bain, B. (1974). Bilingualism and cognition: Toward a general theory. In S. Carey (Ed.), *Bilingualism, biculturalism, and education* (pp. 7-19). Edmonton: University of Alberta.

Bain, B., & Yu, A. (1980). Cognitive consequences of raising children bilingually: One parent, one language. *Canadian Journal of Psychology, 34*, 304-313.

Ben-Zeev, S. (1977). The influence of bilingualism on cognitive strategy and cognitive development. *Child Development, 48*, 1009-1018.

CENTRO. (1980). Social dimensions of language use in East Harlem. Working Papers. (ERIC Document Reproduction Service No. ED 212 751)

Chafe, W. L. (1962). Estimates regarding the present speakers of North American Indian languages. *International Journal of American Linguistics, 28*, 162-171.

Crandall, J. A. (1981). Equity from the bilingual education specialist's perspective. Research and development series No. 214D. (ERIC Document Reproduction Service No. ED 215 160)

Crawford, J. (1987, April 1). Bilingual education: Language, learning, and politics. *Education Week*, 19-50.

Crawford, J. (1989). *Bilingual education: History, politics, theory and practice.* Trenton, NJ: Crane.

Cummins, J. (1977). Cognitive factors associated with intermediate levels of bilingual skills. *Modern Language Journal, 61*, 3-12.

Cummins, J. (1978). Metalinguistic development of children in bilingual education programs. In M. Paradis (Ed.), *The fourth Lacus Forum, 1977* (pp. 1-33). Columbia, SC: Hornbeam.

Cummins, J., & Gulutsen, M. (1974). Bilingual education and cognition. *The Alberta Journal of Educational Research, 22*(3), 259–269.

Daniels, H. A. (Ed.). (1990). *Not only English: Affirming America's multilingual heritage.* Urbana, IL: National Council of Teachers of English.

Duncan, S. E., & DeAvila, E. (1979). Bilingualism and cognition: Some recent findings. *NABE Journal, 4,* 15–50.

Fishman, J. A. (Ed.). (1966). *Language royalty in the United States.* The Hague: Morton.

Frick, E. (1990). Metaphors and motives of language restriction movements. In H. A. Daniels (Ed.), *Not only English: Affirming America's multilingual heritage* (pp. 27–35). Urbana, IL: National Council of Teachers of English.

Glazer, N. (1966). The process and problems of language maintenance: An integrative review. In J. A. Fishman (Ed.), *Language and loyalty in the United States* (pp. 358–368). The Hague: Mouton.

Guitart, J. M. (1977). *Question of language loyalty. Lektos: Interdisciplinary working papers in language sciences.* (ERIC Document Reproduction Service No. ED 135 227)

Hakuta, K. (1986). *Mirror of language. The debate of bilingualism.* New York: Basic Books.

Hakuta, K., Ferdman, B., & Diaz, R. (1986). *Bilingualism and cognitive development: Three perspectives and methodological implications.* Los Angeles: University of California, Center for Language Education and Research.

Howard, R. E. (1988). *Teaching native language and culture in the Indian schools.* (ERIC Document Reproduction Service No. ED 300 151)

Ianco-Worrall, A. (1972). Bilingualism and cognitive development. *Child Development, 43,* 1390–1400.

Juarez & Associates. (1980). *Final report of an evaluation of the Head Start bilingual/bicultural curriculum models.* Washington, DC: U.S. Department of Health and Human Services.

Judd, E. L. (1990). The federal English Language Amendment: Prospects and perils. In H. A. Daniels (Ed.), *Not only English: Affirming America's multilingual heritage* (pp. 37–46). Urbana, IL: National Council of Teachers of English.

Keatinge, R. H. (1984). An assessment of the Carpinteria preschool Spanish program. *Teacher Education Quarterly, 11,* 80–94.

Kim, K., K.-O., Lee, K., & Kim, T.-Y. (1981). *Korean-Americans in Los Angeles: Their concerns and language maintenance.* (ERIC Document Reproduction Service No. ED 205 666)

Krashen, S., & Biber, D. (1988). *On course: Bilingual education's success in California.* Sacramento: California Association for Bilingual Education.

Lambert, W. E., & Tucker, G. R. (1972). *Bilingual education of children: The St. Lambert experiment.* Rowley, MA: Newbury House.

Liedtke, W., & Nelson, L. (1968). Concept formation in bilingualism. *Alberta Journal of Educational Research, 14,* 225–232.

Macias, J. (1987). The hidden curriculum of Papago teachers. In G. & L. Spindler

(Eds.), *Interpretive ethnography of education* (pp. 363–384). Hillsdale, NJ: Erlbaum.

Medicine, B. (1980). Bilingual education and public policy: The cases of the American Indians. In R. V. Padilla (Ed.), *Theory in bilingual education: Ethnoperspectives in bilingual education research* (Vol. 2) (pp. 395–407). (ERIC Document Reproduction Service No. ED 200 005)

Moll, L. (1987). Teaching second language students: A Vygotskian perspective. In D. Johnson & D. Roen (Eds.), *Richness in writing* (pp. 55–67). New York: Longman.

Peal, E., & Lambert, W. (1962). The revelations of bilingualism to intelligence. *Psychological Monographs, 76*(27), 1–23.

Perlman, J. (1990). Historical legacies: 1840–1920. *Annals of American Academy of Political Science, 508*, 27–37.

Phillips, S. (1972). Participant structures and communicative competence. Warm Springs children in community and classroom. In C. Cazden, V. P. John, & D. Hymes (Eds.), *Functions of language in the classroom* (pp. 370–394). New York: Teachers College Press.

Skutnabb-Kangas, T. (1977). *Bilingualism or not: The education of minorities.* Clevedon, England: Multilingual Matters.

Soto, L. D. (1991a). Understanding bilingual/bicultural young children. *Young Children, 46*(2), 30–36.

Soto, L. D. (1991b). Alternate paradigms in bilingual education research. In R. Padilla & A. H. Benavides (Eds.), *Critical perspectives on bilingual education research* (pp. 93–110). Tempe, AZ: Bilingual Review Press.

Soto, L. D. (1991c). *Families as learning environments: Reflections on critical factors affecting differential school achievement.* Unpublished manuscript, University Park: Pennsylvania State University.

Soto, L. D. (1991d, April). *Families as learning environments.* Paper presented at the Annual Meeting of the American Educational Research Association, Chicago.

Sotomayor, M. (1977). Language, culture and ethnicity in developing self-concept. *Social Casework, 58*(4), 195–203.

Spitzer, N. R. (Ed.). (1985). *Louisiana folklife: A guide to the state.* (ERIC Document Reproduction Service No. ED 312 190)

Sung, B. L. (1979). *Transplanted Chinese children.* (ERIC Document Reproduction Service No. ED 192 040)

Torrance, E., Wu, J., & Alliotti, N. (1970). Creating functioning of monolingual and bilingual children in Singapore. *Journal of Educational Psychology, 61*, 72–75.

Underwood, R. A. (1981). *Bilingual education in the developing Pacific area: Why?* Asian Pacific American education occasional papers. (ERIC Document Reproduction Service No. ED 212 748)

U. S. Bureau of the Census. (1973). *1970 census of the population. Characteristics of the population. U.S. summary.* Washington, DC: U.S. Department of Commerce.

U. S. Bureau of the Census. (1984). *1980 census of the population. Characteristics of the population. U.S. summary*. Washington, DC: U.S. Department of Commerce.

Veltman, C. (1978). *The assimilation of American language minorities: Structure, pace, and extent*. Washington, DC: National Center for Education Statistics.

Waggoner, D. (1988). *The undereducation of American youth*. San Antonio: Intercultural Development Resource Association.

Willig, A. (1985). A meta-analysis of selected studies on the effectiveness of bilingual education. *Review of Educational Research, 55*(3), 269–317.

Wong Fillmore, L. (1991a, April). *The loss of native language in minority children as the result of premature exposure to English*. Paper presented at the Society for Research on Child Development, Seattle, WA.

Wong Fillmore, L. (1991b). A question for early childhood programs: English first or families first? *Education Week, 10*(39), 32–34.

Wong Fillmore, L. et al. (1991, January). *NABE's no-cost study*. Paper presented at the National Association for Bilingual Education, Washington, DC.

CHAPTER 11

An African-American Early Childhood Education Program
Visions for Children

Janice E. Hale

A question that is being raised by African-American scholars is whether we can bring about an improvement in educational outcomes for African-American children without recognizing their culture. I have pointed out elsewhere (Hale-Benson, 1986) that African-Americans participate in a culture that has a base in West Africa. The uniqueness of the American slavery experience and the challenge of living thereafter as African-Americans created a distinctive culture that has given rise to distinctive expressive and behavioral styles.

THE NEED FOR ETHNIC IDENTITY

George DeVos (1975) states that ethnicity persists in America because of the individual's need for a sense of continuity—belonging, which, from the perspective of psychology, is essential to the development of the sense of self. DeVos (1975) suggests that ethnic identity provides meaning to the life of the individual:

> Ethnicity . . . is in its narrowest sense a feeling of continuity with the past, a feeling that is maintained as an essential part of one's self-definition. Ethnicity is intimately related to the individual need for collective continuity. The individual senses to some degree a threat to his own survival if his group or lineage is threatened with extinction. Ethnicity . . . includes a sense of personal survival in the historical continuity of the group. (p. 17)

Elsie Moore (1985) has pointed out that ethnicity is essentially a process variable that has its effects in the earliest interactions between mother and child. It continues to have effect as parents shape the child's emerging physical and cognitive capacities. "Therefore, a lifespan perspective on human development requires analysis of how socialization in different ethnic groups affects behavioral development from childhood throughout later life" (p. 102). Moore notes that the significance of ethnicity has been ignored in conceptual models of human development. American social scientists have had a tendency to describe children from various ethnic groups in terms of how they deviate from European-American cultural norms.

Moore conducted a study comparing African-American children who were adopted by white families with those who were adopted by African-American families. She found that the children adopted by the white families scored higher on standardized tests. This was not a surprising finding, given the fact that such tests are highly indexed to language and cultural content found in upper-middle-class European-American families.

However, Moore points out that higher test performance alone does not necessarily mean that those African-American children will be more effective in their adult roles than traditionally adopted African-American children. An adoption agency study of those children at age 4, including data on social and emotional functioning as well as cognitive achievement, indicates that African-American children adopted by African-American families displayed *higher levels of social and emotional adjustment* than did African-American children adopted by white families.

Other scholars have studied the childrearing attitudes and practices of African-American parents and found implications for the construction of a sense of self for African-American children. Margaret Spencer (1985) found that many African-American parents tend to *transcend race* in their socialization efforts. The goal, she points out, "seems to be the rearing of 'neutral' children, or 'human beings' irrespective of the continued salience of race on the macrostructural level" (p. 228). She found in her study that the children who made the most African-American positive choices on a measure of racial preference and color connotation were children who were older and had knowledge of African-American history. The children who made white positive choices had the following characteristics in their background:

1. Parents who do not teach children about civil rights
2. Parental beliefs that integration is an enriching experience
3. Child's lack of knowledge concerning black history
4. Parental lack of knowledge of black history
5. Parental belief that current racial climate is better than the 1950s or 1960s
6. No parental discussion of racial discrimination

Spencer found that in nearly one-half of the children, race dissonance was predicted from specific parental childrearing strategies. She concludes that the "race transcendence" position of some African-American parents is not compatible with the psychological intervention that is required to offset the sociocultural factors that place African-American children at-risk in American society. This "humanistic" or race-neutral posture is at odds with the events the child encounters over the course of the life span.

Leahcim Semaj (1985) points out that a key to helping African-American children construct and maintain a positive self-identity is for primary socializing agents (e.g., parents, relatives, teachers) to present evidence confirming the worth of African-American culture and people for the child. He states further that European-American children growing up in a culture that is pro-white and anti–African-American do not face this situation. The mechanisms of cultural transmission (e.g., the mass media) provide continuous propaganda regarding the superiority of European-American culture and people. The primary socializing agents of the white child would not need to do anything extra to establish a positive self-identity. Semaj (1985) states:

> The dominant position of Euro-American culture enables these agents to draw from other cultures at will without fear of cultural domination. This is because they, on their own terms, filter alien influences through their own cultural mechanisms and discard what they no longer have use for. (p. 183)

Semaj suggests that liberation for African-American children is contingent on a socialization that develops a collective, extended self-identity. There is a need for ethnically appropriate parental socialization and Afrocentric early childhood education that can provide African-American children with a self-identity that will work for them in their existential situation in America.

VISIONS FOR CHILDREN

Early childhood educational and caregiving settings must search for cultural continuity, not intervention. Rashid (1981) states:

> The preschool experience must therefore provide a dynamic blend of African-American culture and that culture which is reflected in the Euro-American educational setting. . . . The African-American child

who only sees the Euro-American cultural tradition manifested in the preschool environment can only conclude that the absence of visual representation of his culture connotes his essential worthlessness. (p. 60)

A developmental psychology of the African-American child is clearly called for. Likewise, there is a need for an educational model that is consistent with African-American child development. Essential components of such an educational model are the following

1. Infusion of African-American culture into the school curriculum
2. Development of a culturally appropriate pedagogy
3. Replacement of "skill and drill" education with an educational process that imbues African-American children with a love for learning, *raison d'être*, intrinsic motivation, and self-actualization through meaningful work

Unfortunately we do not have empirical data to document the long-term effects of Afrocentric programs on children's development and later academic success. However, we do have the data from the research of Jacquelyn Fleming (1985), which revealed that historically African-American colleges do a better job of motivating and preparing African-American students than do integrated schools.

Fleming studied 2,500 African-American and white freshmen and seniors at fifteen colleges, including Spelman College in Atlanta, Ohio State University in Columbus, and the University of Houston. Her study was conducted over a seven-year period. She found that, even though the African-American colleges had very limited resources and many operated under severe financial constraints, students at those colleges gained more intellectually than did their peers at integrated schools. More African-American students are enrolled in white colleges than are enrolled in historically African-American colleges, but the largest numbers of African-American college *graduates* are produced by historically African-American colleges.

Efforts to document the long-term effects of Afrocentric preschool programs have just begun. Visions for Children (VFC) is a preschool program that emphasizes the special characteristics of African-American children, offering a teaching method and curriculum that encourage children to learn the information and skills necessary for upward mobility, career achievement, and financial independence in the American mainstream. At the same time, they feel pride in their own ethnic culture and are able to identify with and contribute to the development of their people.

This program is based on the model described in *Black Children: Their Roots, Culture and Learning Styles* (Hale-Benson, 1986). VFC is a day-care center that is located in a storefront building in Warrensville Heights, Ohio, a suburb of Cleveland with 95 percent African-American population. The research associated with the program is funded by the Cleveland Foundation. The operation of the program is supported by parental fees. A distinctive feature is the emphasis on teaching young children cognitive skills while strengthening their self-esteem and identity as African-Americans.

The teaching method emphasizes African-American culture and integrates it in all of its diversity throughout the curriculum. The children learn about Africa and their rich cultural heritage; they learn about African-American and African arts and crafts; they listen to folktales and stories written by African-American writers; they listen to music and learn about musicians that emerge from black culture; they learn about heroes in black history such as Dr. Martin Luther King, Jr.

Authenticity is maintained by presenting African and African-American culture to the children by using original sources, such as authentic African masks at the art museum, and by involving consultants who have actually visited Africa. For example, I have visited West Africa and formally studied African life and culture. For several years we have had artists-in-residence who teach the children African dance and drumming. They have traveled extensively in Africa and have firsthand knowledge of African culture.

In sum, the children in this program are surrounded with messages that get them started on the right track in realizing that there is pride in being beautiful African-American children who can hold their own in a competitive society.

Visions for Children emphasizes the development of cognitive skills, such as reasoning, memory, problem solving, creativity, and language skills. Progress is assessed using both teacher-made and standardized instruments. Even though standardized instruments can contain inherent biases toward minority children, a goal of this program is to demystify these tests for parents and to help the children perform well on such measures.

There is a strong correlation between language facility and performing well on standardized measures in the professional work world. Therefore, VFC's focus is on language skills. This includes expressive as well as receptive language. Too often children receive language through listening but do not have enough opportunities to engage in expressive language. Expressive language includes holding conversations with adults, telling stories from pictures, engaging in sociodramatic play, and responding to questions in complete sentences.

The teachers in this program are high school graduates. The director is a college graduate. There is also a part-time research coordinator, who is vice-president of VFC. She supervises the director and coordinates the evaluation of the program. The program is being implemented at one site only. Four full days a year are provided for inservice training. The focus of this training is on stimulating creativity in teaching. Additional workshops are provided during the children's naptime throughout the year. The teachers and the director have also attended local, regional, and national conferences that provide training. Presently, the teachers are involved in training associated with the Child Development Associate credential.

CURRICULUM DEVELOPMENT

An important outcome of this project is the curriculum that is being developed to document the planning for increasing the intellectual gains in the children. This is a pioneer effort to pull together a quality early childhood education curriculum that is specifically geared to meet the needs of African-American children.

This curriculum has an easy-to-follow format that can be easily adjusted by individual programs according to the areas of the curriculum they wish to emphasize. The curriculum can also be adjusted to accommodate more or fewer teachers, larger or smaller groups of children, one room or multiple rooms, short or longer days.

Most curriculum schedules in early childhood education texts and activity books designate large blocks of time for ambiguous activities such as free play, small-group activity, large-group activity, story time, or activity time. This curriculum is an advancement over those presently available because it combines flexibility and structure. There is a one-and-a-half-hour period in the morning and an hour-long period in the afternoon that are for child-directed activities. This gives the children an opportunity to select from a variety of choices the activities they will engage in. There is also one half-hour period in the morning and one in the afternoon when the children are engaged in free play or teacher-led gross-motor activities. There are other fixed periods such as breakfast, lunch, snack, and naptime.

The remaining periods of the day are arranged into activity periods during which the children rotate among the teachers and engage in small-group activities in each area of the curriculum. Thus the curriculum offers a balance of child control and teacher direction. Studies show (Berrueta-Clement, Schweinhart, Barnett, Epstein, & Weikert, 1984; Bissell, 1971; Karnes, Schwendel, & Williams, 1983) that children gain most from early childhood education programs in which teachers have clear objectives in mind for the children.

Another feature of the curriculum is that it is being planned for use by teachers who are at the entry level of early childhood education/childcare careers. Certainly each teacher must be trained in early childhood education so that each area is taught properly. However, a feature of the curriculum is that it provides a comprehensive panorama of the components of a quality early childhood education. This support may be important for a teacher with minimum training who might have difficulty structuring the day on his or her own to include all of the things we want young children to know and do.

The teachers in this program, who live in the Cleveland community, were involved in the development of the curriculum. Planning sessions were conducted during which the teachers assisted in formulating the monthly themes, identifying the heroes and sheroes, planning fieldtrips, and coordinating the presentation of various streams of the curriculum to achieve integration.

Planning

There are several organizational features that have been designed to facilitate planning:

1. *Daily schedule.* I design the daily schedule, and it is revised as needed by the director and the teachers in staff meetings. The flexibility of the schedule means it can be altered when the number of groups of children changes because of increases or decreases in the enrollment. It is also altered during the summer when more outdoor activities are planned and the length of the activity periods is shortened.

The daily schedule is designed to be easy for the teachers to follow. The time schedule is given for the entire day, and it designates how many activity periods will be devoted to particular curricular areas per week. This can be easily altered to give more or less emphasis to various areas of the curriculum. For example, preliminary testing revealed low scores for the children in the area of quantitative skills. So, the daily schedule was subsequently altered so more activity periods per week were devoted to activities in the area of mathematics.

2. *Daily activity plans.* The teachers are required to submit these plans for the areas of the curriculum they teach on Wednesday for the coming week. The teachers specialize in particular areas of the curriculum, and the children rotate among the teachers as outlined on the daily schedule. The children have a "home teacher" they eat meals with, but all of the teachers teach all of the children throughout the course of the day. This creates a kind of extended family atmosphere in the center.

3. *Monthly planning forms.* These plans were created to require the teachers to add a long-range dimension to their planning. The teachers are required to submit these plans on the second Tuesday for the coming month. This form requires that the teachers identify the objectives that will be worked on in each area they teach. The curriculum guide designates the objectives to be taught for every month. This long-range planning provides enough time for the teachers to develop the teaching aids and materials needed to teach each unit.

The teachers are also assigned monthly bulletin boards to design. These are designed on the monthly planning forms. The center displays ten bulletin boards. One is designed by the center coordinator. It is labeled "Visions for Parents." It provides "Daily Doings," which give a brief overview of each area of the curriculum, the fieldtrips, enrichment activities such as guest speakers, or the activities of the artist-in-residence. Two of the bulletin boards are devoted to displays of children's work. The remaining seven each represent an area of the curriculum and are teaching bulletin boards.

4. *Monthly themes.* An important goal in early childhood education curriculum development is to achieve integration in the curriculum. We have attempted to achieve this in the VFC curriculum by developing the curriculum component by component and then putting them together with the goal of achieving integration. The monthly themes provide such a mechanism.

Twelve themes have been identified for each year. The themes have been planned on a three-year cycle so that a child who enters the program at 2 years of age will have a variety of themes for each of his or her three years in the program.

The themes include eight of the same themes each year and four different ones. We believe that there are some themes that bear repeating for the benefit of new children in the program and deeper treatment for continuing children. In other words, a monthly theme on Africa that a child experiences for three years will have a different yield for a child at the ages of 2, 3, or 4 years. The repeat themes are generally indexed to the seasons of the year or aspects of African-American culture, such as Black History Month or Africa.

The themes provide integration for all of the diverse areas of the curriculum. The teachers are encouraged to utilize the curricular objectives for determining the goals of instruction and to utilize the theme to determine the content of instruction. In other words, the curricular objectives should guide the skills the children are working on, and the themes should guide the information that is being imparted to the children along with the skills.

The monthly themes should also suggest the selection of fieldtrips and enrichment activities. For example, in October, the monthly theme is Africa. During that month, a fieldtrip is scheduled to the art museum to view an exhibit of African masks. Also, the enrichment activity is an African party at which the children dress in African garb at the time that Halloween parties usually occur. The study of African spirituality replaces the observance of the supernatural usually associated with Halloween. The children also make African drums and masks and participate in African rituals. In this way, the art and music curricula are correlated with the monthly theme.

5. *Heroes and Sheroes*. Each week the children study a different person or significant event in African-American history. These have been identified on a three-year cycle with certain key figures and events represented each year, such as the birthday of Dr. Martin Luther King, Jr., and the Juneteenth celebration. Juneteenth is a holiday that originated in Texas. It is celebrated on June 19. It commemorates the day that African-Americans who were held in slavery in Texas received word of the Emancipation Proclamation. African-American Texans celebrate this holiday much like the Fourth of July is celebrated nationally.

The teachers are encouraged to correlate the heroes and sheroes with lessons in other curricular areas. For example, when the monthly theme is plants and the hero for the week is Dr. George Washington Carver, the science lesson can focus on the peanut and all the products Dr. Carver created in his research. The intent of this integration is to create an incidental, integrated educational process that flows naturally throughout the curriculum.

Pictures of the heroes and sheroes are featured on the center bulletin board devoted to the cultural curriculum. Examples of sheroes are Coretta Scott King, Sojourner Truth, Phyllis Wheatley, Lorraine Hansberry, Jane Kennedy, Mahalia Jackson, Mary McLeod Bethune, Nikki Giovanni, and Marian Anderson.

6. *Fieldtrips*. Fieldtrips are planned once a month. The fieldtrip is correlated with the monthly theme. Occasionally fieldtrips are planned

around important events or exhibits that occur for young children in the community. Examples of fieldtrips we have planned are

Cleveland Zoo
Circus
Dramatic presentation on *The Life of Harriet Tubman*
Peter Pan performance
The Wizard of Oz performance
Children's Museum
Holden Arboretum
Shaker Lakes Nature Center
Malcolm Brown Art Gallery
Afro-American Museum

Organization

A central problem in curriculum organization in early childhood education is managing the diversity of the information and skills we desire to impart to young children. It takes an extremely skilled teacher to give balanced and integrated attention to all aspects of the curriculum.

As a start toward designing a quality early childhood education curriculum, we have selected five organizing components of a comprehensive curriculum: (1) physical, (2) communicative, (3) creative, (4) inquiring, and (5) cultural. The first four areas are adapted from Stephanie Feeney's, (1987) *Who Am I in the Lives of Children?* The cultural component was added to address the unique thrust of VFC. It can be expanded or changed to address the focus of other multicultural programs. Thirty-one curricular areas have been identified within the five components. The areas of the curriculum are listed in Figure 11.1.

At the beginning of each section of the curriculum is a conceptual overview of each area of the curriculum. This is designed to give the teachers a brief orientation to each area they will be teaching and prepare them to use techniques that represent the latest methodology in early childhood education.

Over 120 concepts distributed over the thirty-one curricular areas have been identified; that have been developed into specific lessons and instructional objectives for teaching the children. Additionally, each concept has been broken down into an instructional objective. This is the unit that the teachers enter on their daily lesson plans. In the curriculum guide, an exemplary activity is given for each objective so that it is clear to the teacher what the concept is and how it is to be taught. Following the brief description of the activity is the identification of the book from which the

Figure 11.1 Curriculum Concepts

COMMUNICATIVE	CREATIVE
Listening	Art
Speaking	Music
Perception	Creative movement
Literacy	
Literature	
Writing	

INQUIRING	
Scientific method	CULTURAL
Health	African-American studies
Safety	African studies
Social studies	African-Caribbean studies
Mathematics	Social skills
Physics	Nonviolent conflict resolution
Chemistry	
Geology	
Meteorology	
Astronomy	
Biology	
Human body	
Ecology	PHYSICAL
Computer science	Manipulatives
Nutrition	Gross-motor development

activity is drawn and the page number of the activity in the book. Materials are also listed that are needed to teach the activity. There is an additional indication of other books in the VFC library that the teacher can consult for other activities that teach the same objective.

RESEARCH COMPONENT OF THE PROGRAM

The research component of Visions for Children was funded for two years by the Council for Economic Opportunities of Greater Cleveland. It is presently funded by the Cleveland Foundation.

Comparison of VFC and Control Group

To evaluate the effectiveness of the Visions for Children program, we selected a day-care center in Cleveland, Ohio, to serve as a control group for the study. This center has provided childcare services in Cleveland for eighteen years. The hours of operation are 6:30 A.M. to 5:30 P.M., Monday through Friday, year round. The center serves families with children aged 18 months to 8 years, including full-day kindergarten, after-school and holiday care for school-age children, and a toddler program for children still in diapers.

Children are enrolled in both VFC and the control group on a family self-selection basis. The parents select the program and pay fees. The control group has Title 20 funding that pays for services for lower-income families. Visions for Children provides a sliding fee scale for lower-income families. Up to 30 percent of the slots of the center are allocated for reduced-fee enrollments. The remaining slots are occupied by children from working-class and middle-class families.

There is no claim that either center fits any particular configuration in terms of socioeconomic level. The primary consideration was that there be no significant difference in the configurations of the two groups. An important consideration in selecting the control group mentioned above was matching VFC children on the dimension of socioeconomic status. This is an important variable for black children. Without such controls, it could be argued that any differences in the achievement of the children were due to socioeconomic characteristics of the families. We used the Hollingshead Four Factor Index of Social Status, which creates a score based upon parent education, occupation, sex, and marital status.

An overall t-test was conducted on the age of the subjects in both groups and the Hollingshead scores to determine whether the two groups of children were comparable. The overall age of the VFC children was 47.13 months, and the average age of the control group children was 45.00 months. (Only children who fell within the age groups served at VFC were selected for the control group.) There was no significant difference in age.

The overall Hollingshead score for the VFC children was 42.05 months. The overall Hollingshead score for the control group children was 41.95 months. There was no significant difference in the scores between the two groups.

One reason for selecting the control group was its reputation as a quality day-care center. Observations in the center confirm that impression. The center is an established program, having been in operation for eighteen years.

The staffs of both programs are racially integrated. At the control group, the director (with a master's degree in early childhood education), one teacher assistant, one teacher holding a bachelor's degree, and one teacher holding an associate degree are Caucasian. The assistant director, three teacher assistants, and one teacher holding an associate degree are African-American.

The staff of the control group has a higher level of credentialing than the VFC staff. All of the VFC teachers who are African-American have high school diplomas, which is the minimum standard required by the state licensing agency for a child day-care provider. The center director at VFC, who is Caucasian, has a bachelor's degree in early childhood education.

The structure of the two programs is different. At both programs, the children are divided into small groups. The group sizes range from seven children for the 2- to 3-year-olds to fourteen children maximum for the other age levels. The groups at VFC are named after African tribes: Ibo, Fanti, Zulu, Kikuyu, and Kumasi.

The large room used by the VFC program is divided into six areas, where the following activities occur: gross-motor development, housekeeping/dramatic play, block play, sand play, computers, circle time, book corner, science, manipulatives, math, music, art, cultural, woodworking, writing center, easel painting, chalkboard. The children and teachers move through the rooms on a schedule. Snack and lunch are served in three areas. There is also a large backyard with a beautiful lawn and outdoor play equipment. There are swings, a basketball rim, and a climbing apparatus.

The control group classrooms are self-contained. The children are grouped by age in small groups and have one or two assigned teachers. There is a large motor area that is used by all of the children.

The control group schedule is less structured than the VFC schedule. General time slots are indicated on the schedule. The time slots on the VFC schedule are indexed to a specific area of the curriculum. The menu of activities is more clearly designated in the VFC program.

Activity time begins in the morning at 9:15 at the control group program. Activity time begins at 8:30 at VFC. At the control group, an hour is provided for outdoor play and forty-five minutes for free play in the afternoon. Those who wish to continue free play may do so for another hour and fifteen minutes or they may choose to participate in special activities. VFC provides thirty minutes for free play in the morning and thirty minutes for gross-motor activities in the afternoon. During the gross-motor period the children are taught specific skills that are contained in the curriculum. Obviously the control group children spend more time in unstructured activities.

The control group schedule reflects that one hour and ten minutes are used in preparation for and eating lunch. The VFC schedule devotes thirty minutes to these activities. The afternoon at the control group is relatively unstructured. Preparation for departure begins as early as 3:30. The VFC children continue structured activities until 5:00 each day. They then may select activities until their departure at 6:00. There is no "preparation for departure."

VFC has five Apple IIc personal computers and one dot matrix image writer. The control group does not have computers. VFC children use the computers daily for at least thirty minutes. They may also choose to use them during child-selected activities.

The lesson plan used by the control group basically shows a week at a glance. It indicates the activity with a one-sentence description of what will be taught in each time slot. The VFC lesson plan is more detailed (the daily activity plans described above). It is a one-page planning form that lists the objective (drawn from the curriculum), points to be emphasized, materials, procedure for teaching the activity, and extensions. Each teacher completes an average of three lesson plans daily. Each teaches the same lesson three times on a rotating basis to the groups in the morning and one or two different lessons to the rotating groups in the afternoon.

The VFC curriculum, contained in a four-inch notebook, is over 500 pages in length. The control group curriculum is approximately fourteen pages long and contains statements of educational philosophy and goals. There are three pages each that describe objectives for toddlers, 3-year-olds and 4-year-olds. The objectives are divided into three categories; relationships, self-esteem, and ego skills.

Observations at the control group program reveal that attention to African-American culture varies from classroom to classroom and from time to time. Special attention is paid to Dr. Martin Luther King's birthday and Black History Month. There are a few pictures of African-American children on the walls. African-American dolls are provided, and stories are read that feature African-American children. There is no mention of Africa or African-American culture in the curriculum goals or educational philosophy.

As noted earlier, an emphasis on African-American culture is a central part of the thrust of Visions for Children. Pictures of African-American children are everywhere. The majority of the dolls are African-American, although a few are Asian and Caucasian. The puzzles feature African-Americans pictured in different careers and settings, as do books and puppets. African-American culture is taught three days a week and is infused throughout other curricular areas wherever possible.

Three of the twelve monthly themes are devoted to topics in African and African-American culture. The nine remaining themes cover mainstream topics. All of the heroes and sheroes are either figures in black culture or involved in important events such as the signing of the 14th Amendment to the Constitution.

Standardized Tests

Stardardized tests are used as a data-gathering device in evaluating the responses of children to Visions for Children. Their use is not intended to convey confidence in their assessment reliability for African-American children. Padilla and Wyatt (1983) have provided a fine review of the effects of intelligence and achievement testing on minority-group children. I agree with their suggestion that:

> The major thrust of the testing movement must be the development of criterion-sampling techniques and the elimination of norm-referenced tests. . . . The inclusion of adaptive behavior scales and the consideration of sociocultural factors . . . is the strategy of choice. (p. 435)

However, I also agree with the assertion of Barbara Sizemore in a personal conversation that the best way to assure that standardized tests are abolished in America *is for all African-American children to pass them.* Even though we acknowledge the shortcomings and political agendas surrounding standardized tests, we also must recognize that their use is becoming more widespread. I do not recommend that early childhood education programs "teach to the test." However, children who are educated in a culturally appropriate manner should have no difficulty in scoring well on those tests. A key factor in scoring well is exposure to the experiences and vocabulary that represent the objects and concepts on the test.

Research Design

To implement the research component of VFC, a literature review was conducted of child development measures that could assess the desired outcome of the program. These areas were general cognitive abilities, child behavior, self-concept, delay of gratification, and racial attitudes. Instruments were tentatively selected in each category as a result of the literature review. Four consultants reviewed the instruments and literature associated with them and wrote recommendations for final selection of the instruments of this study. Interestingly, there was no disagreement among the consultants. One consultant might not have had a recommendation in a particular category; another, however, might have had a strong recommendation. In several categories more than one consultant strongly recommended the same instruments.

All children enrolled in VFC are tested each year on the child development measures described below. The control group of children is also tested. All children in the study will be tested each year as they matriculate in the primary grades. These data will be analyzed longitudinally to establish the long-term effects of the program and to revise the curriculum based on these outcomes.

Listed below are the research questions of the study and the child development measures used to investigate each question.

1. *Does exposure to the Visions for Children program result in measurable gains in the cognitive abilities of African-American children?* This was investigated using the McCarthy Scales of Children's Abilities (MSCA) (McCarthy, 1972), which provides a measure of children's overall cognitive skills. It is an individually administered test of general cognitive abilities that can be used with children from 2½ to 8 years of age; administration time for children under 5 years of age is approximately forty-five to fifty minutes. The test consists of eighteen individual subtests, which form six scales: verbal, perceptual-performance, quantitative, memory, motor, and an overall general cognitive index (GCI—made up of the verbal, quantitative, and perceptual-performance scales). While there is considerable, ongoing debate about bias in IQ measures with black children, the test still provides useful information about children's overall cognitive abilities.

The MSCA has many assets that counterbalance some of the liabilities of using IQ measures with black children. (The majority of my reviewers do not call it an IQ measure.) In general, the psychometric properties of the MSCA are good. The standardization sample for the test is excellent and fairly recent. In addition, validity and reliability are acceptable. Another strength of the MSCA is that it is appealing to children. Materials are colorful and stimulating, and the individual subtests are relatively short; thus children do not tend to have difficulties attending to task. Also, unlike other measures, the MSCA contains a motor component, with both gross- and fine-motor tasks.

2. *Does attendance at the Visions for Children program result in African-American children becoming more in-group oriented?* There is a tendency for African-American children to prefer white physical traits and to attribute more positive characteristics to white people than to African-American people. A major question of the study is whether participating in an early childhood education program with an African-American cultural component reverses that trend. We used the Preschool Racial Attitudes Measure (PRAM II) (Williams, 1975), which is a picture test that is designed to assess racial bias among preliterate children. It has excellent reliability and validity.

3. *Are there distinctive styles that characterize the behavior of African-American children in classrooms?* There is evidence in the literature that there is cultural dissonance between African-American culture and the culture of the schools (Rashid, 1981). The Report of Child Behavior (Schaefer, 1987) measure has been administered as a first step in examining relevant dimensions of classroom behavior. This is an instrument that has the virtue of evaluating more normal and less pathological behavior than many of the other instruments that are available. Many of the others are seeking to identify juvenile delinquency rather than normal classroom adjustment. They result in being biased against African-American male children.

4. *Does participation in the Visions for Children program empower African-American children and enhance their self-esteem?* We seek to answer this question by using the Pictorial Scale of Perceived Competence and Social Acceptance (Harter & Pike, 1984). It has four subscales: cognitive competence, physical competence, peer acceptance, and maternal acceptance. There are two assessments in this measure: the children's self assessment and the teacher's assessment. Susan Harter, the author, has done some excellent work in the area of self-concept for older children, and this is a recently developed scale for preschool and kindergarten children.

5. *Does participation in the Visions for Children program enhance the ability of African-American children to engage in sustained effort for delayed rewards?* A technique developed by Schwarz (1981), Delay of Gratification, is used. Teachers rate the children on their ability to defer gratification, an important skill needed for achievement.

6. *Does participation in the Visions for Children program result in measurable gains in reading readiness skills useful for success in kindergarten?* We selected the Metropolitan Readiness Test (1976) as an outcome measure for the children entering kindergarten. The test is a group-administered, multiple-skill battery that takes approximately eighty to ninety minutes for children to complete. There are two levels available, with level 1 being appropriate for the children beginning kindergarten.

The test is used extensively and has good organization and clarity. In addition, a great deal of psychometric work has been carried out that demonstrates its substantial reliability and validity. In general, the test can provide useful screening information pertaining to achievement-oriented skills useful upon school entrance.

7. *Does participation in the Visions for Children program result in measurable gains in achievement-oriented skills?* To answer this question, we used the Stanford Achievement Test (1985). This is an outcome measure for the children entering first grade and at the completion of

each year of the primary grades. The test is a group administered, multiple-skill battery.

The test takes approximately 1½ to 2½ hours for children to complete. It is recommended that it be given in two to three sittings. The test is used extensively and has good organization and clarity. In addition, a great deal of psychometric work has been carried out that demonstrates its substantial reliability and validity. In general, the test can provide useful information pertaining to achievement-oriented skills.

Summary of Data Analysis

A summary of the measures administered during phase 3 are reported in this chapter. An analysis of phase 1 and 2 testing is reported in Hale-Benson (1990b). The VFC children scored significantly higher on five of the six subtests of the McCarthy Scales (perception, quantitative, general cognitive, memory, and motor) (McCarthy, 1972). There was a nonsignificant difference between the two groups on the remaining subtest, verbal.

The control group scored significantly higher on Delay of Gratification (Schwarz, 1981). The VFC children scored higher on two components of the self-concept measure: assessment of their own cognitive abilities and teacher's assessment of their physical abilities. The control group scored significantly higher on two components of the self-concept measure: teacher's assessment of the child's cognitive abilities and teacher's assessment of peer acceptance. There was a nonsignificant difference between the groups on three components of self-concept: own opinion of peer approval, own opinion of physical abilities, and perception of maternal acceptance. The VFC children scored significantly higher on the Child Behavior measure (Schaefer, 1987).

A surprising finding was that even though both groups of African-American children indicated an out-group orientation (more positive characteristics attributed to Caucasians) on the Racial Attitudes measure (Williams, 1975), the control group children showed less of a Caucasian orientation than the VFC children. This is surprising because a major thrust of the VFC program is an Afrocentric perspective.

A conversation with Dr. Harriette McAdoo (Howard University) revealed that African-American preschool children tend to score similarly to white children until they are about 8 years old. Her data reveal that differences made by educational programs on racial attitudes emerge at that age. We also discussed the possibility that children who score higher on cognitive abilities measures may be more astute at reflecting the attitudes of the general society and that more direct instruction is needed to counteract the messages of the media.

Visions for Children has attempted to provide an integrated, subtle approach to incorporating African-American culture in the curriculum. We discussed the fact that it is difficult to counteract Eurocentric cultural overtones with a subtle presentation of African-American culture.

As a result of these data, steps were taken in the program year following the phase 3 evaluation to engage the children in more direct activities that are designed to create an in-group orientation, such as mealtime chants and pledges.

The VFC children scored higher on sixteen of the twenty-two subtests on the Metropolitan Reading Readiness Test (1976), but the difference between the groups was nonsignificant. On the Stanford Achievement Test (1985), the VFC children scored significantly higher on visual recognition and vocabulary than the control group. Even though there was not a significant difference on the remaining four tests (sound recognition, comprehension, language expression, and mathematics concepts and applications), the VFC children consistently scored higher on all except language expression.

The graduates of both programs will be tested as long as the project is funded to determine whether they sustain the gains made through attending this preschool program.

The control group was selected because it is a quality early childhood education center, which has been in operation for eighteen years. As pointed out earlier, the staff in the control group also has a higher level of training than the VFC staff. Therefore the fact that the VFC group scored higher than the control group on over half of the tests administered is a good beginning.

REFERENCES

Berrueta-Clement, J. R., Schweinhart, L. J., Barnett, W. S., Epstein, A. S., & Weikert, D. P. (1984). *Changed lives: Effects of the Perry Preschool Program on youth through age 19*. Ypsilanti, MI: High Scope Press.

Bissell, J. (1971). *Implementation of planned variation in Head Start*. Washington, DC: U.S. Office of Child Development, Department of Health, Education and Welfare.

DeVos, G. (1975). Ethnic pluralism: Conflict and accommodation. In G. DeVos & L. Romanuci-Ross (Eds.), *Ethnic identity: Cultural continuities and change* (pp. 14–24). Palo Alto, CA: Manfield.

Feeney, S. (1987). *Who am I in the lives of children?* Columbus, OH: Merrill.

Fleming, J. (1985). *Blacks in college.* San Francisco: Jossey-Bass.

Hale-Benson, J. E. (1986). *Black children: Their roots, culture and learning styles.* Baltimore: Johns Hopkins University Press.

Hale-Benson, J. E. (1990a). Visions for children: African-American preschool program. *Early Childhood Research Quarterly, 5,* 199–213.

Hale-Benson, J. E. (1990b). Visions for children: Educating black children in the context of their culture. In K. Lomotey (Ed.), *Going to school: The African-American experience* (pp. 209–222). Albany: State University of New York Press.

Harter, S., & R. Pike. (1984). Pictorial scale of perceived competence and social acceptance for young children. *Child Development, 55,* 1969–1982.

Karnes, M. B., Schwedel, A. M., & Williams, M. B. (1983). In the consortium for longitudinal studies *As the twig is bent* . . . lasting effects of preschool programs. Hillsdale, NJ: Erlbaum.

McCarthy, D. A. (1972). *Manual for the McCarthy Scales of Children's Abilities.* New York: Psychological Corporation.

Metropolitan Readiness Tests. (1976). New York: Harcourt Brace Jovanovich.

Moore, E. (1985). Ethnicity as a variable in child development. In M. Spencer, G. Brookins, & W. Allen (Eds.), *Beginnings: The social and affective development of black children* (pp. 101–116). Hillsdale, NJ: Erlbaum.

Padilla, E. R., & Wyatt, G. E. (1983). The effects of intelligence and achievement testing on minority group children. In G. J. Powell (Ed.), *The psychosocial development of minority group children* (pp. 417–437). New York: Brunner/Mazel.

Rashid, H. (1981). Early childhood education as a cultural transition for African American children. *Educational Research Quarterly, 6,* 55–63.

Schaefer, E. S. (1987). Maternal prenatal, infancy, and concurrent predictions of maternal reports of child psychopathology. *Psychiatry, 50*(4), 320–331.

Schwartz, J. C. (1981). Measuring individual differences in self-control and self-regulation in early childhood. (ERIC Document No. ED 204 008) April, 22pp.

Semaj, L. (1985). Afrikanity, cognitive and extended self-identity. In M. Spencer, G. Brookins, & W. Allen (Eds.), *Beginnings: The social and affective development of black children* (pp. 173–183). Hillsdale, NJ: Erlbaum.

Spencer, M. B. (1985). Cultural cognition and social cognition as identity correlates of black children's personal-social development. In M. Spencer, G. Brookins, & W. Allen (Eds.), *Beginnings: The social and affective development of black children* (pp. 215–230). Hillsdale, NJ: Erlbaum.

Stanford Achievement Test. (1985). Monterey, CA: California Testing Bureau, McGraw-Hill.

Williams, J. (1975). Preschool Racial Attitude Measure II. *Educational and Psychological Measurement, 35*(1), 3–18.

PART IV

VOICES FROM THE FIELD: TEACHER NARRATIVES AND COLLABORATIVE WORK

The chapters in this section reflect a growing trend in educational research in which the relationship between the researcher and the researched is made problematic and the voices of teachers and students are emphasized. Such work includes autobiographical life history work, action research, and collaborative work in early childhood settings. Chapter 12 is written by a primary teacher in a Friends school and an early childhood researcher. Beth Blue Swadener and Dorothy Piekielek draw from their collaborative work (i.e., an ethnography of conflict management and peace education with young children and the production of a videotape on social problem solving with children) to discuss the roles of teachers and children in consensus decision making and other aspects of Friends education. The chapter is based largely on teacher voices drawn from interviews and also includes several reflections of adults who were former students in Quaker schools.

Chapter 13 is written by one of the pioneers in our field in terms of early childhood teacher autobiography, voice, collaboration for action research, community advocacy, and curriculum—William Ayers. Ayers has worked directly with urban teachers from diverse backgrounds for much of his career. His chapter in this volume is a vehicle for progressive early childhood educators from Chicago to tell their stories, struggles, and successes. Just as much of the previous chapter was drawn from group interviews with early childhood teachers, this Chapter draws from the dialogue at "Teacher Talk" monthly meetings of progressive Chicago teachers. Several times the Chicago teachers raise similar or identical issues and visions as the teachers in the small, rural Friends school described in Chapter 12. Thus some of the emergent themes in this section are shared, and again the importance of the "recovery of voice" through the telling of such stories is emphasized, as it has been in other chapters.

It is appropriate, then, that the final chapter in this section—and in the book—is written by a kindergarten teacher doing curriculum research in her own classroom. Monica Miller Marsh describes her first year of teaching kindergarten in an urban, culturally diverse setting in which she attempted throughout the year to implement antibias curriculum. Through her daily journal entries, analysis of children's informal enactment of activities, drawings/journals, and conversations, the observations of a collaborative researcher (Beth Blue Swadener), and discussions with parents, Miller shows—largely through the children's own words—many of the issues of race, class, gender, ability, and age that the children are actively, often passionately, interested in learning about. This example demonstrates what one teacher, together with her young students, can accomplish by moving antibias curriculum from the margins to the center of the early educational experience.

CHAPTER 12

Beyond Democracy to Consensus
Reflections on a Friends School
Collaborative Ethnography

Beth Blue Swadener
Dorothy Piekielek

This chapter was coauthored by a kindergarten–first grade teacher, Dorothy Piekielek, and an early childhood researcher, Beth Swadener, who began collaborating in 1987, initially on an ethnographic study of social problem solving and consensus decision making with young children, and later on the production of a videotape, *Teaching Toward Peace*. This chapter draws from data collected during a two-year ethnographic study of the Friends school where Dorothy teaches. The process of working with four teachers and their students is used as a framework for discussing the role of teacher values and Friends (Quaker) ideology, with particular focus on social problem solving and types of collaboration with students and colleagues. Teachers' interpretations of classroom culture and group process are discussed from both "insider" and "outsider" perspectives, drawing implications for collaborative research, teacher empowerment, and alternative social problem solving approaches in early childhood settings. Our chapter title, "Beyond Democracy to Consensus," refers to the fact that much of the social problem solving and decision making used in this school was not based on simple majority rule (Sheeran, 1983). Rather, a consensus decision-making process of coming to a "sense of the group" on matters of importance to young children was used. We offer these reflections on consensus decision making and collaborative research as potential ways of reconceptualizing early childhood education.

As coauthors of this chapter, we continue to struggle with the best way to include and clarify both our separate voices, the voices of the others involved in this research, and our shared interpretations. We begin with two "stories" about how this collaboration began, then share some information on the setting, children, and teachers. The sections that follow juxtapose several direct quotes from Friends school teachers with quotes from a book of reflections on Friends education and highlights from our data that show children engaged in consensus decision making. Much of the dialogue is taken from a two-hour semistructured interview at the end of the second year of the case study of this school, in which teachers discussed their values and practices with a focus on social problem solving, including consensus decision making, and their insights about coconstructing classroom culture with young learners. We then present an example of schoolwide consensus decisions regarding rules for the "Friendly Woods." We conclude with our reflections and suggestions for successful and inclusive collaborative work and describe how the process of producing a videotape is an example of the many possibilities for intensive and mutually fulfilling collaboration between a teacher and a researcher.

DEVELOPMENT OF THE PROJECT

A Step Toward Peace/A Step Toward Collaboration

Beth: During my first year of teaching at Penn State University, I met an incredible woman—a peace and social justice activist, mother, early childhood education advocate, and teacher in the local Friends school. We met in the context of bringing a play, *A Step Toward Peace*, to campus to give my social studies methods students a taste of the "possibilities" for young people through bringing social issues alive with performance and expressive arts. The play was written and performed by young people (fourth- through twelfth-graders) from the public alternative school and from the Friends school where Dorothy taught. Dorothy was one of the adult consultants and organizers for the play and was helping the young actors facilitate workshops for college students following the play when we first began to talk about shared interests. Later, I visited her school and the collaboration began to take shape.

I shared with Dorothy my enthusiasm for research that documents positive practices and possibilities for socially responsible, culturally inclusive, and antibias education in early childhood settings and described briefly my previous case study of two childcare centers that were attempting to implement a more multicultural curriculum. Would she be interested in working with me on a project documenting some of the aspects of Friends education in terms of peace education, conflict management, and teaching about social issues with young people? As an enthusiastic researcher, I was forming my agenda as we talked about possibilities for a collaborative endeavor.

Dorothy: State College is a small community, so the word spreads quickly when a new community activist moves into the area. I had heard about Beth long before I met her. We met briefly during the performance of *A Step Toward Peace*. Then, in the spring of 1987, a mutual acquaintance brought Beth to visit the Friends school. It was during this visit that Beth mentioned her interest in possibly doing research on peace education in our school. I was immediately enthusiastic for two reasons. First, I saw it as a learning opportunity for me. I hoped that Beth would be a resource for information and expertise, and also that she would be an outside, objective observer who could give me valuable feedback about my teaching.

My second reason for excitement was the possibility of collaborating with Beth on the production of a videotape. I had a vague idea about producing a video that could be used in conjunction with a workshop for adults, addressing how to do conflict management with children. Beth was not only enthusiastic about making a video—she could also provide the video equipment! After three years of hard work and lots of learning, both of my goals were met. Beth was the resource I had hoped for, and we completed the production of a video that I have been using success-fully in workshops. There were other unexpected benefits for me that resulted from this project. I acquired knowledge about collaborative research and video production; I was forced to clarify my thinking about peace education and conflict management, with the result that I could communicate it more clearly; I found myself reevaluating some of my beliefs and assumptions about peace education and teaching; and I found a close friend and mentor in Beth.

Getting Started

One of the possibilities that interested us both was the use of video-tape to document some of the typical activities and discussions with the children. As noted, Dorothy was interested in eventually having a video-tape to use in her many workshops with parents and teachers (addressing conflict management) in order to bring the concepts discussed "to life" with real classroom examples. Beth was interested in having more class-room examples for use in teacher education courses and for research purposes. In the months that followed our first meeting, we obtained a small amount of funding for our project and began to discuss our ideas with the rest of the staff at the Friends school.

In May 1987 we met with the entire staff of the Friends school and discussed several potential questions that our study might address. The following questions initially guided the study:

1. What are age-appropriate learning experiences for elementary children that deal with acceptance of human diversity, nonviolent conflict resolution, and other forms of "social knowledge"?
2. How do children create their own learning experiences in these areas, and how do children differ in preferences for social problem-solving strategies? Do these approaches "work" for all children, or do they work "better" for some children than for others?
3. How do the philosophy and values of the school and its teachers influence the curriculum, and what are some of the ways in which a Friends school conveys its philosophy throughout the curriculum and environment?
4. What factors appear to empower teachers to remain committed to a variety of "possibilities" in education (including the possibility for peace and social reconstruction)? What forms of support do teachers provide for one another, and what forms of support do they seek "outside" the school environment?

It should be noted that data and issues related to questions 3 and 4 are addressed in this chapter and data related to the first two questions are reviewed in more depth in an earlier paper (Swadener & Piekielek, 1988).

Initially the teachers had questions about such an open-ended style of research (ethnography), in which themes and further research questions would "emerge" from the observations and other data we would be collecting. There were also some concerns about having the video camera in the classroom so frequently and about how children and parents might feel about the project. We discussed other uses of the videotapes, including some potential uses with parents new to the school and in conflict management workshops. Teachers expressed a desire not only to continue refining and reassessing their human relations, social issues, and peace lessons and curricula, but also to document the process in such a way that it could be effectively shared with other teachers, parents, and community groups from whom they received requests for workshops, ideas, and guidance.

We should also acknowledge that in such a small, private school a collaborative "tone" was already in place and was very advantageous to the type of study we had proposed. As we will describe later, teachers also met together to view some of the videotapes, and we both spent many long hours systematically viewing and analyzing all thirty-six hours of tapes.

In the initial meeting, teachers mentioned that they were trying to plan more units focusing on understanding and accepting individual differences, including special needs, and that a focused unit on developmental differences was planned for the following fall. They also mentioned some of their civil rights and peacemakers units, which might be interesting to document.

We obtained further research support in the form of a preservice teacher who was hired as a work–study research assistant and came to the school twice a week during most of the following year. By September 1987 the collaborative project had grown from one researcher and one teacher to include four teachers, one director, and one research assistant. Several times the school's administrative assistant and parent volunteers assisted in videotaping, making relevant documents available, and assisting our work in other ways. During the second year of the project we were joined by a community member with interests in filmmaking and little experience with young children. He provided both the perspective of a truly "naive observer" and a steadier hand on the videocam than any of us, proving to be a wonderful addition to the team.

As in any project, some members of this collaborative "team" were greater "stakeholders" than others in the project, but certainly everyone cooperated, shared ideas, and generally put up with a research "presence" in the classroom over a two-year period. We decided to keep the videotape equipment at the school, and teachers occasionally asked a parent or colleague to tape activities and discussions that they thought relevant to the project.

SETTING AND METHODOLOGY

The setting of this research is a small Friends school, located (during the period of data collection) in two large downstairs rooms of a Friends meeting house in a rural, central Pennsylvania community (population 40,000). The school has been in operation since 1980. There were forty-three children, ages 5 through 11 years, enrolled in the school during the first year of the project.

One downstairs classroom (typically referred to as the "front room") combined kindergarten and first grades, and the other ("back room") combined second- through fourth-grade children. During the first year of the project each room had a lead teacher and an assistant teacher. In the case of the back room, the assistant teacher, Jane, was doing a first-year internship with an experienced head teacher. In the second year of the study, Jane took over a new fifth-grade class when fifth grade was added that year.

Sheri, the lead teacher in the "older room," had fourteen years of teaching experience, and Dorothy, the lead teacher in the "younger room," had five years of teaching experience at the beginning of our work together. During the first year of the study, Eileen was Dorothy's assistant teacher; during the second year, Eileen and Dorothy each had their own K–1 classroom (and Dorothy had an assistant teacher).

Other staff included a full-time school head and an administrative assistant, both of whom spent some time each week in the classroom, particularly when special activities were being carried out. Additionally, parents, grandparents, and some community members were often present as classroom visitors and volunteers.

All staff at the time of this research were European-American women. During the final year of our collaboration, a male school head with extensive urban teaching experience was hired.

Of the seven staff members in the school at this time, three were actively involved with the Friends meeting. One issue in this school, as in most Friends schools, is the lack of familiarity with Friends principles on the part of teachers who are not involved in the Friends meeting. At this Friends school, non-Quaker teachers were educated about the principles of Friends through reading and group discussions. Also, in the hiring process, teachers were sought who would "fit well" in the school because their beliefs and lifestyles were compatible with Friends beliefs.

The "all-purpose room" upstairs was used by the school for lunch, movement activities, and special programs, and the meeting room was used for all-school meeting for worship and for rehearsals of the school's peace choir.

Of the forty-three children attending the school when we began the collaborative project, seven were children of color, including three African-American boys (one in the younger group and two in the older group), two Asian-Americans (Indian and Japanese-American), and two children in the younger group who were of Latin American background (from Chile). The remainder of the children were European-American, reflecting the relative percentages of cultural diversity in the community in which the school is located. In terms of religious diversity, a number of religious backgrounds, including Christian, Krishna, and Jewish, were represented, with only two families having formal membership in the Friends meeting that operated the school.

In terms of socioeconomic status and indicators, no explicit information on parents' education or employment and income status was collected. In general terms, the school serves middle-class professional families, many of whom commute from rural settings into the community for work or school. The school appeared to be committed to providing access to families with limited incomes and had succeeded to the extent that eleven of the students (during 1987–88 year) received scholarship support. The major fund-raising activities of the school were directed toward this scholarship fund. The commitment to continuing to develop a more culturally diverse and income-balanced enrollment was frequently expressed by both the school head and the two head teachers.

Our research utilized an ethnographic case study approach, with repeated participant observations and both informal and semistructured interviews with children and with teachers. It also utilized analysis of videotapes of activities, discussion, and classroom interactions. As mentioned earlier, the video camera was used not only by the researcher and research assistant but also by the school staff and volunteers in order to document relevant activities and discussions.

Fieldnotes made on each visit by Beth and the assistant were transcribed onto computer disks and often shared with the lead teachers, particularly Dorothy, for "validity checks" and discussion of emerging trends or issues. Over 200 hours of fieldnotes and 36 hours of videotape were collected during the two years of data collection. As discussed earlier, teachers viewed and discussed some of the videotapes at informal meetings both at school and in Beth's home. This helped clarify questions, identify issues, and provide a better sense of the teachers' interpretation of activities in the classroom.

During the spring semester of the 1987–88 school year, all the children were interviewed about their school, how problems were solved, how they interpreted meeting for worship, centering activities, and other unique aspects of Friends education. We also discussed their definitions of peace and their thoughts about what it would take to make the world a more peaceful place (these findings are discussed in Swadener & Piekielek, 1988). Teachers helped in developing the interview questions and also discussed the children's responses at a staff meeting. Among our findings were patterns, by age, of responses to questions concerning how children thought about peace and whether peace was possible. The youngest children tended to think about parents, pets, and places in nature when they pictured peace, and second- and third-grade children discussed an absence of fighting or getting along at school. The oldest children, third- and fourth-graders, discussed peace from a more global perspective, and many held strong views that peace was not possible until racism, hatred between Jews and Arabs, and the arms race were ended. These views reflected many of the discussions and activities focusing on social justice that are typically part of a Friends education.

It was also interesting to interview children about their impressions of meeting for worship, centering, and other activities typical of Friends schooling. Many children recalled vividly the first time they had "centered," including one 7-year-old girl who remembered a visualization done the year before on St. Patrick's Day in which she "saw green everywhere" and got so quiet she could "hear that voice inside." Some children described such quiet times as when they "talked to God" or "held God's hand," but others said they did not view it as a religious thing but liked to just calm down during a busy school day. Some of the older children complained about how distracting it was when the kindergarteners could not sit still or keep quiet during meeting for worship, and others said they did not like this part of the day and found it boring.

In addition to formal observations during the school year, Beth participated in other school-related activities, including two year-end all-school campouts and talent shows, three "Fun Fairs" (the major scholarship fund-raiser held each spring as a major community event), a parent meeting, and several staff meetings.

WHY A FRIENDS SCHOOL?
QUAKER VALUES IN EVERYDAY PRACTICE

In this particular community the Friends school was one of very few alternatives to public education for families. The Friends school was known locally for being child-centered, process-oriented, grounded in principles of justice and conflict resolution, and committed to holistic education, in which social skills of children were no less important than academic subjects and mastery of essential skills. In other words, this project did not set out to be primarily a study of Quaker education per se but sought to find a setting where a number of possibilities for coconstructing learning with children were being actively explored and implemented in daily practice. The Friends school served this role very well, and the teachers, director, and administrative assistant all made suggestions early on about when Beth should come (e.g., on days when all-school meeting for worship was held, when problem-solving discussions were anticipated, and when activities focusing on human diversity and social responsibility were to be introduced).

A contrast between the initial two collaborators was our different levels of familiarity with Quaker practices and Friends education. As an attender of the Friends meeting and a teacher in the Friends school, Dorothy was clearly the "insider"; as a researcher interested in Friends education, Beth was the "outsider" who was attempting to "make the strange familiar." One of the books that Dorothy shared was *Reflections from a Friends Education*, an edited collection of brief personal reflections on many aspects of Friends education (Dorrance, 1982). The following passages may help illuminate further the purpose, general atmosphere, and curricular goals of Friends schools (emphasis added where points were particularly relevant to this research):

> A Friends school offers the chance to share in a community's struggle to transmute an ideal into human fact.
>
> These schools hope . . . to create an environment within which students and staff alike can continue to mature as *companions* in a wide range of experiences. These experiences, both outward and inward in nature, may bring forth in each (as each is ready and in forms appropriate to different age levels) a deepening awareness of the presence of God. Recognizing that response will vary from individual to individual, a Friends school cannot promise results nor catalogue a project.
>
> Since Friends education is religious at heart, it therefore tends to be socially responsible. A person's training and heightened gifts extend to neighbors as well. Peace and war, racism and brotherhood, ignorance and poverty, justice and law and violence, all these are both subjects for study and issues for commitment, now as students and soon as effective citizens.
>
> To be effective, all people must be freed insofar as possible from incompetence and ignorance. They need to be increasingly able to handle the signals of meaning that everyone uses. They should be able to sense, to see, to *listen*, to read with sureness; to write, to speak, and to project their thoughts with clarity. They should be able to respond compassionately, thoughtfully, and critically as appropriate to the material and the occasion. They need a stock of basic information and the *key techniques of problem-solving*. They need constant encouragement and opportunity to be playful and creative and involved. They need the tools and the training and the time to develop their manual and artistic skills. And students, especially, need an environment within which these enterprises of body and mind and spirit can be cherished and strengthened. (pp. 8–9)

With the above emphasis on the strong religious basis of many of the Friends school practices and goals, it was interesting to learn, as mentioned earlier, that of the forty-three children attending Friends school during the first year of our research, only two children's parents were members of Friends meeting. However, all parents were well informed about the ways in which Friends principles were evident and were taught in the school. In fact, most families come to the school because they have social values and beliefs similar to or compatible with those of Friends and they want these values to be encouraged in their children.

Teacher Dialogue and Quaker Values

It was also interesting to compare aspects of this description to ways in which teachers in our project described their views of teaching in a Friends school setting. The idea of teachers and students as companions or equal stakeholders in the classroom was reflected in the following quote from an experienced teacher, Sheri:

> The classroom is a place where students and teachers and anyone who comes into the classroom are allies. They live together in this space for academic kinds of activities and learning, for the routine, and the ups and downs of life. *It's a very full life in that classroom.* The way you do that is to make space for not only the diversity of individuals in the classroom, including the teacher, but the way you do that is to make space for the diversity of things that go on in life. You're not only creating the academic environment, but you're creating the developmental environment for yourself as the teacher, and for the students and the parents that come in and maybe pick up on some other things that they see in terms of interaction. I think the hallmark of that is that it has to be *honest and authentic*, just like your home is. At home you live your life, and the children are in and out of it. As a parent you make demands on them; as children, they make demands on you. It's just a kind of ebb and flow that's real, and the classroom has to be that way.

When responding to the above comments, Beth interpreted Sheri as implying that there was much mutual respect between teacher and children. Sheri's response, which follows, demonstrates the tendency of an "outside" researcher to misinterpret or use prior concepts to interpret inaccurately what the teacher intended to communicate.

> You know when you say there's mutual respect between students and teacher it almost implies a kind of approach. But really what I feel about it is it's the *most natural way* to behave toward another individual—and what you expect to get back is the same. I don't know what I would do if I had to be the font of knowledge in an environment like a classroom, if I couldn't depend on students when I had a headache, or when I didn't have any idea what to do next in a particular situation. I want to have the freedom as a person myself to say,

"Well, I don't know what to do. Who has an idea?" I think
that that's part of that whole environment, that isn't so much
planned as just real life that you allow to happen in a classroom instead of stifling real life in a classroom.

At this point in our discussion, the school's head added her interpretation and perspective, as follows:

I would just supplement that by saying that I think the teachers
set up the classroom by giving respect to the students as being
a part of the learning environment. It may be so natural for
some of the teachers to be doing it, but I think what they are
consciously doing is telling the students that they're sharing in
the teaching that's going on. That the ideas and the direction
of the students are just as important as the ideas and the direction of the teacher, and therefore the *give-and-take becomes natural.* It's not a set-up. I think because it's so natural
and so easy because you do it so much (referring to the
teachers) . . . I think the teachers consciously and deliberately
start off by saying, "This is a team approach. This is the ally
approach." The students are working together. I see that as I
go from class to class in different ways, but I think it's a mutual thing.

The above quote introduces a somewhat "broader" view, with its
comparison of how different teachers interpret a similar quality or value
in this Friends school environment.

Another critical concept used in the initial description of Friends
schools was that of the importance of listening. This was emphasized,
and modeled, many times by the teachers. In the following dialogue
between Dorothy and Sheri, the role of listening in the conflict mediation
or social problem-solving process is emphasized:

Dorothy: I think that probably one of the most important, if not the
most important, skill that anyone can have in resolving conflict
or even just being a teacher is *listening.* It's just so important to
take the time to listen, to really listen to what people are saying.
In the hubbub of the day and trying to get lessons in it's really
easy to say, "Yeah, we'll get back to that." But if you take the
time right in the beginning to really listen to the children or the
adults or whoever is in the classroom, to listen to what they are
saying . . . that's the bedrock. You can't go on solving problems

until you've heard what other people are saying. Until people feel like they've been listened to, they're not willing to be part of the process. I think that's really important. There have been times when I've tried to rush through conflicts and it doesn't work. It doesn't work because those little ones, or whoever, keep coming back and saying, "But wait a minute, I meant . . ." or "Wait, you didn't hear this" or "Wait, I'm still upset about that" or "Wait, my feelings are still hurt." You can't do that. That's [listening] what you're building up from.

Sheri: I really agree with that. It's not just making the space for someone to talk, which is better than not making the space, but that isn't what we're referring to. We're really referring to *hearing* and making the space for that. And making sure that a child knows that he or she is being heard. At a very young age that starts, and later on when the kids get older, they start to think that they aren't being heard if they aren't getting what they want or if they're not getting their way. Then you have to begin to develop the idea that hearing doesn't always mean agreement. I think it's harder for young children to hook on to that concept that you can be heard and still have people say, "Yes, we understand what you're saying here completely, but we're not going to do that, or we don't agree with your perception." And that takes time. It's almost like something that spirals through the ages as the children get older until finally they begin to absorb that end of it.

Another value that teachers discussed and enacted in their teaching was an underlying or *implicit vision for the future* and for the larger world community. Whether learning about apartheid from a black South African teacher, learning about Latin America through their Save the Children partner school in Bolivia, participating in weekly Spanish lessons, taking actions to protect endangered species, or writing letters about the lack of wheelchair-accessible buildings in their community, themes of social justice were often present in the formal and informal curriculum.

A related aspect of this vision for the future is the strong value of acceptance of individual differences and the promotion of a "friendly" environment for shared learning. Again, whether through many types of cooperative learning, mixed-age "buddies" for certain activities including meeting for worship, noncompetitive activities, and collaborative work, this value of working as friends was frequently stated explicitly, as well as present implicitly in the room arrangements, daily schedule, and types of activities chosen by the teachers.

In a section of *Reflections from a Friends Education* titled "The Invisible Curriculum," Harrison (1982) makes the following related observations:

> Nothing, in a sense, can replace the stimulation of inspired teaching, appreciation for the sound use of evidence or the habit of mental alertness; but the morally progressive school will also expose its students, through its invisible curriculum, to a vision of an emergent, nonviolent and just society. The school, itself, is the living model for tomorrow. It is a protected humane environment, an alternative miniworld, encouraging young dreamers to see and feel the possibilities of an expanded peaceable kingdom. Of even greater importance, the teachers and the tone of the Quaker school will inspire in our youth the confidence, the knowledge and the courage to work toward their vision without fear. (p. 16)

This discourse on the school's (and teachers') vision for the future as central to its curriculum and daily practice is relatively rare in much of the educational literature. We more typically talk about the "hidden curriculum" in reference to ways in which the "organization of time, knowledge, students, and instruction, quietly reinforces established social structures positions of authority, and linear, determined ways of knowing within schools," (Miller, 1990, p. 2). The hidden curriculum as many other curriculum scholars have described it (e.g., Anyon, 1981; Apple, 1979, 1986; Apple & King, 1977; Jackson, 1968; Lather, 1986) is often synonymous with the perpetuation of unequal power relations based on race, gender, class, or ability in everyday school practices, curricula, texts, and technology.

In the above quote, however, the implicit curriculum has a decidedly visionary and social reconstructionist meaning. This is, of course, only one of many hidden curricula within Friends, or any other, education. Nonviolent conflict resolution and peacemaking is one of the strongest values in Friends education, as the following quote asserts:

> Our curricula should pulsate with the "basic international literacy" of *global order and peace*. We can lead. In view of the fact the identifiable Quaker community within our institutions (schools) has largely vanished, one might ask if the few remaining Quaker schools have any evolutionary calling of greater importance than the mission of peace education. (Harrison, 1982, p. 16)

It was, in fact, the focus of "teaching toward peace" with young children that brought us together and has been a primary focus of all our collaborative efforts (e.g., previous papers, symposia and national conferences, and the videotape). It is interesting to consider, however, some of the concerns that teachers expressed about the ways in which Friends schools prepare children for conflict resolution and the possibilities for peaceful change.

Friends Education and Diverse Family Values

In this section, Dorothy discusses some of the dilemmas of the Friends school staff in terms of the peace education values of the school and the diverse values of the families. One topic of frequent discussion among the staff was how to teach Friends values while still respecting the diverse values of families in our school community. The philosophy of the school is based on the premise that Friends beliefs will permeate all areas of the school. For example, one of the Friends testimonies is the peace testimony. It is on that testimony that we base our emphasis on nonviolent conflict resolution, our embracing of peace activism, and our stand against war. We teach the peace testimony in developmentally appropriate ways, such as teaching about peacemakers, reading books such as *The Butter Battle Book* (Seuss and Geisel, 1984), discussing the nonviolent civil disobedience actions during the civil rights movement, and enforcing a rule that no weapons can be brought to school because we are a Quaker school.

There is a pitfall, however, in taking such an active stance in teaching the peace testimony. While our school generally attracts families with values compatible with Friends values, our school population is by no means homogeneous. Not all the Friends school families oppose all war or applaud the nonviolent actions of Martin Luther King, Jr., or Gandhi. Where these disagreements occur, there is the possibility of children's becoming confused by conflicting home and school values (e.g., differing opinions about the Gulf war). There is also the possibility of a child's minority opinion being silenced in the classroom. There is no easy answer to this dilemma. It requires the utmost sensitivity and awareness on the part of the classroom teacher. Ideally, children will learn that people have many different opinions, that their families may have different beliefs than Quakers, and that someday they will consider all the opinions and make an informed choice for themselves about what they will believe.

Another concern that gets discussed by the staff surrounds the question of whether the children are *internalizing the values and social skills* we teach in the school or are they only learning to use words as rhetoric that has little real meaning to them but is valued by the adults in the school. In particular, we are interested to know if children solve conflicts in the classroom in the presence of adults in the same way as they solve problems on the playground when adult presence is minimal. Similarly, do the children in our school truly learn to celebrate human diversity, or do they only learn that racist or sexist comments are not appropriate to make at school? This is a complicated issue, since school is only one of the child's socializing agents. However, if the goals of peace education are to teach the values of appreciating diversity, nonviolent conflict resolution, and social responsibility, then educators need some sense as to whether they are successful at instilling these values in the children they teach.

Yet another important dialogue concerns the questions of disempowering children and possibly creating victims, as Dorothy discusses here. In the Friends school there is a heavy emphasis on using words to settle conflicts, on not using any kind of physical violence, such as hitting or pushing. Unfortunately, since these values are not shared by all people in our society, the children are faced with situations in which other children are living and playing by a different set of rules. No one wants to create passive victims. The children need to be taught that true nonviolence is an active role, not a passive one. They also should be taught to use all their creativity, flexibility, and common sense in conflict situations, rather than doggedly hanging on to a set of rules.

Reality and Relevance in Friends Education

Connected to this discussion is the question of how *relevant* peace education is to places very different from a small community in rural Pennsylvania. Does it make sense to teach nonviolent conflict resolution to children who live in high-crime areas and witness brutal violence? Does it make sense to teach appreciation of human diversity to children who are daily victims of racism and classism? Is peace education a luxury affordable only to privileged children who live in safe neighborhoods? These questions are important, and it would be pretentious to try to answer them in this chapter. However, it could be argued that teaching the power of nonviolent conflict resolution, respect for human diversity, and social action is most needed in those areas where are children are at the greatest risk.

One of the reactions we have gotten when we have presented together in the past is that all our ideas are "great—for the isolated, middle-class, peaceful setting of a small private school in a tranquil rural setting"—in other words, the notion that Friends schools in general, or this one in particular, are somehow "unreal" or of limited relevance to schools and children in less protected environments.

In our videotapes and weekly observations, as well as in the issues confronting teachers, children, and parents, this "reality" was quickly apparent. It should also be recognized that the "unreal" label also reflects the potential incompatibility between the curriculum goals and social and political realities in the dominant culture.

Finally, in terms of what makes a school a "Quaker school," we turn to one last quote from the collected reflections on Friends education. Colin Bell (1982) provides the following descriptive criteria for what makes Quaker education distinct:

> Maintaining and creating good private schools, largely for middle income people, may be a worthy thing to do, but is not particularly Quaker unless two things happen. One is that the whole life, the "smell" of the school is redolent of the Quaker testimonies as applied to today's world. The second is that the students leave the school clear in their understanding of the Quaker Testimonies. . . . I would like people to send their children to us in order to expose them to our religious views and how they apply to the world around them. . . . [Students] should be helped to understand our ambivalence regarding material possessions, the economic and social systems, the use and abuse of power and wealth and nature, violence of all sorts, and the universal shame of war. For after all, these are the issues they must face in life, whatever their faith. Our purposes are to help them seek and find what is truth for themselves. (p. 21)

The importance of gaining nontrivial life skills as a result of their education in the Friends school was expressed by Jane in her first year as a teacher there:

> I feel that learning how to get along is as important a concept as reading and writing. This is a lifetime skill that everybody needs, and it isn't thought of all the time that this is what you are doing. When you get out in the real world, some people don't know how to do math very well, but everybody has to know how to get along. In some ways I think that may be the most important thing we do that is different.

The value of learning the life skill of problem solving was one that all the teachers and staff of the Friends school shared. They shared it so deeply and implicitly, in fact, that it was sometimes hard for them to analyze how they put this value into daily practice. Another potential contribution of our collaboration was the detailed description and videotapes of daily practice, which teachers discussed several times throughout the research project.

Last, but not least, was the role of humor in the daily lives of teachers and children at the Friends school. As two of the teachers put it,

> I'm delighted to know that all of what we do we do with humor. You have to have humor with your children, and with the teachers that you are with. It just lightens everything. It is the humor that just takes the edge off of conflict. Then you can go into the process. So, humor is used as a very multifaceted . . . it seems to just permeate for most of the day. And yet the kids come in and really, you know, it makes the class light so they really like it. They know that I am going to joke with them and I do it often.

> Yes, I do it too. You know, if someone is getting upset and there is a conflict that might be brewing . . . it is the way to take the edge off and then you can examine what the problem is.

During one of our meetings to discuss what teachers thought should be emphasized in a videotape that we were in the early stages of producing, the most experienced teacher commented, "Be sure to show our feet of clay! We don't have all the answers, and we sure need to have a sense of humor about that."

This balance of discussions, queries, projects, and study of often significant issues and social problems with a sense of playfulness and fun was visible on every visit and in most of the tapes. The balance of being "deadly serious and playful" at the same time was evident in each of the teachers.

Consensus Decision Making and Problem Solving with Children

In our discussions and observations it was clear that listening to children and helping them more clearly identify problems were critical steps in the problem-solving process as generally carried out. As the teachers discuss below, identifying children's "real" problems sounds deceptively simple, but it can actually be a complex, subtle, and time-consuming process. As discussed earlier, listening is a critical skill mentioned by all the teachers.

> **Jane:** Sometimes when children come to me with a problem, they don't always know what the problem is, so I'll listen and then I'll

say one or two more things and try to bring out how they feel
. . . and I try to get them to state it. I don't know if that's
reflecting, but I think it takes adaptation and sometimes I don't
do that, I forget. But if I take the time, I'll begin to hear what
they have to say and understand.

Eileen: When you reflect what you're finding out usually is, the
problem isn't what you saw. That would be to let go those
emotions and feelings that either have been building up or most
often are connected to something not happening right then and
there. So you really are helping that child and are learning about
that child as to what is really going on for them. It's very seldom
that what you saw happen is really the problem. There's always
something else that's happening for them.

Dorothy: Before we talk about consensus decision making, one thing
I want to say about listening and conflict resolution is that
sometimes *when someone is listened to, that solves the problem.*
It's really that simple. You can go through a whole mediation
process and not get to the root of the problem and spend hours
doing it. Whereas, if right in the beginning someone had said,
"Oh, I see, this is what you're upset about and this is why," it's
solved. I thought that was important to say, since it is the
foundation of conflict resolution. People really want to be heard
and understood. You can't get to consensus decision making or
problem solving until that's been done!

Sheri: It's happened to me in my classroom time and time again. A
child will come with a problem, the child is heard. I don't pick
up the cue that we're now done. I continue and say things like,
"Do you have any ideas for how we can solve this problem?"
and they're getting up and walking away because the problem
has been solved for them.

Eileen: I've had the experience of kind of rushing through and
saying, "Oh, we'll deal with that later," and the child will come
back and say, "You know we still have to talk about that." She
needs her space, she really needs to talk about that. And since I
didn't come back to it, she was going to make sure I did! They
really expect and need and desire and value talking about it and
being listened to. I've seen that a lot.

Jane: I like to walk in on them. It's just the easiest thing to listen to
two kids begin to talk to each other; you think you're acting as a
mediator. All of a sudden they are talking to each other and
walking away. And you think, "What happened?" They got it
out much sooner than I would have.

Sheri: And the teacher not having to be the font of mediation can just be done.

After probing further for concrete steps in the problem-solving process, the dialogue continued. It was interesting to note the different examples—Dorothy's from the kindergarten and first-grade classroom, to Sheri's from second and third grades, and Jane's from the fourth grade. This seemed to be a valuable developmental comparison for the teachers to make as well.

As Dorothy points out,

We've already mentioned the first step in problem solving is listening. When a problem arises you get the people involved together and you get them to listen to each other. For instance, if it's two children fighting over a block, you come over and help the children take turns being talkers and being listeners. One child would say, "I got the block first. I had it in my hand. I was going to build with it, then I put it down and turned away and then he took the block." Then you say, "Now, you be the listener and let the other person talk." And the other says, "Well, the block was on the floor. How was I supposed to know that he was going to use it?" And again, it's the talking and listening part that's so important; that the people involved actually feel that they've been heard. We try to emphasize this a lot, too. *It's not just the adults who are listening.* It's the young people who need to be listeners, too. We think that's as important a skill as being a communicator in the conflict—that the other person says, "Yeah, I really heard the other side of the story." That's the first part.

The teachers then discussed the importance of children having eye contact and staying with the process while the problem is identified. One teacher commented, "You need to be sure that they can see each other . . . that will help them. You might even turn and guide them to stay with the process." They also gave examples of how they reminded children about the steps in the process. For example, "You might have to say, 'Oh, remember, you're the listener now. Listen to what he's saying.' Sometimes, though, we'll have her repeat what the other person said. 'What did the other person say?' When they repeat it back, you know that they've really heard."

Sheri went on to discuss the process with her second- and third-graders:

What I do to gather people together who are having a conflict
is say, "Someone wants to talk to you; you need to talk to
him." Then I, because they're a little older, very often I can
pull back, and I try to get as far away as I can so that it becomes a really genuine dialogue between those two people,
and every once in a while I'll just kind of move forward if it
looks like they're getting off the track or somebody's being
distracted by minutiae that really doesn't impinge on the
problem . . . or if they're dredging up old stuff. Helping to
summarize what they've heard so far. And then in the end I'll
ask them what they want to do now.

Sheri also discussed how she responds when children come up with
and agree to solutions such as "I won't speak to him for the rest of the
day" or "I'll never speak to this person again." She continues with this
example.

When, for example, children agree "We won't be friends any-
more," as the third person involved I don't step in and say,
"Now that's ridiculous." Even though I know that's not one
they're going to hang in there with. That's their decision for
now, and that's what feels good to them. They're getting
some satisfaction out of making a vow to never speak to each
other again. This is an extreme, an extreme example, but it's
all right for them to make a decision that I know isn't going to
work out for them really. *Both parties have to be satisfied.*
Both of them have to agree to what the solution will be.

It was also interesting to discuss how children who had been in this
school since kindergarten had become "expert" at this consensus decision
making process and how older children newer to the Friends school have
more trouble picking these techniques up—at least at first. Jane, who
worked primarily with fourth-graders, put it in the following way:

With the older kids I had a mixture of children who have
been here for a long time, and then children who have come
in maybe at fourth-grade level. And the ones who came in at
the fourth-grade level need to learn the listening skills of the
kindergartners. . . . With the children who are older and have
come into this situation, it's more difficult, and they do have
to learn it. I do have to be there a lot of the time, and I will
have to say, "You're not making eye contact" or "I don't feel

that you are really listening." And I'll ask the other person how he feels. The ones that have learned it, and have been here for a while, and know it really well, can solve their problems a lot of times without me, without ever coming to me. And then the ones that have come, need more help, they need help even with the children that know the process. I see this as something they learn, and they do learn well.

In describing the steps in the Friends school process of consensus decision making with young people, Sheri explained the process in the following way:

We've had so many different issues that have come up in our classroom, issues that need to be addressed by the group. The way we start, in a consensus decision making process, is to have everybody list what they feel the problems are in a situation. We do it in a very organized fashion. We'll make a list on the board or put it on a piece of paper so that it can be saved. People are called on, they know that they're going to be heard. They know what the roster is for people having their say. They're confident in that process. Then, when we get all the problems listed up there, we talk about what problem we want to discuss first. You get a general feel for what problem we want to talk about first. . . . Sometimes you lump problems together and sort of make a category.

We'll brainstorm ideas that kids have for how to solve problem number one and put the list on the board. Then we'll make a decision about which solution the group feels is going to be a good one. Everyone has a chance to say what they think about solution A, the pros and cons. Then we come to some kind of consensus—which *doesn't mean everyone agrees on everything*. It just means that you get a *feel for the group* in general. It's not unanimity. That's real important! Because if you hold out for everybody agreeing on everything, then you never get any action at all. That's a pitfall in the consensus process. So you get a feel for the "sense of the group."

The list of solutions is just a working list. It doesn't mean that this is how it always has to be. You try it out, the kids go out and play. In a couple of days we come back again and say, "Well, how did that work out?" Sometimes they say, "That was great. We don't have any more problems at all there." And sometimes they say, "Well, A and B were terrific, but C was a dud because this and this happened." You have a choice, the students can decide they're going to erase C or maybe they're going to address the problem in a whole new way. You begin the process again.

Beth asked Sheri, "How do you think children feel about this process? How do your kids feel about being consensus decision makers?" Sheri responded, "They love it because they get to have their say. They hate it because it takes time and they don't always like to spend their time that way. Sometimes they yearn for a teacher to come and say, 'No, no you're not allowed to do this.'"

Teachers also told of how they were constantly pleased and amazed at how creative children were in solving their problems. Whether resolving the hurt feelings involved in competing for parts in a play by casting more than one child in each part of *Peter Pan*, making sledding rules anew each year for the big hill, or creating rules for property ownership and rights in the "Friendly Woods" (playground), children did bring a variety of creative ideas to these often lengthy brainstorming discussions. Figure 12.1 includes a list of potential solutions to the "Friendly Woods" problems identified by the children. This example is particularly relevant to the chapter and to social education in that through the resolution of several problems associated with "land ownership" of forts and means of exchange (e.g., nuts and berries), the children essentially re-created the rules of a society through their discussions, creative visualizations, group tour of the woods, and other consensus building activities.

It was also interesting to note that several solutions were proposed that did not reflect the dominant U.S. culture, including "share everything" rather than private ownership of land and "money," which the teachers discussed as a more collective or cooperative solution. Another potential solution was to use a simple barter system instead of having certain berries or nuts represent money. It was also interesting to note that a 7-year-old girl became a self-appointed "public defender" and another first-grade girl took on "prosecuting" some of the second- and third-grade boys who had raided the forts of three of the kindergarten children. After three days of discussion, a guided visualization about the "perfect Friendly Woods," and a shared language experience in which children drew a cooperative picture with a partner depicting how they wanted the Friendly Woods to be, the entire school reached consensus on several interim solutions. In terms of property and ownership issues, the children decided to continue to have a system of group-"owned" forts that would be claimed and clarified through a group tour of the woods. They would not steal, and they would use both money and trading. They

Figure 12.1 Friendly Woods Solutions

ROBBERIES
1. Check to see who owns stuff before taking it.
2. Use guards.
3. Talk to the people, and then talk to the teacher.
4. Share stuff
5. Ask for what you want. Be honest.
6. No stealing.
7. Be honest.

LACK OF COOPERATION
1. Take turns as guards.
2. Share stuff.

FORT DESTRUCTION
1. Talk with the after-school kids.
2. Other solutions will stop this.
3. Say, "I don't like that" or "That's not fun."
4. Need to cooperate.
5. No arresting.

BLAMING
1. Don't yell or blame. Talk instead.
2. Don't jump to conclusions.
3. Ask others is someone did something.

OWNERSHIP
1. Use fences.
2. Label things with your name.
3. Keep stuff in your fort.*
4. Take a tour so everyone knows who owns what.*
5. Share everything.
6. Use signs.
7. Claim and label your own space.*

TRESPASSING
1. Use signs to tell people.
2. Ask if it's OK.

NOT LISTENING
1. Compromise.

MONEY TOO HARD TO FIND (money = nuts and berries)
1. Make money from paper.
2. Use things from woods and agree on amounts.
3. Don't use money. Trade instead.
4. Use both money and trading.*
5. Use walnuts and leaves.

POOR PEOPLE
1. Have a poor fund or place.
2. Give money to poor people.
3. Use trading, not money.
4. Advertise stuff.

WEAPONS
1. No weapons.*

*Solution chosen

would help younger children build forts and find "money," and they would not use "weapons." The banning of weapons was perhaps the only solution that did not reflect dominant culture in the United States and directly reflected the values of Quaker education. As with any other solutions, they would try these out and assess how well they worked, and possibly amend their group decision.

The teachers also talked about how the consensus decision making process feels *different from voting* and is something beyond democracy or majority rule in the classroom. As one 5-year-old kindergartner put it, "When we vote there are winners and losers . . . but this way nobody loses . . . and nobody cries!" Dorothy discussed consensus decision making and voting as different options available to children and teachers:

> I think it's important to keep it in perspective. This [consensus decision-making process] isn't dogma. This isn't the word of God. It's an option for us, and it's an option that we teach the children. Here's another way to solve problems. . . . In my class I'm very careful to teach other options also. Sometimes if there's a decision to make I'll talk about voting. When we bought our hamsters this year, we voted. We had little ballots, and I said, "This is different from when we get together and we all try to agree, so that everyone feels good—this is voting." We actually try to do it around the time of elections. And here we've got the winners and here we've got the losers, and we can talk about how they feel. It's just another way to solve problems. What's exciting is that [consensus decision making] is a way to solve problems that a lot of people don't know. It's an option that has a lot of benefits. But it's not the only one.

During the second year of the research, Sheri's second- and third-graders decided to elect class officers as part of a government unit. Although there were new class presidents and other officers elected weekly, voting was clearly a different experience for the children than consensus decision making. She describes this as follows:

> I think the students see [consensus decision making] as an option that feels very different to them than voting. We also did voting as part of a government unit . . . and the kids talked in great length about how it felt to be elected as class president or vice president. And that was something that just grew out of it, it was what they wanted to do. I had not planned that,

so when they talked about what it felt like to be a loser, I thought it had larger implications for them.

I thought that the process began to be a conscious one where they started to think, well, if you do this decision, it could mean that some people will lose. And that is a different feeling from not completely getting your way. And so they began to see more value to the time you put into consensus decision making, because they noticed that the end feeling was somewhat different from the feeling . . . I mean *nobody cried at the end of consensus decision making*. But people did cry at the end of the election. It also gave them a different feel for . . . what goes on in a presidential election. And I felt that they learned a great deal about what it is to be a candidate and just how difficult it is to participate in that whole process. It was wonderful.

The increased understanding of group process, as evidenced in children's discussions of different forms of decision making, was clearly seen as a benefit to both teachers and children.

REFLECTIONS ON THE COLLABORATIVE PROCESS

In this concluding section, we will end as we began—with two distinct voices and interpretations of our collaborative research process.

Dorothy: Few teachers think of themselves as researchers or have any experience in research. This was true of me, so that I had few preconceptions about doing collaborative research with Beth. I had certain goals and I was eager to learn. I was frank about stating what I wanted from the project, and I was clear about Beth's goals and expectations. An important factor in the beginning of the project was that I felt comfortable with Beth, and we seemed to share similar values and beliefs. I felt assured that the process would be based on open communication and mutual respect. This was especially important to me, as the teacher in the project, for a number of reasons. For one thing, elementary teachers in our society are not given the same status and respect as college professors. This could easily have set up an unequal and condescending dynamic that could have sabotaged true collaboration.

Also, the thought of being videotaped and observed throughout the year could have been very intimidating if I had felt Beth's presence as being critical or patronizing. Teaching young children is unpredictable, and the nature of the job is such that it is difficult to look polished and professional a good deal of the time. I needed to know that Beth understood that and that she would be supportive and nonjudgmental in her feedback to me. (Unfortunately, "teacher bashing" is sometimes condoned and promoted in the academic community.) This is not to say that Beth could not objectively evaluate what was happening in my classroom, but rather that the process could unfold in an atmosphere of mutual learning together.

This is reminiscent of the statements made earlier about the classroom as a place where children and teachers are allies and are learners together. From this foundation, the collaboration of the project could proceed to everyone's benefit.

There were some definite advantages for me and the other teachers in being involved in this research project. Beth has been a constant resource for education articles and books, new ideas, and insights. Talking with Beth about what we were doing forced us to clarify and be able to communicate ideas and procedures that we took for granted. This helped me to better understand what I was doing. It also stimulated new thinking and questioning among the staff and in myself. I began to reevaluate some common practices and ideas I had about teaching. Beth's presence at staff meetings was a catalyst for discussions and more questions. For example, Beth observed a discussion in my room during which a minority opinion was voiced by a boy, and he changed his opinion when many of the children soundly disagreed with him. This drew to my attention the need to support those children in my group who may hold beliefs different from those held by the majority of the school community.

Creating the video required the same rethinking and reevaluating that the research required. Certain procedures and beliefs were inherent in how we did conflict resolution with the children. However, we had never really listed them and stated them in a way that people outside of our environment could understand. This was especially helpful for me in the video production, because we needed to make the process understandable and real for people who would view the video. I needed to be clear and specific in my own thinking before I could communicate this to someone else.

Teachers tend to be active and busy, with little time for reflection on what they are doing. The research and video projects were a stimulus to do some reflecting on some parts of teaching that I had taken for granted.

Beth: For me much of the collaborative process was reflected in the process of actually completing the videotape. As Dorothy described earlier, we were forced to clarify what had been learned or illuminated by the research in her school in order to clearly communicate it to those who would see the videotape. We also were committed to "foregrounding" the teachers' perspectives and using their voices for the narration. As I have shared the tape with many groups of preservice and inservice teachers, I sometimes regret that we used sixty seconds of a male "authority voice" for narration, because other than this, the story is told entirely by the teachers—and by the children, through our frequent cuts and voice-overs between classroom and playground interactions and the teacher discussion. In fact, students in courses stressing multiculturalism and antibias teaching have raised this as an issue and questioned why we thought adding this outside voice near the beginning of the tape was necessary.

I have found that using the videotape in my social studies methods class, for example, is a good way to introduce future teachers to many of the possibilities in working with young children and in helping them solve problems. I also use many highlights from the raw footage or data tapes made during the two-year study for discussion and to provide further examples of classrooms that are moving "beyond democracy" and taking a very inclusive approach to decision making. By frequently bringing the teachers and children of the Friends school into my university classes, I feel that our "collaborative connection" remains strong.

The video editing process was a long and far from smooth one. In many ways we became disempowered in feeling that we both lacked the technical expertise to complete the editing in a way that was consistent with our "vision" for the final tape. After nearly a year of unproductive meetings, we were becoming impatient with the editor we first worked with. We realized, after many months, that we were relying too heavily on "experts" and needed to reclaim our project. This involved going back through most of the tapes and developing our own script, a task to which Dorothy devoted many hours. To further complicate matters, I had now left Pennsylvania and was living in Ohio. Through visits back and forth, many phone calls, and the discovery that Kent State had excellent technical assistance for teleproductions, we completed the tape by the spring of 1990—exactly three years after we first decided to collaborate. It was exciting to return to State College and share the videotape with all the staff who had so willingly participated and to feel that they did feel included in our collaboration.

In many ways the videotape became an important vehicle for transcending the more typical educational research outlets, in that we had to keep in mind a wider audience that included parents, childcare workers, teachers, and future teachers. It was interesting to contrast the making of the videotape with the co-presenting at an educational foundations conference (Swadener & Piekielek, 1988), in which Dorothy had wondered if any teachers ever participated. By involving the teachers in both the research and video conceptualization process as much as possible, we felt that we had not betrayed or exploited them and that the tape was an authentic reflection of at least the problem-solving aspects of this Friends school.

The importance of being clear and open about what we each wanted and needed out of the project was another way in which we were able to work so well together. The role of humor, play, hot soup on winter nights of video viewing, and neck massages should not be underestimated. Finally, the larger focus of our work on peace and social justice, Friends education principles, and antibias education for young children provided critical larger contexts for our smaller projects. Remaining grounded in these social contexts for our collaborative work and continuing to grow as friends and colleagues are perhaps the most empowering aspects of our work.

REFERENCES

Anyon, J. (1981). Social class and school knowledge. *Curriculum Inquiry, 111*, 3–42.

Apple, M. W. (1979). *Ideology and curriculum.* Boston: Routledge and Kegan Paul.

Apple, M. W. (1986). *Teachers and texts: A political economy of class and gender relations in education.* New York: Routledge and Kegan Paul.

Apple, M. W., & King, N. A. (1977). What do schools teach? *Curriculum Inquiry, 6*, 341–357.

Bell, C. (1982). The smell of the school. In C. A. Dorrance (Ed.), *Reflections from a Friends education.* Philadelphia: Friends Council on Education.

Dorrance, C. A. (Ed.). (1982). *Reflections from a Friends education.* Philadelphia: Friends Council on Education.

Harrison, E. G. (1982). In C. A. Dorrance (Ed.), *Reflections from a Friends education* (pp. 15–16). Philadelphia: Friends Council on Education.

Jackson, P. (1968). *Life in classrooms.* New York: Holt, Rinehart and Winston.

Lather, P. (1986). Research as praxis. *Harvard Educational Review, 56*(3), 257–277.

Miller, J. L. (1990). *Creating spaces and finding voices: Teachers collaborating for empowerment.* Albany: State University of New York Press.

Seuss, Dr., & Geisel, A. S. (1984). *The butter battle book.* New York: Random House.

Sheeran, M. J. (1983). *Beyond majority rule: Voteless decisions in the Religious Society of Friends.* Philadelphia: Philadelphia Yearly Meeting of the Religious Society of Friends.

Swadener, E. B., & Piekielek, D. (1988, November). *Teaching toward peace in the early elementary years.* Paper presented at the annual meeting of the American Educational Studies Association, Toronto.

CHAPTER 13

Disturbances from the Field

Recovering the Voice of the Early Childhood Teacher

William Ayers

> Each of us has worked by improvisation, discovering the shape of our creation along the way, rather than pursuing a vision already defined. (p. 1)
>
> The process of improvisation that goes into composing a life is compounded in the process of remembering a life, like a patchwork quilt in a watercolor painting, rumpled and evocatative . . . composing a life through memory as well as through day-to-day choices . . . seems to me essential to creative living. The past empowers the present, and the groping footsteps leading to this present mark the pathways to the future. (p. 34)
>
> —Mary Catherine Bateson (1989)

What are the conflicts, contradictions, and obstacles you face as a teacher, and what resources do you bring to your daily encounters with the reality of teaching? What allows you to be a risk taker, an initiator, an inventor, a teacher who resists the conventional and the taken-for-granted? How did you come to be the teacher you are today? What projects, goals, or dreams fuel your teaching now? Here is how Susan Kilbane, a second-grade teacher, begins to answer these questions:

> I grew up in a child-centered environment. I was lucky to be part of a large, loving family, a place where children were highly valued. Early in life I acquired a sense of children as valuable, children as whole human beings, and that general orientation has been a foundation and a guide for me—a lasting and continuous gift from my childhood. Both of my par-

ents were educators—my mom still teaches kindergarten today—and they are my models.

I believe that the classroom should be modeled after the home; school should be a kind of family/community. Everything should revolve around the kids—they should set the pace and the rhythm, they should find the engaging and meaningful work to do, they should uncover all the ways they need to express themselves. Children need spaces to be children, spaces where life is enjoyed and lived fully.

Alice Brent, a first-grade teacher, responds this way:

I was a fortunate child—I was nurtured and challenged by so many caring and loving people. My first teachers were my wonderful parents, and it is their shoulders I stand on—even today—in everything I do. They made me know I was important, that I could accomplish anything, that I could make a difference in this world. I also had many nurturing teachers in the Chicago Public Schools from 1953 to 1965. I still remember—their encouraging me, sheltering me, and, yes, pushing me when that was necessary. I never felt that being a girl or being black should stand in the way of what I needed to accomplish.

I think of myself today as a nurturing teacher, a teacher who sees the whole child, who works in the intersection of intellectual, social, and moral growth. I try to make my classroom a homelike environment: a patch of rug, an old chair or a couch, a stuffed animal, a few photos of the students themselves, a reading corner, quiet and private space. It's a place I want to be, and a place my kids want to be.

Finally, Sarah Cohen, a kindergarten teacher, frames her reply like this:

I was intensely involved in my own childhood. It was not idyllic, nor even always happy, but it was a strong and rich experience, and I remember it vividly. It was a time of color and energy, a time of strength and also fragility. I think it's that balance that fascinates me: the incredible power children have to face the complexities, even the horrors of life—the vigor and the resiliency—standing alongside the delicate, tentative, breakable side of childhood. How do you respond at once to the vitality and the frailty kids bring to school? I'm interested in the *work* of childhood. I'm engaged with people, and children offer a certain acute entry point into the flow of humanity.

My classroom is challenging and safe, a pleasurable place to be if you're 5, but a place that sometimes asks you to stretch yourself. It is a place where real choices are made by kids, and the real work of 5-year-olds is honored. It is alive with possibilities, and it can support a lot of youthful passion, even conflict.

Each of these teachers works in the Chicago public schools: Alice has taught for twenty-two years, Sarah for four years, and Susan for two. Each has a vision of teaching that guides her efforts, and each is struggling to make that vision a reality, to create a classroom practice that does not make a mockery of her values. Each, then, is a resistant teacher, someone composing a life in opposition to much of the taken-for-granted of teaching and most of the machinery of schooling.

For example, consider the curriculum. Teachers are typically expected to "cover" the curriculum, to complete a textbook, to move children through a prescribed course of study. Teachers are reduced to assembly-line workers, clerks, and worse—they are expected to do their jobs, to ask no questions, to follow orders, to passively convey the stuff of learning to inert and inanimate youngsters. One teacher told me recently that she had two weeks to "cover" rocks in science with her second-graders, but that in their initial foray to see some rocks by a lake, the children's attention and interest quickened when they saw some fish. Throwing caution to the wind and following their lead, this teacher built an elaborate, integrated project around fish: fish stories, fish legends, fish charts, fish maps, fish in art, fish in cultural contexts. It was exciting, vibrant, and yet, as the teacher admitted, "The whole time we were doing fish I was feeling guilty about missing the rocks. I mean, would they be ready for the third grade?"

The assumption, of course, is that some academic, researcher, state official, or genius has determined what ought to be covered by all students at a certain age, how it sequences into further bits and pieces of knowledge, and that everyone needs the same material at the same time to avoid any deficits. Neither the teacher nor the students individually or collectively could possibly know what knowledge or experiences would be valuable. Furthermore, knowledge itself is assumed to be fixed, finite, discreet, immutable.

Sarah, Alice, and Susan struggled on the boundary of a different idea about curriculum and knowledge. Each thought that learning required active choice-making for students and teachers alike; each considered learning a complex process that engaged the heart, the soul, and the body as well as the mind; and each felt that learning is something people do constantly in many different styles and at varying paces. In Sarah's classroom the ongoing care and observation of animals and plants is a natural doorway into science, but there is reading, writing, and charting involved as well. In Alice's classroom block-building involves work with number, space, design, order, and pattern, not to mention language, group process, and democratic living. Susan teaches reading by supporting the development of the child's own voice through fiction and autobiographical writing. Each is interested in interaction and interconnection, in developing such dispositions of mind as curiosity and commitment, and in building a sense of efficacy and agency in learners. Each wants to pursue a few interests and ideas in depth rather than skim along the surface of a lot of topics without thinking or caring much about them.

Or, for example, consider the question of standardized testing and grading, a centerpiece in the business of schooling, a little motor that drives the entire enterprise, an insistent engine inside the school-machine. Teachers routinely object to standardized testing on the grounds that attention to the tests skews teaching and curriculum in inappropriate ways—early childhood teachers are troubled, for example, by the increasing pressure to spend less time with blocks or paints or dress-ups in favor of little worksheets that will presumably prepare children for the real world of school. But their voices are muffled and usually ignored.

Susan, Alice, and Sarah had each independently found her way to resisting the pressure to teach to the test, to sort, and to grade. When they met and began to compare notes, they discovered with satisfaction how much they had in common: each kept a journal or diary, a running record of her teaching experiences and personal reflections; each wrote a more detailed account of the activities and developments of three or four children each night; each saved multiple samples of all children's work. They were each surprised by some of the strategies the others employed.

Susan had convinced her principal, and then several colleagues and parents, that giving letter grades to young children was destructive—"reducing the kids to numbers became a moral issue for me"—and she designed a report card based on thick descriptions of the dynamics of growth. Alice, with humor and confidence, defeated the grading system by simply giving all children A's in everything. "Imagine being 6 and getting your first report card and having a C or an F," Alice says. "Do we grade toddlers when they move from crawling to walking, or from the bottle to the cup? Getting A's delighted each child. No one said, 'But if everyone got A's my A isn't worth as much!' Each was pleased and felt nurtured and positive about their own work in the classroom."

Sarah demonstrated an approach to assessment based on seeing the child as a whole person, an approach she had practiced at the Prospect Center in Vermont. In this approach, assessment is entirely in the service of the child's growth and the teacher's understanding—there is no interest in summative judgment, in sorting youngsters along some assumed objective norm, in ranking teachers according to children's responses. Assessment in this view must be dynamic and interactive, that is, it is always changing and it is expected to be colored by each child's own purposes, values, hopes, dreams, aspirations, and reasons. Assessment, then, accepts the complexity of persons, builds on each child's unique strengths and abilities, and opens up large questions of purpose (What knowledge and experiences are most worthwhile for this child in this situation? How will this child have access to that knowledge and those experiences? Given what I now know, what is required of my teaching?).

Typically, these teachers attach a paragraph or two to the traditional report card sent home in an attempt to embody notions of assessment, to build from strength, and to enlist parents in the dialogue. Here, for example, is Sarah's first quarterly report on 5-year-old Vito:

> Vito is a delight to teach. He is eager, responsive, and enthusiastic. His enthusiasm and interest in the things around him makes him wonderful to be around.
>
> Vito has largely adjusted to the routines and expectations of the school day. His understanding of what is expected of him in various settings is good, though his ability to carry this out in his behavior is still developing. Vito is a good group member. He is sensitive to the needs of others and eager to contribute to discussions and participate in activities. Vito's development of literacy skills in language arts and mathematics is progressing well. He is gaining a strong understanding of pattern and order. Furthermore, Vito is becoming more articulate in telling his own stories and stating his ideas and questions. Vito continues to need support to communicate his needs in appropriate ways to his peers; however, he is responsive to teacher guidance. I have great confidence in Vito's continued growth in all of these areas.

Testing and grading, the predetermined and iron-clad curriculum, of course, are only emblematic of the problems these teachers contend with as they construct their lives in teaching. The entire structure of the school experience—the pledge of allegiance, the lines in the hallways, the intercoms and the bells, the pullouts and interruptions, the obsession with quiet and order, the constant reference to classroom management and misbehavior—seems calculated to defeat their humanistic goals and larger purposes. Each teacher knows that she must decide which fights to fight, which issues to confront, where to accede and where to do battle. Each knows that challenging convention requires energy and that she must defend any step away from the ordinary. That is, she knows that if she lines children up for the bathroom, if she insists upon complete quiet in the hallway, if she assigns worksheets, if she speaks disparagingly of children's families, and so on, no one will challenge her. All of these things (and more) are simply the way things are, some of the "existing regularities," part of longstanding past practice, pieces of the common sense of schooling. If, on the other hand, she allows children to use the bathroom as needed, moves through the hallway purposefully but naturally, and so on, a serious and thoughtful explanation is required, and this will likely be insufficient. This is in part because common sense (or the taken-for-granted) can be as totalizing as any religion or political belief—it needs no explanation, it requires no thought, it is simply obvious. Challenging common assumptions is pushing against a heavy rock. And since each of these teachers could challenge practically every assumption every minute of every day, each could exhaust her personal and collective resources by midafternoon. Each has decided, then, that she must shepherd her strength for those things that matter most.

Shepherding strength, building resistance, choosing battles, challenging the status quo—these are what brought these teachers (and many others) together into a teacher support group. Informally called "Teacher Talk," this group of progressive Chicago public school teachers meets twice monthly to explore issues, exchange ideas, and support each others efforts. One seed of Teacher Talk was a group of nine former students at the University of Illinois at Chicago who began gathering in 1988 as preservice teachers committed to working in Chicago public schools. Looking uneasily at the antistudent, antifamily structures and values awaiting them, these students began to meet in the hope of finding common cause. In a system that is isolating and destructive, a culture that is suffocating and conformist, finding a space for imaginative thought and common purpose is in itself an act of affirmation and insurgency. Teacher Talk is, according to these teachers, a time to be nurtured and challenged, to gain perspective on the upside-down, Alice-in-Wonderland world of school, a place, finally, to feel sane.

Sometimes Teacher Talk is all complaints and criticism, sometimes an exploration of aspects of teaching or curriculum. Teacher Talk is accounts of action, conflict, and contradiction, the daily experiences of classroom teachers, accounts infused with urgency and immediacy. Teacher Talk is always storytelling, always the unwinding of narrative and the locating of oneself within. It is connection and identity—among people, between thought and conduct, between inner and outer selves. As teachers tell their stories, their stories also tell them. There is, of course, not a single story to tell, but a crazy-quilt of stories: there are tales of humiliation and triumph, of failure and success, of cowardliness and courage. Connie describes her frustration with herself for losing her temper more than once in class and asks for suggestions for doing better; Chris tells about her isolated and embattled position among her colleagues and seeks advice; Jackie relates with some awe the impact she feels she has had on the teacher next door and wonders how to consolidate the gains and take next steps. The stories change and grow, build on one another and merge, connect, and rupture. The stories are never adequately summed up, never reducible to a single story. The storytellers are singular, the stories unfinished and expanding.

No one, of course, entirely invents a story from scratch: each is part of a physical, cultural, and social world, each existing in a situation not of his or her own making. What one makes of the given world, who one becomes within our shared and specific surrounds—this is a large part of the content of our storytelling. And so exploring contexts and understanding the world is also a part of Teacher Talk. Sometimes the group chooses a concept for focused reflection—"democracy," say, or "racism," or "peace." Participants think quietly and then write for fifteen minutes or so on the concept. "It's a way of staying intellectually alive," says Sarah. "It saves us from an exclusive focus on the everyday details and demands. It allows us to be in touch with larger purposes and the higher goals of our teaching."

Several projects have emerged from Teacher Talk: ongoing explorations of integrated approaches to math and language, challenges to standardized testing, participation in organized teacher advocacy groups and co-authoring a book. Perhaps the most ambitious project has been the attempt by a subgroup within Teacher Talk to articulate their vision of what an urban, public school could look like and their attempts to create a space (an annex to an existing public school, a school-within-a-school, a new public school in an overcrowded area of Chicago) where that vision could become a reality. Susan, Sarah, Alice, and a few other teachers wrote, in part:

> Our aim is to create a school that will empower children, parents and teachers alike. We hope to establish a school that will draw on all members of the school community to foster the social and intellectual growth of each student. We will build a vital learning environment by linking the child's interests to existing subject matter. We will support each child's strengths and needs by bridging between the school and the family. And we will enlarge each child's sense of being a responsible and active contributor to society by making visible the connections of the community and the larger world to the work of school and its culture. . . .
>
> Children come to school with a multitude of experiences and a wealth of knowledge, making them vital contributors to the education of each member of the class. A child's culture as well as the surrounding community will be viable entry points into any topic of study. For example, the study of history and geography could arise out of the origins of the students' names. Trips to the post office, the public library, or the grocery store could all be starting points for in-depth, interdisciplinary studies. We will learn from the community by inviting community members to share their knowledge and experiences and by welcoming them as audience for the work of students. We will participate in the community through service projects such as singing or reading with senior citizens. . . .
>
> Assessment will reflect the whole child and serve to illuminate the child's strengths, interests, and areas of need. Ongoing evaluation will be based on narrative records, . . . careful observation of the students, and portfolios of each child's work throughout the year . . .

What these three teachers propose for elementary education borrows heavily from the guiding principles of early childhood education. In a sense they are proposing a kind of "trickle-up" process of school improvement as opposed to the traditional "trickle-down." They are saying that the kinds of things that make sense for young children—to be active, to explore, to feel safe and unafraid, to know that people care about them, to be understood and trusted—in fact make sense for all children.

While "good teaching" is typically defined in terms of classroom control and test score results, these teachers are redefining good teaching. In their approach, the child's activity is central and the teacher is a guide and co-discoverer. Democracy is practiced, not merely ritualized, and the wider community (including multicultural and international perspectives) is both content and audience for classroom work. Everything is connected, and so the old saying "You can learn something from anything" is reconceptualized: you can learn everything from anything, if you are willing to pursue it deeply enough and follow it far enough.

Proposing to create a school based on a different vision and a larger purpose has pushed these teachers to ask one another a wide range of big questions: Who are we? Why are we here? What are our strengths and weaknesses? What kind of teaching do we have in mind? In other words, their work has propelled them toward autobiography as a method of self-understanding and collective growth. Each recollects a childhood of care, nurturance, intensity; each draws on a life story as she constructs a teaching identity. This, of course, is based on an assumption that teaching is neither objective nor something easily prescribed. Teaching is, rather, emotional, affective, and subjective. Teaching is interactive and intersubjective, like friendship, like love. Teaching is hard to explain—it is complex, changing, intense, and mysterious. It has an undeniable existential dimension, as Peter Abbs (1981) has argued, and can only be understood inside itself. It is, then, hopeless to aspire to teaching as a concept divorced from persons, since "we can only teach out of our own being" (Abbs, 1981, p. 495).

Teaching out of our own being is both hope and burden. It pushes us to be more thoughtful, more reflective, more analytical, more careful. It demands self-scrutiny, self-awareness, and a willingness to hold judgments and choices contingently. It promises a deeper fulfillment, perhaps, and a larger personal payoff—a greater intentionality for teachers.

An assumption here is that teaching is voluntary, intelligent, and collective work that is typically enacted in situations that are indifferent at best and often coercive. Teachers are patronized and infantilized in structures not of their own making, socialized into cultures that run counter to their students and even their own best interests. Teachers are silenced in their own worlds, rendered powerless and thoughtless. And yet teaching remains so complex, so person-specific and situationally grounded, that it is impossible to fully understand it outside of itself—it cannot be adequately described outside of doing it. This being the case, teachers are the central (though largely ignored) sources of knowledge about teaching, and teacher self-awareness is a critical part of successful teaching.

Recovering the voice of the early childhood teacher involves challenging the "laws and causes of social physics" (Geertz, 1983, p. 3) that still dominate research on teaching. It requires that teachers speak in their own voices and struggle to legitimize their own knowledge and perceptions. And it demands that we turn the world of research on teaching upside down—didactic, intimidating, and oppressive approaches can be scuttled in favor of interpreted, shared, and creative ones; all the pseudo-scientific accouterments—the authoritative third-person accounts, the flood of footnotes, the leaden expert conclusion—can be thrown out in favor of a more straightforward, honest, and autobiographical stance. This stance need not be the property of academics, university-based scholars, or sanctified researchers. On the contrary, autobiography belongs to everyone—the researcher and the researched are one. The requirements are these: a willingness to begin, time and space to sustain effort, a collective in which each participant is both author and audience. There must be trust, something that can build over time, and there must be courage, the ability to give as well as demand, to nurture as well as challenge, to probe for detail as well as for pattern.

The telling of many stories—the recovery of voice—will be worth the effort. It will potentially expand the space in which choices are made, revealing wider and different perspectives, illuminating diverse meanings, creating opportunity for broader interpretations. In this way story-telling, as it expands, will become mirror and window both—reflecting back knowledge and understanding for a widening circle of teachers, and opening possibilities for all. Further, it will, as it grows, perhaps offer an antidote to arid research and break the logjam on voice and choice. A kaleidoscope of views may at last challenge the sanctity of a single lense. Finally, multiple stories may successfully challenge a narrow and static view of children and childhood. The stories of teachers, after all, are stories of children, and they can, therefore, expand the natural history of children—they can show us children in elaborate detail, case by case. This knowledge enriches our understanding, complicates as well as makes truer our conclusions about children's lives.

Who understands the demands and rewards of teaching young children? Who knows the back-breaking and gut-wrenching aspects of it, the surprise and joy and confusion in it, the despair and epiphany that can simultaneously share center stage? Who recalls the humorous incident or the profound discovery, can tack back and forth with relative ease between detailed description and larger context? To say that these and other teachers understand, know, and recall would be beneath comment were it not for a powerful, sanctified research community that dismisses the voice of the teacher outright. Teachers, it seems, are mere practitioners, not thinkers. They are subjective, emotional, involved, caring, and, therefore, somehow suspect. The voice of the teacher—full of commitment, compassion, and action—is diminished in favor of the distanced voice of the developmentalist, the psychologist, the academic researcher. And in the course of this shift a rich and valuable source of knowledge about young children and teaching is distorted or completely lost.

Early childhood education is a field in search of direction. It is a profession-in-formation, moving decisively toward neither the largely discredited trade-union model of elementary and high school teachers nor the distanced and elitist medical model. Early childhood education is in flux and under pressure: from the educational system to "prepare" children for kindergarten, from politicians and policy makers to be accountable in terms they can accept, from business to solve the "problem" of workers with children. All of this pressure occurs, of course, in larger contexts of international competition, war, economic instability, massive governmental retreat from supporting the needs of children and families (and the abandonment of urban poor children in particular), and the ongoing struggle of women and people of color for equity and justice.

Recovering the voice of the teacher—usually a woman, increasingly a person of color, often a member of the working poor—is an essential part of reconceptualizing the field of early childhood education. There is beginning to be a popular literature that illuminates teachers' lives, insights, and knowledge, but the scholarly research and writing fail to make a comparable contribution. Policymakers and scholars tend to speak for teachers, never with them. The question "What can these teachers tell one another and the world about teaching and about children?" has largely been ignored in favor of more distanced questions, such as "How shall we explain what these teachers ought to know and what it must be like for them?" At some point the goal must become an accurate portrayal of action as teachers themselves experience it, an account infused with immediacy, conflict, and contradiction as teachers actually live it. Autobiography, then, may prove essential for the progressive reconceptialization of the field of early childhood education.

REFERENCES

Abbs, P. (1981). Education and the living image: Reflections on imagery, fantasy, and the art of recognition. *Teachers College Record, 82*(3), 475–496.

Bateson, M. C. (1989). *Composing a life*. New York: Atlantic Monthly Press.

Geertz, C. (1983). *Local knowledge: Further essays in interpretive anthropology*. New York: Basic Books.

CHAPTER 14

Implementing Antibias Curriculum in the Kindergarten Classroom

Monica Miller Marsh

During the summer of 1990, I had many things on my mind. In addition to planning an October wedding, I was making a job transition. In the fall I would be teaching in a new school district and making the switch from fifth grade to kindergarten. As if that were not enough, I was contemplating the number of ways in which I could fulfill the requirements for my master's thesis. After several conversations with my thesis advisor, we decided that a collaborative action research study would best meet my needs.

I had made the choice to implement antibias curriculum in my kindergarten classroom. I felt that collaborative research would provide me with an opportunity to systematically observe kindergarten children immersed in antibias curriculum for one academic year, as well as provide a vehicle for my reflections as an early childhood teacher.

As I was initially preparing lessons and activities for the upcoming school year, I made a conscious effort to eliminate as much bias as possible from the kindergarten curriculum. I had received my class list and was able to determine that at least 30 percent of the students in my classroom were not of European descent. I revised and designed lessons and activities that would reflect the diversity of my students. I created an environment that was culturally inclusive. Pictures and posters of children and families representing a variety of backgrounds adorned the walls. The bookshelves were laden with books that also depicted a variety of cultures. The dramatic play area contained both male and female dolls that were culturally diverse and anatomically correct. Presenting children with this type of curriculum would offer each child the opportunity to have more meaningful and relevant experiences.

THE RATIONALE FOR ANTIBIAS CURRICULUM

According to census information and predictions of demographers concerning population growth, by the year 2000 one out of three Americans will be nonwhite, and at least fifty-three U.S. cities will have become predominantly nonwhite ("Today's Numbers, Tomorrow's Nation," 1986). Immigration is now America's major source of population growth. United Nations statistics show over 14 million foreign-born people living in the United States in the early 1980s, and the total number of new immigrants as totaling between 11 million and 13 million for the decade (Carroll & Schensul, 1990). By the end of the 1990s, many of our schools will have populations in which minority-group members form the majority.

These statistics call for a reconceptualization of the educational process in the schools of the United States. In order for educators to meet the challenges in the 1990s, they need to acknowledge that racism, sexism, handicapism, and classism exist in their schools. These issues need to be confronted by educators on both a personal and professional level. All students need to be engaged in activities that inform them about these social issues so that they are empowered to discuss, explore, and take action to make lasting social changes. Until the issues of racism, sexism, handicapism, and classism have been addressed in the classroom, the needs of each student will not be met. Failure to meet the needs of all students could cause serious societal repercussions, including a high incidence of school dropouts and the creation of a generation of adults not prepared to become fully participating and contributing members of American society.

One comprehensive approach to curriculum that addresses the diverse needs of America's school-age children is antibias curriculum. Antibias curriculum is an integrated curriculum that is culturally inclusive. It is based on children's developmental tasks as they construct identity and attitudes. Antibias curriculum not only addresses the race and ethnicity of a child but includes the dimensions of gender, religious diversity, sexual orientation, physical ableness, and socioeconomic status. Antibias curriculum challenges existing prejudices, stereotypes, sexism, classism, racism, and discriminatory behavior in young children's development and interactions (Ramsey, 1982). Not unlike multicultural education, which grew out of the multicultural movement, antibias curriculum incorporates lessons and activities that directly address cultural diversity.

The multicultural movement was a public effort to address the social inequalities that existed in the United States during the time of the civil rights movement of the 1960s. Various racial and ethnic groups resided in the United States, yet equal opportunities were not shared by all. The civil rights movement challenged educational institutions to make education more equitable for minority groups. Movements such as desegregation, special education, bilingual education, and the use of mainstreaming were developed in order to make public schools accessible to more students. Multicultural education has been a reform movement aimed at changing the content and processes within the schools (Sleeter & Grant, 1987). Originally, those advocating multicultural education were concerned primarily with racism in the schools. It has been expanded to address sexism, classism, and handicapism (Sleeter & Grant, 1987).

Several approaches to multicultural education have evolved from the 1960s through to the 1990s. Sleeter and Grant (1987) have categorized and identified five major approaches to multicultural education, as follows:

1. *Teaching the culturally different* focuses exclusively on the needs of minority students, students with low socioeconomic backgrounds, and students with special educational needs in an attempt to meet their individual needs within the regular classroom setting.
2. *Human relations* emphasizes communication and interaction among diverse groups of students in order to reduce tension and conflict while simultaneously fostering positive attitudes among students.
3. *Single-group studies* looks at the history of each minority group and identifies specific social concerns and problems that face these groups in order to sensitize and promote social change.
4. *Multicultural education* gives top priority to race and ethnicity, although this approach is for all students, not just minorities.
5. *Education that is multicultural and social reconstructionist*, an extension of multicultural education, promotes an understanding of social problems and active work against sources of oppression in our society.

Multicultural education seems to be the approach that is most popular with educators, although full implementation of multicultural education is still the exception, not the rule (Sleeter & Grant, 1987; Swadener, 1989). The goal of multicultural education can be defended on logical grounds. If children are taught about different cultures and learn to respect and appreciate the differences as well as the similarities among cultures, then prejudice and discrimination will be decreased (Derman-Sparks, 1989). However, educators often fall into the trap of teaching a tourist curriculum that uses a less authentic, "additive" approach.

Tourist curriculum is the term used to define the teaching of cultures through the use of "food, traditional clothing, and household implements" (Derman-Sparks, 1989, p. 7). Multicultural activities become isolated or contained in one unit rather than being infused into the daily curriculum. Students are misled into thinking that various cultures are based on holidays and celebrations rather than being a part of everyday life. Ramsey (cited in Derman-Sparks, 1989) highlights other problems that may characterize a multicultural curriculum:

1. Focusing on information about other countries—learning about Japan or Mexico rather than about Japanese-Americans or exploring the diversity of culture among Mexican-Americans
2. Standardizing the curriculum, with the assumption that there should or can be one set of goals and activities for all settings, ignoring the importance of taking into account the background of the children, their experience or lack of experience with people from other groups, and their attitudes toward their own groups
3. Restricting it to classrooms with diverse student populations, when, in fact, children in all-white classrooms may be the most in need of learning about the differences that exist in American society

The multicultural approach incorporates activities that are similar to those advocated in antibias curriculum. The danger of falling into a tourist curriculum is lessened as antibias activities are infused into existing units of study. Antibias curriculum goals are to "enable every child to construct a knowledgeable, confident self-identity; to develop a comfortable, empathetic and just interaction with diversity; and to develop critical thinking and the skills for standing up for oneself in the face of injustice" (Derman-Sparks, 1989, p. *ix*).

Educators choosing to employ antibias curriculum must plan and implement activities that will meet the diverse needs of the students in their classroom each year. Teachers need to explore the backgrounds and experiences of the children in their classrooms in order to plan activities that will help each child reach her or his full potential. Early childhood educators, parents, and caregivers have a large responsibility. Children enter early childhood programs and, for the first time, experience playing and learning with peers from many different backgrounds. It is crucial that early childhood educators help young children to feel positive about themselves and others.

BACKGROUND INFORMATION ON THE STUDY

In order to better understand the strengths and limitations when implementing antibias curriculum with kindergarten children in a public school setting, a collaborative action research study was undertaken. This study systematically analyzed the quality of antibias activities that were planned and implemented in the classroom. There were three major questions that guided the study:

1. How do children from ethnically and racially diverse backgrounds respond to formal and spontaneous antibias curriculum?
2. What are ways in which children enacted the antibias curriculum in their play, questions, and conversations?
3. What happens to the teacher who designs and implements antibias activities?

Methodology

The study was based on one academic year of data collection. As the teacher–researcher, I began a professional journal on the first day of school and made daily journal entries. The journal focused on the children's questions, concerns, and responses to planned and spontaneous antibias activities. An analysis of children's dialogue and interactions was conducted. The university collaborator (Beth Swadener) was responsible for observing my teaching of selected antibias activities and recording the responses and interactions that occurred between the children and me. Fieldnotes were shared with me immediately following most observations in order to clarify what was observed. The children provided another source of data as they illustrated and responded to selected antibias activities in their journals and through artwork.

As I collected and analyzed data from these multiple sources, the information was categorized into five primary areas: (1) race/ethnicity, (2) gender/sexual orientation, (3) holidays/religious diversity, (4) individual differences, and (5) socioeconomic status. Observations were made by me and the university collaborator at various times throughout the school day (e.g., during learning centers, large group activities, and snack), and data were coded.

Setting

The setting of the study was a full-day, tuition-based, enriched kindergarten classroom in an urban/suburban public school system located in a midwestern state. The elementary school in which the enriched kindergarten is located serves a population of approximately 461 students in grades K–5. The demographics of the elementary school mirror those of the district. Approximately 284 students are classified as African-

American, 162 as Caucasian, 13 as Asian, and 2 as Hispanic. The total number of minority students is 299, which is 65 percent.

Twenty students participated in the enriched kindergarten program. These students were accepted into the program based on evidence of high intellectual potential. Each child was given the Kaufmann Assessment Battery for Children (Kaufmann & Kaufmann, 1983) by the school psychologist. In order to qualify for admission to the enriched kindergarten program, a child had to score 2 standard deviations above the mean minus the standard error of measurement on any one or a composite of the following processes: simultaneous processing, sequential processing, and mental processing. The choice to teach antibias curriculum was my choice as an educator; it was not part of the enriched kindergarten program.

The names of the twenty kindergarten students have been changed to ensure confidentiality. The students ranged in age from 4½ to 6 years old. Twelve of the students were male and eight, female. Six, or 30 percent, were considered minority-group members, including three African-American students (two males, one female), two Asian students (one Korean male, and one Indian), and one biracial female student. The remainder of the students were classified as being European-American; however, one of these students was an Arab-American female. The Korean student and one African-American male are adopted. The dominant religion is Christian. Four of the children practice both Jewish and Christian traditions.

Socioeconomic status ranged from upper-income to lower-income. Many of the parents were professionals. This accurately reflected the socioeconomic status of the school district.

The elementary school where the enriched kindergarten was housed was an open school. The physical layout of the classroom itself consisted of two adjoining rooms. One room was comprised of the dramatic play area, block area, three computers, the art center, and the science center. The other room contained tables for various centers and a reading corner. This room opened into a classroom referred to as the Developmental Educational Program. There were nine students in this classroom. These students were either physically or mentally impaired. This classroom was the "buddy" classroom of the kindergartners. These two classrooms were located in a wing that was fairly isolated from the rest of the school.

I had one aide for three hours a day, an African-American female in her mid-fifties. She helped facilitate centers and activities as needed and supervised the children during the lunch hour. Several parents acted as volunteers. Parent volunteers helped with computer instruction, journaling, and various special activities.

Program Description

The children began their school day at 8:45 A.M. As they entered the room, they organized themselves and chose an arrival activity. There were usually three arrival activities from which to choose. Arrival activities lasted for approximately twenty minutes and included such things as puzzles, games, or simple art projects. Students were then asked to clean up and proceed into the adjoining room for a large-group discussion. Discussion topics varied according to integrated units of study. The units of study that were taught that year were:

Getting Acquainted
I Am Special
Safety Is Important
It's Fall
Pioneers
Native Americans
Immigration
Friends from Around the World
Knights and Castles
Resolutions, Cooperation, and Peace
Tools and Simple Machines
Inventions
Careers
Space
Our Planet Earth
Plants
Animals

Toward the end of group discussion, learning center activities were described to the children. Students could choose from a total of eight learning centers. These eight learning centers were math, reading readiness, snack, fine-motor skills, listening, science, art, and computer. Free play was also an option for the children during center time. They could play in the block area, in the dramatic play area, or at the sand table. Center time lasted from one to one-and-a-half hours, depending on the day of the week.

Learning centers allowed each child to work at her or his own pace on a level that was developmentally appropriate. Children could choose to work individually or cooperatively. In the learning center approach, children are responsible for choosing an activity and following it through to completion. Children exercise decision-making skills as they move freely from one center to the next.

Before lunch, students were involved in music and rhythm activities for twenty minutes. The students had one hour for lunch and quiet activities, plus twenty minutes of rest.

The afternoon consisted of sharing time, recess, and various language, math, or art experiences. The children were dismissed from school at 3:05 P.M.

The children's schedule allowed freedom of movement throughout the classroom for most of the day. Each child was empowered when given the right to make her or his own decisions. As a group, the children were empowered as they practiced concensus decision making. Group decisions were made regarding everything from generating classroom rules or choosing topics of discussion to the type of refreshments that should be served for a celebration. Children also engaged in social problem solving (for a more detailed discussion, refer to Chapter 12).

The antibias activities and lessons that were infused into the kindergarten units of study came from two major sources: (1) *Anti-Bias Curriculum: Tools for Empowering Young Children*, by Derman-Sparks and the A.B.C. Task Force (Derman-Sparks, 1989) and (2) the children. The children generated many questions that led me to create and/or search for more activities that would meet their specific needs.

ENACTMENT OF THE ANTIBIAS CURRICULUM: CHILDREN'S VOICES

The following examples describe the infusion of antibias activities into existing units of study. Direct quotations of the students illustrate their reactions and interactions during both formal and spontaneous antibias activities and discussions. The anecdotes and excerpts are taken from the multiple data sources.

Getting Acquainted

We began our kindergarten year with a unit entitled "Getting Acquainted." I had planned a number of experiences that would help the children learn more about themselves as well as one another. The activity body tracing and painting was planned to address race. I began the lesson with a discussion regarding skin color, eye color, and hair texture. The terms *melanin* and *pigment* were introduced to the children. We discussed hair follicles and the fact that hair was wavy, straight, or curly based on the shape of individual follicles. The follow-up activity, body tracing and painting, was completed over a two-week period.

Each child chose a partner to trace their body on butcher paper. Students then helped one another cut out the tracings. The next step was to visit the art table and to closely examine their skin color so that they could mix paint as close to the color of their skin as possible. The following excerpts were recorded in my journal while children were involved in this project.

9/12
The body painting continues. They really enjoy mixing colors and matching them to their skin. They don't seem to be aware of the fact that there are some large differences in skin tone.

Larry (African-American): Scott [Caucasian], mix your color like mine. Make it the same.

Mrs. M.: Which of you has more melanin?

Larry: I have less. Well, maybe we have the same.

9/14
I think I've made a breakthrough. We colored pictures of our families today. Stephanie (African-American) colored the faces and bodies of her family members with brown crayon. Prior to this, pictures of her family were merely outlines in blue, red, or green.

9/17
Patrick (African-American): My mother has more melanin than I do. She has freckles and I don't.

9/24
The children really want to help each other to get the right color. Kevin [Caucasian] and Robert [Caucasian] were talking today.

Robert: Look, I think that's the right color. Maybe should I add a little more yellow?

Kevin: Make it exactly like your skin. (*holding his arm up to Robert's*) It *is* like my color! Let me help you!

The children finished painting the body tracings. As they were drying, one of the students exclaimed, "Our bodies are naked!" The university collaborator suggested that we use fabric to make clothing. The students readily accepted this idea, and the next day they began bringing in fabric scraps to glue onto the tracings for clothing.

As we were designing our clothing, I saw that the children had already formed attitudes and opinions regarding males and females.

9/25
Jeff and I were busy cutting out some pink felt pants for his body painting. Scott, who was gluing fabric onto his body tracing/painting, came over to watch.
Scott: Pink is a girls' color! You can't have pink pants!
Jeff: Yes I can! *Pink is not a girls' color!*
Scott: Yes it is!
Mrs. M.: Who says there have to be boy colors and girl colors?
Scott: No one. But there is!
Jeff: Hu-uh! (*Jeff continued to work.*)

We concluded our body tracing/painting activity, but this was only the beginning of many more antibias discussions that would take place this academic year. On several occasions, differences in skin color were referred to in a natural and positive manner. The following excerpts give me reason to believe that the body tracing/painting activity had made quite a positive impact on the children.

10/1
It was raining this morning, and the children were allowed to enter the building early. Kevin, Emily, Stephanie, and Patrick walked into the classroom together.
Kevin: Look, Mrs. M., two black kids and two white kids. Two big white kids and two little black kids. We're the first ones!
They all smiled and ran off to play together.

1/31
Patrick drew a picture of himself in his journal today.
Patrick: Look, I'm taking a Valentine home to my mother. Can I rip this page out?
He had drawn the same blue and black shirt he had on today and the same black pants. His skin was colored a beautiful shade of brown. He was carrying a large heart in his hand.

4/25
Meredith made a picture of Carli picking flowers in her garden.
Carli: Meredith, I don't have any hands! How can I be picking flowers?
Meredith: Hand me that brown crayon over there. I'll give you some.

Stephanie [African-American]: Those aren't Carli's [Cauca-
sian] hands, they're my hands! I mean they aren't my
hands, they are Carli's but my hands are brown.

Pioneers

Several weeks after the body tracing/painting activity, we were
discussing pioneers. I was planning an autumn field trip to a historical
farm, so the topic of pioneers needed to be addressed. This is my journal
excerpt.

10/22

Pioneers. We began our discussion by brainstorming what the
children knew about pioneers. I received many of the typical
responses: Pioneers made their own clothes. Pioneers didn't
have cars. Pioneers made their own food.
Larry: The pioneers killed black people.
Mrs. M.: What do you mean, Larry?
Kevin: The black people were slaves. They were beat and
treated badly so they would do all of the work.
Emily [Caucasian]: No, the pioneers didn't kill the black man,
they killed the red man—the Indian.
Anna [biracial]: The reason some black people don't have
very much today is because they were slaves. Some black
people like our neighbors have a really nice house and
car, but others just want to eat and they can't. They don't
have as much as white people. They don't get as many—
what's that P word?
Mrs. M.: Opportunities?
Anna: Yes, opportunities as white people do.
Kevin: Some people think that black people steal and cheat,
but I don't think that is true.

We discussed these issues, and the children agreed that slavery was
wrong. That afternoon I went to the library and checked out the book
Follow the Drinking Gourd. The following day we read the story and
discussed the Underground Railroad. I introduced Harriet Tubman to the
children. It seems that Sean's mother lived in a home that was a stop on
the underground railroad. He eagerly explained this to us. It was during
these discussion that I realized that these 4- and 5-year-olds were conscious of race and well aware of existing social situations.

Native Americans

Our unit on pioneers led to our next unit centered around the theme of Native Americans. We again began our unit with brainstorming.

11/5
Mrs. M.: Today we are going to talk about Native Americans. What can you tell me about Native Americans?
Children: They got behind white men and chopped off their heads!
They had bows and arrows.
They wore feathers.
They made *woo, woo* noises.
They had pow wows.

These answers sounded to me as if the children believed that Native Americans were a people of the past. This thought prompted my next question.

Mrs. M.: Do you think there are still Native Americans living in the United States of America?
Children: No, they are all dead.
No, they were all killed a long time ago.
Meredith: Some of them might still be alive but they are very, very old.
(*Jack and Kevin agreed that they were still alive.*)
Kevin: I went to a Native American dinner at the Natural History Museum. There were lots of Native Americans there. I talked to them and a little boy danced for us.
Alex: I have friends, lots of them, who are Native Americans.
Jack: Of course they are still alive! Look around we have an Indian in here—Nirij!

Nirij feverently denied this by shaking his head and saying "Uh-uh." He refused to say anything else.
We briefly discussed Christopher Columbus and the fact that upon "discovering" America, he mistook the Native Americans for Indians because he thought he was in the West Indies. I explained that Nirij was from India and that it was different from being a Native American. We located India on the map.
It is interesting to note that only three out of twenty students believed that the Native Americans were still existent. When I asked how

they knew so much about Native Americans in the past, their responses were television and books. Only two students had ever been in contact with someone that they knew was a Native American. We came back to the topic of Native Americans several times throughout the year.

Immigration

Nirij had an opportunity to share more about his heritage when we studied immigration. His parents volunteered to present a slide show and bring in clothing and toys that they had brought from India to the United States. Other parents and guest speakers were invited into the classroom to share their ethnicity. We learned words and phrases in several different languages. I began teaching the children songs and how to count in Spanish. We discussed ethnic customs and traditions and shared special family stories.

In November we constructed a large tree in the classroom on one side of the room. This was "Our Class Tree," and everyone had a branch. On their branch each child taped a picture of him- or herself and a small piece of colored yarn. We then wrote their names, the names of their parents and grandparents, and the place from which the grandparents or parents had emigrated. Below the class tree, we hung the world map. The students used the same color of string they had taped on their branch to map out the path their predecessors' had followed to the United States.

I sent a Family History Questionnaire (Derman-Sparks, 1989) home with the children two weeks prior to the immigration unit. The children couldn't wait to share their information with the class. The following are highlights from my November journal entries:

11/16
Kevin: My grandparents were from Poland and so were
       Carli's. Anybody else from Sweden?
Anna faced some laughter today when she shared her father's
African name, Muyundu.
Mrs. M.: Yes, this name is different, and it may sound funny
       to us. It is an African name.
Sean: It sorta sounds like the name *grand bubu*. (*Grand bubu
       was the name that we learned for a type of African gar-
       ment we had discussed with one of our guest speakers.*)

The topic of slaves again came up during this discussion. The children reasoned that because slaves came to the United States and crossed the Atlantic Ocean, they, too, must have been immigrants. At this point we reiterated the fact that slaves did not choose to come to the United States; they were captured and taken against their will. I reminded them of when a guest speaker had shared slides of the "door of no return," where captured Africans were forced onto slave ships in Senegal.

Billy, who was reluctant to share that he was adopted, decided to list Korea, his place of birth, as one of his places of origin as well as the background of his adoptive parents. Now he could claim he had come the farthest if he had flown over the Atlantic Ocean or "maybe I came over the Pacific Ocean. I'm still the only one."

This unit concluded with an international Thanksgiving feast that most of the families attended. Families brought traditional ethnic foods, and children explained where the dishes originated and, in some cases, how they were prepared. A short speech was written by the class. Four children presented the speech before the meal.

11/20

Colleen: Welcome to our international Thanksgiving feast.

Larry: At the first Thanksgiving meal, not everyone was happy. The Native Americans were sad because the Pilgrims were taking their land away. Many of the Pilgrims were sick from the long trip and missed their families back home.

Kevin: Today we are thankful to eat together. We are celebrating because our families have come from all different parts of the world. We are happy to be eating together.

Scott: Now let's eat!

Inventions

The process of inventing was a unit of study for several weeks in the spring. I had set up an inventors' table and supplied it with a variety of odds and ends. I left the rest to the children's creativity. We discussed several inventions and their inventors. During this unit, the following discussion was recorded.

Mrs. M.: I'm wondering if women really can be inventors. We've been talking about inventors for over a week now, and we haven't once mentioned a woman. What do you think?

Alex: I think women can be inventors. My mom really invented the thing that I brought into school. We helped each other.

Jack: Well, my mom tried to invent something and it didn't
work for her. I don't think girls can be inventors.

Three boys said that females could not be inventors. Some other children disagreed.

Anna: I've also seen a woman make things.
Kevin: Just because we haven't talked about them doesn't
mean there aren't any. Most crossing guards are boys, but
my sister's a crossing guard.
Meredith: It doesn't feel fair to me to say that girls can't be inventors. I might invent something, and he (*pointing to a
male classmate*) might not know about it.
Carli: I think girls can be inventors because remember when I
came up with something?
Emily: I think girls can because I saw boys and girls and little
and big kids make things.

At this point, the children started putting thumbs up and thumbs
down, as if they were voting for the idea.

Mrs. M.: Most of the inventions we have discussed so far were
invented quite a while ago. Women were not allowed to
have businesses or even own their own home or property.
Even if they came up with an invention, they would have
their father or husband or brother claim that they had invented the product. This was the only way they would be
able to sell or manufacture the invention. Carli, whose
name would you like on that invention you came up
with? Patrick's or Sean's?
Carli: I wouldn't like it.
Mrs. M.: H. J. Heinz's wife really invented the pickle jar, and
supposedly it was Eli Whitney's landlady who gave him
the idea for the cotton gin. We will be talking about other
women inventors including Ruth Wakefield, who invented
the chocolate chip cookie.

As I dismissed the children from the group discussion, four boys and
one girl ran over to the inventors' table. After a few minutes the female
left the table. In order to give girls an opportunity to work at the
inventors' table, I limited the number of inventors to two boys and two

girls. It eliminated the girls' complaints that "he takes too long!" and the boys continually prodding the girls to "hurry up!"

We also worked in mixed groups of inventors for pretend corporations. Students had to come up with ideas and a prototype of a new product. Some of the product assignments were: make a device that would keep a puppy in the bathtub while it was being bathed, design an exercise machine for a puppy that was home alone all day, and design a way to iron clothes without an iron. This activity seemed to help both boys and girls work together while also exercising problem-solving and decision-making skills.

Resolutions, Cooperation, and Peace

Kevin, who made the comment during the invention discussion that "most crossing guards are boys but my sister's a crossing guard," is very aware of the crossing guard situation because he and his sister walk to school together every morning. Kevin often waits with his sister at her post. One morning in February Kevin ran into the classroom looking very agitated.

Kevin: I have to talk to Mr. G. [The school counselor].
Mrs. M.: Kevin, what's the matter?
Kevin: You wouldn't understand! You can't do anything about it! Can I go?
Mrs. M.: Mr. G. isn't here this morning, but this seems to be urgent. Is it something we could write him a note about and leave in his mailbox up in the office? When he comes in he'll contact you.
Kevin: Well . . . I think so.
I went to get a pen and sheet of paper to write on. Kevin dictated the following note.

Dear Mr. G.,

Why are there no black boy crossing guards? If this school is peaceful and you're making conflict managers and we want freedom, we should have black boy crossing guards. They need to feel like a part of our school.
Please send me a note back after you know.

Signed,
Kevin

Together we took Kevin's note down to the office and deposited it in Mr. G.'s mailbox. That afternoon Kevin received a short reply.

Dear Kevin,

I asked some of my black male students if they would like to be at the door(s) of the school *or* if they would like to be outside at the corner. They preferred to be guards at the door(s) inside. They feel like a part of our school. Thank you for your concern.

Mr. G.

Kevin seemed to be comfortable with this answer. He listened to the response from Mr. G., then continued his work at the math center.

Kevin was not the only student in our classroom to become a social activist. There were many occasions when individuals or the entire class took action against things they felt were unjust or unfair. On two occasions, the kindergarten children were excluded from assemblies, based on administrative judgments that the content was "inappropriate" or too advanced for kindergartners. All kindergarten children were excluded from a peace assembly and an assembly about Dr. Martin Luther King, Jr. (based on the belief that if children saw a bus boycott or a sit-in role played they might react negatively), they were excluded from a peace march that included two representatives from each classroom in grades 1–5. These representatives were members of the school's conflict manager program. Conflict management training begins in the first grade.

When they were excluded from the peace march and the representatives from other classes came around marching with banners, they were upset. Without my input, they organized their own peace march on the playground.

Carli: Come on, let's march for peace! We want peace! We want peace!
Anna: Peace on earth! We want peace!
The line got longer and longer. Jack, Kevin, and Patrick ran to get on top of the monkey bars.

Jack: Look, Mrs. M.! We made floats for the parade! Peace on
   Earth!
There was one student who started shouting: "We want war!
We want more!"
Carli: Scott, be quiet! Get in line!

Scott did not join in the march, but he did stop shouting. The march lasted for the rest of the time we were out on the playground. The children relayed the details of the peace march to the principal when she came in to say "hello" that afternoon.

During our school's designated "Peace Week" in May, all of the students were asked to participate in an "all"-school peace march. The kindergartners were very excited. They collaboratively designed a banner and proudly displayed it as they "marched" the two blocks around the school.

Carli's ability to organize a class peace march and Kevin's desire to maintain equity indicate that young children are ready to actively participate in antibias curriculum. After discussing my curriculum and the reactions of the children to these exclusionary practices with the principal, we agreed that the kindergarten teachers should have the option to participate in these school functions with their classes.

Administrators who feel young children are not developmentally ready for antibias curriculum are not uncommon. Many teachers and parents also share the belief. They believe that young children are color-blind, oblivious to differences in class, and, although noticing handicaps, not in need of information regarding handicapping conditions.

Religious diversity, like physical differences, is often problematic in public school districts. Many school districts prohibit discussions or activities pertaining to holidays. It has been my experience that holidays play an important part in young children's lives. They seem to be natural times for children to compare and contrast religious and ethnic celebrations and traditions.

TEACHER-RESEARCHER REFLECTIONS

The teacher who chooses to teach antibias curriculum is a risk taker on both a professional and personal level. Personal limitations included admitting to myself that there was much I still needed to learn. In order to present accurate information and "authentic" experiences, I gathered as many resources as possible. My biggest resource proved to be the parents of the children in my classroom.

According to the findings of this study, young children are very aware of differences in color, gender, religious orientation, physical ableness, and socioeconomic status. The knowledge they possess seems to have been transmitted primarily through the media and the beliefs and values of their immediate families.

The children's level of awareness and their interest in certain issues led to the spontaneous generation of many discussions and activities. This evidence indicated that young children are "ready" for antibias curriculum.

Antibias curriculum has been successfully implemented in several school districts in the United States, including Portland, Oregon; Chicago, Illinois, Atlanta, Georgia; and Rochester, New York. Information regarding these districts and their successful antibias programs should be disseminated throughout the country and made more easily accessible to teachers.

Once committed to antibias curriculum, I found that most of my time was spent searching for and planning activities. I learned on the job which types of antibias activities worked best with young children. If coursework and field experiences in antibias education were required for preservice teachers, educators would graduate from the university with accurate information that they would feel confident to teach. The development of a clearinghouse would also make it less difficult for educators to acquire antibias materials.

Teachers choosing to implement antibias curriculum need opportunities to discuss ideas and concerns with one another. I will never forget the feeling of professional isolation as the other kindergarten class went running down the hall in their freshly made Indian headbands making "whooping" noises. I had just spent the entire week helping my class unlearn these stereotypes about Native Americans. It would be less frustrating and mutually beneficial for teachers implementing antibias curriculum within the same school to identify themselves and meet on a regular basis. These meetings would allow teachers to share thoughts and concerns, brainstorm and revise the curriculum, while, at the same time, providing peer support for one another.

Journaling did serve as an outlet for the frustration and isolation I often felt. As Holly (1989) describes, through keeping a journal, I watched myself grow. At first the entries consisted mainly of my fears and apprehensions about teaching antibias lessons and activities for the first time. As I grew more confident, I focused on the reactions of the children.

Through making daily entries, I was able to watch the children grow and mature. Patterns in their behavior and thinking began to emerge on paper that I never would have connected without the documentation to review and analyze. At times, I could make predictions based on the information I had collected in my journal. The dictated journals of the students proved to be invaluable to me. Through serving as scribe for the entries and viewing the illustrations, I gained insights into what was meaningful to the students. For example, many students had intense feelings about the war in the Persian Gulf and included comments about the war in their journals. This helped me gauge what knowledge the students were internalizing and how they were interpreting that knowledge.

Teachers need to be cautious when implementing antibias activities with young children. When children were involved in a Rosa Parks–Montgomery bus boycott role-play activity, they were asked to take on some powerful roles. Teachers need to debrief children immediately after they are engaged in these types of activities. The process of debriefing allows teachers to bring out and discuss the feelings of the children and to clarify the concepts being taught.

The study suggests a number of avenues for future research. There has been a paucity of research in the area of the antibias approach. There is need for further research, particularly in the primary grades. Collaborative research is one way in which teacher–researchers and university collaborators can work together to identify and analyze critical incidents and classroom data (Lytle & Cochran-Smith, 1990; Swadener & Piekielek, 1991).

A second direction that research might take is to investigate how children from both ethnically and racially different backgrounds in a more typical kindergarten class respond to the antibias curriculum. As stated earlier, the kindergarten children in my classroom were assessed and admitted to the enriched kindergarten program based on their intellectual potential. Therefore the responses to antibias curriculum by the kindergarten children in my classroom may have been enhanced by this specific group of children's characteristics, but the success of the activities is not attributable to the level of intelligence. The antibias lessons and activities need to be investigated at multiple sites in heterogeneous as well as more homogeneous settings.

Third, there is a need for further exploration of how one's life history affects the way antibias curriculum is approached. Research needs to be conducted addressing how specific characteristics and qualities, gender, socioeconomic status, and cultural background impact the way antibias curriculum is taught by an individual. Findings from this type of study would help educators to define certain areas of focus that might be more meaningful for them. Teachers could benefit from sharing life experiences and perspectives.

Young children are very aware of differences in color, gender, socio-economic status, and physical ableness. It is important to educate young children and help them to understand why these differences exist so that they can accept and affirm human diversity, notice bias, and take appropriate action. It is also important to inform young children about social issues through discussions and planned activities. Children are aware of racism, sexism, classism, and handicapism. They need to feel comfortable discussing their thoughts and feelings about these issues. Acknowledging that these social "isms" exist is the first step to breaking down social barriers. I feel confident that antibias curriculum is the most effective approach for preparing young children to actively participate in a diverse society.

REFERENCES

Carroll, T., & Schensul, J. (1990). Visions in America in the 1990s and beyond: Negotiating cultural diversity and educational change. *Education and Urban Society, 22*(4), 339–345.

Derman-Sparks, L. (1989). *Anti-bias curriculum: Tools for empowering young children.* Washington, DC: National Association for the Education of Young Children.

Holly, M. L. (1989). *Writing to grow: Keeping a personal-professional journal.* Portsmouth, NH: Heinemann.

Jipson, J. (1991). Developmentally appropriate practice: Culture, curriculum, connections. *Early Education and Development, 2*(2), 120–136.

Katz, P. A. (1982). Development of children's racial awareness and intergroup attitudes. In L. G. Katz (Ed.), *Current topics in early childhood education* (Vol. 4) (pp. 17–54). Norwood, NJ: Ablex.

Kaufmann, A., & Kaufmann, N. (1983). *Kaufmann assessment battery for children.* Circle Pines, MN: American Guidance Services.

Lytle, S. L., & Cochran-Smith, M. (1990). Learning from teacher research: A working typology. *Teachers College Record, 92*(1), 83–102.

Mathison, S. (1988). Why triangulate? *Educational Researcher, 17*(2), 13–17.

Phillips, C. B. (1988). Nurturing diversity for today's children and tomorrow's leaders. *Young Children, 43*(2), 42–47.

Ramsey, P. G. (1982, September). *Racial differences in children's contacts and comments about others.* Paper presented at the annual meeting of the American Psychological Association, Washington, DC.

Ramsey, P. G. (1986, April). *Young children's understanding of social class differences.* Paper presented at the annual meeting of the American Educational Research Association, San Francisco.

Ramsey, P. G. (1987). *Teaching and learning in a diverse world: Multicultural education for young children.* New York: Teachers College Press.

Sleeter, C. E., & Grant, C. A. (1987). An analysis of multicultural education in the United States. *Harvard Educational Review, 57*(4), 421–444.

Swadener, E. B. (1989). Race, gender and exceptionality: Peer interactions in two child care centers. *Educational Policy, 3*(4), 371–387.

Swadener, E. B., & Piekielek, D. (1991, February). *Interpreting classroom culture: Reflections on a Friends school collaborative ethnography.* Paper presented at the twelfth annual Ethnography in Education Forum, Philadelphia.

Today's numbers, tomorrow's nation. (1986, May). *Education Week,* p. 14.

Watson, M., & Fisher, K. (1980). Development of social roles in elicited and spontaneous behavior during the preschool years. *Developmental Psychology, 16*(5), 483–494.

Whaley, K., & Swadener, E. B. (1990). Multicultural education in infant and toddler settings. *Childhood Education, 66*(4), 48–50.

Epilogue

In the Introduction we invited readers to consider a number of major issues and questions in the reconceptualization of the early childhood curriculum. We now return to these questions, drawing upon some of the themes raised in each section of the book as well as issues that will also need discussion and debate in the collective efforts to reconceptualize early childhood education.

This book has taken the view that curriculum must be made problematic. To us this means we must make it an object of study, rather than assume we know what it is. One of the most important aspects of studying the curriculum is to examine it *in context* and see it from a personal and political perspective. What is taught and how it is taught is largely dependent on the structural and cultural contexts of the classroom and school. As Bloch pointed out in Chapter 1, the beliefs about the importance of psychological and child development research, carried out within a positivistic methodology, coupled with the practice of separating early childhood teacher education programs in schools of home economics and schools of education, resulted in distinct orientations toward curriculum: one assuming knowledge as that which socializes the young; the other, the critical science orientation, making knowledge problematic. We must continually ask ourselves how knowledge about children and their ways of knowing is constructed and how our perspectives on what is known and worth knowing depend on beliefs about how one constructs and acquires knowledge. These questions lead inevitably to issues of evaluating what is "known." What criteria do we use to determine the validity of knowledge? Is one way of knowing better than another? Are all equal?

This issue of knowledge construction is likewise at the heart of Graue's work on readiness (Chapter 4). Her data highlight the need to question our assumptions about the categories we use and to be aware of how our categories influence the way we group children for instruction, as well as what and how we teach them. We believe the early childhood community must address fundamental epistemological questions such as these in order to reconceptualize the early childhood curriculum.

Making the curriculum problematic also requires us to examine the curriculum as it is enacted in classrooms and schools. We can no longer assume that we understand the process of schooling on the basis of occasional visits, nor on the basis of the examination of textbook manuals, workbooks, or what is written in the teacher's planbook. The task of observing, understanding, and describing the early childhood curriculum in specific settings is no simple endeavor. We must spend much more time than we typically do in examining the process of curriculum construction in a social and cultural context. As King states in Chapter 3, "the full array of context variables continue to be largely ignored in the research literature." Furthermore, examining the curriculum in use requires that we see it from multiple perspectives, further complicating the issue. To reconceptualize the early childhood curriculum, we must see curriculum as a vital object of study in a specific context if we are to understand and change early schooling for young children.

Another important aspect of making curriculum problematic is the question of *whose knowledge* is represented in what we teach. As Jungck and Marshall indicate in Chapter 5, knowledge is not value-free. It is tied to the interests of individuals, and one's interests underlie what is perceived as well as what is prescribed. How do we determine which, as well as whose, interests serve the common good? Further, we must ask ourselves to what extent the selection, organization, and construction of knowledge is legitimately the purview of our students. As Jipson demonstrates in Chapter 8, individual students create unique learning experiences for themselves based on choice and past experiences. To what extent is this approved, encouraged, or planned for? Where do we impose specific standards on learners and require certain experiences? Where do we open opportunities for learners to make their own educational experiences? A major question in reconceptualizing the early childhood curriculum is whose knowledge is represented in the events that occur in the classroom or in other informal early childhood settings.

In addition to examining the interests underlying the curriculum we enact, the question of *voice* needs to be examined from diverse perspectives. In terms of the curriculum question of whose voices are represented by what is taught and experienced, and whose interests are being served, the critical and feminist perspectives included in Part II are extended in Part III, *Issues of Cultural and Linguistic Pluralism*. Gomez, in Chapter 9, raises issues and questions regarding the importance of teachers' understanding their own cultural heritage and class background and what that brings to their teaching. Such cultural self-interrogation is important in embracing diversity (e.g., McIntosh, 1992).

Chapters in this part also address issues inherent in pluralism, including the balance and dynamic tension between the diversity inherent in our history and the maintenance of a common set of core values necessary to sustain us as a nation. Or, as James Quay (1990) asserts, "We should not have to choose between a common legacy and cultural diversity—especially in a nation where cultural diversity is a legacy" (p. *xiii*).

Chapter 10 extends the dialogue concerning pluralism to focus on linguistic diversity, placing early childhood curriculum in the larger political, pedagogical, and historical contexts of early bilingual education. This chapter extends curriculum questions of whose knowledge should be included and what form pedagogy should take to include issues of the official language of instruction and ways in which assimilation to dominant culture beliefs and language have been used in oppressive ways, including the issues of the cultural and linguistic genocide inflicted on Native American children. Young native speakers, in Soto and Smrekar's reconceptualization of the early childhood curriculum, are viewed as "at promise" versus "at risk," another reconceptualization (e.g., Swadener & Lubeck, in press).

Authors such as Soto, Gomez, Hale, and Polakow urge us to consider ways in which we can learn to understand and value individuals outside of our own affinity groups and better perform as allies across affinity groups for social change. A related question concerns how we can create classroom communities in which differences are cherished and members of the dominant culture are willing to modify their traditions to incorporate what is valuable to others and necessary for the existence of true pluralism. Such questions have their roots in the early childhood curriculum, during a time in when children are first learning about difference and beginning to form life attitudes.

Another growing movement within curriculum studies and education reform is the recognition that many of the unexamined assumptions about what should be learned and how it should be taught are grounded deeply in a Eurocentric world view, including assumptions about how children learn. This is particularly problematic in a field such as early childhood education, in which many of the prevailing assumptions of child development theory and "best practice" advocacy have been either "color-blind" or based on Eurocentric, often middle-class, notions of optimal early childhood experiences, communication with children, and what should be at the center of programs for young children.

Both the voices and audiences for an Afrocentric approach to curriculum and pedagogy have been growing rapidly for the past decade (e.g., Asante, 1987, 1988; Delpit, 1988; Hale, 1991; Hilliard, Payton-Stewart, &

Williams, 1990; Kunjufa, 1984, 1987; Williams, 1991). Visions for Children, the Afrocentric preschool program described by Janice Hale in Chapter 11 is an example of a growing phenomenon in the United States—an early childhood program designed both to honor the rich history and cultural diversity of African-American children and to enhance the likelihood of later academic success in dominant culture institutions (i.e., public schools). In a time in which growing numbers of African-American young people have begun to equate being smart with "acting white," (e.g., Fordham, 1988; Fordham & Ogbu, 1986), there is growing concern that the strong tradition of valuing education, literacy, and academic achievement in the African-American community is being eroded. Programs such as Visions for Children may function as a new generation of freedom schools in their commitment to helping children of African heritage to first, know themselves and their history so that they may take pride in their culture and heritage, even as they become increasingly bicultural and bidilectal.

The final part, *Voices from the Field: Teacher Narratives and Collaborative Work*, foregrounds teacher voices and provides concrete examples of ways in which early childhood teachers are collaborating for empowerment and curricular transformation. As William Ayers states, "Recovering the voice of the teacher—usually a woman, increasingly a person of color, often a member of the working poor—is an essential part of reconceptualizing the field of early childhood education" (Chapter 13). We share with Ayers the belief that autobiography, authentically collaborative research with teachers and students, and *listening* to what early childhood teachers have to tell us are essential for not only the reconceptualization of the early childhood curriculum, but for its *enactment*.

Through their shared, as well as separate, reflections on their collaborative research, Swadener and Piekielek in Chpater 12 raise several possibilities for the reconceptualization of early childhood curriculum in the area of social problem solving through consensus decision making. This chapter includes an implicit view of the future, as reflected in Friends ideology, and is an example of education for democracy—and beyond. This exemplifies another major issue in curriculum, the view of the future implied in what we teach. What kind of society are we helping to create by the curricular events that occur in the classroom? What practices serve the common good and our view of the just society? Reconceptualizing the early childhood curriculum requires that we address a fundamental question in curriculum making—"to what end?"

In the final chapter, Monica Miller Marsh describes her personal reconceptualization of the kindergarten curriculum to move multiculturalism and antibias pedagogy from the margins to the center of her planned curriculum. Her kindergarten children are not only "ready" to discuss issues of justice, inclusion, peace, and social activism, but virtually demand it. This chapter provides an example of social reconstructionist education as enacted by an early childhood teacher *and her students*; it also exemplifies how the curriculum points to a vision of the future—a future where children practice justice, inclusion, and peace to promote a better life for all. This chapter offers a powerful example of collaboration with children for the reconceptualization of the early childhood curriculum.

As Mara Sapon-Shevin states in the Foreword, this book may raise more questions than it answers. We feel that the sorts of curriculum questions raised in this volume will need to be asked of early childhood researchers, teachers, policy makers, advocates, curriculum developers, parents, and other stakeholders. Since this work began, in 1989, two national conferences focused on reconceptualizing research, theory, and practice in early childhood education have further expanded the dialogue.

If knowledge is power (Apple, 1982; Wexler, 1990), the *nature* of knowledge, as well as practices that are valued or privileged in the early childhood curriculum, must be examined within a number of larger contexts as well as from multiple perspectives. In order to reconceptualize the early childhood curriculum, we will need to become better listeners, so that we can hear the stories, honor the voices, and come to better understand the lives of our potential allies in this work. We will also have to learn how to make the "familiar strange" and many of our prized assumptions problematic. The dialogue around deconstructing and reconceptualizing the early childhood curriculum is only beginning, and there are many ways of knowing.

REFERENCES

Apple, M. W. (1982). *Education and power*. New York: Routledge & Kegan Paul.

Asante, M. (1987). *The Afrocentric idea*. Philadelphia: Temple University Press.

Asante, M. (1988). *Afrocentricity*. Trenton, NJ: Africa World Press.

Delpit, L. D. (1988). Power and pedagogy in educating other people's children. *Harvard Educational Review*, 58(3), 280-298.

Fordham, S. (1988). Racelessness as a factor in Black students' school success: Pragmatic strategy or pyrric victory? *Harvard Educational Review*, 58(1), 54-84.

Fordham, S., & Ogbu, J. U. (1986). Black students' school success: Coping with the "burden of acting white." *The Urban Review*, l8(3), 176-206.

Hale, J. E. (1991). The transmission of cultural values to young African-American children. *Young Children, 46*(6), 7–15.

Hale-Benson, J. E. (1986). *Black children: Their roots, culture, and learning styles* (rev. ed.). Baltimore: Johns Hopkins University Press.

Hilliard, A. G., Payton-Stewart, L., & Williams, L. O. (Eds.). (1990). *Infusion of African and African-American content in the school-curriculum.* Morristown, NJ: Aron Press.

Kunjufa, J. (1984). *Developing positive self-image and discipline in black children.* Chicago: African-American Images.

Kunjufa, J. (1987). *Lessons from history: A celebration in blackness.* Chicago: African-American Images.

McIntosh, P. (1992, January-February). White priviledge: Unpacking the invisible knapsack. *Creation Spirtuality,* 33–35, 53.

Quay, J. (1990). Foreword. In E. C. DuBois, & V. L. Ruiz (Eds.), *Unequal sisters: A multicultural history of women in the United States* (p. *xiii*). New York: Routledge.

Swadener, B. B., & Lubeck, S. (in press). *Children and families "at promise": The social construction of risk.* Albany: SUNY Press.

Wexler, P. (1990). *Social analysis of education: After the new sociology.* New York: Routledge.

Williams, S. (1991). Classroom use of African American language: Educational tool or social weapon? In C. E. Sleeter (Ed.), *Empowerment through multicultural education* (pp. 199–227). Albany: State University of New York Press.

Index

About the Contributors

Shirley A. Kessler is Assistant Professor in the Department of Interdisciplinary Studies in Curriculum and Instruction at National-Louis University in Evanston, Illinois. She graduated from the University of Wisconsin–Madison with a degree in curriculum and instruction and early childhood education. Her interests include examinations of the curriculum in use and the history of curriculum. She is currently co-editing (with Marianne Bloch) a book on alternative paradigms in early childhood research, and has published articles on curriculum theory in early childhood education.

Beth Blue Swadener is Associate Professor in Teacher Development and Curriculum Studies at Kent State University. She received her M.S. in Child Development and her Ph.D. in Curriculum and Instruction from the University of Wisconsin–Madison. Her work focuses on antibias, culturally inclusive early education, social policy affecting children and families, and early education in African settings. She is currently co-editing (with Sally Lubeck) *Children and Families "At Promise": The Social Construction of Risk*, and guest edited (with Shirley Kessler) a special topic issue of *Early Education and Development* (April, 1991) on "Reconceptualizing Early Childhood Education."

William Ayers is Associate Professor of Education at the University of Illinois at Chicago. He received his M.A. and M.Ed. in Early Childhood Education from the Bank Street College of Education and his Ed.D. in Curriculum from Teachers College, Columbia University. His interests include teacher education, school improvement, and early childhood education—all with an emphasis on issues of social justice and the ethical dimensions of teaching. He is author of *The Good Preschool Teacher* and co-editor (with William Schubert) of *Teacher Lore*.

Marianne N. Bloch is Professor of Early Childhood Education in the departments of Curriculum and Instruction and of Child and Family Studies at the University of Wisconsin–Madison. She has written numerous articles related to the history of early education, as well as various articles that focus on the cultural ecology of children's play and development. She edited, with A. Pellegrini, *The Ecological Context of Play* (1989), and is in the process of editing several other volumes related to the history of early education and reconceptualizing research in early education.

Mary Louise Gomez is Assistant Professor in the Department of Curriculum and Instruction at the University of Wisconsin–Madison, where she co-directs an experimental teacher-education program aimed at preparing elementary teachers to successfully educate low-income children of color. Her research focuses on how prospective and inservice teachers learn to teach diverse populations of students. She is particularly concerned with the preparation of teachers of writing and is the Associate Director of the Wisconsin Writing Project. She is currently co-editing (with Carl Grant) *Making Schooling Multicultural: Campus and Classroom.*

M. Elizabeth Graue is Assistant Professor in the Department of Curriculum and Instruction at the University of Wisconsin–Madison. She specializes in early childhood policy and research methodology. Her chapter is taken from her dissertation, *Socially Constructed Readiness for School in Three Communities*, which won the 1990 Outstanding Dissertation Award in qualitative methods and early childhood education from the American Educational Research Association.

Janice E. Hale, Ph.D., is Professor of Early Childhood Education at Wayne State University in Detroit. She is the author of *Black Children: Their Roots, Culture, and Learninq Styles* and *Unbank the Fire: Visions for the Education of African-American Children*. She is the founder and president of Visions for Children, a research demonstration program that is designed to facilitate the intellectual development of African-American children. Presently she is a member of the governing board of the National Association for the Education of Young Children.

Janice A. Jipson received her M.S. in Educational Psychology and her Ph.D. in Curriculum and Instruction from the University of Wisconsin–Madison. She was awarded the American Educational Research Association Women Educators Research Award in 1991 for her research on feminist pedagogy and collaborative process and the University of Oregon Phi Delta Kappa Outstanding Community Service award in 1990 for her work with homeless families. She has published in several journals and is currently completing a book on feminist theory and education entitled *Positions on Imposition: Multiple Cultural Realities*. She is currently Associate Professor of Education at Sonoma State University.

Susan Jungck is Associate Professor and Chair, Department of Interdisciplinary Studies in Curriculum and Instruction, in the National College of Education at National-Louis University. She also teaches in the Foundations and Research Department. Her interests are in curriculum studies and ethnography.

Nancy R. King is Associate Professor in the College of Education at Towson State University, where she teaches graduate and undergraduate courses in curriculum and instruction. Her research interests and many publications address issues related to play, the hidden curriculum, gender roles with regard to war and peace, and developmentally appropriate homework. Her publications include *School Play*.

Monica Miller Marsh has taught preschool, kindergarten, and a fifth-grade gifted program; she is currently teaching an enriched kindergarten program in a Cleveland-area school. She has recently completed her M.A. degree in Teacher Development and Curriculum Studies through the Early Childhood Education program at Kent State University. She presented papers at the 1991 Reconceptualizing Research in Early Childhood Conference in Madison, Wisconsin and the 1992 Ethnography in Education Research Forum in Philadelphia, and is a coauthor of a chapter in *In Praise of Diversity: A Sourcebook for Multicultural Education* (2nd ed.), edited by Carl Grant.

J. Dan Marshall is Associate Professor in the Department of Curriculum and Instruction at The Pennsylvania State University. His professional interests include textbook selection and adoption practices, teacher-education reform, and curriculum studies. In addition to having published various journal articles and book chapters, he is co-editor (with James T. Sears) of *Teaching and Thinking About Curriculum: Critical Inquiries.*

Janet L. Miller is Professor at National-Louis University. She received her M.A. in English Education from the University of Rochester, New York, and her Ph.D. in Humanities Education–English and curriculum from Ohio State University. She serves as Managing Editor of *JCT: An Interdisciplinary Journal of Curriculum Studies* and as a program coordinator for the annual Bergamo Conference on Curriculum Theory and Classroom Practice. Her research and writing interests include curriculum and feminist theories, qualitative inquiry, and teachers' knowledges. Her book *Creating Spaces and Finding Voices: Teachers Collaborating for Empowerment* won Hofstra University's annual Stessin Prize for Outstanding Scholarly Publication for the 1990–1991 academic year.

Dorothy Piekielek has a B.A. in Sociology and Teaching Certification in Early Childhood from Pennsylvania State University. She has taught kindergarten and first and second grades. She is currently working as an educational consultant for a demonstration research intervention project in central Pennsylvania. She is particularly interested in peace education, social learning in the classroom, and conflict management and mediation. She leads workshops and training for parents and teachers in conflict management with children and young adults.

Valerie Polakow is Associate Professor of Teacher Education at Eastern Michigan University and teaches in the Early Childhood and Educational Psychology Programs. She is the author of *The Erosion of Childhood* and *Lives on the Edge: Single Mothers and Their Children in the Other America* as well as numerous other publications dealing with women and children in poverty, critical pedagogy, and interpretive qualitative research.

Jocelynn L. Smrekar is a Ph.D. candidate at the Pennsylvania State University specializing in early childhood education in the Department of Curriculum and Instruction. She has a background in social work, holds an M.A. in Comprehensive Bilingual Early Childhood Education from Pennsylvania State University, and teaches at the Cedar Child Development Center there.

Lourdes Diaz Soto is Associate Professor of Education at Lehigh University. She has twenty-five years of experience as a researcher, teacher, and advocate on behalf of young bilingual/bicultural learners and their families. Her research interests include the realities of growing up Hispanic, and she is currently Chair of the Early Childhood Special Interest Group of the National Association for Bilingual Education, Chair of the Bilingual Caucus of the National Association for the Education of Young Children, and served as Director of an Early Childhood Bilingual masters program of Pennsylvania State University.